GEOGRAPHIES
of TRAVEL

GEOGRAPHIES
of TRAVEL

Impressions of America in the
Long Nineteenth Century

Susan L. Roberson

TEXAS A&M UNIVERSITY PRESS
College Station

First edition

♾ This paper meets the requirements of ANSI/NISO Z39.48-1992
(Permanence of Paper). Binding materials have been chosen for durability.

Library of Congress Cataloging-in-Publication Data

Library of Congress Control Number: 2024945394
Identifiers: LCCN: 2024945394
| ISBN 9781648432583 (hardcover) | ISBN 9781648432590 (ebook)
LC record available at https://lccn.loc.gov/2024945394

Cover designed by Noah Van Soest

CONTENTS

ACKNOWLEDGMENTS

I would like to thank the Interlibrary Loan staff at Texas A&M University–Kingsville for helping me access sources for this study and the American Literature Association for providing an early venue for my ideas.

I would also like to thank these presses for allowing me to use material already published or scheduled to be published: University Press of Kansas ("Geographies of Expansion: Nineteenth-Century Women's Travel Writing," in *Inventing Destiny: Cultural Explorations of US Expansionism*, edited by Jimmy L. Bryan Jr., 2019); University of Georgia Press ("'The Ancient City' and the Ethics of Sightseeing," in forthcoming *Secret Histories: A New Era in Constance Fenimore Woolson Scholarship*, edited by Kathleen Diffley, Caroline Gebhard, and Cheryl Torsney, 2025); J. Wiley ("Travel Writing," in *A Companion to American Literature*, edited by Susan Belasco, Theresa Strouth Gaul, Linck C. Johnson, and Michael Soto, 2020); and Penn State University Press ("Jumping Frogs and *Roughing It Out West*," in *Studies in the American Short Story*, vol. 1, No. 2, 2020).

GEOGRAPHIES
of TRAVEL

Introduction

IN MANY WAYS THE story of America is a story of roads and travel. When Walt Whitman figuratively led his readers "upon a knoll," pointing to "landscapes of continents and the public road" as he set his readers out on the open road to discoveries of self and nation, he tapped into an important icon of the American story. Just as "Song of Myself" imagines the diverse geographies of the nation and invites readers to undertake their own journeys of self-discovery, the road has persisted as a metaphor for America's idea of itself. If, as Ralph Waldo Emerson declared, "everything good is on the highway," then the road conjures ideas of mobility and discovery as important elements of the national identity. The stories that arise from mobility, from the highway or open road, Alfred Bendixen and Judith Hamera argue, participate in constructing the American ethos, the imagined geographies the nation has about itself. The road story, Deborah Paes de Barros claims, "is almost a manifesto of American cultural consciousness; it is the mythic representation of history and ideology." As she suggests, our nation's story about itself is informed by the imagined public road that Whitman set us on and by the accumulated imagined geographies of individual travels. Together, the metaphor of the road and the actual experiences of individual journeys shape ideas of the self, the nation, and its geographies. As Edward Said explains, space is poetically endowed with "an imaginative or figurative value we can name and feel . . . whereby the vacant or anonymous reaches of distance are converted into meaning for us here." This is the geographic imagination, the impulse to convert space, geography, into meaning, that emerges as writers confirm, contest, and recast assumptions in texts that are themselves sites, rhetorical locations of exploration and contestation. Notoriously on the road, in movements of "circulation, motion, and boiling agitation," American writers have shaped imaginative geographies to tell the story of the nation as it extended its borders and plotted its identity.[1] By following the trails of some of the nation's most astute writers as they explored sections of the country, the familiar grounds of the Northeast and those that were new to them, the Midwest, Far West, the South during the long nineteenth century, *Geographies of Travel* maps the multiple imagined geographies of the nation through time and space as it maps identities that are forged on the road and in the writing.

Heeding Whitman's call and creating what George Pierson calls the "M-factor" of the American character, nineteenth-century travelers from all walks of life took to the road. Following diverse motives for journeying, "movement, migration, [and] mobility," seeking change and transformation, the great mix of peoples that comprise the American scene contributed to debates about the national imaginary in their travel narratives. Travel writing is complicated, like any writing is, by purpose and audience. Some travel writing, like the early texts by explorers Christopher Columbus, Cabeza de Vaca, and Thomas Harriot, is clearly imperialistic and intent on describing the land and its peoples with a mind to conquering them. Some, like the travel sections of William Bradford's "Of Plymouth Plantation" and Caroline Kirkland's *A New Home, Who'll Follow?* (1839) relate the hardships and rewards of settlement. Some take the forms of diaries and letters meant to be shared with family and friends, like those women wrote about the Overland Trail or Union soldiers wrote about the Civil War South. Some travel writing is embedded in other forms of discourse, like captivity narratives, slave narratives, and "escape-to-freedom" stories by African Americans in which the road figures as an avenue to freedom.[2] Geographic surveys like John Wesley Powell's *Exploration of the Colorado River and Its Canyons* (1895), military narratives, and cowboy narratives map the landscape and the hardships of traversing it. Memoirs, autobiographies, and spiritual narratives like African American itinerant preacher Jarena Lee's *Religious Experience and Journal* (1849) relate geographic and imagined journeys to self-fulfillment or self-realization. Immigration and migration narratives write of relocation, of new identities forged in the going forth, of assimilation and deracination. Fictional and poetic texts may also double as travel narratives, like Susan Warner's wildly popular novel *The Wide, Wide World* (1850). Travel abroad to Europe, the Caribbean and South America, Africa, and the Pacific Rim, whether for leisure, health, missionary, or commercial reasons, constituted another category of travel writing that contributed to ideas of national identity in the nineteenth century. Through these diverse narratives, readers witness the ways race and class and gender, the motives for travel, and experiences on the road inflect the geographic imagination and contribute to the debates about the meanings of mobility and the American character.

One of the popular forms of nineteenth-century travel writing focused on journeys that were prompted by the desire for a holiday, leisure, adventure, a tramp across the continent, a road trip to the West Coast, or even a ramble about the familiar countryside. These are the narratives this book examines as it takes this slice of the greater travel writing experience for its subject. While the more touristic narratives are implicated by imperialism in terms of sightseeing, by the prejudices and imagined geographies authors bring with them, and by the impulse to measure and contain, they are meant primarily to relate an enjoyable (by and large) trip to new places or home travels around familiar locations, to entertain, to share an American version of the Grand Tour, and to provide information about the expanding nation during a period when the national identity was becoming increasingly complex. Ignited by the increasing ease of travel during the long nineteenth century, as the steamboat replaced the flatboat and the railroad replaced the stagecoach, during a period that Henry Tuckerman in 1844 declared "might not inaptly be designated as the age of travelling," these kinds of narratives entertained and informed their readers as they helped shape an American identity. Indeed, travel writing was the most popular genre in the nineteenth century. Nearly eighteen hundred travel books were published in the United States between 1830 and 1900. Publisher James Harper (Harper & Brothers) said early in the century, "Travels sell about the best of anything we get hold of."[3] Travel writing was so popular because it enabled readers to join the writer-narrator in adventures of the road and become voyeurs, experiencing secondhand the peoples and places the writer visited. Readers could imagine a horseback tour of Illinois, escapades in mining country, mountain hikes through the Sierras. They could savor the exotic landscapes of the Great American Desert, the swamps of Florida, or the Maine woods and become acquainted with the people and cultures that the travelers encounter. As the century progressed, they could imaginatively visit the tourist destinations that began popping up—the extravagant hotels and resorts of Southern California and Florida. In these ways, travel writing allowed readers to become armchair tourists, following travelers like Constance Fenimore Woolson's fictional tourists seeing the sights on the Great Lakes and in St. Augustine, Florida.

The travelers featured in this study wrote for readers much like themselves, educated people who had access to the newspapers, magazines, and books in which their narratives were published and who were "curious about their expanding and fast-filling land." These travel narratives were often first published in newspapers and journals as dispatches from the road, William Cullen Bryant publishing his letters in the *New York Evening Post* (which he edited), Catharine Maria Sedgwick writing for *Putnam's Monthly*, and Charles Fletcher Lummis sending dispatches to the *Los Angeles Times* and the *Chillicothe (Ohio) Leader*. Alan Nevins claims, "The most striking feature in newspaper correspondence of the forties was the prominence given mere travel." This contributed to "the age of *travel literature*" that Benjamin Moran praised in his 1859 *Guide to American Literature*. Like those examined here, many were written by professional authors skilled at conveying what they saw and did and thought in lively prose. As Bendixen and Hamera state, "Travel writing has consistently attracted the talents of major authors, many of whom produced travel books either as early apprenticeship works designed to launch a literary career, or as part of their later roles as public intellectuals."[4] Such is the case with the authors of this study.

By and large, the authors considered here come from the educated classes, five of them attending or taking degrees from Harvard University and Margaret Fuller tutoring Harvard men even though as a woman she was unable to attend the university. Many, like Francis Parkman, Mark Twain, and Helen Hunt Jackson, traveled extensively, for leisure, for curiosity, for the sake of their art. But even as their narratives are shaped by their education, class, race, and gender, by their leisure and privilege, and by the geographic imaginations shaped by their social group, they also, in the words of Jen Jack Gieseking, "pry open the power in assumptions, stereotypes, and expectations associated with space and place." When travelers ponder what the word "West" sounds like, when they picture romanticized versions of Native Americans or listen to the "latent poetry of the South," they illustrate the ways the imagination shapes how they perceive the geography. Like Henry James's "inquiring stranger," his "restless analyst," these writers not only expose some of their own prejudices, they also interrogate the myths of the past, the gilded glimmer of materialism, the ideologies of progress, and the humbuggeries of race that bolster America's ideas of itself. From Margaret Fuller, who criticized the racism and materialism that degraded Native Americans, to W. E. B. Du Bois, who pronounced that "the problem of the Twentieth Century is the problem of the color-line," these authors enact what Jimmy Bryan calls a kind of "literary intervention" into the national imagination even as they help shape it. Larzer Ziff claims, "Travel's capacity to compel personal self-definition leads to cultural self-awareness, a reevaluation of what in American life may be exceptional and what common, what worthy and what reprehensible." This capacity by some of the nation's most capable travel writers makes their writing important for us to read and consider today. Like other great literary texts, they enable us to understand, as Scott Slovic explains, how our personal, cultural, and national values and beliefs were formed as they reveal and question their own assumptions.[5]

Confronting new terrains and challenging transportation systems, inter-acting with the country's racial others, the travelers examined in *Geographies of Travel* were prompted, as Ziff would put it, to not only reconsider personal identities and expectations but also to think carefully about the national iden-tity and ethos. Experiencing different cultures, they heard their stories, learned their myths, and ate their foods. Francis Parkman lived with the Oglala Sioux for nineteen days, hearing such stories as the one about the thunder-fighters who shoot their weapons in the air to frighten the thunder; Charles Lummis relates Patapalo's story of being bewitched by a *bruja*; and Bryant listened to "negro ballads [and] negro jokes" and ate "bushels of hominy" during his tour of the South. These travelers discover alternate histories and cultures and hear a new poetry of America emerging from the mix of peoples, prompting one of Wool-son's tourists to remind the other sightseers that Florida was "settled more than a century before Plymouth or Jamestown." They also confronted new terrain in which one could get lost, lose one's bearing as Parkman did or as Henry David Thoreau did at Ktaadn (Mount Katahdin), or formulate new ecologies to account for the South's "spikey sub-tropical things."[6] Even when describing travels close to home or returns to homesites reshaped by time, travelers call our attention to the complexities of multiple geographies. Traveling roads that took them to locations near and far, these restless analysts constructed narratives that partici-pated in more than the construction of American identity. They actively adjusted concepts of American identity to include the diverse peoples of the nation.

Traveling during the century of the great revolution in transportation sug-gested the progress the nation was making in other domains. When travel evolved from the "confusing and chaotic" travel arrangements of the early part of the century to the well-appointed Pullman car that Henry James rode and the private motorcar that took Emily Post from New York to San Francisco in 1915, it seemed the ethos of the nation was also evolving. Lewis Perry asserts, "Travel literature, American-style, was much concerned with the ease or difficulty of getting from one place to another," with relative ease being a sign of "progress" and advancing civilization. So taken was Catharine Maria Sedgwick by the pro-motional Great Excursion and the extension of the railroad to the Mississippi River in 1854 that she pronounced that the rail lines marked the "advancement of true civilization." By joining geographic areas and extended populations into one united nation, the rail line suggested to her ideals of unity, equality, democracy, and piety. Frederick Law Olmsted also saw connections between transportation systems and national ideals: "There is nothing that is more closely connected, both as cause and effect, with the prosperity and wealth of a country, than its means and modes of travelling, and of transportation of the necessities and luxuries of life." But what he found in the South was a system of intentional incompetence that kept it tied to the ideologies of cotton. When Mark Twain revisited the Mississippi River in 1882, he bemoaned the loss of the old romance of the river since his earlier days as a steamboat pilot. But he also saw how the river had been refined by "progress, energy, prosperity." Even so, traces of "inflated language and other windy humbuggeries" of the South rubbed up against "the wholesome and practical nineteenth-century smell of cotton factories and locomotives," giving the lie to the connection between technological and social progress seemingly promised by the transportation revolution.[7] The Jim Crow train cars in which W. E. B. Du Bois and other African Americans in the South were forced to ride testify to this disjunction between technological and social progress. Connecting the road, transportation, and ideas of progress to cultural ethnographies, the narratives in *Geographies of Travel* join discussions about the nation and the directions it is going—or not going.

Travel writing, like the travel it relates, is fluid, mobile. Not only does travel writing fuse multiple genres—geography, nature writing, history, fiction, poetry, autobiography, ethnography, and travelogue—each writer also has a style, tone, rhetoric, or multiple rhetorics, that make the writing fluid. As it traces and recounts the journey, the travel narrative often shifts between modes of discourse and points of view in ways that can perplex. Practicing an ethics of reading, I have tried to listen carefully to each writer, to peel back the surface to uncover what lies under it, to respect the individual text for what it says and does. Employing close readings to analyze the ways writers map their travels, experiences, and themselves in the narratives, I heed the ways Twain creates a dialogic blend of travel writing and humor to critique the myths of the West and American exceptionalism. I pay attention to the ways Helen Hunt Jackson juxtaposes speed and distance, motion and repose, composing a dialectics of movement and place that rhetorically suggests the experience of speed. I follow the currents and bends of thought in Henry David Thoreau's *A Week on the Concord and Merrimack Rivers* to think about how he defies the strictly rational to write a narrative that is always in motion. I have listened to the quiet commentary about slavery by the visiting Bryant. I have looked at the ways Parkman and Lummis map their journeys of masculine testing and the ethnographies they record. I have examined ways Margaret Fuller's narrative is itself a territory in which competing views of the West, as well as her own competing voices and attitudes, create textual tension. I have unraveled James's complex sentences to find the ways he both deploys and critiques the geographic imagination. And I have thought about how Audubon's sketches of birds imply his own autobiographical brief. Doing so, reading ethically, I have tried to honor each text rather than make them fit into a singular interpretive model.

Even so, the narratives I read share some concerns and common themes as they relate some of the nuts and bolts of travel. Writers share their routes, sometimes recording miles covered and dates of travel. They mention the conditions of the road, oftentimes the mud they encounter or the lack of a true road when they head across country on their own. They relate the kinds of transport they used, giving readers a sense of what it meant to travel by flatboat or steamboat, on foot or on horseback, in the early trains of the Baltimore and Ohio line, the more luxurious Pullman cars or the Jim Crow cars of the segregated South, atop a western stagecoach, or in an automobile in one of the early transcontinental road trips. And they describe the people they meet along the way, fellow passengers going to the Midwest, guerrilla forces roaming the postbellum roads of the South, riverboat characters, and families that take them in for the night. They tell us about their accommodations, indicating how the rustic inn where Audubon shared a room with five other men gradually gave way to hotels outfitted with private bathrooms by the time Emily Post tested how far one could comfortably travel. They pay attention to what they ate, meals shared with locals that often featured bacon and corn products, the wild game that was shot and eaten, and then as restaurants began to spring up along the route, the fried chicken and sandwiches they could pack for roadside picnics. Many tell us what they wore during their travels, Parkman and Twain regaling in western outfits, Lummis describing his walking boots, and Post sketching the duster and veil she wore to protect herself from the sun and dust. And they tell us what they carried with them, the provisions they found necessary for the journey, Twain's "pitiful little Smith & Wesson's seven-shooter" and six pounds of unabridged dictionary, Muir's plant press, and the silver set that Post finally left along the way.[9]

They tell us about the places they visited, Mackinaw Island, Fort Laramie, San Francisco, the Confederate Museum in Richmond, Fort Marion, Acoma Pueblo, Salem (Mass.), and New York. Sometimes they pause to sketch the history of place, as Woolson's fictional tourists do in St. Augustine or as Lummis does when he writes of the Pueblo Revolt. Going to new terrains, the writers remark on the landscape and the flora and fauna, Fuller and Bryant describing the Illinois prairies, Jackson and Muir giving lyrical, scientific descriptions of the Sierras, and Muir and James startled by the exotic southern plants. Audubon lists and describes the birds that make up so much of his journey and journal, and Parkman counts the buffalo and other animals of the West. Even those who traverse familiar terrain describe the plants and animals they encounter, the house wren that lives under the eaves or the moose of Maine. They also comment on the ruined environment, the burned Cuyahoga River, the remains of mining camps, the cotton fields of the South spoiled by overplanting, the damage to forests by farmers intent on clearing the land. As visitors, many of the travelers were also sightseers, tourists, gazing at the sites, the environment, the local people, the racial others. While they try their hand at writing brief ethnographies, they also view the native people as part of the tourist experience. Fuller employs some Native American men to take her on a canoe ride down the rapids of the Sault, Twain peers at the Mormons of Utah, Bryant enjoys listening to the enslaved people sing their songs. As the century progressed, writers describe the developing tourist industry, the commodification of the road and its attractions by such enterprises as the Fred Harvey hotels and restaurants. And they develop an ethics of sightseeing that Fuller exemplifies in the intellectual use she makes of her summer on the Great Lakes and that is implied in Woolson and James's satirical critiques of the self-absorbed tourist class.

Finally, more than just telling us about their own adventures on the road, their escapades, and giving their texts autobiographical content, these narratives share their author's point of view about what they have seen and what they have to say about the sociopolitical situation of the places they visit and the nation as whole. As James understands, the key activity of the traveler is to see: traveling is an act of perception and insight. Relying on "the agent of perception" and "freshness of eye, outward and inward," James shapes what he has seen into impressions, into scenes of meaning. Traveling through the South, "spying" on it as an outsider, Olmsted discovered a more complex, nuanced Black society and economy than he had expected. In addition to seeing things afresh, the travel writers experienced a changed perspective because of their experiences. At the end of her narrative Fuller muses, "I feel that I have learnt a great deal of the Indians," and Parkman remarks, "We had seen life under a new aspect."[10] The mobile eye of the traveler, alert to new sensations and ready to adjust its line of sight, prompts these restless analysts to discoveries of self and nation that resonate in the travel writing and in subsequent projects such as Bryant's poem "The Prairies," Twain's story "The Celebrated Jumping Frog of Calaveras County" (and the novel he returned to after his trip down the Mississippi, *Adventures of Huckleberry Finn*), Woolson's short stories, Jackson's popular novel *Ramona*, and Lummis's creative collecting after his transformative sojourn in the Southwest. Positioned at the ends of some of the chapters as interludes, my brief analysis of these familiar works suggests how the travels and travel writing influenced other literary or artistic endeavors and the ways the traveler's imagination reverberated beyond the narrative at hand.

The narratives examined in *Geographies of Travel* open a window on the road and the nation across geographic regions and through time. A pathway to "landscapes of continents," the road cuts through meadows, over mountains and rivers, and through the burgeoning cities, small towns and villages, and farms and homesteads, enabling readers not only to visit specific locations with some favorite writers but also to get firsthand reports and commentary about "a nation on the move." By stitching these accounts together, this book tells a story of America from the road, the multiple roads and stories that comprise the "hotchpotch" of the nation. As Cecelia Tichi has argued, the road is "a place in and of itself, a fundamental defining part of an American experience," a metaphorical space where the rhetorics of the nation are shaped and debated.[11]

Geographies of Travel is organized by region, with essays examining travel writing about local journeys in the Northeast before setting off on jaunts to the Midwest, the Far West, and the South. Arranging the contents around the regions gives us a chance to think about the geographic imagination of each region and the kinds of travel it invited. It also gives us a chance to hear the ways Americans react to regional landscapes, both natural and social, to see how these travelers think about the peoples, cultures, and politics of the region. Because several of the travelers visited multiple regions—Bryant, Woolson, Muir, Twain, and James—we can see how they shape the differing geographic imaginaries or how they carry similar concerns with them in their travels. Then, within each geographic unit, the travel writing is arranged chronologically so that we can see how the region changed over time, how transportation technologies and the tourist industry evolved. We can also watch how travelers' perspectives on each region's environmental and social landscapes as well as their concerns about place and travel change over time. Following American visitors chronologically we witness how they think about their own nation as it transformed during the long century.

The opening section examines the local travels and geographies of Susan Fenimore Cooper and Henry David Thoreau. Writing at midcentury, both writers explored the most established region at the time, the Northeast. Tracing rambles about the woods and gardens of Otsego County, New York, Cooper's

1850 *Rural Hours* extends ideas of home and the domestic sphere, demonstrating that, like travel, home "is a complex and multilayered geographical concept."[12] Following the multiple trajectories of her home travels and metaphoric travels through time and space, she shapes an imagined geographic home, an ecosystem that extends from the local environment to the universal ecosystem. Likewise, Thoreau recounts his extensive regional travels in *A Week on the Concord and Merrimack Rivers, Maine Woods,* and his great work *Walden.* Although he did not travel far in these books, travel was such an essential element of his life that, even when he was not writing explicitly about his journeys, he deployed the material conditions of travel as metaphors for self-exploration, knowledge, and wayfinding through the physical terrain and the interior geographies of the self. Complicating what we mean by travel, place, and the traveler's imagination, Cooper and Thoreau merge literal travels with metaphoric travels to create imagined geographies for interrogating the American scene. This section launches the themes of the book, and the region it examines was a launching ground to the other sections of the nation for many of the travelers examined here.

The first section of travel beyond the familiar terrain of the Northeast analyzes travel to the Midwest and the Great Lakes region. Beginning with William Cullen Bryant's 1832 journey to Illinois to visit family and Margaret Fuller's summer on the lakes, the section follows travelers who witness the transformation of the west of the Midwest during a time of rapid change. When Catharine Maria Sedgwick journeyed as a guest on the Great Excursion in 1854 to celebrate the extension of the railroad to the Mississippi River, she witnessed the progress the nation was making. By the time Constance Fenimore Woolson wrote her fictionalized narrative of tourists on the Great Lakes and Emily Post drove through the region in 1915 on her way to San Francisco, grand hotels had popped up in the major cities, and the tourist industry was emerging as part of a national push to see America first. These "transient" tourists witnessed not only the growth of cities into commercial and industrial hubs and the increasing sophistication of transportation and communication technologies, but also the consequences of expansion and the materialism associated with it on the settlers, Native Americans, the environment, and the nation.[13]

The next section examines travel to the Far West and Southwest, together comprising a vast region that eastern travelers found geographically and ethnologically different, intriguing, and daunting, the open spaces, desert landscapes, and mountains suggesting freedom and danger. The section follows Francis Parkman, who spent the summer of 1846 among Native Americans, living with them and hunting the great herds of buffalo. When Mark Twain went west to rough it among the miners, he was beginning to mock the myth of the West exemplified in Parkman's adventures. The California Sierras summoned John Muir, who made momentous geologic discoveries, and Helen Hunt Jackson, one of the early tourists to Yosemite. Leaving the East for a newspaper job in Los Angeles, Charles Lummis tramped through the ethnologically diverse South-west: "We stepped into a civilization that was then new to me." By the time Emily Post completed the western leg of her journey, "the West of yesterday" had been converted into an annual celebration of the past, the Frontier Days Celebration of Cheyenne, Wyoming.[14]

The following section traces travel to the South along two main routes, down the Mississippi River and down the eastern seaboard to Florida, as they chart journeys into a land both lush and troubled. It floats along with John James Audubon down the Mississippi to New Orleans in 1820 in search of birds and employment. Then it turns to Bryant's visit to the antebellum South as the guest of poet and novelist William Gilmore Simms. His gentle sketches of slavery contrast with Frederick Law Olmsted's more critical analysis of the deleterious effects of cotton and the slaveocracy on life, land, and economics in the South. John Muir, among the earlier travelers to the postbellum South, gives readers glimpses of the ravages of the war as well as the natural environment that nudged him toward a biocentric ethos. Then the section goes down the Mississippi River with Mark Twain as he reminisces about the past and points to technological progress along the river. Taking in the tourist sights of the South, Woolson's fictional tourists visit the monuments and mementos that mark the incursions of the Spanish and French, the British and the Americans. For her, the South seemed haunted by time and memory and race. Writing the southern paradox, these travelers note the tension between the ideals of America and the promises of its natural world against the violence and brutality fed by greed and racism. The section ends by contemplating W. E. B. Du Bois's travel chapters in *The Souls of Black Folk*, giving him the last word about the South and the impact of race, the institution of slavery, and the post-Reconstruction era that conspired against the progress of the New South by imposing multiple forms of immobility on the Black population. This social, economic, and geographic immobility troubles the promises of the open road and journeying that Whitman had seemed to offer. Yet they too participate in the debate about the nation and the direction it is headed at the beginning of the twentieth century.

The study ends with an examination of Henry James's *The American Scene* in a coda that brings together his astute observations of the Northeast and the South. Recounting his return to the United States after twenty-one years abroad, James is unsettled by what he finds. Deploying the geographic imagination to analyze the social geography etched in the built environment, he finds an uncanny gap between his imagined past and the material present, between memory and experience, between the promise of the nation and the moral emptiness he finds. Revisiting the familiar scenes of his youth in Boston, Salem, Newport, and New York, and taking in the tourist sites of the South, he writes a narrative about the importance of seeing "straight," in a social commentary of a nation shifting from the nineteenth to the twentieth century.[15]

As Alfred Bendixen and Judith Hamera claim and the works examined here illustrate, "Travel and the construction of American identity are intimately linked." The narratives examined in this book demonstrate that travel writing participated in the "complex ideological and cultural work" of creating multiple "American 'selves' and American landscapes."[16]

The NORTHEAST

$\mathcal{E}$xamining narratives of home travels in the Northeast, this section looks at the ways Susan Fenimore Cooper and Henry David Thoreau explore familiar terrain, finding pathways through the landscape and the interior geographies of the self. Recounting physical and metaphorical travels, these writers join the present to the past, map new identities, and interrogate social and cultural relations as they stitch forays into deep time to their local rambles. This section follows these nature writers through the forests and paths of Otsego, New York; Concord, Massachusetts; the Maine woods; and along the Concord and Merrimack Rivers. Writing from a geographic imagination shaped by a home geography, a "complex and multilayered geographical concept," from what Thoreau calls a "home-cosmography," they reveal the complexities of place and travel. Following differing trajectories, literally across the landscape, vertically into the past and to mythic space, and metaphorically into interior geographies of the self, they create working reveries that reveal divergent, innovative ways of thinking. Keen and patient observers, Cooper and Thoreau also carefully delineate the changes of the seasons and the changes of the times. Writing of the natural and social environments, they craft early versions of an environmental ethics as they witness the stresses of progress and "American environmental transformation" at midcentury.[1]

Home Travels in Susan Fenimore Cooper's *Rural Hours*

IN 1850 SUSAN FENIMORE COOPER published *Rural Hours*, a book she described as notes "in a journal form" of "those little events which make up the course of the seasons in rural life."[1] It recounts one year of her experiences rambling about her local environs, beginning with the spring of 1848. Her father, the famous novelist James Fenimore Cooper, expressed his "great satisfaction" when he first read her manuscript, noting its "purity of mind, the simplicity, elegance and knowledge they manifest," and worked to secure US and British publishers for the book (though he noted, "At first, the world will not know what to make of it"). Published by Putnam's, it enjoyed initial success and garnered positive assessments as an "admirable portraiture of American outdoor life." It went into six distinct editions within the first four and a half years and came out again in two new editions in 1868 and 1876 before disappearing, like many other women's narratives, from the public eye. Rediscovered by environmentalist scholars in the late twentieth century, it has been hailed as a first in environmental writing in the United States. Lawrence Buell called it "the first major work of American literary bioregionalism"; Vera Norwood announced that Cooper was "the first woman to enter [the] company [of nature essayists]"; and the editors of the 1998 edition, Rochelle Johnson and Daniel Patterson, claimed that Cooper "became the first American woman to publish a book of nature writing." Commenting on its journal format and attention to the natural world, Buell notes that Cooper is a precursor, perhaps even an influence, on Henry David Thoreau, who likewise structured his great book *Walden* around the seasons, his excursions around the local landscape, and "an encyclopedic passion for bringing bibliographical resources to bear on one's native township."[2]

Focused on the ways women pay attention to the environment, Norwood discusses Cooper's work in terms of domesticity and class, claiming that "the

gardens and woods of Otsego were an extension of her domestic sphere," and
Nina Baym argues that *Rural Hours* "showed how scientific knowledge contributed to an ideal of gracious country living for women." Placing Cooper and her
writings in other contexts, the essays in *Susan Fenimore Cooper: New Essays on
"Rural Hours" and Other Works* "situate her in relation to nineteenth-century
conservationist thought about the relative claims of unmodified nature versus
responsible domestication; debates about women's rights and women's sphere;
religious controversies and the state of biblical interpretation; the critical reception of European ideas in the nineteenth-century United States; and the
natural and social history of Cooperstown, New York, from its founding to the
present day." Mirroring Cooper's "encyclopedic passion," scholars have looked
at *Rural Hours* from a range of cultural and intellectual perspectives, enriching
our understanding of the narrative and its multiple contexts.[3]

Even though the book is structured around her rambles and excursions, no
one has really teased out their important role in *Rural Hours*. Baym points out
that *Rural Hours* "merges accounts of excursions in the Cooperstown environs
with associated material pieced together from a huge array of print sources,
most of them scientific, . . . making travel a textual affair." Norwood indicates
that Cooper describes the "changing, seasonal landscape in an area within
walking distance, or occasionally a day's carriage ride," making of "the familiar
round of home, garden, and local neighborhood" her exploratory journeys. In
his hefty study of Thoreau and the environmental imagination, Buell posits that
"the notion of writing a book of local travels did not originate with Thoreau"
and says that "Thoreau was anticipated in this . . . by Susan Fenimore Cooper."
He then outlines "three primary ways of organizing environmental material,
all seemingly inchoate: as seasonal chronicle, as episodes in an excursion, and
as items in an inventory. Each approach invites atomization: a catalog of spring
events, a series of things seen, a bestiary."[4] All of these we find in *Rural Hours*.
Even as they acknowledge Cooper's local excursions and her more metaphorical
or "textual" travels and situate her in the context of other nature writers who
likewise rambled about their home landscapes, these scholars do not follow
the thread of travel in *Rural Hours* to see where it leads Cooper and the reader.

Beyond recognizing the excursions as organizing strategies for her nature
writing, important as that is to do, I want to think of *Rural Hours* as a text about
travel, a travel narrative, albeit a unique one. Usually, when we think about
travel writing, we turn to accounts of journeys to new and distant lands, to
adventures on the road, to the trials and tribulations the traveler endures, and
lessons learned from the experience. Nineteenth-century travelers to the West
like Meriwether Lewis and William Clark, Frances Parkman, and Margaret

Fuller, and tourists to Europe like Washington Irving, Catherine Maria Sedgwick, and James Fenimore Cooper, often come to mind when we think about the travel narrative. So it is not surprising that readers have not placed Susan Cooper's accounts of local excursions around Otsego County in the tradition of travel writing.

Clearly, *Rural Hours* exemplifies a different kind of travel writing, one that records and privileges home travels instead of journeys to strange or foreign lands. Her excursions take her around the village of Cooperstown, through the local woods, and out onto Lake Otsego, all local destinations, which she describes and uses as inspiration for more metaphorical journeying. Even though Cooper's use of scientific texts, Baym contends, "turns the local into the global," Cooper does not recount actual physical excursions beyond the familiar terrain of her extended home sphere. Rather, her travels remain close to home, and her geographic imagination, that part of the imagination "which affords ways of thinking about space and place," is informed by the geography of home.[5]

Like Thoreau's "home-cosmography" that details his tramps around Walden Pond and Concord and Emily Dickinson's geographic imagination that "sees New Englandly," Susan Cooper's home geography and home travels are shaped by the local geography that she encounters on her almost daily outings. She describes the creatures and flowers she meets along highways and pathways as well as some of the local folk and their habits, asking us to think of the home geography as a heterogenous space made up of not only domestic and environmental spaces but also the social, historical, and cultural relations that accrue to them. Exploring this extensive home geography, the text's literal travels along roads and paths intersect with and inspire metaphoric travels backward in time and forward to forecast the future shape of Otsego County under the stresses of progress and "American environmental transformation." At times, her home travels evince what Ralph Waldo Emerson calls "sallies of the spirit," as she attaches spiritual orientations and mythical, abstract meanings on the geography and follows a vertical trajectory to cosmic or mythic space. These are the kinds of journeys one finds in traditional travel writing (as well as nature writing), regardless of how far one journeys. Following the multiple trajectories of her home travels and the metaphoric travels through time and space, she shapes an imagined geographic ecosystem that extends from the local environment to the universal ecosystem. As Annie Dillard so eloquently shows us, you do not have to travel far to witness the beauty and power of the universal ecosystem, the "waste and extravagance" of nature that are played out at Tinker Creek—or Otsego County.[6]

Travel writing is a fluid and capacious genre, generous enough to include *Rural Hours* in its purview. As Alfred Bendixen and Judith Hamera note, "It exists betwixt and between the factual report and the fictional account, personal memoir and ethnography, science and romance. The genre is itself in motion and, in the process, reveals much about the changing cultural desires and anxieties both of the traveler and the American reading public." Letters gathered from abroad like James Fenimore Cooper's *Gleanings in Europe* or sent as dispatches to newspapers, like those of William Cullen Bryant to the *New York Evening Post*, count as examples of travel writing as do the diaries kept by women going west on the Overland Trail and Caroline Kirkland's autobiographical novel about settling the Michigan backwoods, *A New Home, Who'll Follow?* In some ways, *Rural Hours* exemplifies women's travel writing that Mary Louise Pratt explains as "emplotted in a centripetal fashion around places of residence from which the protagonist sallies forth and to which she returns," as Cooper sets off from her residence and returns to it each day. And if Michel de Certeau is right, that "every story is a travel story—a spatial practice," then we can think *of Rural Hours* as a travel story because of the ways it deploys "a spatial practice" in recounting the day's events and the musings inspired by her outings.[7] Even though Cooper does not range far from home, there is some precedent to thinking about *Rural Hours*, the journal of a year's explorations around Otsego County and corresponding contemplations, as an example of travel writing, of writing about home travels.

Although she does not travel great distances or forage in strange lands, there is something audacious at work in her narrative as she disrupts expectations about genre, time and space, and home. Taking a cue from Norwood, who claims that "the gardens and woods of Otsego were an extension of her domestic sphere," that the county counted as "home" to Cooper, I argue that Cooper expands our definition of home to mean not just the house and its intimate spaces but also a wider home geography that extends beyond the particular and local to the universal. Imagining a home geography that breaks through the boundaries of public and private, the local and the universal, she stakes a claim not only to the open roads of her travels but also to a larger, universal ecosystem. In many ways *Rural Hours* is like nineteenth-century women's domestic novels that take their heroines out on the road where "the simple dichotomy of gendered assignments to places—the public sphere to the male and the private sphere to the female—is contested as women authors claim the road not only as a location for female activity and mobility but as another site of domesticity that is shaped by women's values."[8] For Cooper those values pertain to an ethos of care and relation that the ideology of domesticity and an ecological perspective both promote. A pioneering work in environmentalism, *Rural Hours* also blurs boundaries between nature writing and travel writing, between the domestic sphere and the public spaces of intellectual activity.

Making the rounds of the familiar "home, garden, and local neighborhood," Cooper exemplifies what I am calling home travels.[9] Her sorties from the home base constitute not only an abiding routine in her life, but they also form important thematic and structural motifs in her narrative about a year's observations of her local region. In it she notes the outings—walking, riding, boating, sleighing—that become vehicles for seeing and thinking about the world as home. These were almost daily excursions, as her comments that she "walked as usual" (*RH* 318) and that a ramble over the hills was "so different from our every-day rambles" (*RH* 60) would suggest. Looking more carefully at the journal entries, I find that they record 119 specific outings. By my count, 39.4 percent of the entries explicitly mention travels, with ninety specific references to walking, twenty references to driving in the carriage, six to rowing on Otsego Lake or the Susquehanna River, and three to sleighing in the winter. These do not include entries that imply without explicitly stating an outing as she observes local birds or plant life. Nor, obviously, can I account for those outings that were "usual" but not recorded. Nonetheless, we can see that her travels form a persistent motif in *Rural Hours* and lay the foundation for the more metaphorical journeys she also undertakes.

Even though the *Rural Hours* outings were confined to the environs of Otsego County, often to sites already familiar to Cooper in "an extension of her domestic sphere," they sent her out to multiple locations. For example, she mentions walking on the outskirts of the village, wandering in the woods, walking the highway and byways, going to Great Meadow and Hannah's Heights, rambling around Mill Island, taking a moonlight walk on the Mount, rowing on the Susquehanna River and Otsego Lake, and riding off to a neighboring hamlet. Though she does not travel far and returns home each day to Otsego Hall, the mansion built by her grandfather, she travels often, making her rambles a part of her daily life and a key motif for her book. And though she often returns to favorite locations, she is always curious about what she sees, the likes of the "Turk's-cap lily [that] belongs to our neighborhood" (*RH* 107) and the nests of birds that had left for the winter, counting 127 of them during a winter walk (*RH* 322–25). Like Dillard, who proclaimed, "I explore the neighborhood," Cooper finds joy in her home travels, in visiting the familiar plants and creatures to see

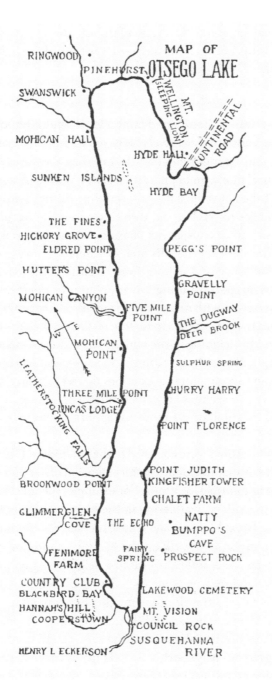

Map of Lake Otsego, by Henry L. Eckerson, from *The Story of Cooperstown*, by Ralph Birdsall (1917)

how they are doing, in finding new things in the familiar haunts, and residing in and returning to the familiar.[10]

Using the map of Otsego Lake, with its references to locations in her father's Leatherstocking novels, we can follow some of Cooper's ramblings from Otsego Hall in Cooperstown to some of her usual haunts, the Fenimore Farm on the southwest side of the lake, Hannah Hill, the southern point where the Susquehanna River meets Lake Otsego, Mount Vision just to the east, and the Chalet Farm north of it.

Although she does not say much about the conditions of travel and transportation systems, as does Caroline Kirkland, whose protagonist Mary Clavers must slog through the Michigan mud, Cooper does briefly comment on walking after a snow, the lack of the "new-fashioned plank-walks" in the village, and winter roads that caused the stagecoach to take ten hours to go twenty-two miles from the railroad (*RH* 236, 237). The absence of commentary on the conditions of travel may indicate that the roads and paths she traversed generally posed no challenge to her. She likewise does not tell us about her travel garb beyond a few mentions of a parasol to shade her from the sun, suggesting again that her home travels did not prompt the kinds of costume changes that some travelers to the West like Mary Alice Shutes described: "I am dressed like Charles and straddle of my horse."[11] We can only imagine that while she got out almost daily for some kind of ramble or drive, hers was a more genteel travel than those going west experienced. By relying on walking or riding in the carriage rather than public transportation, fairly nonexistent in Otsego Valley in 1850 (*RH* 318), she enjoyed an intimate relation to the landscape, allowing her to wander and linger at will. Though she also walked in the woods and forests and rowed on the lake, an illustration from *The History of Otsego County, New York* by Hurd D. Hamilton (1878) can give us some idea of the condition of the roads and the types of carriages she might have ridden in. It depicts manicured lawns, wide roads, fenced-in farms and gently rolling hills, a farmer in the fields with his horse, and an open carriage pulled by a proud-looking horse.

Even though she does not tell us much about the condition of traveling, she writes about it as an activity that engaged not only her feet and body but also her senses, imagination, and intellect. As Shane O'Mara in *In Praise of Walking* reminds us, "When we're walking our brains are in motion too"; and "acts of imagination are exactly that: *acts*." When Cooper punctuates her accounts of excursions with active verbs such as "saw," "observed," "found," "met," and "gathered," she indicates the dynamic quality of both the ramble and her mind. Her mind was engaged, set in motion by her physical mobility, as it was in the

Residences of Francis Hecox and C. Childs, from *The History of Otsego County, New York* by Hurd D. Hamilton (1878)

entry for September 8: "*Passed* a charming morning on the Cliffs. The wych-hazel is in bloom; brown nuts and yellow flowers on the same twig. *Gathered* some speckled-jewels, partridge-berry, and squaw-vine blossoms. *Found* a purple rose-raspberry in flower; it is always pleasant to *meet* these late flowers, un-looked-for favors as they are.... *Found* also a few red raspberries, whortleberries, and the acid rose-berry" (*RH* 176, emphasis mine). As well as telling us what she does (passed and gathered), she tells us what she sees or observes (found and met)—demonstrating how perception is connected to locomotion and with the "mobile body" of the traveler.[12] Though she does not travel far or to unfamiliar territory, she engages in some of the essential activities of travel, moving about the terrain, seeing, observing, and thinking about what she sees.

Mobility, as Eric Leed demonstrates, is also linked to curiosity and new knowledge, the freedom to move, and the innovative mind "that explores new ways of looking at things," which include the material, physical world and the interior landscapes of the self. Spending a "pleasant morning in the woods," Cooper finds a "little chipmuck, or ground squirrel . . . holding something in his fore paws, which he was eating very busily." She was "curious to know what [the squirrel] was eating, and moved toward him"; it "proved to be the heart of a head of a half-ripe thistle" instead of the chestnut she had supposed (*RH* 177). This simple episode indicates the relation between mobility and curiosity, seeing new beings or events and stopping to pay attention. It also indicates the relation between travel and new knowledge as she learns what the squirrel was eating. Indeed, one of travel's axioms is that it is equated with new awareness and under-standing. For Cooper, that enlightenment is not so much of new lands or peoples but more new or fresh insights into what Jessie Ravage calls the "minutiae of na-ture" and the particulars of her home geography. The other part of the equation between travel and knowledge is power, as thinkers like Michel Foucault have recognized and that Cooper quietly both claims and unsettles when she situates herself in the scientific (male) domain of nature writing. In the incident with the squirrel, she expands on the moment to share her knowledge of different tribes of squirrels, their habitats and migrations, to write the kind bestiary Buell finds in environmental writing. In another example, she writes: "Pleasant day. *Walked* some distance along the bank of the river. *Gathered* handsome berries of the cranberry-tree. *Found* many vines . . . *Observed* several soft maples. . . . *Saw* a handsome thorn-tree vivid red" (*RH* 214, my emphasis). Again, active verbs signify her nimble, curious mind as she looks carefully at the natural world, describing and naming plants and illustrating what Buell calls "the excursion as a form of environmental interaction." The excursion connects mobility not only to perception but also to interaction by letting the natural world act on her. She not only records what she did and saw; following the track of her mind, she makes associations that take her beyond the present moment. Continuing the September 14 entry, she writes: "Altogether, the shrubs and bushes strike us as more vividly colored than usual. Every season has some peculiarity of its own." (*RH* 214). Here she makes an obvious jump from describing the specific plants to generalizing about the seasons. This is a quick example of the creative side of mobility, the mind-wandering, "divergent thinking" or "collision of ideas" that O'Mara claims occurs with walking and that abounds in *Rural Hours*. Citing a passage from Thoreau, "the moment my legs begin to move, my thoughts begin to flow," O'Mara claims that mind-wandering allows "us to integrate our past, present and future, interrogate our social lives, and create a large-scale personal narrative." More than the set pieces or textual travel that Baym describes, Cooper's mind-wandering, divergent thinking is constructive, creative, integrative work.[13]

When Cooper diverges from the physical path through the woods or along the lake to follow the track of her mind, she sets off on metaphorical journeys that are as important to her and her text as the geographic ones. Her riffs on such topics as the environment, American history, and biblical themes integrate the seasonal narrative of rural life with other times and peoples to create a "large-scale" narrative that expands "the notion of community" and reveals a "deepening sense of place." These digressions reveal the thickness of place and time, the interconnections between past and present, and double modes of thinking that follow physical and metaphoric trajectories.[14]

Coooper writes, "One likes to come upon a spring in a walk. This afternoon we were seldom out of sight of one." Then she lists the different places one can find a stream—near the bank of the river, falling over a cliff, along the highway, and "bubbling through the ditches by the road-side." Listening to the gentle, cheerful voice of the "unfettered" stream, she muses that there is something about streams that is "soothing to the spirit." Letting the environment, the stream, act on her, she first considers its effect on her spirit and then conjures scenes of the past: "When standing beside these unfettered springs in the shady wood, one seems naturally to remember the red man." Like the unfettered stream, her imagination journeys back in time when Native Americans and "the wild creatures" stopped to slake their thirst at a spring like the one she describes (*RH* 57–58). Writing history on the terrain, she also demonstrates "movement's relationship to creative" thinking. In a scene much like one Margaret Fuller imagined on the shores of Niagara Falls, Cooper writes that "the flickering shadows of the wood seem[ed] to assume the forms of the wild creatures" and that "a crash of a dry branch" summoned an image of "the painted warrior, armed with flint-headed arrows and tomahawk of stone." Although the tomahawk-wielding Native American seems to pose a threat to her, she claims a common humanity when she realizes that indigenous peoples have "as much of life as runs through our own veins." Integrating the past and the present in this entry, deepening a sense of place, she also expands the "notion of community" to include the Native American, and quietly, quickly interrogates "our social lives" as she enters the national conversation about the fate of Native Americans and the loss of native wildlife: "yesterday they were here, today scarce a vestige of their existence can be pointed out among us" (*RH* 57–58).[15]

In another entry, she dives into what Wai Chee Dimock calls "deep time," a "set of longitudinal frames, at once projective and recessional . . . binding continents and millennia into many loops of relations." Reaching beyond historical time to mythological time, Cooper connects the present and the past as she contemplates the trees that are being felled in her home territory. Walking in the Great Meadow, she notices, "The old trees which bordered this fine field in past years are fast falling before the axe" (*RH* 146). Linking her own history to that of the trees, she remembers, "Few summers back, this *was* one of the most beautiful meadows in the valley." Using the past tense here and when she recalls that "it *was* favorite ground" (emphasis mine), she records the passing of time and the deleterious changes effected by the "axeman" that have disrupted the balance between "the sweet quiet of the fields, and the deeper calm of the forest." She remembers the mix of new-growth trees and the noble older trees whose "great trunks" lighted by the sun made "forest colonnades" that she could view from the highway. Using personal and local history to pry open interrogations about environmental conservation in the face of a growing human population, she sketches the history of the ash tree and its uses. Reminded that the black ash is "much used by Indian basket-makers" and forms the small bows and arrows boys now play with, she embarks on a metaphorical journey through time to think about how the ash was used in weaponry by the "heroes in the ancient world" and the "knights of the middle ages." Going further back in time, to mythological time, she thinks about how the ash figures in the mythologies of "several different nations." Figured as a "tree of life, or an emblem of the world," the ash connects people and story through time and place. Citing a passage from the *Edda*, the medieval Icelandic manuscripts that recorded Norse legends, that describes the

ash as "the first and greatest of all trees," Cooper concludes that although there
are many versions of the Scandinavian tale, they "are all connected with the good
and evil in man." Integrating the past and the present, she expands the "notion
of community," finding a shared morality in "faint gleams of great truths" (RH
146–47) in myth as she quickly interrogates "our social lives" and the ways we
use the natural world.[16]

In one of her most extensive metaphorical excursions, Cooper takes her reader from the recently harvested crops of Otsego County to the Old Testament to
contemplate the place and role of gleaners, those who come to harvested fields
to glean the leftover stubble and remains. Reflecting that while there are poor
people in her region, she has never seen a gleaner because there are other ways
of caring for the poor, including letting them beg. Leaving the local customs of
providing for the poor, she imaginatively crosses over to the Old World, citing
examples of the ways gleaning is regulated in Europe and Asia. Going further,
she reaches down into Mosaic law and biblical history to recall the story of Ruth,
her relations to her mother-in-law, Naomi, and to her relative Boaz and the ob-
ligations of Jewish society to take care of its poor. As she says at the beginning
of this entry for August 21, "Walked some distance" (RH 158), this passage has
covered much ground physically and metaphorically. While she takes the opportunity to show off her knowledge of the Bible and ancient customs, to situate
herself in the tradition of biblical exegesis, she also uses the entry to connect
present and past, the local and the global in "loops of relations."[17] She employs
it to contemplate the social issues that the practice of gleaning brings up, like
what to do about poor people, something that she would personally undertake in
founding the Orphan House of the Holy Saviour in Cooperstown. Connecting
her physical wanderings to the imaginative journey, she says at the end of the
entry, "We have meanwhile strayed a wide way from our own ungleaned fields."
She justifies the long divergence from the present time by saying that the story
of Ruth, "seen amid the ancient frame-work of the sacred historian, never fails to
delight the imagination, to refresh the mind, to strengthen the heart, whenever
we turn to it from the cares of our path of life" (RH 166). Like more physical
journeys, this mind-wandering has delighted, refreshed, and strengthened her,
and it has connected her to a community of care that goes back millennia.

Eliding the details of her mobility in the July 28 entry by simply saying "Passed
the afternoon in the woods," she travels through time as she contemplates the
ages of the trees, sketches the effects of settlers on the woods, and projects a
future of environmental conservation. Doing so, she not only describes the
ecosystems of the forest, where "there dwells a sweet quiet, a noble harmony"

(*RH* 127), but also places the forest in the contexts of human history and ethics. As in the July 23 entry, in which, according to Buell, she "reinvents the whole cultural ecology of Cooperstown" when she "repeats the epochal events of public memory," here she outlines the effects of human encroachment on the forest in the last sixty years by men "whose chief object in life is to make money" (*RH* 132).[18] But she also places the forests in a wider, moral context as "a noble gift to man" and the "handiwork of God" (*RH* 125). Criticizing the "unsparing," indiscriminate felling of the trees by the early colonists and the wasteful use of trees during her own time, she urges "some forethought and care" in their use. Finding that true progress lies not in the clearing of the land but rather in "the preservation of fine trees already standing," she connects an environmental ethics to human ethics, saying that "a careless indifference to any good gift of our gracious Maker, shows a want of thankfulness, as any abuse or waste, betrays a reckless spirit of evil." Extending her journeying from an afternoon poking about the woods to rambling through time, she also expands her home geography to a vast spiritual ecology when she wraps "his Almighty economy" (*RH* 132–34) into her imagined home geography.

"Seeing things new, seeing new things" on her excursions around Otsego County, Cooper expands "the notion of community" to include the natural ecology of the woods and God's ecology that extends beyond "Time" (*RH* 134).[19] I can imagine Cooper flushed from walking her favorite paths, perhaps with a notebook in hand, returning to the homestead to write in her journal as she brings to life the world around her and takes off on intellectual, imaginative travels through an enlarged home geography that takes in the forests, meadows, and springs, and the locals she visits, and that extends through time and space to include vanished Native Americans, ash trees, and biblical figures.

Geographers Alison Blunt and Robyn Dowling argue that home is "a *spatial imaginary*: a set of intersecting and variable ideas and feelings, which are related to context, and which construct and connect places and extend across co-existing spaces and scales." Theorizing about home like Dimock theorizes about time, they posit that home can be read in multiple ways—as a "a place/site, a set of feelings/cultural meanings, and the relations between the two." They elaborate, "Home is both a place/physical location and a set of feelings." "Material and imaginative geographies of home are relational . . . each infusing the other with concepts of home." Like Dimock, who argues that "scale enlargement along the temporal axis changes our very sense of the connectedness among human beings," Blunt and Dowling argue that home is likewise multi-scalar, extending "across diverse scales—body, household, city, nation, empire, and globe."[20] In both readings of time and space, porous boundaries reveal the importance of "connectedness," of relationships, and the intersections between material and imaginative geographies. This is important in our reading of Cooper because, while her material home geographies are regional locations, her imagined geographies range through time and across multiple sites. In both cases, the connections, the relations, and the shared humanity and beingness they reveal are important to her. To get an idea of Cooper's home geographies, her ideas of home, and how they figure in her home travels, I want to look at a few examples to see how home and its values are not confined to a house but extend across multiple scales.

Beginning the entry for May 29 by referring to the "varieties of birds flitting about our path," she reminisces about a house wren that for several summers "had a nest built under the eaves of a low roof" of the house. Remembering that their "little friend" would often sing "while the conversation within doors hushed to hear him," she brings the little wren into the family sphere. Domesticating the wren, as she does other birds, she comments on his house-building and parenting styles. From this observation of the house wren from the vantage point of her own home, she makes global connections when she refers to the European wren, the international migratory paths of the wren, and then to the habitat of the "mandrakes, or May-apples" that extend from local meadows to Central Asia. She ends by musing, "One likes to trace these links, connecting lands and races, so far apart, reminding us, as they do, that the earth is the common home of all" (*RH* 55–56). In this entry, she constructs a chain of associations that connects her home travels along a familiar path to the home spaces of the wren and her own family, and then out across the globe, reminding readers that the earth itself is a "common home." In this quick move, she claims her share in the wider home geography and domesticates the earth, as she did the wren, by echoing religious, domestic, and ecological attitudes of belonging and connection.

In another example of home geography, Cooper takes readers on a tour of the farm of her good friend, Mr. B—, joining the physical spaces of the farm with ideas of work and gender. From the vantage point of the window in the sitting room of the little house, Cooper looks out on the fields where the farmer along with a boy and another man are busy in the hayfield. Following her hostess, she inspects the garden, where the family grows food for the table, and the barn, where the dairy cows are kept. As she relates, tending the milk pans, butter, and cheese fell to the women of the home as well as "all of the cooking, baking, washing, ironing, and cleaning" (*RH* 97). Returning indoors, Cooper guides readers to the sitting room, describing the ways it is arranged and decorated, and then takes them to the kitchen, with its cooking utensils, festoons of red peppers and dried herbs hanging from the ceiling, and the great spinning wheel in the corner where the women do the spinning and weaving for the family. Sketching the customs of rural life and the gendered identities constructed in the farmer's homesite, she opines, "Home, we may rest assured, will always be, as a rule, the best place for a woman; her labors, pleasures, and interests, should all centre there, whatever be her sphere of life" (*RH* 100). Clearly articulating conservative ideas about home, women, and the value of rural life, this entry connects Cooper's travels to the farm and the ideology of domesticity, of a "home system" and "political economy" that is "healthier and safer for the individual" (*RH* 99–100), as she returns to her own home at the end of the day. As this example illustrates, home for Cooper is "a place/site," the farm, "a set of feelings/cultural meanings" about women's sphere and the value of rural life, "and the relations between the two," the ways meanings and identity are shaped by farm life.[21] For her, home represents ideas of care and relation, as each family member has tasks, gendered though they are, that contribute to the material and moral well-being of each individual and the family unit.

Likewise, her descriptions of the natural world often figure it as home, a place and a set of feelings and cultural meanings. As Blunt and Dowling explain, their concept of home "moves beyond the dwelling and alerts us to other sites, feelings, and relationships that are called home." Deploying the rhetorics of domesticity and religion, Cooper describes the natural setting she visits on May 16 as a place of repose and comfort, a home, where she is reminded of God's mercies. Strolling "in quiet fields by the river, where sloping meadows and a border of wood shut one out from the world" and embowered in this charming scene, she feels a sweet calm enhanced by her sense of God's presence. She muses, "At hours like these, the immeasurable goodness, the infinite wisdom of our Heavenly Father, are displayed." Meditating on the calming effect of the river, the meadows, and the "birds flitting quietly to and fro, like messengers of peace," she uses words that are often associated with religious and domestic languages to describe the site and her feelings about it: "goodness, "merciful and gracious," "friendship," "sympathy," "gentle harmony," "hearts," "love" (*RH* 45–46). Considering the language and images that describe her stroll along the river, we can see that they make "the transition from the human home into nature's household an easy one."[22] It is no wonder that she would feel at home in this natural location. Or that she would find a spiritual home in the "works of

God" (*RH* 46). Joining the material, environmental, and the imagined, spiritual, geographies through feelings of calm and repose, Cooper shapes an extensive, interrelational idea of home.

These are the kinds of home geographies that Cooper travels in her physical and metaphorical excursions—the local paths, the home, the farm site, the natural environment, and eternal regions of the spirit. Following multiple trajectories in her home travels, she traverses the diverse landscapes and locations in her region along a horizonal line and explores imagined historical, mythic, and spiritual spaces along a vertical axis that reaches into "deep time" and what Yi-Fu Tuan calls "mythical space." Seeing things new on her home excursions, she sees the commonalities that exist through time and space, the "loops of relation" that stitch "a densely interactive fabric" from the physical and imagined, the present and the past.[23] Audaciously gathering these diverse domains, these multiple home geographies into a bundle, like the wildflowers she gathered on her rambles, she imagines a vast interconnected ecology that joins natural, social, and moral systems. Doing so, she figures an inclusive home geography that reverberates with spiritual, domestic, and ecological perspectives.

Donald Worster reminds us that for nineteenth-century Romantics, an ecological perspective, even before the term "ecology" was coined in 1866 by Ernst Haeckel, comprised a "search for holistic or integrated perspective, an emphasis on interdependence and relatedness in nature, and an intense desire to restore man to a place of intimate intercourse with the vast organism that constitutes the earth."[24] This is what Cooper does when she reminds us that the earth is the common home of all and integrates historical, literary, and moral explorations in her nature and travel writing. She does this when she reads human history in the stands of trees and the spring where an imagined Native American refreshed himself. She does this when she traces stories of the ash tree back to mythological time. And she does this when the harvested fields prompt imaginative wandering to the stories of the Old Testament. In her hands, the past has not vanished but instead is a part of the world, of the home geography, through which she wanders. Most importantly for her, the geographies she explores evince the intersections of an ecology of faith with the natural and social systems she recounts.

Stitching together an ecological perspective with an ideology of domesticity "that celebrates human connection, both personal and communal" and spiritual, she audaciously brings natural, social, and moral geographies under the aegis of domesticity and stakes a claim in public discussions about them.[25] Blurring the lines between home and the environment, between material and metaphorical geographies and travels, Cooper demonstrates the porousness of the public and private spheres. Along the way, she disrupts narrative expectations about travel writing when she explores the local landscape and follows the metaphoric tracks of her imagination. Like the birds of passage, the flock of wild geese flying southward and the golden-crowned kinglets who raise their young in northern regions and then fly south for the winter, Cooper tracks an extensive geography that encompasses not only her house, the domains of her rural neighbors, and the local environment but also, like the wren outside her window, flies metaphorically through the larger domains of earth and time. Although assessments of *Rural Hours* have often pointed to her conservative Christianity, politics, and domesticity, we can also think about how it disrupts narrative expectations, blurs boundaries, and positions her as a daring, creative wanderer through far-flung home travels.

Metaphoric Traveling with Henry David Thoreau

EVEN THOUGH HENRY DAVID THOREAU announced, "I have not been much of a traveller" in one of his last publications, "Life without Principle," he journeyed quite a bit, as his travel books *A Week on the Concord and Merrimack Rivers*, *Maine Woods*, and *Cape Cod* as well as his many rambles and boating around Walden Pond and Concord attest.[1] While he claimed a "home-cosmography" (*Walden* 320), he also understood the importance of travel: "True and sincere travelling is no pastime, but it is as serious as the grave, or any other part of the human journey" (*Week* 306). Known primarily for his "social activism and his defense of nature," his "ferocious curiosity" sent him out into the world, even if it was in his "own backyard," to explore nature, society, and himself. Prompted to write up his excursions, he became, Barbara Packer asserts, the "first Transcendentalist to publish a travel narrative" with two essays on walking published in 1843. And, as William Stowe outlines, he was "an avid reader of travel accounts," the most popular genre of literature in the nineteenth century. Travel writing, Stowe further claims, helped shape some of his "work as a writer"; like travel itself, thinking about travel was an integral part of his "intellectual and literary life." Travel was such an essential element of his life that, even when he was not writing explicitly about his journeys, he deployed the material conditions of travel as metaphors for self-exploration, knowledge, and way-finding through the physical terrain and the interior geographies of the self. A complex of objective reporting and meditations about the journey, Mario Cesareo argues, travel writing invites the conversion of experience into language and metaphor, the "traveling eye to the writing gaze," to open more esoteric geographies to exploration.[3] I contemplate that this complex of travel writing and physical and metaphoric journeying helped shape Thoreau into a divergent, innovative thinker.

If metaphors transfer or transport ideas, as Georges Van den Abbeele reminds us of the original Greek meaning for "metaphorein," then we can see how metaphors of travel transport Thoreau into contemplations of the "principal powers" of self and cognition (*Week* 306). Not only does the metaphor of travel "conjure up the image of an innovative mind," Van den Abbeele argues, we can also "invoke the metaphor of thought as travel," because travel and metaphors prompt "new ways of looking at things" that move one beyond preconceived assumptions and values. Similarly, we can invoke travel as a metaphor for thought. Ilan Stavans and Joshua Ellison put it this way: "Travel writing is a form of thinking aloud, with the journey as the narrative frame. This elision of travel and thought—of travel as a metaphor for thought—has a long history." In *The Mind of the Traveler*, Eric Leed claims that "the flows of passage not only provide information about the world," they also provide "information about the self of the passenger" through activities of movement and observation. Contending that the mind of the traveler is not separate from the body and the physical conditions of travel, he theorizes that "the metaphor of travel . . . conjures up the image of the innovative mind that explores new ways of looking at things," which include the material, physical world and the inner world of the self. For Thoreau, who moves "gracefully among scientific information, verbal pictures, and 'contemplations,'" Stowe contends, writing about travel likewise invites contemplations that extend beyond the physical journey to more imaginative, interior excursions.[4] Because travel as a metaphor transports the mind to new terrain just as the material fact of travel transports the body to new geographic locations, it is an apt metaphor for prying into the imaginary geographies of self and mind that Thoreau constructs in his vast oeuvre.

Conjuring up the great explorers Mungo Park, Lewis and Clark, Sir Martin Frobisher, and Christopher Columbus in the "Conclusion" of *Walden*, Thoreau invites associations between physical exploration across the terrain and inner trajectories of self-exploration that he will track in other narratives. Transferring tropes of actual movement—exploration, mapping, and wayfinding—to spiritual, intellectual examination and discovery, Thoreau calls on readers to become explorers of the moral world of the self, to be explorers "of your own streams and oceans . . . your own higher latitudes" (*Walden* 321). As he invokes the "discoverer" of America, he encourages an interior voyage of discovery, enjoining his readers, "Nay, be a Columbus to whole new continents and worlds within you, opening new channels, not of trade, but of thought." Following a cue from

Columbus's journey of discovery, Thoreau figures the interior geography of the self as continents and oceans. Imagining a "moral world" in which "each man is an isthmus or an inlet, yet unexplored by him," a tenuous land mass or secret inlet, he figures a private, solitary, dangerous voyage of self-discovery (*Walden* 321). Using geographic metaphors to imagine the interior being, he suggests that the soul, the conscience, and the mind likewise comprise a place, a location, where one can journey and discover new worlds of thought and identity, the law of "your own higher latitudes." Diving into the empire of the self and charting new territory, he recognizes, is dangerous work that demands "the eye and the nerve," especially when the self-explorer finds truths that open "new channels . . . of thought" that counter socially acceptable avenues (*Walden* 322, 321).

Like the admiral who plotted a new course across the ocean, the admiral of the self must chart new courses, forge new paths, against not only the conformity of society but also one's own past and habits. Having asked readers to plumb the depth of the soul and scout out new moral terrain, Thoreau enjoins readers to follow an *"extra-vagant"* path, to "wander far enough beyond the narrow limits of [your] daily experience, so as to be adequate to the truth of which [you] have been convinced." Like the "cow which kicks over the pail" to run after her calf, he would have readers travel and speak *"without* bounds," to get out of the "ruts of tradition and conformity." Asked why he left his hut at Walden Pond, Thoreau replied that he "left for as good a reason" as he went there: he had "several more lives to live." As well, he mused about the ways we fall into physical and mental ruts: "It is remarkable how easily and insensibly we fall into a particular route, and make a beaten track for ourselves. I had not lived there a week before my feet wore a path from my door to the pond-side" (*Walden* 562). Instead of continuing to live out a known life path, he wanted new adventures, new possibilities, "to go before the mast and on the deck of the world," to follow the "direction of his dreams" and chart new journeys of self-discovery (*Walden* 323–24). Thinking of cosmic journeys, he wants "to walk even with the Builder of the universe, if I may—not to live in this restless, nervous, bustling, trivial nineteenth century, but stand or sit thoughtfully while it goes by" (*Walden*, 329–30). Using tropes of mobility, mapping, and freedom, Thoreau ties the linear, material activity of travel to a vertical, spiritual trajectory of self-discovery and self-reliance. For Thoreau that means following and making new paths, stepping to the music of his own drummer, practicing *"Extra vagance!"* and going outside the bounds and fences that attempt to keep him "yarded" (*Walden* 324). Self-exploration requires not only self-examination, sauntering "abroad in the Great Fields of thought" ("Walking" 215), but also plotting new maps ("to travel the only path I can, and that on which no power can resist me") (*Walden* 330).

This kind of way-finding is difficult because it involves not only exploratory dives into the self but also mapping a new cognitive terrain that situates the self and traces the trajectories of thought. As Thoreau charts the material roads, paths, trails, and tracks that he follows, as he attends to geographic maps of place in his narratives, he is also crafting a cognitive map, a "topography" in the mind, as he writes in *Maine Woods* (200 [hereafter *MW*]). According to psychologist Edward Chace Tolman, a cognitive map is "the abstract map of the environment created by the brain which allows us to navigate the three-dimensional world." Shane O'Mara explains, "It provides a map of the possibilities for movement in the world, giving you the constant 'what and where' you need to move about." He further explains, "At the heart of navigating our world is knowing where we are, where we want to go, and then going there."[5] In many ways these definitions of cognitive mapping connect to Thoreau's injunction to explore the self, since one must know "where we are [and] where we want to go" at the metaphysical level. In Thoreau's hands, geographic signs of way-finding point as well to the project of mapping cognition, for plotting locations and processes of knowledge and thought.

Indicating this injunction to explore the self, Thoreau infuses his narratives with references to maps and way-finding. As Rick Van Noy points out, "The word 'map' appears forty times" in *The Maine Woods*, demonstrating Thoreau's concern with way-finding, literally over the unfamiliar terrain and metaphorically into the "the space of his mind." Venturing into the Maine woods, Thoreau consulted a "map of the Public Lands of Maine and Massachusetts" (*MW* 91), followed established roads like the Houlton Road, and hired the Native Americans, Joe Aitteon and Joe Polis, to guide him. Attending to the waterways, paths and markers, and animal tracks and trails, Thoreau plots the narrative through space. In "Ktaadn" he notes the "traces of bears and moose, and those of rabbits" and relates how he traveled along the "faint paths" the moose had made, "like cow-paths in the woods" (*MW* 57). In "Chesuncook," as he and his companions are looking for moose, he pays attention to tracks, paths, and markers—moose tracks, a pair of moose horns, a log marked with "W-cross-girdle-crowfoot," and the "well trodden paths by which they had come down to the river"—to assure that he is going in the right direction (*MW* 97–98). In "The Allegash" he remarks on a tree in the fork of the path with the letters "'Chamb. L.' written on it with red chalk" and a "musquash trail," the human and animal trails overlapping (*MW* 215). He names the waterways Moosehead Lake, Lobster Lake, the Penobscot, Mud Pond, and Chamberlain Lake and describes the numerous swamps they slogged through, not just for tourists who might follow but as a way of locating himself. By plotting his journeys in these ways, he not only provides spatial movement through the narrative, taking the reader with him as he tramps, slogs, and portages his way through the dense woods, but also locates himself in space, finds himself, and creates a cognitive map of the self. Indeed, place-identity, according to H. M. Proshansky, "is a sub-structure of the self-identity of the person consisting of broadly conceived, cognitions about the physical world." Thus, one way of knowing or identifying the self is to "locat[e] oneself in the geographical ecology."[6] In essence, this is what Thoreau is doing when he records place names and charts the tracks and trails he follows in the wilds of Maine. He is locating himself geographically and psychically.

These paths and trails, animal tracks, and human markers are also signs, a semiotics of knowledge, such as where the moose are and where the travelers are located or headed. They should be reliable ways for finding location and direction, for finding and mapping the self. But when Thoreau fails to read the signs, relies too much on Western knowledge—using maps and compass—and is separated from his guides, he gets lost. In contrast, the Native guides rely on different sources of knowledge, the rocks and trees and some internal navigational system that Thoreau lacks. For instance, as Joe Polis tells him about hunting in the "solemn bear-haunted mountains," Thoreau asks how "he guided himself in the woods." Polis replies that he looks at the hillside to tell north from south or at the rocks to find direction. Unable to explain exactly how he finds his way, it seems to Thoreau that he exercises "his Indian instinct," that he "relies on himself at the moment," that he has a different "sort of knowledge" than the white person (*MW* 184–85). In another instance, Thoreau and his companion become separated from Polis when he goes ahead of them up the trail. They follow his directions, taking a path on the south side of Webster Stream, "a wild wood-path, with a few tracks of oxen . . . mingled with the tracks of moose." Even so, the two men become lost: "without a compass, or the sight or noise of the river to guide us, we could not have kept our course many minutes." In contrast, Polis just seems to know where he is and can "go back through the forest wherever he had been during the day" (*MW* 249–51). He knows how to read the signs of the woods of this environment and the routes that crisscross it in ways that Thoreau, trained to use map and compass, cannot.[7] Without his guide in the dense forests and swamps, Thoreau would have been helplessly lost.

Not only do these episodes demonstrate two different methods of reading the signs, the rational and what seems to Thoreau to be the intuitive, they also suggest that getting out of the ruts of the known unsettles the self. Indeed, Thoreau implies that finding oneself may require getting lost. As he commented in *Walden*, "Not till we are lost, in other words, not till we have lost the world, do we begin to find ourselves, and realize where we are and the infinite extent of our relations" (*Walden* 171). These episodes suggest that getting out of the worn paths of society may require relying on the kind of intuitive way-finding of the Native who follows an abstract map of the environment, geographically and intellectually. And they suggest that navigating the universal questions of where I am and where I am going may be more a matter of intuitive than rational thinking, of Reason rather than Understanding in the Transcendentalist lexicon, the work of the poet rather than of the surveyor. Exploring the inner terrain of the self, Thoreau suggests, requires veering off the built roads of society and plunging into the wilderness of the imagination and drinking from the fountain of inspiration: "The poet must, from time to time, travel the logger's path and the Indian's trail, to drink at some new and more bracing fountain of the Muses, far in the recesses of the wilderness" (*MW* 156).

These paths, in which moose tracks are overlaid with Indian trails, the logger's path, and then by roads and railroads, map cognition onto the spatial environment, creating an archaeology of the road and of knowledge that not only follows linear routes forward but also plumbs a line downward into history. In *Through Other Continents*, Wai Chee Dimock advocates for a new way of reading American literature that is uncannily presaged in Thoreau's writings about travel. She writes: "Rather than being a discrete entity, it is better seen as a crisscrossing set of pathways, open-ended and ever multiplying, weaving in and out of other geographies, other languages and cultures." Using metaphors of transit—pathways and networks—she argues for a new term, "deep time," to describe the "set of longitudinal frames, at once projective and recessional" to describe American literature's more global contexts. Similarly, Thoreau's motif of the "crisscrossing set of pathways" and paths overlaid on each other suggests a reading of "deep time," a longitudinal strategy that informs his travel narratives and the global knowledges he explores. When we consider how the paths and byways Thoreau treks are overlaid, one on top of another, we can see both the longitudinal and the linear at play in his travel narratives. When Thoreau muses in "Ktaadn" that they "probably followed the trail of an ancient Indian carry around these falls" (*MW* 30), he gets at the thick history of the roads. Seymour Dunbar summarizes in his history of American travel: "When the Indians travelled they moved by water if their purpose made it possible. For their land travel they created paths leading from one stream to another. . . . Practically the whole present-day [1915] system of travel and transportation in America east of the Mississippi River, including many turnpikes, is based upon, or follows, the system of forest paths established by the Indians hundreds of years ago." He goes on to say that these trails "when they led through regions where native travel was particularly heavy and long continued, were worn a foot deep by generations" of foot travel. Literally, then, the paths and roads Thoreau followed had a physical depth that hinted at the historical depth of New England and American history that included Native American traditions. Following these tracks, Thoreau contemplates travels back through time as he shapes a geographic imagination that joins the terrain with history.[8]

Overlaid and embedded in the terrain, the arrowheads Thoreau finds during his tramps around Concord, that he turned up hoeing his beanfield, or that he gathers on treks through the woods and along the rivers, comprise another marker of the complexities of place and time. Literally embedded in the landscape and along the trails, the arrowheads represent the ways history is riveted into the terrain and the geographic imagination. When Thoreau notes, "This variety of hornstone I have seen in every part of New England in the form of Indian arrow-heads, hatchets, chisels, etc.," he is signaling the ways the arrowheads mark both the literal paths of the Natives and his own imaginative journey into deep time (*MW* 176). He makes explicit the reading of the arrowheads as markers of the trail in his journal for 1856: "August 12. An arrowhead in Peter's Path. How many times I have found an arrowhead by that path, as if that had been an Indian trail! Perchance it was, for some of the paths we travel are much older than we think, especially some which the colored race in our midst still use, for they are nearest to the Indian trails."[9] As well, they prompt him to dive into the past to ponder the Indian villages and the lives they mark, relics on which the history of New England is built. In his journal for October 22, 1857, he mentions the preponderance of arrowheads and then moves imaginatively to the "far back time" to think about the civilization they signal: "Why, then, make so great ado about the Roman and the Greek, and neglect the Indian?" (*I to Myself* 336). In other words, the relics suggest a civilization as ancient and as important as the Greek and Roman as they figure the transnational sediments in American history and thought. The arrowheads Thoreau finds during his rambles reveal a past that haunts the present, the "ancient battle between the Eastern Indians and the Mohawks" (*MW* 12), the "extinct nation [that] had anciently dwelt here and planted corn and beans ere white men came to clear the land" (*Walden* 156).

More than representing an ancient, to his mind extinct, civilization, they conjure up the humanity, the philosophers, and poets, whose "fossil thoughts" the arrowheads also represent. They are, as Laura Dassow Walls puts it, "Objects as mindprints."[10] Like metaphors, they transport him imaginatively to the past: "I would fain know that I am treading in the tracks of human game,—that I am on the trail of mind,—and these little reminders never fail to set me right" (*I to Myself* 390–91). Like the tracks in the mud that led his party to the moose in "Chesuncook," arrowheads are tracks to the minds of the ancients and his own mind and to his way of thinking. Like the arrowhead that wings its way through the ages, "bearing a message from the hand that shot it," his imagination transports him back through time to contemplate past cultures, philosophies, and poets (*I to Myself* 390–91). Markers of trails past and present, the arrowheads signify a way of thinking that is both linear, following a "philosophy of . . . progress" (*MW* 30), and longitudinal, with dives into "deep history," which suggests two trajectories of thought and writing: forward and inward.

We can see these trajectories in "Walking," a rumination on "the art of Walking" in which Thoreau joins the physical activity of sauntering with spiritual journeying to the Holy Land of the self. Plotting the essay around actual walks and expeditions, he moves the essay forward before he brings it "round again" to the beginning metaphor of the "*sainte terrer*," the saunterer, at its conclusion ("Walking" 185). Structurally, the essay hinges on the material journeys he recounts and the reflective, inner voyages they suggest to him. Weaving horizontal and vertical trajectories, the material and the metaphorical, he aims to "take that walk, never yet taken by us through this actual world, which is perfectly symbolical of the path which we love to travel in the interior and ideal world" ("Walking" 195). The journeys he takes through the "actual world" and the "interior and ideal world" illustrate the way thought for Thoreau moves, forward and inward, kinetically and metaphorically. In this and other essays, he consistently moves between the linear, horizontal mapping of the actual journey and the vertical, deep, internal journeys they call up, to what Dimock calls "deep time" and Yi-Fu Tuan calls cosmic or mythic time. Tuan postulates three kinds of mythic time: cosmogonic time of origin stories; astronomic time that follows the seasons; and human time that follows the course of human life, all of which appear in this essay as Thoreau joins his jaunt to etymological beginnings with the approach of autumn.[11]

Beginning with a quick discussion of the excursions of the Crusaders, he describes his almost daily treks in the woods, connecting his walks "into a nature" with those of "the old prophets and poets Menu, Moses, Homer, [and] Chaucer" in an early example of the movement between the horizontal and the historical-vertical trajectories ("Walking" 192). Another plot point arrives when he remarks, "When I go out of out of the house for a walk . . . I finally and inevitably settle southwest" ("Walking" 195). Inviting the reader to follow him in a southwest direction, he leads us to other roads west and southwest where the "future lies." In a long section in which he contemplates what the West and "the Wild" mean, he activates images of movement, claiming "I must walk toward Oregon" ("Walking" 196). Describing the migrations of birds, quadrupeds, the "Great Western Pioneer" as well as himself as a potential migrant ("Walking" 196–97), he joins moving westward to "a new country or wilderness" to "hope and the future" ("Walking" 204), to "free and wild thinking" ("Walking" 207). He begins with actual travel southwesterly when he leaves his house and then follows a vertical line of thought to the mythic space of the West, an "ideal" space constructed by the national geographic imagination.[12]

Another plot point arises when he thinks about "saunters abroad into the Great Fields of thought." Shifting to more spiritual journeys, he imagines a geography where he can "bathe [his] head in atmospheres unknown to [his] feet." There he will find the "higher knowledge" of "Sympathy with Intelligence" ("Walking" 215). Concluding the essay, he references a walk on Spaulding's Farm as the sun was setting. Recollecting his impressions of "some ancient . . . and shining family" that may have resided there, he weaves the possible with an imagined past as he describes the activities of this supposed family ("Walking" 218). Next, he recounts a climb up a pine tree, from which vantage point he could look out over the land and out to the horizon. He ends the essay by remembering a November meadow walk just as the sun was setting. Imagining the last "saunter toward the Holy Land" and the "great awakening light" ("Walking" 222), he joins literal, earthbound jaunts with metaphysical journeys to enlightenment as he turns toward the celestial Holy Land in this essay that was published a month after his death. Thoreau calls this activity "a true sauntering of the eye."[13] In other words, it encompasses two journeys—through the material world and into the mind.

Even in the more traditional travel narratives, we can see the twin trajectories of forward movement and inward contemplation. In the narratives of *Maine Woods*, which are primarily charted spatially and chronologically along his tramps through the forests, there are moments when he maps a more esoteric journey. One of these comes in "Ktaadn." As he approaches the mountain, he prepares readers for the vertical ascent the essay will take when Tom, one of his companions, climbs a spruce tree to locate where they are and ascertain which direction they should take. Unable to determine their course even from this lookout, the group follows some fresh moose tracks to find their way. Deftly deploying horizontal and vertical paths as the lost men attempt to find themselves, Thoreau anticipates the cosmic questions of location that his journey into the Maine wilds will prompt. At the "Burnt Lands," which had an air of both the familiar and the strange, he shifts the plot from the horizontal project of way-finding to the vertical trajectory toward the mythic forces of Power, Chaos, Nature, Necessity, and Fate. Attempting to locate himself by surveying the horizon and following animal tracks, he becomes lost for a wild moment as he grapples with how to understand the meaning of the universe. He shouts, "Talk of mysteries! Think of our life in nature,—daily to be shown matter, to come in contact with it,—rocks, trees, wind on our cheeks! the *solid* earth! the *actual* world! the *common sense*! *Contact*! *Contact*!" Lost philosophically as he was geographically, he asks the Titan Nature, "*Who* are we? *where* are we?" before he turns his attention to the more familiar landscape (*MW* 71). Indicating that both paths, the vertical and the horizontal, are required for true journeying and finding oneself, one's identity, he quietly comments after his outburst: "Ere long we recognized some rocks and other features in the landscape" (*MW* 71). In this section of existential crisis, he deploys twin methods of locating the lost self, cognitive mapping and mapping cognition, the process of acquiring knowledge. By calling out "*Contact! Contact!*" he indicates that visceral contact with the natural, material world and imaginative contact with the cosmic, mythic realm are both important aspects of spiritual way-finding and thinking.

A Week on the Concord and Merrimack Rivers likewise charts the two trajectories of movement, the horizontal travel of the river journey and the vertical excursions into deep history, as, according to Linck Johnson, he "established the intimate connection between literal and figurative travel, outward and inward exploration." Calling rivers "the natural highways of all nations," Thoreau figures the Concord and Merrimack Rivers as metaphors of travel and imagination and as structural devices that take the reader through the narrative (*Week* 12). Condensing the two-week journey into one, *A Week* begins as many travel narratives do by situating the journey chronologically and spatially: "On Saturday, the last day of August, 1839, we two, brothers, and natives of Concord, weighed anchor in this river port." He describes the boat, lists the provisions they brought on board, and then sets off, "floating past the first regular battle ground of the Revolution" (*Week* 15–17). Thus, the journey and the narrative that recounts it get underway. Throughout, he describes the material aspects of the journey and the physical adventures shared by the brothers. Paying attention to the details of life along the rivers, he inscribes a geographic imaginary of river life, the pickerel and bream, the bittern and the tortoise, the willow, the "rose-colored polygonum," a man fishing on the shore, his dog beside him (*Week* 20). As the journey continues, he recites the towns and landmarks they passed (Ball's Hill, Carlisle Bridge, Dunstable, and Litchfield), the falls and locks they navigated, and the locations where they camped, the first one seven miles from their start at "a little rising ground" near Billerica, until finally, at the end, they made "about fifty miles" on the last day to bring them back to Concord (*Week* 39, 393). Like other travel narratives, *A Week* follows the adventures of the author and records his observations of life as he and his brother, John, float along the two New England rivers. And like other travel narratives it records the inner journey into "the author's brain" and invites the reader to her own imaginative journeys.[14]

Complicating the trajectory of the narrative and the geographic imagination, *A Week* also plots vertical forays into history and exposes "the complex of culturally and historically situated geographical knowledge and understanding" that contribute to the imaginary of place. Rehearsing events of New England history and the conflicts between the settlers and the Native Americans, Thoreau exposes social and spatial relations of power that were played out in the past. For instance, passing Dunstable, he is reminded that it was the jumping off place for "the famous Capt. Lovewell," who "marched in quest of the Indians on the 18th of April 1725" (*Week* 19). On March 31 he recalls that 142 years earlier Hannah Dunstan had made her daring escape from her Indian captors. At Pawtucket he relates the story of "the famous Sachem Passaconaway," who "restrained his people from going to war with the English." As he says, "Every town which we passed . . . had been the residence of some great man" (*Week* 252, 254), and so he infuses the narrative with sketches of the people and events that made them "great." These stories suggest the ways the past inhabits and haunts the present as well as the ways the geographic imagination is "mediated, even conditioned, by previous knowledge," the deep history that he plumbs along the vertical axis.[15]

Although Passaconaway's grave remains unmarked, history and the past are entrenched not only in accounts Thoreau recites but also in the riverscape itself, creating a sedimented geographic imagination. Gliding along the Merrimack between Chelmsford and Dracut, he notes that the area had been the "ancient and capital seat of the Indians": "It was in fact an old battle and hunting ground through which we had been floating, the ancient dwelling-place of a race of hunters and warriors. Their weirs of stone, their arrowheads and hatchets . . . lay concealed in the mud of the river bottom" (*Week* 80, 82). Inscribed by these relics, the landscape bears witness to history through the weirs, the "dents in the earth" where the first white settlers erected their homes (*Week* 160), the "ruins of a mill" (*Week* 233), the arrowheads, and the "money buried everywhere" (*Week* 198). Of the graves of some "aborigines" near Bedford, he writes, "The land still bears this scar here, and time is slowly crumbling the bones of a race" (*Week* 237). Guiding readers into deep history on a vertical journey through time, these memorials mark the uncanny meeting of past and the present where the geographic imagination of space and place meets the historic imagination of the past.

Exemplifying the global, transnational crosscurrents of knowledge that Dimock advocates, Thoreau extends his foray into the past to the Greek and Roman classics, Chaucer, Goethe, and Hindu philosophers, bringing their poems, plays, and sayings into the present time of his narrative. Layering the literary past on the present, as he did when he layered the scars of New England history on the route of his journey, he demonstrates the ways time and thought are overlaid on each other. Remembering the passage in which Antigone asserts her duty to her dead brother Polynices, a question of "the burial of a dead body," Thoreau pairs it with passages from the Hindu philosopher Menu and the New Testament to think about conscience and the law, a question to which he will return throughout his career (*Week* 135). Copying a handful of poems by "the Teian poet," Thoreau likens reading them to a "tour" that is more pleasurable than an actual excursion through the scenery of Greece or Italy (*Week* 226). As he suggests, these references to literature and philosophy comprise a deep intellectual journey that is as exciting and rewarding, if not more so, as the physical adventure of travel. More, he indicates how the authors and the works he brings up are layered century upon century, country upon country, thickening the terrain of the mind. These works become directional signposts along the intellectual, aesthetic "highway" he will travel as he goes "from Homer and Hesiod to Horace and Juvenal" (*Week* 226). Like the sedimented remains of the past embedded in the geography, "Everything that is printed and bound in a book contains some echo at least of the best that is in literature": "Homer had his Homer, and Orpheus his Orpheus" (*Week* 90, 95). Narratively constructing a past "concealed in the mud" of the present, he imagines yet another direction along the longitudinal trajectory in the celestial journeys launched by the ancients: "Reading the classics . . . is like walking amid the stars and constellations, a high and by-way serene to travel" (*Week* 226). More than a display, these "learned allusions and quotations" are road maps along a vertical trajectory down into the past and upward to mythic, spiritual locations in the larger project of wayfinding, of answering the questions "*Who* are we? *where* are we?" (and "where are we going?") (*MW* 71).[16]

In the quest of self-exploration, Thoreau charts yet another avenue for way-finding. Inspired by the fluidity of the river, he figures a curve of thought that meanders and undulates with the water's current. Theorizing a more liquid, associative arc of thought, he uses the metaphor of the river and the ways its currents and winds carry him and his brother along to compare the ways his mind works to the flows of the river. Playing around with the Latin words one could use to describe the Concord, *fluvius* (running water) and *lacus* (basin or tub), and the Latin word to describe the Merrimack, *amnis* (deep-flowing), he connects the flow of the rivers to the flow of writing, another meaning for *amnis* (figuratively, "the flow or pouring out of a piece of writing") (*Week* 10). Prefiguring William James's metaphor of "the stream of consciousness" for the ever-changing and layered consciousnesses that "melt into each other like dissolving views," Thoreau writes, "our thoughts flowed and circulated" (*Week* 331).[17] As he puts it, "The current of our thoughts made as sudden bends as the river" (339). Flexible, always moving, thought for Thoreau in these passages is transient, leading him around its contours to new dreams and visions: "The most glorious fact in my experience is not anything that I have done or may hope to do, but a transient thought, or vision, or dream, which I have had" (140). Thoreau hints that rivers take him to more than physical adventure. They lure and transport him to adventures of imagination and reverie: "Rivers must have been guides which conducted the footsteps of the first travellers. They are the constant lure, when they flow by our doors, to distant enterprise and adventure" (12). Contemplating "the charm of fluent writing," he muses, "We should consider that the flow of thought is more like a tidal wave than a prone river, and is the result of a celestial influence, not of any declivity in its channel" (102). This kind of writing and thinking takes Thoreau and his readers to "higher levels" of intuition and inspiration as "our critical brains" are washed away (103). Writing, he asserts, that follows the currents and bends of thought, that explores associations and defies the strictly rational, is truer because it is alive, always in motion: "Give me a sentence which no intelligence can understand. There must be a kind of life and palpitation to it, and under its words a kind of blood must circulate forever" (151). Like the currents of blood and the flows of the river, there is something alive and present and nimble about this kind of writing and thinking.

Letting the currents take him along, he contemplates journeys of imagination and dream: "We seemed to be embarked on the placid current of our dreams, floating from past to future as silently as one awakes to fresh morning or evening thoughts" (*Week* 19–20). In *The Poetics of Reverie*, Gaston Bachelard muses that "cosmic reveries" "situate us in a world" apart from society and out of time, a

world that "teaches us the possibilities for expanding our being in the universe."
Reverie takes us places beyond the geographic terrain and "extend[s] history
precisely to the limits of the unreal," to places between "history and legend,
between memory and imagination," where "consciousness subsists." This is
where Thoreau as author wandered as he followed the arc of memory and dream
to construct a narrative taking him back in time to when his brother was alive
and they ventured out on the rivers. Indeed, Johnson makes a case for reading *A
Week* as an extended elegy for John. Borrowing the language of the river journey,
"floating" and "gliding" (*Week* 21), Thoreau imagines thought as likewise wandering and meandering in the stream of consciousness as he "floated in imagination
further down the stream of time" (366) and realized "the power of thinking like
a river."[18] Conjuring the "current of our dreams," he travels out of time to a world
apart, to "higher levels" of intuition (103). By comparing thought to the flows of
the river, he suggests that not only is there room for reverie, imagination, and
dream but also that they reveal our truest selves free from the learned constraints
of society and the worn paths of habit: "Our truest life is when we are in dreams
awake" (297). Merging the actual flows of the river with his own contemplative
movement, Thoreau is transported to more metaphoric rivers of thought that
he follows in the narrative.

   As he charts the physical river adventure and as he dives into history, he
also maps the imaginative and intellectual reveries that transport him beyond
history and geography to the empire of idea. Bachelard calls the state "when
we are in dreams awake" (*Week* 297) the "*working reverie* . . . the reverie which
prepares works [like books and art as distinct from our sleeping dreams]." This is
the awake, working reverie that Thoreau follows like the current of the river and
that gives *A Week* "the charm of fluent writing" (102). Using ideas and concepts
as signposts of the imagined journey, he plots an interior course of way-finding
and discovery, converting ideas into locations, places along an "abstract map"
that allow him to navigate more than the "three-dimensional world." As a form
of "divergent thinking," "mind wandering," O'Mara argues, allows us "to integrate our past, present and future, interrogate our social lives, and create a
large-scale personal narrative." The divergent mental excursions that Thoreau
takes in the narrative help him navigate more than the physical world; they
guide him through a geo-philosophical terrain where he can locate himself
intellectually, imaginatively, and plot his way forward as a thinker. Some of these
geo-philosophical landmarks include references to the books that "make us
dangerous to existing institutions" (96), the ways Friends live in harmony
and melody (266), how dreams "are touchstones of our characters" (297), how

the true genius is "an originator . . . who produces a perfect work in obedience to laws yet unexplored" (328), and, at last, silence, "when we hear inwardly" (391). Not random ideas or simply "learned allusions," these side routes mark the mind-wandering that O'Mara calls "creative problem solving" needed not only for dealing with grief and memory after the death of his brother but also for exploring identity and mapping the route to the future. Like travel and travel writing, these metaphors conjure up "the image of the innovative mind that explores new ways of looking at things." While readers may be more interested in the actual adventures of boating, the metaphoric journey of the working reverie transports Thoreau and the reader beyond geographic locations to what Bachelard calls "the world of the soul . . . a soul which is discovering its world, the world where it would like to live."[19]

These journeys, the physical and the metaphoric tours, were transformative for Thoreau. During his travels, he learned such practical things as how to read the bends in the rivers and the moose tracks in the forest, how to portage around difficult water passages, what it is like to kill a moose, and how to camp out in all weathers. His travel experiences provided fodder for intellectual and spiritual transformations. Encountering the great wilderness of Maine, much of it still "unsettled and unexplored," he understood that much of the nation was likewise unsettled, "unmapped and unexplored" (*MW* 81, 83). The Native Americans who navigated the intersections between the Maine woods and the great cities, using ancient trails and modern transportation, "confounded everything Thoreau knew" about "the Indian."[20] Together, the recognition of the interconnections between the wild and the civilized complicated easy definitions of the nation, history, and progress. His confrontation with the raw materiality of Mount Kta-adn unsettled him, causing him to rethink his relation to nature and the cosmos. And writing his narratives, delving into the memory of past excursions, helped him learn how to grieve for his brother and to anticipate his own last journey.

More, wandering and way-finding "abroad in the Great Fields of thought" ("Walking" 215) and imaginative, creative, "divergent thinking" promoted the kind of self-reliant, innovative thinking that would counter tradition and point the way to social reform. Following the currents of his thought, Thoreau progressively moved toward "the active mode" of social reform that would lead him to critiques of "political, spiritual, and physical oppression." A surveyor of more than highways and forest paths, Thoreau maps a geographic imagination that "plays a central role in envisioning and enacting just [,] possible futures" in order to "produce social and spatial justice." Tracing Thoreau's excursions and mental, imaginative jaunts, we can see not only the conditions of travel in antebellum New England but also, more importantly, how travel as a metaphor runs through his narratives and charts the directions his thinking will take him. As Thoreau demonstrates literally and figuratively in his writings about travel, "Fundamental [to being free] is the ability to transcend the present condition," which is "most simply manifest as the elementary power to move." This ability to move beyond the present condition, to travel intellectually, philosophically, and politically, will contribute to transforming him into one of virtue's heroes.[21]

The
MIDWEST

*C*alled to the Old Northwest, the Midwest, to summers on the Great Lakes, travelers during the long nineteenth century witnessed the transformation of the terrain and the geographic imaginary as settlers moved in and pushed the line of the frontier farther west and southwest. Charmed by the open prairies and the clear waters of the Great Lakes, travelers in the early decades of the nineteenth century discovered a region that seemed to promise refreshment, rejuvenation, and reward. By the end of the century, some of those promises were less sure, as the natural landscape gave way to the built environment. As travelers across the Midwest during the nineteenth century, William Cullen Bryant, Margaret Fuller, Catharine Maria Sedgwick, and Constance Fenimore Woolson, and Emily Post in the early decades of the twentieth century were poised to make firsthand observations and comment on the settlement of the land, the growth of cities into commercial and industrial hubs, and the increasing sophistication of transportation and communication technologies. As their narratives chart the march of progress, they also question its meanings, what it means for the burgeoning cities of the Great Lakes and what it means for the individual, at times conflating technological improvement with ideological movement.

Looking for the possibilities of a "new poetry" born of the transitions on the frontier and the intermingling of voices, these writers also sketch the consequences of expansionism on the settlers, Native Americans, the environment, and the nation. From the rude cabins of the early settlers to the posh mansions of Euclid Avenue in Cleveland, from the violence of Black Hawk's War to the gathering of the tribes to collect their annuities and the eventual disappearance of Native Americans from the narratives, these travelers provide perceptive observations of a location and a nation undergoing transformation. As Margaret Fuller's *Summer on the Lakes, in 1843* demonstrates, the ideal of living in nature often grated against the realities of human materialism and racism.

Tracing the changes in travel from William Cullen Bryant's chaotic 1832 journey to Illinois to Emily Post's motorcar trip in 1915, these tourists, vacationers, people looking to refresh their lives through travel, delineate the evolution of modes of transportation, the accommodations available to travelers, and the emergence of tourism in America. Doing so, they demonstrate what it means to be an ethical sightseer, to realize the productive potential of travel that Dean MacCannell defines in *The Ethics of Sightseeing*. Reading these narratives, we can see how looking at the Midwest from the road reveals the ways geographies of travel and the geographic imagination move in tandem with transformations in the geographic and the social terrain.

William Cullen Bryant's
Summers on the Lakes

THE 1832 ILLINOIS JOURNEY

An inveterate traveler, a man who enjoyed hiking, rambling, and walking, William Cullen Bryant recorded his many travels in letters and poems that evince his poet's sensibilities, his delight in the natural world, and a cultural commentary that bring to life the locations he visited. Known today primarily as a poet of the "Fireside" school, Bryant was an important newspaper editor and essayist as well as travel writer. Drawn to the west of the Midwest by a desire to see the country that had enticed his brothers to emigrate, in May 1832 Bryant set out on the first of four journeys (1832, 1841, 1846, 1851) he would make to Illinois and the Old Northwest. The impetus for his first journey to Illinois was to visit his brother John Howard Bryant and take a horseback journey on the prairies. John Bryant had recently immigrated to Illinois, joining his brother Arthur, who had left Massachusetts for Illinois in 1830 as the Bryant farm in Cummington, Massachusetts, "became less productive." Within three years of this first trip, his "four brothers, mother, and sister Louisa were all settled in the West near Princeton, Illinois," and the temptation to join them recurred and prompted Cullen not only to visit on several occasions but also to "invest periodically in land."[1] He never moved to Illinois, remaining a resident of Massachusetts and New York, but his travel writing about the Old Northwest provides a picture of an area undergoing transformation from a frontier to a more settled region marked by towns and cities and the displacement of the wild.

Bryant would become a leading voice for America and the editor of the *New York Evening Post* from 1829 to 1878. But in 1832 he had just managed to increase the paper's profits enough to allow him to leave for a few months' visit to his brother. Founded in 1801 by Alexander Hamilton as an organ for the Federalists, the *Post* was one of New York's "oldest and most prosperous journals" when Bryant took over the editorship in 1829. As editor for almost fifty years, Bryant took up a variety of social and political issues. Michael Branch asserts that he was "the nation's most distinguished newspaper essayist" and that he used his position at the *Post* to "take positions on every major issue affecting American life—issues such as Jacksonian economics, the Mexican War, temperance, the annexation of Texas, slavery, the Civil War, Reconstruction, urbanization, and women's rights" as well as "environmental education, preservation, and protection." So vocal and influential was he about the issues that concerned nineteenth-century America, that James Fenimore Cooper proclaimed, "Bryant is the author of America"; George William Curtis said, "Whoever saw Bryant saw America." Because of his insistence on avoiding sensationalism and his high moral sense, James Boylan asserts, Bryant created a "reputation as the nation's most distinguished essayist."[2]

In addition to essays advocating for the causes he cared about, Bryant included travel pieces, his own and those of other journeyers, giving curious readers a view of America and abroad. Although Bryant did not use the *Post* to publish extensive book reviews or literary essays, according to Allan Nevis, he did use it to comment on "British travels in America" by Mrs. Trollope and Harriet Martineau and to closely follow Charles Dickens's 1842 tour of America. Nevins notes, "The most striking feature in newspaper correspondence of the forties was the prominence given mere travel. Americans were more curious about their expanding and fast-filling land . . . and the expense and hardship of travel made its vicarious enjoyment greater." Indeed, travel writing was the most popular form of writing in the nineteenth century. Among travel sketches by Americans, Bryant published those sent to him in 1841 by a friend, the novelist Catharine Maria Sedgwick. He made room for his own multiple and perceptive travel sketches, sending letters to the *Post* describing many of his trips to the West, the South, and abroad to Cuba and Europe. Although he did not send notices of his first trip west in 1832, the poem "The Prairies," first published in the *Knickerbocker* magazine in 1833, filled in as a testament to his experience.[3]

Geographies of travel, his travel sketches are descriptive accounts of his adventures and of the people and landscapes he encountered. The firsthand observations of an astute observer and careful writer, they record the cultural, social, economic, and political realities of particular places at a particular time. Taking the reader along with him as he moves across the terrain, Bryant's Illinois and Old Northwest letters compose images of America at the beginning of the movement west that enable Bryant and his readers, then and now, to convert space "into meaning," into ideas of nationhood, the environment, and pro-gress.[4] In the nineteenth century, those meanings were fraught with contested and fluid ideas of what America meant and what its future would look like. Reading his and others' accounts of the Midwest, from the early decades of the nineteenth century to the early days of twentieth-century auto travel, allows us to see how the imagined geography of the region and the nation changed as templates of meaning changed with time.

Bryant's first journey west is recorded in letters written to his wife, Fanny, who stayed behind in New York with their young children. The letters were later collected and edited as "Illinois Fifty Years Ago" by his son-in-law, Parke Godwin.[5] Although he begins each of these letters with a salutation to Fanny, "My dear Frances," the journey rather than familiar or familial matters organizes the epistolary narrative. By carefully noting the place and date of composition, "Hagerstown Md. May 24, 1832" ("Illinois" 3); "Steamboat Water Witch on the Mississippi twelve miles above the mouth of the Ohio, June 3, 1832" ("Illinois" 7), and so on, the letters map out the journey in real space and time. Unsurprisingly, accounts of the travel itself form a major motif of the letters. Bryant writes not only of the various modes of transportation he uses and the conditions of the roads, but also of accommodations along the journey—his lodgings and the food he ate. Answering questions of where he went and how he got there, the travel narrative also maps out the movement or progress of a nation that dramatically expanded its boundaries during the nineteenth century and experienced tech-nological revolutions that would transform it from an agrarian to an industrial nation. Anne Baker reminds us that "during the first half of the nineteenth century, the United States more than doubled in size"; she further contends that "geographical knowledge and nation formation were inextricably connected in the United States." Much of this knowledge was facilitated by travel, travel accounts, and the transportation that conveyed travelers to their destinations. As travelers and readers learned "about a nation on the move," "travel literature, American-style," Lewis Perry asserts in *Boats against the Current*, "was much concerned with the ease or difficulty of getting from one place to another" as a sign of the "progress," technological and geographic, the nation was making. Be-cause ideas of civilization and progress in the nineteenth century were joined to the transportation revolution, roads, steamboats, and railroads stand in as signs of advancing civilization. Paying attention to systems of transportation in travel writing thus reinforces the interfaces between technology, travel, travel writing, and nationhood. Noting the different methods of transportation he uses, Bryant participates in this meaning-making as he bears witness to the conditions of travel in the early nineteenth century that were made "confusing and chaotic" by the "different methods of making any . . . journey of length, and [the] many possible conditions to be encountered during its progress."[6]

On the cusp of this revolution in 1832, Bryant's attention to the transportation system satisfies curiosity about the hardships of travel, but it also signals the nation's technological progress, chaotic as it may have been at the time. He begins by writing that he "left New York on the steamboat New York early in the morning" of May 22 and then "transferred to stage-coaches" to Bordentown, where he embarked "on a little boat" for Philadelphia. The next day, he traveled by boat and railroad to Frenchtown, covering "sixteen miles and a half . . . at the rate of ten miles an hour." At Frenchtown, passengers were "put on board the Carroll" and sailed down the Chesapeake to Baltimore. Leaving Baltimore by rail, he engaged in conversation with "three Virginia planters," and he remarked, "This mode of travelling is agreeable and rapid" ("Illinois" 3–5). In 1832 the Baltimore & Ohio Railroad, which connected Washington, D.C., to Baltimore, was one of the few early rail lines, having been opened to steam-powered locomotive in August 1830 with the *Tom Thumb*. In 1835, 97,786 passengers would travel on the sixty-to-seventy-mile line of the B&O as the rail system in the United States rapidly grew.[7] Bryant was an early adapter of this modern technology, no doubt sitting in cars much like the *Tom Thumb*'s open-air cars. If "chaotic" because of the "different methods" of travel, the 1832 trip was unremarkable in terms of danger or adventure, a point not to be lost on an eastern reading public that might have been hesitant about travel to the frontier.

In addition to giving readers a view of the technology of transportation, Bryant sheds light on the sociology of travel, of the classes of people who travel and those who serve travelers. The "Virginia planters . . . remarkably intelligent men—slovenly in their dress, but gentlemanly in their manners" and the women of the "ladies' cabin" ("Illinois" 4, 8) testify to a traveling public of middle-to-upper-class citizens. The farther west Bryant travels and the further off the beaten track he goes, the ruder the class of citizens he meets. While he is able to stay at Barnum's Hotel in Baltimore, where he meets a fellow editor and the secretary of state for New York, the taverns beyond the eastern seaboard are less sophisticated, if not downright "filthy" ("Illinois" 16). He relates that, in one, several men, notably "two brawny, hard-breathing fellows" ("Illinois" 13), shared the same room with him. Bryant also stayed with farm families who provided for travelers. He writes of one such place with its "sweaty hostess" and a cabin so occupied with family and travelers that in addition to occupying all the indoor space of the one-room log cabin, "the floor of the piazza was also occupied with men wrapped in their blankets" ("Illinois" 18–19). Such was the practice in the rural areas of the country: "Every house on the great road in this country is a public house, and nobody hesitates to entertain the traveler or accept his money" ("Illinois" 21).

These public houses also provide most of Bryant's contacts with local residents—the sweaty hostess, the Kentuckians who served him bread and milk, and the "tall young wife" who gladly served him food and coffee even though she was so poor that she had "but one spoon for every purpose" ("Illinois" 21–22). Replicating the dialect of his Dutch hostess who asked if he was "in yearnest" about eating cornbread with milk, Bryant uses language to code her as immigrant and lower-class. Likewise, his rendition of a tale about the murderous Cottrells of the Cumberlands uses dialect to place the storyteller demographically at the same time that he creates a regional identity through language: "They got near whar yon driftwood lays, and thar they killed him in a thicket" ("Illinois" 6). Doing so may betray his own upper-class inclinations, as his use of dialect seems to poke fun at his hosts, but it also provides a geographic imaginary of the region and the people who inhabited it.

Likewise, the farther west he goes, the ruder and simpler the meals become. From the dinner of "corned beef roasted, pickled eggs, and boiled potatoes, with gravy poured over them on the dish" at Smithfield in the Alleghany Mountain region ("Illinois" 6), he goes to being served "a rasher of bacon, a radish, bread and milk," "warm cakes, bacon, coffee, and lettuce, with bacon-grease poured over it," and "cakes of corn-bread" and milk ("Illinois" 18–21). Cornbread and bacon, inexpensive and readily available, were staples of the frontier diet and all there was to share with the wanderer. Recounting what he ate provides Bryant with a way to mark or remember the journey, creating "edible chronotopes" of "time, place, and memory,'" but it also helps to shape an image of the regional or cultural identity he imagines.[8] What we find in Bryant's 1832 journey to Illinois is a rural population ready to share the little they have but also one for which the niceties of middle-class, urban society, like the spoons Bryant notices, are lost in the effort to manage on the edge of the frontier.

In her novel A New Home: Who'll Follow?, Caroline Kirkland would also make distinctions between the realities of frontier living and the expectations of her middle-class immigrant, Mary Clavers, who learns to simplify her living arrangements as she adjusts to life in rural Michigan. Her narrator comments that in her early days in Michigan, she "was surprised by the dearth of comforts.

... Neither milk, eggs, nor vegetables were to be had." "[But after only] fourteen days from the city ... my ideas of comfort were by this time narrowed down to a well-swept room with a bed in one corner, and cooking apparatus in another." As sojourners, Kirkland and Bryant represent the foods, accommodations, and speech patterns of the area as they also create a regional identity that is "other" and coded by class, by the distinction between the "city" and the "country," which Bryant and Kirkland read as "a place of backwardness, ignorance, limitation," in the words of Welsh author Raymond Williams.[9]

In the early nineteenth-century, the prairies east of the Mississippi River represented to many "the West," the edge of the frontier. Frederick Jackson Turner defined the frontier as a place that "lies at the hither edge of free land" between settled and so-called unsettled land. Turner defined the frontier as both a line one could cross between savage and civilized and a forward, westward-moving wave that demonstrated the progressive Americanization and industrialization of the nation. According to Turner, as the frontier environment was changed by progressive waves of settlers, so too the vanguard into the wilderness was changed as it adapted to the environment and Indian ways of life. As Turner explained, the frontier represented the "meeting point between savagery and civilization" as Euro-Americans made incursions into the land claimed by Native American tribes. When William Cullen Bryant visited Illinois in 1832, it was in the process of being settled by people like his brothers and those with whom he stayed. Speculation in public, "un-settled" land, which could be purchased for $1.25 an acre, prompted many, like the Bryant family, to buy land in the hopes of starting a new life or of making profits from their investments. The settlers' homes that Bryant saw were crude, often log cabins with dirt floors, and the town of Jacksonville, where he stayed for a night, is, in his account, "a horribly ugly village" with "the ugliest of possible brick courthouses." Adjacent to the plains, which are "partly enclosed and cultivated, and partly open and grazed by herds of cattle and horses" ("Illinois" 13–14), the town, founded in 1825, is situated on the border between the wild and the pastoral, between openness and enclosure, between the unrefined or "ugly" and a future of respectability. When he revisits the Old Northwest in 1846, these areas have become settled, replications of "bustling Yankee town[s]," and the line of the frontier has moved on.[10]

Situated on a cultural border between settlers who were moving in, claiming land, and building towns, and the Native Americans they were displacing, the Illinois frontier of 1832 was marked by violence. Bryant writes to his wife of the murder of several families by Indians near Kaskaskia, the violent reaction of St. Louis residents to a stabbing of a white man by "Indian Margaret," and his encounter with the "Illinois militia," a "hard-looking set of men" ("Illinois" 20). He notes, "There is much talk in St. Louis concerning the Indians," and he mentions the families murdered on Rock River, their bodies "left to be devoured by hogs and dogs" ("Illinois" 11). What he does not tell her is that in the summer of 1832, Black Hawk and the Sac Indians he led engaged in what is known as Black Hawk's War in a gambit to return to their homes in Illinois. Seymour Dunbar, who sees "a very close relation between the Indian problem and white travel," relates that when Black Hawk led his band back across the Mississippi River to their lands in Illinois to raise "a crop of corn," a band of "frontiersmen" shot at the band, provoking Black Hawk. Twelve "frontiersmen" were killed, and, in an uneven display of force, Governor John Reynolds ordered three thousand militia "to subdue the Indians and drive them out of the state." Sioux Indians, "hereditary enemies of the Sacs," were brought in to route the Sacs, who, fleeing to Wisconsin, killed more settlers and were overtaken in the Battle of Bad Axe. There a massacre of Indian women and children trying to recross the Mississippi River ensued, made worse by attacks by the Sioux on the west side of the river. After the war, thirty million acres were transferred to the United States, and the Sacs were promised an annuity of $20,000.[11]

As Black Hawk later told it, "[I had heard that] three families of whites had arrived at our village [during the winter], and destroyed some of our lodges, and were making fences and dividing our corn-fields for their own use." Ronald Satz explains that the tribes of the Old Northwest had a history of migrations and were "close enough to their old domiciles to return whenever the hunting or crops in their new location proved insufficient for their needs." Such was the case with Black Hawk's tribe, who had returned to their old homes only to find them claimed by the new settlers. Bringing together "about two hundred warriors," Black Hawk explains how they "attacked their fort" and took what provisions they could get, killing "several men and about forty horses." After another skirmish, Black Hawk directed his people, reduced and starving, to recross the Mississippi River where "a party of whites" "commenced *slaughtering* them!" In this "Battle of Bad Axe," many of the women and children were shot in the river or drowned. Of those who made it across the river, "a large body of Sioux" pursued and killed many. Black Hawk relates that, in two hours, sixty of his band were killed, "besides a number that were drowned," with about sixteen whites killed.[12]

This is the violence that Bryant quickly inserts into his June 19 letter to Fanny, placing it among descriptions of the prairies, the "sweaty hostess," and his inclination to "purchase a quarter section" of land. He does note, "Every few miles on our way we either fell in with bodies of Illinois militia . . . or saw where they had encamped for the night." Calling them a "hard-looking set of men," he nonetheless deflates their danger by saying that "some of the settlers complained that they made war upon the pigs and chickens" ("Illinois" 20). Perhaps he did this to avoid alarming his wife, whom he had left at home in New York with their children. Perhaps he did not calculate the danger to himself, since he continued with his journey despite the violence. Because the war was reported in newspapers, including the Galena, Illinois, *Galenian*, Bryant was well aware of the war and its costs for both whites and Indians. One then wonders why he did not use the travel narrative to contemplate the meaning of the war for Black Hawk's tribe, the settlers, or the nation. It may be that the war played into his and the nation's narrative that Indians should give up their land (and their way of life) to the encroaching settlers. It also supported a narrative of the Indian as congenitally, racially violent and hence "doomed."[13] Indeed, some of the stories that the *Evening Post* had run in the winter of 1830 pointed to "deeds of cruelty and barbarity" by the Southern Cherokees against "unoffending white women and children" (March 4, 1830). It seems that the violence that Black Hawk's War generated may have supported rather than contested these readings of the Native American.

Although Bryant usually advocated progressive, democratic ideals in his *Evening Post* editorials, he also "supported [Andrew] Jackson's harsh removal policies." For scholars like Carl Ostrowski and David Baxter, Bryant's support of Jackson's removal policies is troubling because it suggests his reconciliation to the "displacement and possible extinction of the Indians." Looking at the situation of the southern tribes from the point of view of a Euro-American committed to ideas of progress and development, Bryant believed that the land held by the tribes "would remain in a state of nature" and that the "unproductive" Indians, would "decline in numbers, morals and happiness." Quoting and reiterating much from a January 9, 1830, *North American Review* essay by Lewis Cass, governor of the Michigan Territory, Bryant averred that the southern Indians had "made not actual progress towards civilization" and instead had "acquired the most reprehensible vices and evil habits of the whites." He also followed up his review with stories of violence conducted by the southern Indians, perhaps as a way of supporting Cass's claim that even with their close proximity to whites, the Indians remained "a barbarous people."[14]

The answer to the situation in Georgia was to offer them a "new country." Bryant writes, "[There] we may hope to see that improvement in their condition, for which we have so long and so vainly looked." As well, removal was thought to protect the natives from the "dangers to which they [were] exposed," President Monroe wrote in 1825. "Under [these] causes . . . it will be difficult, if not impossible, to control, their degradation and extermination." Removal would "not only shield them [the Indians] from impending ruin, but [also] promote their welfare and happiness." As biographer Gilbert Muller notes, in the face of the "impending doom" Bryant and Jackson foresaw for Native Americans, Bryant used his editorials to urge, in Jackson's words, that "Congress should set aside a tract of land, to be guaranteed to the Indians as long as they should choose to occupy it." Because of the violence between whites and Cherokees in the South and the push for land, Bryant saw the removal policy as "universally commended for its humanity and justice." While the fate of Black Hawk's tribe may rationalize the humanistic concern that bolstered his support of the removal policies, paradoxically the Natives were not safe on either side of the river boundary, or, for that matter, in the in-between space of the river. It is disappointing that Bryant did not pause in his narrative to contemplate questions about the place of the Indian and conflicts with settlers, simply commenting that he had to "relinquish [his] projected route to Chicago, which [was] said to be unsafe" because of "the savages" ("Illinois" 10). But Bryant's lacuna mirrors that of a nation that did not see a place for Native Americans in their conceptions of citizenship or nationhood. As Lucy Maddox reminds us, "Nineteenth-century analyses of 'the Indian question' almost always end . . . at the virtually impassable stone wall of the choice between civilization and extinction for the Indians."[15]

Similarly, questions about the use of the environment do not appear in the 1832 letters. Bryant was an enthusiastic amateur scientist who would go on to advocate for city parks and an early version of national parks—"tracts of forest" in "the public domain." He was instrumental in creating New York City's Central Park, lamenting as early as 1833 the "deficiency of public squares in the lower part of the city."[16] As a traveler, Bryant carefully described the environment, naming the animal life and plants that he observed. Passing through Cincinnati, he named the trees along the shore of the Ohio—the "oak, sugar-maple, hickory, buckeye . . . the tulip-tree, the button wood." Commenting on his "first look at a natural prairie," he noted wild plums and wild gooseberries; the "prairie-hen," "prairie-rattlesnake," and "prairie-wolf," and "the violet, wood-sorrel, and the phlox (*Divaricata lychnidia*)." He called attention to the prairie landscape with its "coarse grass and thinly scattered trees" ("Illinois" 6–15).

Yet his depictions of the natural environment are at odds with his support for "western settlement" that will, perhaps irrevocably, change that environment. As Leo Marx might suggest, this scene exemplifies the contradiction inherent in the pastoral ideal and the idea of America.[17] While the naturalist in him could appreciate the natural environment, Bryant also promoted westward expansion in his editorials and in his actions. His family moved west to Illinois as part of that movement West, turning the prairies into farmland, and he was so taken with the area that he wrote to Fanny, "I am strongly inclined to purchase a quarter-section in this place" ("Illinois" 15, 19). This particular piece of land is attractive to the visiting Bryant in part because of its proximity to a market and sawmills, indicating an impulse to improve the natural environment with farms, towns, and markets and to make it commercially viable. Just such is the work of the settler-farmers, like his brothers. And just such is the work of "civilization," which quite literally converts the natural environment to the city, the *civitas*.

The tension between an appreciation for the environment and the desire to settle the land repeats a nineteenth-century dialectic that is also evident in Henry David Thoreau's essay "Walking." There Thoreau looks west, toward Oregon, as the direction he and the nation must move, for there lie the future and freedom, "enterprise and adventure," progress and wilderness. Demonstrating the dialectic that informed much of the national rhetoric about the West, Thoreau promotes the natural, saying, "The West of which I speak is but another name for the Wild; and . . . in Wilderness is the preservation of the World." But he also celebrates movement west as a sign of progress, the direction the nation is taking in which the farmer "displaces the Indian . . . because he redeems the meadow" as the wild is tamed and settled.[18]

This tension points to what historian Donald Worster has called the "Western paradox." According to Worster, there are "two dreams . . . tugging at our feelings [about the West]: one of a life in nature, the other with machines; one of a life in the past, the other in the future." Similarly Marx examines the two great conflicting metaphors of the nation—the pastoral and the technological— perhaps exaggerated by the promise of "the West" to the American geographic imaginary. As Worster points out, the West has called Americans to its landscape and ideas of freedom associated with its wide open spaces. But the West has also been a site that has encouraged a "technological" future, what Thoreau and others would call "progress." In the nineteenth century, this idea of progress, of "expansion, change, [and] development," was complicated. As Lawrence Buell has noted, the word "progress" means "literally a procession or transit, which the democratic and industrial revolutions of the nineteenth century taught us to equate with 'improvement,' first with political liberation and then with technological development." In addition to technological advancement, the idea of progress was tied to the republican virtues of piety, prosperity, and patriotism.

As Catharine Marie Sedgwick wrote, "[Travelers on the Great Excursion of 1854 to the Midwest were able to see] the inappreciable riches and untold beauty of our own country—our own inalienable possessions; to have our piety and our patriotism kindled . . . by the first revelation to our senses of the capacity of our country, the first intimation of its possible glorious future." Echoing Thoreau's exclamation "Westward the star of empire takes its way" and the term John L. O'Sullivan coined when he named what many had been thinking—"the right of our manifest destiny to overspread and to possess the whole of the continent," Sedgwick (and many other Americans) equates geographic, technological progress with political and religious ideals. In fact, O'Sullivan wrote in 1839, "We are a nation of human progress, of individual freedom, of universal enfranchisement," equating progress not just with imperialistic motives but also with liberation.[19]

Asking who can "set limits to our onward march," O'Sullivan tied geographic movement with something more ephemeral than land, for "progress" in the nineteenth century was also a metaphor for a philosophical, religious ethos of self-improvement. In his lecture "Self-Culture" (1838), the Unitarian minister William Ellery Channing persistently employed spatial metaphors and the rhetoric of mobility to encourage his audiences toward self-improvement. "Self-culture," he declared, is "the care which every man owes to himself, to the un-folding and perfecting of his nature." It is accomplished by the "turning of the mind on itself," the "discovery" of the "self-forming power treasured up in themselves," and the control by the mind of the "animal" appetites of the body. The result of this inward focus is "growth, expansion, [and] progress"—the very words John O'Sullivan would use to describe the nation's political and racial "manifest destiny." Relating the unfolding of a person's nature to movement and "the advances of society" "from brutal degradation," Channing connected individual and social improvement to the inevitable forces of history: "The past and the present call on you to advance." Ralph Waldo Emerson too tethered self-cultivation to progress and forward, linear movement, to power over an untamed self and the power gained from self-control. In his Unitarian sermons he described self-reliance as "the progress of a good man when he begins to feel the unworthiness of finding his rule right out of himself," as being "led" by God to self-sufficiency and freedom, and as the advancement of the soul. He told his Boston congregation, "God is setting before every soul that he hath made a great work, an interminable progress." Speaking of self-improvement in part as the control over the body and the animal appetites, Emerson also employed a rhetoric joining movement forward in space and time with the advancement of civilization over the "savage." Thus, ideas of moral self-improvement and personal self-reliance mirror, complicate, and are complicated by metaphors of geographic and political movement. For naturalists like Bryant and Thoreau, these metaphors play into the "western paradox" that Worster mentions and into the brutal destruction of indigenous peoples, who like the personal appetites that Channing and Emerson admonished listeners to tame, were called "savage." As Roy Harvey Pearce pointed out, no one "thought to denounce American civilization."[20] The dilemmas or paradoxes about the West, the Native American, and the environment that we see in Bryant's 1832 letters also inform his imaginative rendition of his experience in the poem that he wrote after returning to the East from his first visit to the prairies.

INTERLUDE

"The Prairies"

Lawrence Buell calls Bryant's "The Prairies" "one of the first of many attempts in verse and prose during the second quarter of the nineteenth century to celebrate the prairie as a region of the American imagination."[21] Not only does the poem paint the prairie environment ("The unshorn fields, boundless, and beautiful"), it is also a poetic extension of Bryant's travels in which he takes the reader along with his narrator on a journey of discovery and through a reverie, a "dream," of the past. The poem gives him the space to contemplate and order what he saw and experienced on the journey, what he did not take the time in his letters to Fanny to explore. It also enables him to use poetic language to construct metaphors that move or transfer the immediate, firsthand experience of the journey into a new form and meaning.

Like the epistolary travel narrative, the poem is organized by journeying and by movement across space and time. The poem is told from the point of view of the traveler who beholds for the first time the prairies, his heart swelling as he "takes in the encircling vastness" of the undulating grasses, the surface "unchained" and moving with the clouds. As he moves onto the prairie it seems to be in motion, to undulate like the vast ocean and the clouds. Verbs like "sweep," "rolls," "glide," "toss," and "pass" punctuate the movement of the prairies and the poem's progress. Looking about, the speaker contemplates the "prairie-hawk" "poised on high," who "flaps his broad wings, yet moves not." Motionless, the "prairie-hawk" nonetheless conjures up distant places, Mexico, Texas, Sonora, and the "calm Pacific"—all places associated with the American West, the American desert, and the westward movement of the nation, prefiguring the military conflict with Mexico to come in 1846.

Continuing, the speaker guides his "steed" over the "high rank grass" of the prairie. As he does so, the speaker contemplates the "mighty mounds" and "a race, that long has passed away," extending the travel motif chronologically through time—to "deep" time—as he imagines a majestic culture, one to rival the Greeks, now "forgotten" and "unremembered." These "mound-builders" vanished when the "red-man came— / The roaming hunter tribes." In Bryant's poem, history is told in terms of movements, what Baxter calls the "passing-of-empires theme."[22] The coming of the "red-man" precedes the vanishing of the "mound-builders," the forms of death encroaching on the scene in the form of vultures until finally a "solitary fugitive" approaches the victors and makes a new life with them. Here Bryant is thinking about the cycles of time, the "changes" of "forms of being" not only for the forgotten race but for also the indigenous people who leave "the blooming wilds" for the region of the "Rocky Mountains." Recalled from this reverie of the past, the poet contemplates the life before him and the colonizing bee with "his domestic hum" as he thinks of the "advancing multitude / Which soon shall fill these deserts" (the settlers like the Bryant brothers who will domesticate the land). Having viewed in his mind's eye the movements of peoples onto and out of the prairies, the speaker brings himself and the reader back to the present moment in which he finds himself "in the wilderness alone."

"A region of the American imagination," as Buell puts it, Bryant's prairie connotes a geographic imagination haunted by the past, both a mythical past of mound-builders and the nearer past of the violence of Black Hawk's War. Even as it mimics the travel narrative, recounting the journey of the traveler, the poem contemplates the movement of the Native Americans and their presence and absence on the prairie. Although he had heard about Black Hawk and the Indians and seen the Illinois militia, he does not tell us (or Fanny) in his 1832 letters that he actually saw or encountered any Indians. Thus, the Native American remains absent physically and ontologically in his letters and his poem, present only in his imagination as loss—historically and eminently in the future. Even the monuments of their past civilization, the mounds, denote not the remains of Native Americans but those of a mythic tribe displaced by the "red-man."[23] The absence of both the mound-builders and the "red-man" from Bryant's travel experience allows him to imagine them from his point of view, a standpoint that knows only the violence and disappearance, not the subjectivity of the Indian. Had he written the poem after his 1846 trip to the Great Lakes, when he saw Native Americans in various stages or degrees of assimilation, he might have featured women gathering wild rice, the two men who guide his canoe through the Sault rapids, scenes of wigwams on the beaches, inhabitants drunk on whiskey or going about their daily routines. But in 1832 he writes of the mythical Indian, not the real one. Rather than reading the poem strictly through the lens of Bryant's support of Jackson's removal policy, we should think of it as a meditation on the displacement and massacre of indigenous peoples, the violence of the frontier, the movement of settlers onto the terrain, and the removal of the tribes across the Mississippi River to the reaches of the Rocky Mountains.

While he seems to think that the displacement of the wild, the Indian, is inevitable in the face of the march of progress, the poet returns his gaze in the last stanza to the details of life, the "myriads of insects," flowers, and "graceful deer." Death and life are juxtaposed in this poem just as he juxtaposes the hawk, which conjures the vastness of the west, with the little colonizing bee. Doing so, Bryant illustrates the western paradox: the dream of "a life in nature" in conflict with the progress that tames the wild, the romanticization of the past against a future wrought by the violent transformations of the present.[24] Ironically, the free flight of the "prairie-hawk" extends across the lands that the United States will soon contest and colonize as the nation pushes west, as it wrenches lands from Mexico and more indigenous tribes. Wistfully, sadly, the speaker who has seen the past and the future wakes from his reverie to find himself alone in the wilderness with his thoughts. The unresolved ending of the poem may reflect Bryant's own mixed emotions about movement into the West, what is lost in the march of empire. Although the last stanza is alive with the "laugh of children, the soft voice / of maidens, and the sweet and solemn hymn / of Sabbath worshippers," it is prefaced by loss, the haunting of the land by the "ancient footprints stamped" into the ground.

"THE EARLY NORTHWEST"

The changes Bryant had predicted in "The Prairies" are evident in the 1846 letters about his third journey to the Old Northwest. Just as the poem had posited the "domestic hum" of the bee and the "advancing multitudes," so his travel account focuses on settlement, the domestication of the land and the Native Americans. He points several times to the changes he has witnessed from his 1841 visit five years earlier: the number of travelers to the area, the growth of the towns, and the multinational, multicultural mix of inhabitants. As readers, we can also see the changes since his 1832 journey, fourteen years previous. The chaotic quality of travel of 1832 has been simplified by steamers that ply the Great Lakes, the rustic accommodations replaced by hotels (even in the small towns), the focus on food has disappeared, and the only real danger to Bryant is the fog on the lakes and the possibility of thieves in Detroit. The landscapes that Bryant now describes are a mix of the natural environment, neighborhoods, villages, and cities, with the natural framing the built landscape. Of the western shore of Lake Michigan, he notes the "high bank presenting a long line of forest" broken up by the "little town of Sheboygan" with "its cluster of houses just built" and its two hotels.

"[Milwaukee]," he writes, "which is rapidly becoming one of the great cities of the West . . . lies within a semicircle of green pastoral declivities sprinkled with scattered trees." Chicago, a city of "more than fifteen thousand" is described by "its long rows of warehouses and shops, its bustling streets . . . and its suburbs" stretching out to the prairies ("Early Northwest" 58–60). Throughout the 1846 narrative, he points to the growth and development of the built environment, the growth of cities (*civitas*), the settlement and domestication of the area, the fort at Mackinaw Island that is now a tourist attraction, and the Indians who are gathered in villages of log cabins and wigwams rather than roaming in marauding bands.

Still attentive to the environment, Bryant describes the transparency of the lakes, their "clean sands" and shoals of fish easily seen through the clear water ("Early Northwest," 58). As he did in 1832, he names the trees he sees, the locust tree and the peach tree, but now he also remarks on the damage done to the trees by settlers who "had girdled them and left them to decay and fall at their leisure" and the clouds of smoke from burning "woods or prairies" as farmers clear the land ("Early Northwest" 54–57). Not only has the landscape changed, a new kind of immigrant, "copper-mine speculators," has significantly changed the area around Lake Superior with houses and warehouses, to say nothing of the mines. While speculation in land was not new, speculation in copper was. The boom in copper had begun in 1843, and, as Donald Ringe notes, Bryant visited Sault St. Marie at the height of the boom and the rapid development of the Sault into a "bustling boom town."[25] Bryant writes about the purity and size of the copper taken from the mines, one "estimated to weigh twenty tons" ("Early Northwest" 66), instead of any damage to the environment. Rather, his attention is caught by the people drawn by the copper boom and the rapid development of the Great Lakes region. He notes the environmental damage being caused by careless farming practices and copper extraction, but Bryant the naturalist does not linger on these scenes. It will be left to Constance Fenimore Woolson in 1872 to pointedly critique the destruction of the natural resources that brought settlers to the area in the first place.

Describing the "men of all ages and complexions . . . a party of copper-mine speculators . . . mixed with a few Indian and half-breed inhabitants of the place" who came to the copper mines at the Sault ("Early Northwest" 66), Bryant notes the demographic changes since his 1832 letters. The burgeoning towns and cities of the Great Lakes are home to the new German and Irish immigrants, who are bringing their traditions, "their holidays," and a Roman Catholic college to the West. Visitors from Virginia, New York, and Massachusetts journey to

Mackinaw in search of health and recreation, and emigrants from Scotland, London, and France make their way into his narrative. As well, the influence of the French, through the French Canadians, the "*voyageurs*" who established the fur trade ("Early Northwest" 79), and the mixed-blood Indians with French Canadian heritage, who speak a mix of Indian languages, English, and French, suggest the international quality of the region. There is even a hint at transnational cosmopolitanism in the example of an Indian who was educated in Rome to become a priest, a "learned savage who talks Italian" ("Early Northwest" 80). Bryant is witnessing not only the settlement of the West but also the development of a kind of transnational citizenship that is different from the West of 1832 that was populated primarily by poor emigrants from Kentucky and New England.

Perhaps the most striking difference between the 1832 account and the 1846 one is the situation of the Native Americans. Although Bryant relates an account told to him by "an intelligent gentleman" about the Pillagers, "a fierce and warlike race" ("Early Northwest" 73), the Native Americans that he encounters occupy various degrees of assimilation and domestication. While the earlier account focuses on violence, here he pays attention to the lives of the Indians and the effects of assimilation. He mentions some of their everyday tasks—Indian women gathering wild rice, men building a log cabin, and fishing. He draws a quick sketch of Indian children playing in the water "like seals." He writes about their homes, the Chippewa village with log houses, the wigwams of the Potawatomi people, "pyramids of poles wrapped around with rush matting," the "humble cabins of the half-breeds" at Sault St. Marie, "with here and there a round wigwam near the water" ("Early Northwest" 55–65). He writes about their clothes or "costumes," noting the blend between Native and European modes of dress: "an Indian woman, in a blue dress and bareheaded"; "a very large man, who wore a kind of turban, and a white blanket made into a sort of frock." He notes their handicrafts—weaving, embroidery, and the birchbark canoes that made him "wonder at the ingenuity of those who had invented so beautiful a combination of ship-building and basket-work" ("Early Northwest" 55, 56, 69). He tells us about their graves and their attendance at Sunday services, providing a quick ethnography of the Great Lakes Native Americans, the majority of whom are mixed-blood— "half-breeds" he calls them. Commenting on their lives and culture, Bryant nonetheless objectifies the people; while he seeks to bring them to life on the page, he constructs them as part of the tourist spectacle, presaging the stance of later tourists to the West.

These mixed-blood Indians evidence to him a curious blend of European, often French, influence with Indian physiognomy and culture. When he visits the home of a mixed-blood woman on the Canadian side of the lakes, he remarks on her "decidedly Indian features, but light-complexioned [skin]" and the "blue embroidered leggings . . . the only peculiarity of Indian costume about her." During a walk through an Indian village, he talked to a "half-breed" man married to "a squaw of the pure Indian race," prompting him to postulate: "The fusion of the two races in this neighborhood is remarkable . . . Some of the half-caste ladies of the Falls of St. Marie, who have been educated in the Atlantic States, are persons of graceful and dignified manners and agreeable conversation" ("Early Northwest" 70, 74–75). Like the burial ground he visited, a mix of Indian traditional graves and wooden crosses, their villages of log cabins and wigwams testify to the hybridity of northwestern Native American culture.

While proximity to the whites has promoted their assimilation into European culture, it has come with cultural and individual costs that Bryant observes. Chief among these is alcoholism. When Bryant tries to recruit some men to paddle him over the rapids of the Sault, he encounters many who are much too drunk for the undertaking. In his "search of a canoe and a couple of Indians, to make the descent of the rapids" ("which is one of the first things that a visitor to the Sault must think of"), he finds three men and two women in the first wigwam "as drunk as they could be." The women were so drunk that they were "speechless and motionless—too far gone." At the next door he finds a woman who speaks "a little English" and says that her husband could paddle them, but he is currently drunk. She sighs, "'Oh! The whisky.'" Her comment causes Bryant to postulate that "when an Indian could get whiskey he got drunk as a matter of course." Bryant is later told that traders are determined to disregard laws against the whiskey trade to "sell spirits to the savages" ("Early Northwest," 67–73).

Another consequence of contact with Euro-Americans is the loss of their land and the payments by the US and British governments to assuage the Indians. The thirty million acres of land that were ceded to the United States after Black Hawk's War, made up part of the one hundred million acres of Indian land the United States had acquired during Andrew Jackson's presidency for approximately $68 million. As a result of removal policies and treaties, nearly forty-six thousand Indians, including those who journeyed the Trail of Tears to Indian Territory, emigrated to the West during Jackson's term of office.[26] Other Native Americans migrated within the northwestern region between their tribal locations and the places where they would receive their government annuities. As a visitor to the Great Lakes, Bryant heard about the gathering of northern tribes to receive their annuities. Although he is unable to walk out among the seven thousand Indians gathered on Madeleine Island, an informant tells him about them and criticizes the "starving" Indians who do not ration their food but "eat it up in a week" ("Early Northwest" 73), seeming to blame them for their own victimization.

Neither the informant nor Bryant realized the cultural loss to the Indians associated with the annuities, which not only went to pay for the loss of land but were also used to promote the acculturation or "civilization" of the "savage." Ronald Satz tells us that "American officials quickly recognized the potential inherent in the use of annuities as a device to weaken Indian cultural patterns" and coerced the Indians "into applying their annuities toward the upkeep of educational and religious instruction by whites." The "Civilization Fund" established in 1819 explicitly connected the removal of Indians west of the Mississippi and the acculturation of the tribes: it had the "purpose of providing against the further decline and final extinction of the Indian tribes, adjoining the frontier settlements of the United States, and for the introduction among them of the habits and arts of civilization." These proposals, Satz reminds us, "fully reflected the ethnocentrism of nineteenth-century Americans," including Bryant and his informants who expected to reinvent Native Americans through a template of European ideals.[27] Mrs. Speight, a missionary wife, gives Bryant a "rather favorable account of the Indians under her husband's charge," noting their industriousness and piety ("[even if] it is difficult to make them send their children regularly to school") ("Early Northwest" 76). Letting his informants speak for him, Bryant does not comment on the cultural loss of the Indians or the effects of acculturation on them, beyond the deleterious effects of alcohol. Rather, he views the Native Americans as part of the touristic experience for Euro-Americans, as people in the service of the European geographic imagination.

As he is bringing his travel letters to an end, summing up his impressions, Bryant opines that "the manifest fate of Mackinaw . . . is to be a watering-place" and that for some tourists, "the savage visitors [who come for their annuities] . . . will be an additional attraction" ("Early Northwest" 81, 82). Mackinaw has changed from being a fort to being a tourist destination, with its "limestone cliffs" ("Early Northwest" 57) and the natural formations at Sugar Loaf Rock and the Arched Rock. Even the Native Americans have been transformed to some extent to being part of the vacation package as guides for tourists who want to shoot the rapids of the Sault and as exotic sights for visitors. A far cry from the violent Black Hawk, these Indians are nonetheless, in Bryant's words, destined "while in the presence of the white—[to] decay and gradual extinction" ("Early Northwest" 77). Like the natural landscape, they too will be lost to "progress": "Two or three years ago this settlement of the Sault St. Marie was but a military post of the United States, in the midst of a village of Indians and half-breeds. . . . But, since the world has begun talk of the copper mines of Lake Superior, settlers flock into the place. . . . Five years hence, the primitive character of the place will be altogether lost, and it will have become a bustling Yankee town, resembling the other new settlements of the West" ("Early Northwest" 67). Bryant ends his narrative with the same wistful tone with which he ended "The Prairies": "I cannot but think with a kind of regret on the time, which I suppose is near at hand, when [Mackinaw's] wild and lonely woods will be intersected with highways, and filled with cottages and boarding-houses" ("Early Northwest" 82). As the wild areas become settled, they will lose their distinctiveness and begin to look like the places settlers and visitors have left, like Yankee towns. As he writes these last reflections, the line of the frontier has moved on to Mexico along with the soldiers from the garrison at La Pointe who have been reassigned "to the Mexican frontier" ("Early Northwest" 73–74) as part of the effort to wrest southwestern territory from Mexico.

Margaret Fuller's "Wests"

WHEN MARGARET FULLER VISITED the Great Lakes region in the summer of 1843, she saw and experienced many of the same things that William Cullen Bryant would in his 1846 visit. With friends Sarah Ann Clarke and James Freeman Clarke, Fuller set off on a tour after finishing her essay "The Great Lawsuit: Man versus Men, Woman versus Women." Going first by train to Niagara Falls and then by steamer to the Great Lakes in May 1843, Fuller saw this summer vacation as a chance to rest after a busy schedule of writing and editing. She had written to Ralph Waldo Emerson in 1842, "I am tired to death of dissipation," and she complained that she had "no inspiration" after having edited *The Dial* since 1840, written several essays for it, translated two works (*Conversations with Goethe* and *Gunderode*), and established her Conversations series of discussions for the women of Boston. Now with proof sheets for "The Great Lawsuit" finished, she was "quite free" to go away. During the journey she wrote letters to friends and family and kept a journal of her experiences, but the product that marks the trip is her travel narrative, *Summer on the Lakes, in 1843*, published by Little and Brown in 1844 with the encouragement and assistance of Emerson.[1]

Her observations of life on the prairies were bolstered by much reading before she departed and then after the journey in the Harvard College library, making her the first woman to read there. Thomas Wentworth Higginson, a student of divinity at the time, later wrote, "I can well remember Miss Fuller sitting, day after day, under the covert gaze of the undergraduates who had never before looked upon a woman reading within those sacred precincts." She read extensively in the exploratory literature of the West and whatever she could find about American Indians. In some ways her reading in the Harvard library extended her summer's journey, as she crossed new thresholds and imaginatively and intel-

lectually continued to roam the prairies and the lakes. Including summaries of
her sources in the narrative enriches and complicates her firsthand observations
in *Summer on the Lakes*, making it what Nicole Tonkovich calls "a library in
miniature." The seven etchings by Sarah Clarke, inserted in the second printing, visually complement what Fuller has written. A complex narrative, Fuller's
travel writing challenges readers trying to classify it since it is at once "travelogue, autobiography, social criticism, sketchbook, and journal."[2] Nonetheless,
it provides a firsthand account of the Great Lakes region, its environment, and
people as well as Fuller's commentary on and critique of westward expansion,
materialism, and patriarchy.

   Like Bryant, who would visit some of the same sites three years later, Fuller
saw the lakes, Lance Newman observes, at a period of transition, "at the moment
of its most breakneck settlement and development," as more settlers poured into
the region, as towns like Cleveland, Milwaukee, and Chicago were becoming
cities, as Native American tribes were being displaced and deracinated, and as
the natural environment was being reshaped by the forces of "progress." It was
a period when the two dreams of the West were grating against each other before the line of the frontier moved further on. It was also a time when the crude
"mob" was being transformed into "men," when the "solitude" of the frontier
was becoming "enlivened" as homes were springing up from "the rich soil."[3]
Attending to these transformative forces, Fuller complicates her narrative and
the geographic imagination that informs it, a mix of aesthetic-spiritual appreciation of the landscape and pointed critiques of the materialism and racism she
witnessed. More than Bryant's letters, which are mainly descriptive, *Summer on
the Lakes* is itself a territory in which these competing views of the West as well
as her own rival voices and attitudes create a textual tension that reveals an ethic
that is both sentimental and political.

   The geographic and social transitions underway in the Midwest are mapped
in Fuller's discussion of the Rock River region as she looks out over the landscape
and burrows down to find traces of the past in the land. Arriving at Rock River
on the western edge of Illinois, the edge of the frontier, she describes the natural
landscape, the river that flows between "high bluffs" and the swallows' nests
"clustered among the crumbling rocks," before her eye moves to the manicured
landscape of an "Irish gentleman" who has built his country estate along the
river. Here humans and nature, the European and American, seem to coexist
in an ideal pastoral landscape; "the plash of some fish," wild strawberries on the

lawn, and Scottish harebells commingle to enhance the beauty of the scene. Yet, while the Irishman's country estate represents "enlivened" living, other homes belie the "spirit of the scene" because of "the slovenliness" of their own- ers who "had no thought beyond satisfying the grossest material wants." In this transitional frontier space, the graceful and the rude sit side by side. She sees the crude dwellings that Bryant and Kirkland commented on, log cabins with dirt floors, one-room homes that evince the utilitarian outlook of a settler class. Members of what she calls the "Gothic" invaders, the lower classes of settlers "obliterate the natural expression of the country" in their rush to conquer the landscape and its original inhabitants. These "Gothic" settlers evince the ugly side of expansionism in their disregard for the land and others and in their lack of an aesthetic appreciation of the environment. The Rock River country was also home to Black Hawk, the location to which he "returned with his band 'to pass the summer' when he drew upon himself the warfare in which he was finally vanquished." Finding traces of their lives, their history in the geography, she notes, "Here are still the marks of their tomahawks, the troughs in which they prepared their corn, their caches" (SL 27–33). By pointing to the geography and history of Rock River, Fuller encapsulates much of what she sees about the Midwest and the changes it is undergoing, putting in close proximity the natural environment, settlements by whites, and the vanquished if not quite vanished Native American.

Other moments in *Summer* demonstrate the transformation of the frontier. One of these occurs when she contemplates the growth of the cities and the lure of wealth that draws settlers to the Great Lakes. Anticipating that she would not welcome this growth, Fuller writes, "[I came] prepared for the distaste I must experience in its mushroom growth. . . . where 'go ahead' is the only motto." The idylls of former times when woodcutters and shepherds could draw a "moral and its meaning" from their tasks have given way to more concerted efforts to extract the gold of Midas from the environment (SL 18). On the boat out of Buffalo she had encountered immigrants whose only thought was what they could "get in the new scene" (12), how they could gain materially rather than how the West would provide them with experiences in self-cultivation. Like Kirkland, who critiques speculators in Michigan and their "madness" for accumulating land and building cities, Fuller understands the lure of wealth the frontier seemed to offer.[4] She even admits, "[We,] like other emigrants, went not to give, but to get, to rifle the wood of flowers for the service of the fire-ship" (19). But unlike the gold-minded migrants, Fuller and Clarke hope to accumulate not only the flowers, species of the natural environment, but also intellectual and spiritual self-cultivation. A disciple of William Ellery Channing, Fuller understands that in a place where "the clash of material interests is so noisy," settlers will need the "spirit of religion" to leaven their greed (12).

Even with this hustle of material interests, she predicts that a "new order; a new poetry is to be evoked from this chaos" (*SL* 18). By bringing together the influences of divergent peoples, this poetry represents a new identity forged on the borderlands and shores of the new Midwest. As Chicago, Buffalo, and Milwaukee, all port cities, have become "thoroughfares" through which passes "the life-blood" of the East and West, back and forth (19), they have enticed a different set of immigrants who will change the character of the region. "There are lures enough in the West for people of all kinds" (70), she writes, listing the Germans, Norwegians, Swedes, Swiss, Dutch and Irish coming to the West. Like Bryant, Fuller sees a cosmopolitan mix emerging on the American Great Lakes. More, she sees a blending of cultures that will create a new poetics, a new ethos, an intermingling of the Europeans' "tales of the origin of things" (102) with those of the Indians, a hybrid voice born of the transitions on the frontier.

Another sign of the transition of the Great Lakes region is the transformation of Mackinac Island from a military and fur trading center to a tourist location. Although the island and Mackinaw City would not become really popular vacation destinations until after the Civil War, by 1838 Mackinac Island had already been "fully described," Fuller writes, "by able pens." Her comments about Mackinac and the arched rock, which surprised her even as "much as [she] had heard of it" (*SL* 106), demonstrate that the tour of the island and its features were already scripted by tourist traditions and itineraries. Indeed, the costs and distances of travel by rail and steamboat from New York to Chicago along the Great Lakes with stops at Detroit, Mackinac, and Milwaukee were calculated in table form in Warner's *Immigrant's Guide and Citizens' Manual: 1848* to help regularize travel to the region.[5] Like Bryant, Fuller mentions Fort Holmes, the old fort that provides a view of the lake for visitors, and the old French town marked by its white houses, "the white fort with its gay flag," and the "Indian, French, half-breeds, and others." With a history, as Fuller relates it, that goes back to the naming of the island Michilimackinac, the word for Great Turtle, Mackinac in 1843 is also the site where the Chippewa and Ottawa tribes come to receive their government annuities and where visitors can view the "fascinating picture" that they make (107). Just as Bryant observed that the Indians add to the attractions of the island, so too Fuller views them along with the natural sites as part of the experience of visiting Mackinac. Observing their domestic activities, Fuller goes out among them to watch the women "preparing food out of doors," children playing, girls carrying babies and cutting wood, "talking and laughing" (108, 107).

In a scene of "gipsy charm," the Indians gathered at Mackinac also evidence the degraded situation that many Native Americans faced during Fuller's era: "The men of these subjugated tribes, now accustomed to drunkenness and every way degraded, bear but à faint impress of the lost grandeur of the race" (*SL* 113). The Indians provide for her a dual view—of the "gipsy charm" of an exotic other and the effects of poverty and alcoholism—both elements of her tourist's gaze of a people in transition. As John Urry has argued, the tourist's gaze is "socially organized"; it shows us how "social groups" (New Englanders like Fuller and Bryant) construct their gaze and decide what to see and how, but the tourist's gaze also shows "what is happening in the 'normal society.'"[6] In the mid-nineteenth century, the place of the "other"—Native Americans, African Americans, and women—was increasingly debated by political thinkers like Fuller and Bryant. Like Fuller's tourist's gaze, the transformation of the old fort to a tourist site metonymically figures the larger transformation of the Native American from warriors like Black Hawk and the Greek-like Indians Fuller imagines to tribal peoples who gather on the shores for their annuities, suggesting a future for them that counters romanticized versions of the First Peoples.

These glimpses of the Great Lakes in 1843 illustrate a place and time in transition from the early settlers who lived in log cabins, competed with the Native Americans for space and dominance, and worked to cultivate the landscape with farms and mid-nineteenth society accoutrements. They also indicate the movement from individual settlements to the growth of the great cities of the American Midwest and the changing population as immigrants from New England and the Atlantic States mingle with a variety of European immigrants as they push the original inhabitants to the margins, socially and geographically. It was an unsettling time, one when the rewards and costs of progress were becoming evident.

Even though *Summer* shares similarities with Bryant's 1846 letters as it sketches the region and its people, it diverges from them because of its multiple voices and perspectives. Fuller's narrative is at once a poetic, imaginative description of the environment and the possibilities for living in it and a critique of the social institutions that interfere with the possible, the two impulses competing with each other as they describe a West of promise and materialist consumption. To the extent that Fuller is what Ken Egan calls a "poetic traveler," she writes imaginative geographies of an ideal West where humans live in harmony with a picturesque nature. Approaching the West with a poet's eye, she hoped to gain poetic rather than quotidian impressions from her journey: "What I got from the journey was the poetic impression of the country at large; it is all I have aimed to communicate" (SL 42). Yet even as she desires to sketch a poetry of the West, she also exposes "the violence and ugliness of empire-building" in clear-sighted critiques of materialism, racism, and the situation of women on the frontier.[7] Mixing poetry with social criticism, Fuller employs different habits of mind, different voices, to portray the Great Lakes, the transcendentalist aestheticism competing with sharp political criticism.

Incorporating poetry and poetic renderings into her narrative rather than composing separate texts as Bryant did, Fuller announces her aesthetics in the opening poems, epigrams to the larger work. In the first poem, "Summer days of busy leisure," she imagines a way of seeing that is different from that of the "scholar," one that gazes "on a magic glass" to a past that the "dull words" of the scholar cannot convey. Instead, "hints," "mottoes," and visions of "knights behind their shields" revealed among the "dried grasses, blooming fields" of the prairie imply the work of a "wizard spell" (SL 1). Rather than using the language of guidebooks or science as other travel writers do to describe her journey, she announces that she will rely on poetic impressions (42). Employing language and images that remind one of medieval tales of heroism, she sets out to describe a summer's tour of the lakes as another kind of heroic, magical venture, as indeed it must have been for her. More than a summer's vacation, her journey will take her to imagined geographies where the mystical or magical is possible amid the everyday.

The second poem, "To a Friend," offers tokens of the prairies, "dried grass-tufts," "a mussel shell," some "antlers," and "an eagle's feather" as well as the gift of her writing to sustain her friend during "weary hours" of her absence (SL 2). Keepsakes, an element of the sentimental tradition, evince the "ethos of human connection" in which separation and loss resonate with personal and political meaning.[8] The tokens she gives reconnect her to her friend and provide remembrances of their friendship. They also evoke sympathy through memory and loss of the "Brave" who is "the last of his despairing band," of the "tall woods which never more" provide a safe retreat for the deer. Providing her reader images of the vanished Indian and the pristine forest, she invites a sympathetic, sentimental reading of her narrative, which she terms a "gift." A "brief refreshment" from the present "dwarf day" (2), the poem takes readers to a time when gods entertained giants, a place where the actual and the imaginary worlds meet, a place Nathaniel

Hawthorne would term the location of Romance, a location for sentiment. Here Fuller can give her imagination play as she sketches the realities of life on the prairies. She will also use the ethos of sentimental writing, the sympathy that could lead to social and political reforms, when she makes an emotional appeal on behalf of Native Americans: "Let every legislator take the subject to heart, and if he cannot undo the effects of past sin, try for that clear view and right sense that may save us from sinning still more deeply" (144). As these two poems suggest, the sentimental, the poetic, and the imaginary make strong claims on Fuller's way of seeing and analyzing the West.

One mode of the poetic imaginary, the picturesque is an aesthetic approach to viewing and describing the landscape. Despite its potential for organizing, controlling, and colonizing the scenes it depicts, the picturesque poetically sketches vistas that are pleasing to the eye. In Fuller's hands the scenes she labels "picturesque" also suggest harmony between humans and nature and, like sentimental tropes, invite connectedness and sympathy. For instance, when Fuller describes "the beauty of the scene" where the Rock River is "interspaced by halcyon isles on which nature had lavished all her prodigality in tree, vine, and flower" (*SL* 32), she indicates not only her emotional connection to the "enchanting" spot but also sentimentally muses, "How happy the Indians must have been here!" Having made imaginative connections between the landscape and the Indians who lived there, Fuller shifts her focus to announce that they were driven away, leaving only traces of their lives in the earth, their arrowheads and pottery. This move invites readers likewise to extend their imagination and sympathy to the vanished Indians, to Black Hawk's band that was vanquished a decade earlier. She makes a similar move when she sketches "a picturesque scene" of an Indian encampment on Silver Lake. Here she points to the Indians' fires smoldering in the sudden rainstorm, an "old theatrical Indian" with arms folded and "looking up to the heavens," and Indian ponies "much excited ... careering through the wood" (74–75). Sarah Clarke literally sketches the scene, featuring an Indian, blanket folded about, sitting in the foreground with his or her back to the viewer while horses race in the windblown woods, their tails flying behind them. Like Fuller, Brigitte Georgi-Findley notes, who "abstracts most views into emotion and feeling," Clarke draws a simple line sketch that is a more emotive than detailed rendition of the scene. As the word "picturesque" suggests, these scenes are pictures, framed not only by the point of view of the observer but also by more physical frames, in much the same way that Clarke's sketch is framed by the edges of the page. When Fuller takes the reader with her into one of their lodges to escape the storm, she poetically frames the scene with the imagined contours of the lodge. But she also steps into the picture, relating how the inhabitants made

Indian Encampment, by Sarah Clarke

room for her despite their sickness and "extreme poverty." Her entrance into the Indians' space exemplifies the dangers of the picturesque, the temptation to colonize her subjects or to treat them as "topography," part of the view.[9] But Fuller also uses the occasion to contemplate the poverty of the wandering band of Potawatomi people who had come to collect their government annuities and to invite sympathy for their situation. By calling attention to the sick children in the lodge and their concern for her comfort, Fuller gestures toward connections of shared experiences of sickness and grace among her readers.

On other occasions Fuller uses the picturesque to compose the landscape as a natural paradise inhabited by just and thoughtful humans. After crossing a river and evading a thunderstorm in the home of an instant host, Fuller and her party leave the "solitary house," which she describes as set off by "a Provence rose" and locust trees, signs to Fuller of the mixing of the Old World with the New. Continuing her trek across the prairie, Fuller uses religious language to describe the natural scene. She writes that after the rain shower "no heaven need wear a lovelier aspect" and then compares a grove of trees to a cathedral, a "place for vespers." Already infusing the mythic onto the landscape, she describes "the blooming plain, unmarked by any road," in which the "friendly track of wheels" did not leave marks of their passing (*SL* 25). Looking at the scene through a "magic glass" (1), she imagines the groves to be "blue islands" floating in the distance. Even when she realizes they are not images of a fairy land, her descriptions are still infused with the romantic, as she sketches pastoral scenes of "fair parks" and "little log houses . . . with their curling smokes" in which the human "harmonized

beautifully" with the natural scene. Taking her reader through the picturesque
scene, from the host's home and over the "blooming plain" to a view of the "little
log houses" before coming at the end of the day to cathedral-like stand of trees,
Fuller draws her reader into a world where natural and human objects coexist
in a semireligious relationship (25).

More than an aesthetic landscape, this picture suggests an ideal life of beauty and religiosity in which humans harmoniously live with nature. In another
instance, when she draws the English gentleman and his home, she notes that
his house is filled with books, and the woods that surround the house "have a
very picturesque and pleasing effect." Here she finds a "mixture of culture and
rudeness" that she reads as a "feeling of freedom, not of confusion," of an orderly
and just relationship: "This habitation of man seemed like a nest in the grass, so
thoroughly were the buildings and all objects of human care harmonized with
what was natural" (SL 24). She sees in this example the possibility of living in
the West based on a mix of an appreciation for culture—poetry, history—and
a peaceful coexistence with the natural world, as if one's home were like a nest
built from and in the natural setting. This kind of living suggests to her the ideal
of freedom, "the liberty of law, not license; not indolence," one informed by "ge-
nial and poetic influences" (66) and self-cultivation, one in which "all should be
fitted for freedom and an independence by his own resources" (77). What she
hopes for is a West that fits these idealized descriptions—a picturesque place
where humans can live in harmony with nature and each other and pursue their
own self-cultivation. Even though the picturesque can be problematic, in Fuller's
hands it is an aesthetic, imaginative, emotive way of seeing or framing the world.

Against these depictions of an ideal West rendered through the language of
the picturesque, Fuller nonetheless understands that "the great problem of the
place and time" (SL 65) is the need for thoughtful stewardship of the natural
and human resources. Thus, even as she extols the Edenic qualities of the Great
Lakes region, she also sees its problems, the materialism that values use over
care, a racism that denigrates and impoverishes the Native Americans, and the
pinched lives of pioneer women. So stark is the contrast between the ideal of the
West and the damage caused by materialistic expansion on Native Americans
and women that Lance Newman calls Summer on the Lakes "dystopian." Newman writes, "Summer on the Lakes is structured by the tension between a vision
of a just society rooted in nature and the stark reality of America's westward
expansion, between an abiding faith in the human potential to live up to the

Log Cabin at Rock River, by Sarah Clarke

beauty of picturesque landscapes and a clear understanding of the cold social calculus of immediate profit."[10] These competing perspectives and Fuller's rival voices, the aesthetic and the critical, create a geographic imaginary that mimics the tensions of a West at a moment of uneasy transformation.

Early in the narrative, when she is visiting Niagara Falls, overwhelmed by the sublime images of "the full wonder of the scene" and fantasizing about "naked savages stealing behind me with uplifted tomahawks," a man comes also to look at the falls. Instead of admiring the natural wonder, he looks about "with an air as if thinking how he could best appropriate it to his own use" and spits into it, claiming and using the environment for his personal aims (*SL* 4–5). This man represents the acquisitive nature of many of the setters and the nation at large that Fuller will criticize. At Cleveland, where she has a fine view of the lake in which "the waters presented kaleidoscopic varieties of hues" and sees Native Americans for the first time, she describes her fellow steamboat passengers as "New Englanders, seeking their fortunes." They talk only of "what they should get in the new scene," their minds not on the natural or human view before them but instead on "accumulation." Rather than projecting hopes for freedom or self-cultivation, these immigrants, trained in "habits of calculation," see the West as an arena for their "material interests" (12).

While Fuller understands that these New England immigrants will need "the spirit of religion" to guide them (*SL* 12), near the end of the narrative she criticizes the so-called religious person who "sacrifices" his own brother to

Mammon and enslaved African Americans. Worshiping the material more than the human, the religious hypocrite "turns in loathing" from the rituals of the Indians (114), cheats them in trade, and degrades them with rum. At her angriest moment in the book, she cries out, "Our people and our government have sinned alike against the first-born of the soil. . . . Yes! Slave-drivers and Indian traders are called Christians. . . . Wonderful is the deceit of man's heart!" (114). Here she resoundingly criticizes the racism and materialism that have shaped government policy, reminding one of Emerson's angry open letter to President Martin Van Buren in 1838, in which he calls the removal of the southern Indians "a dereliction of all faith and virtue," "a denial of justice," and a crime of "fraud and robbery" that asks Americans to question the "*moral* character of the Government."[11]

Even as her sightseeing gaze may colonize the Indians for her own enjoyment and edification, Fuller is irate at the blatant racism against them that she witnesses. While one can take Michaela Bruckner Cooper's point that in her descriptions of the Native Americans Fuller "occupies the position of the colonial observer" with all its issues of domination of the other, an ethics of sightseeing asks us to rethink the implications of Fuller's gaze. Dean MacCannell, who argues that seeing is the essential act of the tourist, lays out an ethics of sightseeing. He argues that "the ultimate ethical test for tourists" is the ability to "acknowledge the gap that separates them from the *other-as-attraction*," to be able to use their imagination "to bring fresh meaning to a tourist experience," and to understand the "responsibility we take, or do not take, for our sightseeing choices." Given this definition we can see the ethical quality of Fuller's sightseeing of the Native Americans because she goes beyond "accepted" attitudes about them to bring out the human elements in the scenes she sketches and to use her observations to articulate a critique of America's behavior toward them. She looks beyond the dirt that disgusts other travelers to see the injustice practiced by a seemingly well-intending woman who spurns the Indian child she was "bringing up" because of her appearance and odor. Against the stereotyped remarks of other travelers, Fuller muses, "All their claims, all their sorrows quite forgot, in abhorrence of their dirt, their tawny skins, and the vices the whites have taught them" (*SL* 113). She uses this moment to think about the Native American and to bring new meaning to her touristic journey and its effect on her "conscience and character" as she speaks out against the cruel hypocrisy of others.[12]

When she visits Nomabbin Lake, formerly site of "one of the finest Indian villages," her host tells of how he had once seen an Indian gazing out on the scene there. "[When] the Indian saw him, [he] gave a wild, snorting sound of indignation and pain, and strode away." The same host hoped that Indians could be prevented from "straggling back...to their old haunts" there: "They ought not to [be] permitted to drive away *our* game." Fuller understands the imperialistic audacity of her host as she muses, "I scarcely see how they can forbear to shoot the white man where he stands" (*SL* 72). Even though she sums up this anecdote by contemplating the fate of the Indian ("the power of fate is with the white man, and the Indian feels it"), she acknowledges the human and political injustices endured by the Native Americans. They are not merely attractions on her tourist itinerary but are also imbricated with political and social meaning. Reiterating the common notion that the Indians must either "conform to the institutions of Europe' (become civilized) or "disappear," she contemplates that "had they been truly civilized or Christianized" rather than unjustly treated "by masses of men," their situation might have been different (143).[13]

The best she can hope for the Indians is that "a national institute" (*SL* 143) will be formed to save the remains, the stories of the Indians, as she has attempted briefly in this narrative with her tales of Flying Pigeon and Muckwa. In fact, the American Ethnological Society had recently organized in 1842, and the Smithsonian Institution would be established in 1846 to gather information to scientifically study Native Americans. For Fuller, as for Bryant and much of white America, the future for Native Americans is bleak; they seem fated to vanish, to give way before the tide of white settlement and imperialism. What Fuller can hope for is the preservation of their relics, their stories, in a "reinvention of tribal cultures as archeological objects," even if the people themselves seem doomed.[14] Meanwhile she calls on the missionary, the trader, the legislator, "every man and every woman," to redirect their energies and thoughts, to avoid "embittering, by insult or unfeeling prejudice," the Indian (144). In these incidents Fuller demonstrates an ethics of sightseeing; having gained a clearer understanding of Native Americans, she has taken on the responsibility of speaking out against their mistreatment. They are more to her, finally, than a picturesque scene or a portion of the landscape, even if her understanding of them is still informed by nineteenth-century rhetoric regarding Native Americans and "manifest destiny." She sums up the narrative, "I feel that I have learnt a great deal of the Indians, from observing them even in this broken and degraded situation" (153), indicating that her experiences, the sights she has seen, have had a moral, political, and imaginative effect on her.

Fuller also directs her criticism of the West to the situation that many pioneer women find themselves occupying. After idealizing the life of settlers, Fuller learns that the frontier has been harder than her idyllic dream of plenty in which "nature still wore her motherly smile" (*SL* 38). She recounts the reality of pioneer life for women, commenting on the unfitness of most migrant women for their situation: "The great drawback upon the lives of these settlers, at present, is the unfitness of the women for their new lot." Following their men "for affection's sake," many women find they have the hardest part of the enterprise, one for which "they are least fitted." Ill equipped by their eastern educations and without "aid in domestic labor," these women find themselves confined to the cabin and domestic chores without the resources men have "to ride, to drive, to row alone" or to go out fishing and hunting. The wives of the poorer settlers "very frequently become slatterns" (38–39), overworked with hard labor. Concerned as well with the role of women in converting the wilderness into a settlement and the emotional and physical costs that accrued to women, Caroline Kirkland in *A New Home, Who'll Follow?* observed, "Woman's little world is overclouded for lack of the old familiar means and appliances. The husband goes to his work with the same axe or hoe which fitted his hand in his old woods and fields . . . But he finds the homebird drooping and disconsolate. She has been looking in vain for the reflection of any of the cherished features of her own dear fire-side. . . . Women are the grumblers in Michigan, and they have some apology. Many of them have made sacrifices for which they were not at all prepared."[15] In addition to thinking about the lives of frontier women, Fuller contemplates the situation of Indian women, pondering their place in their society and their "habits of drudgery" and submission. Though she is charmed by the women she visits, who tease her about her "little sun-shade" and admire her locket, she still decides that "their place is certainly lower, and their share of the human inheritance less" (111). In these sections Fuller looks at the circumstances of women of different classes and races to make the point about the difficulty of their lives, to call attention to their place in patriarchal and racist societies.

Having just brought to press "The Great Lawsuit," Fuller was primed to remark on the situation of women in ways that apparently did not occur to Bryant. In "The Great Lawsuit" she had observed, "[The woman's] circle, if the duller, is not the quieter. If kept from 'excitement,' she is not from drudgery." She compares the lot of middle-class women to that of the Indian woman who "carries the burdens of the camp." Her observations on the frontier validate what she had earlier written. As she did in "The Great Lawsuit," advocating that "every barrier" be "thrown down" and "every path laid open to woman as freely as to man" ("GL" 394), in *Summer* she turns her new knowledge of frontier life to a call for action—a more enlightened education for western girls that would prepare them for the actualities of pioneer living. As many scholars have noted, after her summer on the lakes Fuller returned to her feminist reading of society, extending "The Great Lawsuit" into *Woman in the Nineteenth Century*. Annette Kolodny remarks, "[*Woman in the Nineteenth Century*] was informed by the new insights (and the frustrated fantasies) awakened on the prairies but only imperfectly analyzed in *Summer on the Lakes*." An "autobiographical account of personal change" and "a major turning point in her thought on national identity and its significance," *Summer* evinces the ethical quality of her sightseeing trip to the lakes and suggests the direction her feminist activism will take. In many ways, as Anne Baker argues, *Summer* "is a book in which Fuller carries on an extended conversation with herself about the best way to see, as well as about the moral implications of seeing, which she recognizes as one form of possession and control" but which, as we have seen, is also a form of ethical decision making.[16] She would turn her conversation about seeing into action, going on after her summer's interlude to write journalistic dispatches uncovering other social and political ills suffered by women. As well, *Woman in the Nineteenth Century* will call on a force of women, of *exaltadas*, to change the moral landscape of America.

More than Bryant's letters, Fuller's work exposes the tensions between an imagined West and the realities of expansion during a period of rapid transition in what Worster calls the "disjunction between fantasy and reality." Countering a fantasy of living in harmony with nature and creating a "new poetry" with pointed criticisms of the reality of reckless materialism and the hardships of life on the frontier, Fuller has written a complex narrative that mimics these disjunctions. While she hopes to render "poetic impressions" of a delightful journey, she is also prompted to rethink her ecological and political stances toward the prairie and its inhabitants. Speaking out against corruption, materialism, and prejudice, Fuller provides a strong voice in debates about the nation and the direction it is taking in the nineteenth century. She remarks at the end of the narrative, "Although I have little to tell, I feel that I have learnt a great deal," (*SL* 153), but she has in fact told much in a text that is "a polyvocal, dialogic, multi-perspectival 'experience of the co-presence of cultures.'"[17]

Catharine Maria Sedgwick's Great Excursion

IN 1854 CATHARINE MARIA Sedgwick was an invited guest on the Great Excursion to celebrate the "first railroad to unite the Atlantic with the Mississippi River." William J. Peterson reports that leading citizens invited by the "firm of [Joseph E.] Sheffield and [Henry] Farnam, contractors for the construction of the Chicago and Rock Island Railroad" included such dignitaries as former president Millard Fillmore, historian George Bancroft, Charles A. Dana of the *New York Tribune*, and other representatives from the political arena, elite universities, the press, and the clergy. More than twelve hundred excursionists gathered in Chicago with plans to leave on June 5 on "two trains of nine coaches each gaily decorated with flowers, flags, and streamers" to go from there to Rock Island, Illinois, situated on the Mississippi River. There they transferred to steamboats to continue the journey to Minneapolis, where excursionists could take side trips to Minnehaha Falls, the Falls of St. Anthony, and Fort Snelling. Along the way, they were fêted and treated to parades, fireworks, dancing, and speeches extolling the nation's "internal improvements and the Great West." Connecting the East to the West as far as the Mississippi River by rail facilitated fashionable tourism and westward expansion, but it also signaled the nation's commercial and technological progress. Indeed, on a similar excursion in 1857, Governor Salmon P. Chase of Ohio named "the Railroad, the Locomotive and the Telegraphy—iron, steam and lightning—[as] the three mighty genii of modern civilization."[1] It was an auspicious occasion, bringing together the forces of technology, tourism, and nationalism and forecasting the future of travel in America as the West became more accessible.

Catharine Maria Sedgwick, "one of the more notable women to make the trip," wrote her impressions of the journey in an open letter published in *Put-*

nam's Monthly (September 1854) to Charles Butler, an excursionist who gave her tickets for the tour but was unable to complete the journey. Although she effaces her talents as a writer, her "woman's diffusive pen," Sedgwick was a popular and respected author, ranked by her peers with Washington Irving and James Fenimore Cooper and hailed as "one of our national glories—our Sedgwick."[2] The author of six novels, including *A New England Tale* (1822), *Redwood* (1824), *Hope Leslie* (1827), *Clarence* (1830), and *The Linwoods* (1835), Sedgwick helped to forge a national literature in which she tackled "the social and political debates" of a nation negotiating its identity. Carolyn Karcher argues that we should consider her "an early political novelist" who questioned the "limits to legitimate authority" in novels that looked at the situation of Native Americans, questioned slavery and patriarchy, extended the possibilities for women, and, as Patricia Kalayjian claims, critiqued the "destructive qualities of capitalism, consumerism, and commodification." Kalayjian further claims that "Sedgwick's fiction always has an improving message" and that she "engages every theme as a citizen, a patriot, a social critic, a moralist." An avid traveler who journeyed to the US South, to Europe, and, as we shall see, west to the Mississippi River, she infused her travel writing with many of the same concerns that she brought to her fiction, particularly her concern with promoting "the culture of a *genuine* nationality," as an 1849 reviewer of her novel *Clarence* put it. Written on the cusp of the revolutions that were brewing in Europe, her travel book *Letters from Abroad to Kindred at Home* (1841) conflates "aesthetic touring and political discussion." Indeed, Lucinda Damon-Bach argues that *Letters from Abroad* includes "'unadorned fact' aimed at educating her readers in sociopolitical contexts and European culture" even as it provided "armchair entertainment" for her readers at home. Written as letters to her brother Charles, the narrative displays Sedgwick's keen eye and descriptive talents, but it also illustrates "the importance of travel writing about abroad [*sic*] for America's imagination of itself as a nation" as she addressed issues of economics, politics, and human rights that were roiling in Europe and the United States. Terry Caesar has argued that writing about travel abroad prompts writers to think about home, about America, and national identity.[3] In similar ways, Sedgwick's essay about travel to the Mississippi River and the Falls of St. Anthony, all new territory for easterners like herself, gives her space to think about the nation and the direction it is taking at mid-century.

Sedgwick's article for *Putnam's* in many ways illustrates the literary nationalism the journal actively and consciously promoted. During its short life (1853–1857), the editors of the magazine supported and published American authors like Henry Wadsworth Longfellow, James Russell Lowell, Henry David

Thoreau, Herman Melville, and James Fenimore Cooper to encourage a national literature. The editors also urged writers to mine the "uncultivated but rich field for the American genius" in topics taken from the American experience. As part of their effort to promote an American literary nationalism, they published work by regional authors to do justice to "the peculiarities of the several parts of the nation," including accounts of western travel and adventure. The democratic nationalism, the "ingenuous and idealistic optimism," that characterized the magazine, as Notley Maddox observes, reflected "the expansive, forward-looking spirit which permeated the whole nation during the greater part of the three decades immediately preceding the Civil War."[4] In many ways, Sedgwick found a compatible home for her article that described the West's natural beauties as it simultaneously praised the "enlightened industry" that was transforming it ("Great Excursion" 320).

For Sedgwick and the other excursionists, the extension of the railroad to the Mississippi was more than a convenience; it was a cipher of the nation. As the railroad stretched "over the vast prairies," it joined the "free West to the East in inevitable and indissoluble Union." The rail lines marked not only the "advancement of true civilization," the technological advances of mid-century, but also all that the term "true civilization" means for Sedgwick ("Great Excursion" 320). By joining geographic areas and extended populations into one united nation instead of feudal "*patches*," the rail line suggests to her ideals of unity, equality, democracy, and piety. At a time when the indissolubility of the nation was not as sure as it may have been, when debates about slavery and what Sedgwick called the "misfortune of Missouri" (325) were becoming more divisive, the rails provided a proof of the Union and union and the spirit of democracy. In his brief history of the Great Excursion, Peterson speculates, "Slavery probably was the chief topic of conversation." He reminds his 1934 readers of the Kansas-Nebraska Act of May 30, 1854, and the unsettling events revolving around "the Boston slave case" of Anthony Burns that tested the legitimacy of the Fugitive Slave Act.[5] Peterson also reminds his readers of the Gold Rush of 1849 and the dash to California for wealth, the kind of materialism and speculation that Sedgwick critiques as she praises the "enlightened industry" of the builders of the line, "our *fellow-sovereigns*" (320). Quoting the line from the Declaration of Independence, "that all men are created free and equal," she imagines a nation of equals joined together as one, symbolically enacted during the excursion by the ritual act of "mingling the water taken from the Atlantic . . . with the water of the Mississippi" (321, 324).

She further states that this "land of promise" was "prepared for them by the universal Father," conflating technological change, geographic movement, ideas of nationhood, and religion in a kind of Christian republicanism. She writes that travelers on the Great Excursion were able to see "the inappreciable riches and untold beauty of our own country—our own inalienable possessions; to have our piety and our patriotism kindled . . . by the first revelation to our senses of the capacity of our country, the first intimation of its possible glorious future." Seeing the "abounding vitality" in the growth of the West and the progress of a "democratic republic" evidenced by the "railroads, telegraphs, aqueducts, and gaslights" (320–22), Sedgwick also insists on a principled nationalism founded on "intellectual and moral development." While she articulates a version of manifest destiny, that God had promised the continent to the descendants of the Puritans who came with "their Puritan armor, the Bible and the school-book," she also insists on the necessity of "improving morals" that will raise the nation "above the vortex of speculation and mere material acquisition" ("Great Excursion" 320–22). Charles Babcock, an excursionist who sent dispatches of the journey to the *New Haven Palladium*, focused on the "business resources" of a West that was saved by "a mysterious Providence . . . until He directed the enterprising, indomitable people [to possess it and bind its] towns and States into one people and one interest," a more imperialist and materialist version of manifest destiny than Sedgwick's.[6] For her, the impulses of nationalism were tempered by Christianity, republicanism, and democracy and were not as blatantly imperialist as other commentaries.

John Austin defines Sedgwick's Christian republicanism as "a belief in Christian virtue as a positive moral force that transcends party politics and factional interests." Damon-Bach and Clements refer to her principled nationalism derived from her contact with the "poor and defenseless." Deborah Gussman sees evidences of "classic republicanism" in *Married or Single?*: "the sacrifice of individual interests to the public good . . . the subordination of individual liberty to civil liberty, the rejection of luxury, and the exaltation of independence, reason, benevolence, and public virtue."[7] These versions of nationalism are apparent in her descriptions of what she finds in the West, the honor of labor, the establishment of schools and churches in the newly settled towns, the generosity of Farnam and Sheffield, the physical achievements that raise the standard of living. Indeed, the technological and commercial improvements, and the fructifying labor of the farmer on the prairies, were evidence to her of the "advancement of *true* civilization" ("Great Excursion" 320, emphasis added).

Even as Sedgwick extolled the conversion of the prairies into cultivated farms, the settlement of the western landscape into cities replete with the comforts of modern technology, she also admired the natural environment. Indeed, one of the aims of travel west was to gaze upon the West's vast and unusual landscapes, to "daguerreotype new pictures on the mind" of unique land formations. Like other travelers to the west of the Midwest, like William Cullen Bryant and Margaret Fuller before her, she looked out on the "rich prairie turf," the grass "brilliantly embroidered with flowers," and admired the "gentle declivities, or sharp precipices" along the Mississippi River. Like other mid-nineteenth-century writers, she saw the picturesque, the "new charm" and "new beauty" in the natural, exclaiming of the view of excursionists clambering about the Falls of St. Anthony, "what a picturesque domain the saint possesses!" ("Great Excursion" 322–24).

Despite Sedgwick's clear delight in the natural beauty of the West, her view is tempered not only by an aesthetic of the picturesque but also by ideological paradoxes. As Judith Fetterley has commented, there is a curious "entanglement" in her views, a kind of paradox that is evident in her appreciation of the natural environment and celebration of the advances of technology that have transformed it and also in her treatment of Native Americans in her fiction and travel writing.[8] The author who created the Pequot Indian woman Magawisca, a strong "sister" of Hope Leslie, an articulate spokesperson for the situation of Native Americans in early America, Sedgwick also elided the place of Native Americans in her Great Excursion narrative. As she did when she sent Magawisca to the West at the end of her novel Hope Leslie, even after she rescued her white friends from danger, Sedgwick removes and marginalizes the Native person here. When she celebrates the young missionary who comes to Minnesota to bring education, she notes that the New England woman "hired two Indian girls to row" her to her future charges, "two white families and eight white children" ("Great Excursion" 322). Although education is an important element of her version of Christian republicanism, apparently it is not extended to the Native American.

No longer the threat they had previously been in the Midwest, Native Americans now serve the white advancement that displaces them. When Sedgwick catalogs the warehouses, shops, and "beautiful private residences" in St. Louis and "the social shouts of civilized men, at the warehouses and huge hotels" ("Great Excursion" 324), she also reminds readers of Black Hawk's War. Noting that "a few years since was heard only the yell of the savage[,] . . . tomahawk in hand in quest of his foe" (322), she joins the disappearance of the Native with the advancement of the white. In fact, one of the steamboats that conveyed the

tourists up the Mississippi was named after the great chief. As well, the Falls of
St. Anthony is haunted by disappearance. As Lydia Maria Child recounts the
legend of the falls, an Indian woman, betrayed by her French husband who had
taken her daughter to be raised in Canada, went over the falls in a boat with her
son in an act of revenge: "The Indians believe that the spirits of the drowned
ones . . . still hover over the fatal spot." A romantic tale in Child's hands, the
legend nonetheless marks the disappearance of the Indian with the incursion
of the European that haunts and complicates western expansion. A writer who
advocates equality and union, Sedgwick also evinces the paradoxical attitudes
about the environment and the Native American that entangle the nineteenth
century as both are displaced by the advance of white settlement. As Fetterley
notes about *Hope Leslie*, it is the "entanglement that makes the text worth recov-
ering in the first place," the "engagement with the actual mess of America" that
makes the novel powerful.[9] The "mess" rather than the neatness of Sedgwick's
descriptions demonstrates not only the paradoxes of the West but also the
fraught efforts of travel writers to shape a national identity out of new territory
at a very complex time.

Tourism is another entangling factor, its aims of pleasure grating against the
aims of social and political commentary. The purpose of Sedgwick's excursion
to the Falls of St. Anthony was not so much to critique American expansion as
it was to enjoy a twenty-day vacation to the West with her brother Charles, to
ride on the new rail system, float on steamboats adorned with flowers and an
accommodating crew, eat well, and sleep comfortably. As an elite member of
the Great Excursion, she wanted to enjoy herself and to socialize. She notes that
at the Tremont Hotel in Chicago where the travelers gathered before boarding
the train to Rock Island, everyone had a "festal air" about them: "Gladness was
in every voice, pleasant expectation on every countenance" ("Great Excursion"
321). In 1854 the Tremont Hotel was the "leading hotel in the West." Situated on
what is today called the Magnificent Mile of Chicago, the Tremont boasted five
stories and 260 rooms. In 1858 it was the site where Stephen A. Douglas launched
his presidential campaign; in 1861 he would die there after a brief illness.[10] A far
cry from the rude homes Bryant stayed in during his first trip to Illinois, the
Tremont was the epitome of the luxury hotel in America when Sedgwick and
the excursionists gathered there.

Once aboard the steamboats that would transport them up the Mississippi
River, their "creature-comforts . . . were munificently provided." Sedgwick mentions the French cuisine, the "ices, jellies, cakes, and pyramids . . . of candied
sugar" and "the civil lads who waited on us" ("Great Excursion" 323). The meals

enjoyed by the excursionists were grand: reporter Babcock notes, "We have had oysters and lobsters daily, though two thousand miles from the sea." As a member of the Great Excursion, Sedgwick gives us a glimpse at the most exclusive travel of her time and of the possibilities for future travel, commenting: "The fashionable tour will be in the track of our happy 'excursion party, to the Falls of St. Anthony'" (323). Indeed, "In the years that followed, hundreds of excursions were made to this garden spot of the West." Peterson lists the excursion of 1858 with the completion of the Milwaukee and La Crosse Railroad, the 1860 trip of William H. Seward, Charles Francis Adams, and Charles Francis Jr., and 1866 when scores of boats ran excursions to St. Paul and the falls. "Probably no other single factor was so important in popularizing the fashionable tour with Easterners as was the grand excursion of the Rock Island Railroad in 1854." Sedgwick and the other excursionists of 1854 were in the vanguard of rail travel to the West in what "could be considered a late phase of the eighteenth-century Grand Tour of Europe" and a precursor to the "See America First" campaign that would begin at the end of the nineteenth century.[11]

Although she glimpsed the West and enjoyed herself immensely, Sedgwick was satisfied to return home ("[to] our own Berkshire") and leave the task of settling the West to the young who "go in troops and caravans" just as she leaves the task of fighting slavery to a "*young* man eloquent" whom she met in St. Louis ("Great Excursion" 325). Touring and writing from a perspective of privilege, Sedgwick found the trip to be charming and comfortable, conforming to ideas of American expansion and exceptionalism that overlooked the costs to others and the environment. As Paul Fussell notes, "Tourism soothes you by comfort and familiarity and shields you from the shocks of novelty and oddity. It confirms your prior view of the world instead of shaking it up." Just so, Sedgwick avoids shaking up her own or her readers' views about the nation, expansion, and tourism. Even as she tangles with "the social and political debates" with which Americans of her period grapple, at the end, the sixty-five-year-old woman turns over the business of empire building to the young, who may "perfect an empire of which their Puritan Fathers sowed the seeds" (325).[12] Asking them to remember the poverty of their fathers against the riches of materialism, her view is shaped by the ideals of purity, piety, and patriotism that she brought with her on a very enjoyable excursion to the Falls of St. Anthony.

Constance Fenimore Woolson

Nostalgia on the Lakes

CONSTANCE FENIMORE WOOLSON WOULD make a career writing travel narratives and fiction about her travels to the US South and Europe, but her first travel sketches were not so much about explorations of new places as they were narratives of remembrance. Her first narratives of place were home geographies, home travels that were set in the place where she was raised, Cleveland and the Great Lakes region. Revisiting the haunts of her youth, Woolson infuses her Great Lakes fiction and travel narratives with nostalgia, a keen understanding of the ethos of place, and a biting critique of the national ethic of use that squandered lives and the environment for commercial and political gain. Largely forgotten today, Constance Fenimore Woolson was a popular writer in the waning decades of the nineteenth century, an important voice in the debate about women's role as an artist, and a valued friend of Henry James. Prodded into writing commercially by the death of her father, Woolson began her public writing career with pieces that probed the landscape and people of the Great Lakes region, which were first collected in *Castle Nowhere: Lake Country Sketches* (1875), noted for its realistic, unromantic depiction of the area and its characters.

Unpublished during Woolson's life, her poem "Detroit River" is an apt introduction to a review of her travel narrative "Round by Propeller."[1] The four-stanza poem, a formal apostrophe to the river that runs between the United States and Canada and through the border city, Detroit, sweeps the reader along the river through space and time. Addressing the river as "Thou brimming river," the poet puns on the word "brimming," suggesting both a river full to the brim or edge of its "velvet" and teeming shore and one that is brimming with activity as a "freshwater fleet" glides past idyllic "Canadian farms," an "old-time mill," and "grey small churches." The river and the passing landscapes form a picturesque view of harmony between a fruitful natural environment and an "indolent" human society, now aged and fading away. A nostalgic tone sighs through the rest of the poem as the river and the poem take readers to a past when French fur traders first sailed to the lakes and mingled with Native Americans. As the poem takes us to the past, as it drifts by "deep-grassed church yards" where "the old French habitans lie asleep," it elegizes what has been lost, a simple life denoted by the farms and churches along the river's banks. While the poem expresses a desire for unity, for blending, it acknowledges what is lost. The mix of French and Indian created a new métis or mixed-race people, but now the old French empire exists only in Gallic place names and the "vowelled Indian tongue." By extension, the Native American language rings "fainter, fainter, fainter," "forgotten" and "dying away." While the poet figures the waters of the lakes—Huron, Superior, Michigan—coming together as the Detroit River "bind[s]" the silver, blue and green waters of "the mighty Lakes," the desire for national and geographic union that informed Catharine Maria Sedgwick's view of the Mississippi must surely have been questioned by Woolson when she wrote this poem, nearly a decade after the Civil War. The confident, forward-looking rhetoric of Sedgwick's "Great Excursion" essay has turned to nostalgia for a vanished past in Woolson's poem.

To some extent the nostalgic tone of the poem voices the poet's lost youth as she asks the river to "stay where / I Love thee, remember thee, evermore." With the sudden death of her father, Charles Jarvis Woolson, in 1869 and the loss of his income to support her and her mother, Constance Woolson was urged to seek publication of her writings as she tried to recover from the loss of a beloved parent. As her biographer Anne Boyd Rioux notes, the first pieces that she took to the *Cleveland Herald* newspaper "contained a little bit of her father and the trips they took together" around the Great Lakes and to Mackinac Island. Although the poem to the Detroit River does not contain specific reference to her father, it is a reminiscence of an earlier, idyllic era that resonates with memories of a simpler childhood. Like "Round by Propeller," it was most likely written after she revisited Detroit, Lake Huron, and Mackinac Island, some of her "favorite haunts" as a girl, enabling her to relive the past and refresh her memory as she began to pursue her writing career.[2]

An oblique tribute to her lost youth and to her father, the poem is also a eulogy for a ruined environment. Raised in Cleveland after her parents tried to escape the personal and financial crises they experienced in their old home in New Hampshire, the deaths of three children, and the financial depression of 1837, Constance grew up with a city that was once called the "Forest City." Rioux notes that the "residential east side of the city, where she lived, felt like a town surrounded by woods. Elm-lined Euclid Avenue was the city's jewel." Cleveland's sylvan quality would begin to change as the city grew in population and became an industrial center. Between 1840 and 1873, the period when she lived there, Woolson witnessed its transformation from a town of seven thousand into a city with a population of ninety-two thousand. Later, in 1915, Emily Post would refer to Cleveland as "the Sixth City," suggesting its place among American cities. Attracted to Cleveland because it had already been established as an important transportation link between the resources of the West and the markets of the East, manufacturers like her father, owner of the Woolson stove foundry, and John D. Rockefeller, owner of the much larger Standard Oil Company of Ohio, contributed to the city's growth. But they also contributed to the pollution of the natural environment at a time when little thought was given to the conservation of the environment. Before Woolson turned thirty, the Cuyahoga River, which runs through Cleveland, "caught fire for the first time, its banks crowded with smoke-belching iron mills and oil refineries," ruining the shoreline where she used to picnic in her youth. Later earning the reputation as the most polluted river in the United States, the Cuyahoga River would catch fire thirteen times between 1868 and 1969. The 1969 fire helped spur national efforts to control water pollution and the establishment of the National Environment Protection Act and the Environmental Protection Agency in 1970. It is no wonder that when Woolson wrote her poem to the Detroit River it would "mourn the passing" of what opportunity-seeking Americans had altered in their rush to "progress," the loss of the wilderness and the early peoples who inhabited it. This poem and "Round by Propeller" demonstrate her commitment to the environment. Like her famous great-uncle, James Fenimore Cooper, and Susan Fenimore Cooper in *Rural Hours*, Woolson "would fill her fiction with laments for the disappearance of the wilderness."[3] While the poem ends with a plea, "haste not, river;—stay where I / Love thee," its lament changes to a critique of the imperialism that caused the disappearance of the wilderness in the more satiric and biting travel narrative.

Blending fiction with travel writing, "Round by Propeller" follows the excursion of a band of tourists on board the *Columbia* around the Great Lakes. Woolson invents a first-person narrator, Aunt Ruth Varick (Aunt Rue), who tells the story of the excursion and comments rather sardonically about the goings-on of her fellow travelers and the destruction of the natural landscape by careless industrialization. Published in the same year that Yellowstone Park was established as the first national park (1872) and three years before Mackinac

Island would be named the second national park, "Round by Propeller" can be read as a "travel narrative cast as environmental jeremiad." The jeremiad, Sacvan Bercovitch explains, has a long tradition in American literature, beginning with the early Puritan ministers' "cries of declension and doom" as colonists became more secular, to Frederick Douglass's warning of future retributions for a slave-holding society, and on to current warnings of the disastrous effects of global warming.[4] At a time when the nation was just beginning to understand the need to set aside parcels of wilderness for public enjoyment, even as it promoted industrialization as a sign of progress, Woolson fuses the rhetoric of the jeremiad to her travel writing to expose the damage to the natural environment and critique the national ethic of land use in an early example of eco-feminism.

When Woolson's tourists arrive in Cleveland after sailing all night from Buffalo, they are greeted by "a cloud of smoke" produced by the "iron mills and oil refineries" shrouding the city.[5] Rather than go out onto the prairies to see the wildflowers as former travelers had done, these tourists are eager to see the built and industrialized environment despite the gray sky that greets them. Deciding to tour the oil refineries rather than "Euclid Avenue . . . where the big houses are," the narrator and Major Archer, another excursionist, view firsthand the refining process and the pollution of the flats, the Cuyahoga River, and the Ohio Canal. Compared to the cauldrons of hell, with its "choking odors" ("sulphurous in origin") and shimmering "crude green petroleum," the refinery, marked by rows of stills and pipes, is a "parable" of the commercial destruction of the environment. The allusion to hell is continued as the river itself is described; the pollution has transformed the "clear stream" of the Cuyahoga into a river that is "'more petroleum than water'" and that earlier "took fire, and . . . fairly blazed as it flowed down to the lake." Even though "the risk from fire and explosion is great," Major Archer explains, fortunes are being made from the oil business ("Round" 13–15). With this comment, Woolson connects the degradation of the environment to American greed and imperialism. To punctuate her point, she has one of the travelers cite "Westward the star" (15), a reference to the course of empire that has brought "civilization" to the West at the cost to the environment and the original inhabitants. One is reminded of Andrew Melrose's 1867 painting *Westward the Star of Empire Takes Its Way*, in which the "star" is the light of a train making its way through a landscape marred by clear-cutting, and of John Gast's 1872 painting *American Progress*, which features a gigantic female figure with a gold star at her forehead hovering over the landscape, holding a book and trailing telegraph wires behind her as the wildlife and Native Americans flee westward. In more pointed ways, Woolson's sketch of Cleveland illustrates the costs of "progress" on the environment, the light of empire figured as "a river on fire" (15).

Later, as the tourists sail through Lake Huron, they are told by the ship's mate about the fires of 1871 that destroyed much of the forests that had been clear-cut by settlers: "We was coming down then, and we couldn't see a thing for miles, the smoke was so thick." From Lake Michigan to Mackinac, it seemed "the hull country was afire" so that "the islanders thought the rest of the world must be having a judgment-day" ("Round" 20). During that same season in 1871, the city of Chicago was ablaze, killing approximately 250 people and destroying seventeen thousand buildings. Whether or not the Chicago fire was actually started by Mrs. O'Leary's cow kicking over a lamp, Woolson reads the destruction of the environment in biblical terms, with references to "judgment-day," hell's sulfurous cauldrons, and "original sin" (14). In jeremiad, she figures pollution as both a cosmic and a national problem, implying that environmental destruction is a portent of human punishment to come. If the traditional jeremiad threatens punishment to revitalize the original errand of America to build a moral city on a hill, Woolson's jeremiad seeks to conserve a pastoral landscape and ideology against the ruthless consumption of the post–Civil War era. As Bercovitch has pointed out, the American jeremiad joins politics, ideas of sacred and secular progress, and national identity to suggest an ideology of American exceptionalism. Woolson likewise fuses politics with images of a biblical hell to comment upon national identity. But for her that identity is not one of exceptionalism; rather, it is one of promises broken. Understanding "the centrality of physical environment as a ground of personal and social identity," Woolson critiques a politics complicated by imperialism and commercialism and a national identity that is polluted by national and ecological politics.[6] To drive home her point, she juxtaposes these scenes of environmental damage with views of the Detroit River, its "beautiful shores and islands" (16) and the crisp, "delicious air" of the lakes to remind us of what was and could have been.

Not only has the landscape been changed over the years with the industrialization of the Midwest, the growth of urban areas, and growing signs of affluence—the "large, costly houses" of Euclid Avenue ("Round" 15). The nature of tourism has also changed as travelers seek cities, buildings, refineries, and social institutions as tourist sites rather than the natural landscape. Although Aunt Rue reminisces about old Detroit, "frontier life, and gay legends of the early French settlers," the tourists are guided to the new city hall, built after the "Italian order of architecture" out of "sandstone quarried near Cleveland" (17). Overhearing Miss Key expound on the architectural details of city hall to her young charges, Aunt Rue and the other tourists are visiting at a moment when the natural sights are giving way to the built, when the nation and the West are being reimagined, and when the process of site sacralization, the collective sense of what must be seen, is adding new sites to the tourist's map.[7] When they visit Milwaukee, "the best harbor on Lake Michigan," the tourists take in the courthouse, the opera house, the Plankinton Hotel, and the National Asylum for Disabled Soldiers. The National Asylum, built for casualties of the Civil War, is home to six hundred men, "not a hospital, a prison, or a reform institution" (26–27) but apparently a place where visitors can poke their heads into the private lives of the nation's wounded. In Detroit, the "pale women" tourists shop in "search of new patterns for worsted work," which they craft on board the steamer rather than enjoy the natural views and as they dream of the "cheap goods of Canada"—"gloves, collars and ribbons" (16–17). As her tourists are in the process of changing the nature of American tourism into a consumerist activity, hence reflecting the changing American social scene, Woolson satirizes them and what they stand for.

The pale women seem more concerned about the food they are served, the comforts of travel, and sexual conquests than learning about the places they visit. Dennis Berthold makes the point that Woolson's first-person travel sketches allow her to satirize "the social customs of tourism and expose the superficiality of travelers." The "delicate widow," Mrs. Peyton, comes under especial scrutiny. Although she admits to feeling "very weak," and hence delicately feminine, she immediately asks the waiter for "roast beef, rare, and a spoonful of beans." As she maintains the image of fragility, she also heartily enjoys the food on board, adding cabbage, potatoes, biscuit, and chops to her first request for food ("Round" 10–11). Clearly her pose is a hypocritical version of the "true woman" of earlier decades, focused now on her own pleasure, not on the needs of others.[8] Rather than tour Detroit, these women are more interested in shopping or sitting inside the steamer cabin; wrapped in shawls against the cold, they protect themselves against the natural world. Later, after Sunday services, Mrs. Peyton does "full justice to every dish," including the peach meringue (21), appeasing her overblown appetite rather than adhering to principles of self-control the Sunday service might have suggested.

Even though Mrs. Peyton's hypocrisy seems evident to her fellow travelers, Major Archer asks her to go out on deck with him, thinking that having "done his duty at the candy store," he would be rewarded with her favors ("Round" 21). Indeed, much of the narrative follows the flirtation of the tourists, Morris, Persis, Faust, Mephisto, Miss Key, and the schoolgirls in her charge—Curlylocks and Blackeyes. Even Aunt Rue is not immune to a moonlight outing with Major Archer. Cast together in a small community of travelers, these tourists pair up as part of the travel experience. While the flirtation may be a temporary reprieve from the world they have left, the young schoolgirls seem to have taken them more seriously than the men have. Aunt Rue muses, "Those gentlemen are only amusing themselves, and those poor children [the girls] are in earnest'" (27). Cast as consumers of pleasure rather than travelers who seek knowledge of others and themselves, and as parodies of true men and women, Woolson's travelers exemplify the kind of self-centered and ignorant tourist that Mark Twain had satirized in *Innocents Abroad*. Indeed, Will. B. Mackintosh claims, "tourist satire" that targeted "the stock figure of the tourist" who "quickly and thoughtlessly" moved through the landscape had begun in the early decades of the nineteenth century as travel became more and more a commodified experience.[9]

While it is tempting to poke fun at a group of tourists, as if they are a separate breed, they are, after all, people, representatives, in this case, of the new American tourist class. MacCannell writes, "The tourist is an actual person, or real people are actually tourists. At the same time, 'the tourist' is one of the best models available for modern-man-in-general." The tourists on board the steamer *Columbia*, as its name suggests, are models of "Americans-in-general" and represent the emerging post–Civil War American society. If that is so, then the America they represent is one that is interested in the built environment and consumption, in viewing the pollutions to nature and the wounded men, shopping, eating, and flirting. It is a society that ignores the costs of westward expansion, the disappearance of Native Americans like Chief Pontiac, who lives only as a history lesson for Miss Key's charges, and the costly Indian campaign west of the Mississippi. Ending the narrative by noting that "the Burnt River stage was attacked last week by Indians, and the passengers killed," among them Major Archer ("Round" 29), Woolson leaves readers with a final note on the costs of progress for both the Native Americans and the settlers.[10] While Bryant and Fuller go out among the Indians, no Indians actually appear in Woolson's narrative. They exist as secondhand stories related to Aunt Rue and the other travelers, punctuating by their absence the disappearance of Native Americans on the heels of the drive westward. Like the Indians in Gast's painting, those in Woolson's piece have been written out, pushed farther west, their territory invaded by whites attempting to "civilize" them.

If "Round by Propeller" is a satire of the social customs of tourism, as Berthold contends, it is also a satire of the social customs of middle-class America and the ideologies it supports. Because the genre of fiction allows Woolson to write beyond the firsthand experiences of more conventional travel writing, to extend her view beyond "where I went and what I saw," she can include events that she did not witness, like the death of Major Archer at Burnt River, a location of historical unrest between the indigenous peoples and the advancing phalanx into their territory. Doing so allows her to more pointedly control her satire of American customs and the ideology of progress that the tourists represent. More, it is an early example of ecofeminism that joins an ethos of environmental accountability to a critique of capitalism, racism, and a patriarchy that has left a nation wounded and converted women into thoughtless consumers. Nostalgic for a lost past, a cultural community in harmony with nature, Woolson's ecofeminism laments the destructive forces of patriarchy and capitalism.

INTERLUDE

Woolson's short story "Jeannette," which appeared in *Scribner's Monthly* in 1874, may be read as an allegory of the patriarchal and imperial desire to change or rescue the female and the wild. Figured as a reminiscence of a year spent at Fort Mackinac, the story tells of the romance between Jeannette Leblanc, a woman of French, English, and Indian blood, and the fort's surgeon Rodney Prescott, a taciturn Bostonian. Charmed by Jeannette's "strange beauty" and wild ways and against his upbringing and prejudices, Dr. Prescott falls in love with her. Not content to love her as she is, he attempts to rescue her, first on the great Arched Rock, even though she is the one adept at crossing its narrow pathway, and then by offering to marry her, to take her away with him to give her the "silk dresses and ribbons" that he assumes she desires. But Jeannette refuses him, preferring instead Baptiste, a Métis, to a lover who sees her as Other, a child, unequal to him. In this story we see how the East, represented by the doctor, is enchanted by the beauty and spirit of the West but, embarrassed by its very wildness, attempts to improve it so that it resembles the East. Here we see the tension between the wild and the civilized, the efforts of the West to retain its identity against the imperialist drive to manage and control that which it sees as inferior, as the doctor sees the uneducated Jeannette. Set at the old fort during an interlude between the imperialist war against Mexico and the terrible Civil War, the story reminds readers of the destructiveness of "manifest destiny" and the incivility of the nation. This peaceful interlude is disrupted when the troops and Dr. Prescott are called to Florida, to the Third Seminole War (1855–1858), another reminder of the nation's history of violence, acquisition, and racism that does not recognize or honor the identity of the Other. When Jeannette refuses Prescott for Baptiste, she also refuses his offer to pay the young man for his boat, declaring "He love me more than boat and silver dollar."[11] A regionalist story like "Round by Propeller," this tale laments the destructive forces of patriarchy, capitalism, and imperialism against a nostalgia for a past that was never as peaceful as imagined.

Emily Post's Transcontinental Motor Tour, New York to the Mississippi

WHEN NEW YORK SOCIALITE Emily Post set out on Sunday, April 25, 1915, to drive from New York City to San Francisco, she was not the first motorist to make a transcontinental motor trip, nor was she the first woman to make the trip. In 1915 "cross-continental motoring was all the rage," in part because tourism to Europe was severely curtailed by the war raging on the continent and in part because motoring was promoted by automobile manufacturers and the See America First campaign. Andrew S. Gross observes that "major magazines of the day ran countless stories about driving, intercalating advertisements for cars and automobile products in an early example of 'synergy' or product placement." So persuasive, "so optimistic" were these advertisements that Post could not resist their suggestions to make a transcontinental motor car journey even if she was not doing so "to advertise the endurance of a special make of car or tires."[1]

Before the popularity of automobile travel, scenic tourism was promoted by such publications as William Cullen Bryant's *Picturesque America* (1872–1874) with its "gallery of landscapes" and descriptions of American natural sites. Published by D. Appleton and Company, who would also publish Post's travel book, the massive two-volume set showcased the natural beauty of America through visual and literary sketches, including several of Constance Fenimore Woolson's Great Lakes stories. Major railroad lines promoted tourism to the areas they served, extending the promotional tour that Catharine Maria Sedgwick enjoyed on the Chicago and Rock Island Railroad to the larger groups of upper- and middle-class tourists that were emerging in tandem with the extension of the rail systems. With "their vast systems of influence, distribution, and finance," rail lines like the Northern Pacific, Marguerite Shaffer explains, promoted travel to Yellowstone National Park, and the Santa Fe line in partnership with the Fred

Harvey Company, owner of "popular eating facilities," "romanticized" travel to the Grand Canyon. Combining travel with a complex hospitality infrastructure, including resort hotels on park property, these corporations subsidized and promoted tourism in America, joining recreation, patriotism, and progress in their messages. Additionally, spokespeople for the western states waged See America First campaigns to bring tourists and their money to see the natural wonders of the West. In 1914 the Page Company launched a series of "See America First" travel guides arranged regionally, with the first extolling "Romantic and Beautiful" California. Charles Lummis, who tramped from Cincinnati to Los Angeles in 1884, became another voice encouraging travel across America in the *Land of Sunshine* magazine he edited. These are just a few of the ways that the See America First campaign flooded the tourism market so that by the time Emily Post set out on her journey she would appropriate its message, saying that while she "had driven across Europe again and again . . . our own land . . . was an unopened book" (*Motor* 3) that she meant to read.

As advertising piqued Americans' enthusiasm for seeing their own country, roads for motor travel were being improved and extended to the West. One of these was the Lincoln Highway, the brainchild of Carl G. Fisher. In 1912 he understood the need for a transcontinental highway, a "coast-to-coast rock highway to be completed by May 1, 1915, in time for the Panama-Pacific International Exposition in San Francisco," which Post was determined to see. As the cost of owning a Ford was falling (from $480 in 1908 to $290 in the mid-1920s) and as the number of driving enthusiasts was growing, the country realized the need for good, reliable highways that would link the country together. As part of the Good Roads Movement that hoped to improve existing roads or trails, like the Old Trails Road, the Lincoln Highway Association was established on July 1, 1913 by a group of automobile enthusiasts. The members of the association selected a route from New York to San Francisco, running from Times Square and connecting "major urban areas" of the North to Chicago and points west. They also solicited private funding for the project at a time before the federal government realized the need to regulate and regularize a unified highway system. By the time Post decided to travel the Lincoln Highway, the most famous of the competing trails, other women like Effie Price Gladding had already made the transcontinental journey. Detailing her journey from San Francisco to the East Coast in *Across the Continent by the Lincoln Highway* in 1914, Price wrote: "The Lincoln Highway is already what it is intended to be, a golden road of pleasure and usefulness, fitly dedicated, and destined to inspire a great patriotism and to honour a great patriot."[3]

In 1915 Emily Post was a divorcée with two sons to care for. Her ex-husband, Edwin Post, a playboy of New York City, had lost money in bad investments, and Emily had to earn a living. Raised in the upper-class society of New York, Post had received the best education for a young woman of her time and was used to the perks of the wealthy. Post would go on to become the maven of etiquette, establishing a multimedia empire that provided advice on social mores. But before she found her métier in etiquette, she had to find ways to support herself. One way was to write. A *New Yorker* profile of 1930 described "a prolific and salable novelist, one of a group of headstrong matrons whose daring was buzzed about in Best Society." She had written several society novels and numerous essays in her pre-etiquette days and had established herself as a writer among the New York elite. At a social gathering in early 1915, her friend Frank Crowninshield, soon-to-be editor of *Vanity Fair*, suggested she chronicle a drive across the United States and submit her writing to *Collier's* magazine. Post and her sons Ned (Edwin Jr.) and Bruce had recently returned from a 1914 driving tour of Europe just as things were becoming dangerous, so, as a writer and seasoned traveler, she was up to the challenge. Used to traveling in style, Emily proposed to Condé Nast of *Collier's* that she investigate whether it was possible to drive across the continent in comfort. With the Panama-Pacific International Exposition being held in San Francisco to celebrate the completion of the Panama Canal and the recovery of the city from its devastating earthquake nine years earlier, Post had another purpose in making the trip—to visit the vast exposition. *Collier's* had already run a double issue on automobile travel in January 1915, and Post's contribution would fit their publishing agenda. She sent *Collier's* three articles in September 1915 shortly after she had completed the journey and then reworked her notes into book form, with photographs, hand-drawn and annotated maps, and a daily expense account, which Appleton's, noted for its series of travel guides as well as the earlier *Picturesque America*, published in 1916. As Post writes, "Although I had promised an editor to write the story of our experience, if we had any, we were going solely for pleasure, which to us meant a certain degree of comfort, and not to advertise the endurance of a special make of car or tires. Nor had we any intention of trying to prove that motoring in America was delightful if we should find it was not" (*Motor* 2). Here she announces that she is not going to participate in the commercialization of travel, nor was she going to test herself or her auto (the Mercedes she had driven in Europe), though she did learn that a Mercedes was not the best car for the trip.[4] Her purpose was to travel in comfort and to report on the comforts (or lack thereof) she encountered. As she does so, she gives readers glimpses of America—its landscapes, peoples, cities—from her own elite perspective and in her own spirited style.

"What We Finally Carried," from Emily Post, *By Motor to the Golden Gate* (1916)

Once determined to make the journey, she engaged her son Edwin (Ned), a twenty-two-year-old junior at Harvard, to do the driving and take care of repairs. At the last minute, her cousin Alice Beadleston decided to join the adventure. On that April morning, Emily, Ned, and Alice and their luggage and supplies headed out of New York City for an adventure that would last forty-five days. The Lincoln Highway Association estimated that the trip would take twenty to thirty days, assuming an average rate of eighteen miles an hour. Taking into account the side trips and delays because of weather and car repairs, the Post entourage made the trip within the estimated time, as only twenty-seven days were actually spent driving.[5] True to her purpose ("to find out how far one *can* go pleasurably" [*Motor* 8]), Post relates the comforts and accommodations in this first leg of the trip that takes her from New York to the Mississippi River.

In a narrative that combines guidebook commentary, touristic details of scenery and sites, and personal reflection, she produces an automobile narrative that combines "discovering America and consuming America."[6] Focusing on what it takes to travel pleasurably, the necessary supplies and clothing, nightly accommodations, and eateries, her narrative not only details her own consumption of America but also shows the extent to which the geography of travel—the nation's countryside and cities, accommodations for travelers, and the purposes of travel—had changed since William Cullen Bryant made his first horseback journey through Illinois. While Bryant had to rely on the generosity of farming families for lodging and food, Post enjoys the benefits of a tourist and hospitality industry that catered to travelers wanting to tour in comfort. Early in the journey, she remarks, "Our great surprise has been the excellence of the roads and the hotels, and our really beautiful and prosperous country" (*Motor* 26).

Her friends, aghast at her adventure, sent presents and supplies to help the tourists survive: a "dark blue silk bag," which was "the most useful thing"; a lunch basket equipped with "silver-laden contents" and "food paraphernalia" fit for the "kings of Europe," which they replaced in Chicago for a more practical "tin breadbox"; block and tackle; and canvas "African water buckets" (*Motor* 12, 61, 13). They did not pack tire chains that would have helped them through the Illinois mud, though they did buy a set in Rochelle, Illinois, before they continued their journey west. In addition to these supplies, they packed a typewriter, two cameras, a medicine chest, and various trunks and rugs. As to the clothes one needs for an open-air auto trip across the continent, Post seems to have learned through experience which clothes are better suited for the journey. Hats, gloves, goggles, veils, and dusters were necessary for keeping the dust off. She discovered that a silk duster was preferable to linen or cotton because it sheds dust even if it wrinkles. She also learned that a veil with cutouts for eyes would shield her in the hot desert sun. As for her outfits, she was initially overly ambitious about how much they could carry and rather naïve about the kinds of clothes that she would need. The taffeta afternoon dress and the coat and skirt of a basket-weave material she had made for the journey were "a trial and disappointment" (*Motor* 38). Almost like packing instructions appearing in travel guidebooks, these comments inform her readers of the kinds of things they ought to carry at the same time that she is able to poke fun at her eastern expectations about travel to the West. The first photograph of the book, "What We Finally Carried," is framed by Emily, Ned, and a pile of luggage on one side with the car poised to head out. Featured in most of the photographs of the trip and an important character of the journey, their car, the Mercedes they had driven in Europe and had shipped to the United States, an elegant machine with a powerful engine, did not fare well because of its narrow tires and low-set chassis once they got off the improved roads of the East.

Because they were traveling in comfort, the group stayed at some of the best hotels on the way to Chicago. With an eye for décor (her father Bruce Price was a famous architect, and she would try her hand at interior decorating), Post comments on the various places they stayed, noting the size of rooms, the furnishings, and the location of the bathrooms. The "brand-new Hotel Utica," she writes, had large rooms that were "charmingly furnished" with "damask hangings" and "English chintz." In addition to the physical quality of their accommodations, Post comments on the service they received from the hotel and restaurant staff. At the Utica, the food was good and reasonably priced, and the desk clerk greeted everyone "with a hearty 'How do you do?'" (*Motor* 21–22). In Buffalo and again in Cleveland, they stayed at a Statler Hotel. The Buffalo Statler, which lived up to her expectations of "faultless service" and comfort, was the first in the Statler chain and exemplified its purpose of providing moderately priced rooms and a standardized code of service for business and middle-class travelers. Statler hotels were the first major hotel chain to provide a bathroom in every room, which, along with an automatic dispensing machine for toiletries, delighted Post (49–50). In Chicago she stayed at the Blackstone, "America's best hotel" which she likens to a "tower of chocolate cake" (46), noting its "beautiful interior" and dining room decorated in cerise and cream colors. She gushes about the real linen on the beds, the reading lamp with a pink shade lined in white, and her room's view of the lake (*Motor* 48). Even in Rochelle, Illinois, she writes, she was able to find a "small-town commercial hotel" with rooms and a "new little bathroom attached" (*Motor* 71). As promised, she looks to comfort in travel and in so doing she relates the extent to which other modern travelers can expect the amenities that will make their journeys enjoyable. Though she may admire the pioneers who crossed the plains in the 1850s, she does not mean to replicate their hardships. Nor must she do so in the age of auto tourism.

Food is another continuing concern. Although equipped with the prodigious lunch basket, which, she writes, they hauled out once for a roadside picnic, they took most of their meals in hotel dining rooms, where they were treated to some first-rate dinners. She notes the delicious crêpes Suzette in Utica and the "perfectly cooked chicken casserole and the hollandaise sauce on the asparagus" in Cleveland (*Motor* 32), marveling at finding European delicacies in the hinterlands. She learns that the head chef was from Chicago and the maître d'hôtel was from New York, rather than Europe as she suspected, showing that America was capable of training first-rate chefs. She also tells how the Blue Book guide led them astray in expectation of a fried chicken dinner between South Bend and Chicago. Instead of the delicacy her hungry mind had conjured, the "chicken dinner proved to be some greasy fried fish, cold bluish potatoes, sliced raw onions, pickled gherkins, bread and coffee" served in a grimy tavern (44). From this experience she formulates "a motor philosophy"—"that in motoring, as in life, since trouble gives character, obstacles and misadventures are really necessary to give the *trip* character!" (44). In Chicago, Alice (whom she refers to in the narrative as Celia) decides to send back the silver lunch set and purchase the tin breadbox, which they outfit with paper plates and disposable spoons. They stock it with such essentials as containers of chicken, ham, tongue, pheasant, and pâté de foie gras. Although the food items are rather precious, the decision to forgo the silver set and opt for something more practical indicates that they are adapting to and learning from their journey. When they are delayed in their departure because of rain, the two women opt to have a picnic in their room, eating the pâté sandwiches and lobster salad they had had prepared for them by the hotel staff. Rather than suffer from not eating well on the journey, Post, who loves chocolate, declares that she is putting on pounds and getting "as fat as butter" (60). While her tastes are clearly upper-class, her discussion of food shows the extent to which the cities west of New York had become cosmopolitan and able to serve a distinguished and discerning clientele.

In addition to good hotels and food, the auto tourist must have at hand an infrastructure to support the automobile, especially garages where mechanics can repair the early makes of cars. One of the markers in the narrative is the number of times the auto breaks down, gets stuck, or gets a flat tire. Similarly, Theodore Dreiser kept count of blowouts on his journey from New York to Indiana in *Hoosier Days* (1916). The Posts' first breakdown occurred a mere two hundred miles into the trip when they needed to replace a bearing. As the chauffer and lone male on the trip, Ned becomes acquainted with various garage mechanics along the way, leading Post to declare, "If he can only find a mechanic or two to talk to, he is perfectly happy" (*Motor* 72).

Although Ned can escape the women and talk with the local mechanics, the women are unable to strike up quick acquaintances with the locals. Indeed, Post notes, "The disappointing and unsatisfactory thing about a motor trip is that unless you have unlimited time . . . you stop too short a while in each place to know anything at all about it" (*Motor* 52). Although roads take one up "the best avenues of the cities" and "past the front entrances of farms," unlike the trains that hug "the ragged outskirts of a town" (24), Post is nonetheless a tourist who may stay a night or two in a town before hitting the road for the next destination. She may view the scenery and the buildings, but she does not really get to know the people or the place. As she says, "The observations of a transient tourist are necessarily superficial, as of one whose experiences are merely a series of instantaneous impressions" (*Motor* vii); as a transient she misses out on the character (and characters) of the nation. When they are forced to stay longer for repairs or weather, she and "Celia" go to the movies, go shopping, or are entertained by people they already know.

What Post, a keen observer, does learn about travel and the nation in this first part of the journey is that outside of New York City the scenery is quite nice—the fruits, the farms, and "in every barn, a Ford." Reiterating the theme of the See America First campaign, she declares, "One thing that we have already found out; that we are seeing our own country for the first time!" (*Motor* 23). Finding more prosperity in the country than in the city, she begins to see the nation in a new light. Cleveland, "the Sixth City" is prosperous-looking, with "wide, roomy streets with splendid lawns and trees and houses." Euclid Avenue remains the site of the large homes as it was in Constance Fenimore Woolson's day, and the older mansions speak of fat bank accounts. Chicago, which competes with New York for bragging rights, is the home of boosters, self-made millionaires who like recounting their rags-to-riches stories. She says, "There is something big, wholesome, and vitalizing out here"; she finds Chicago a good place to bring up children, providing "the ideal soil and sun and climate for young Americans to grow in" (59). She discovers that she has come to like Chicago and what it stands for, its pride, its self-made men, its vitality. Kris Lackey may be right that she has consumed America, eating her way across the states, but she also discovered America in the rural farms she views from her auto, in its small towns, and its large midwestern cities. More than a litany of hotels and edibles, the narrative conveys a sense of the spirit of the Midwest—an idealized spirit, certainly, but one that offers a counter to the ethos of New York and Boston.

When the travelers get stuck in the mud outside of Rochelle and consider shipping the car to San Francisco, they are reprimanded by the mechanic and decide to continue their journey. "To finish what you have begun, to see it through at whatever cost, that seems to be the spirit here . . . the spirit of the West." And so they continue, crossing the Mississippi River to Davenport, Iowa. This spirit of "indomitability," of not giving up, Post says, settled the West and "doubled and trebled these towns in a few years" (*Motor* 76). Caught up in the infectious boosterism of the Chicago millionaires and the indomitable citizens of Rochelle, Post reiterates their optimism about the course of the nation. At this point in the journey, hampered in the easy run to the coast and the Panama-Pacific International Exposition only by some minor repairs and the mud, it is easy for her to conjure an imagined geography of prosperity and progress, the end of the frontier, and the celebration of national power. Supported by an infrastructure of good hotels, thriving cities, and helpful mechanics, Post's America is a comfortable place, a place in which the disasters that support her "motor philosophy," the mud in western Illinois and the awful fried "chicken" dinner, do not disrupt her sense of optimism and well-being. Like the tourist Fussell describes, she has not gotten out of her comfort zone, physically or imaginatively, to question herself or the state of the nation.

We will continue to follow Post's journey in the next section as she goes across the Mississippi River to the Far West.

The FAR WEST

*W*hen travelers first encountered the Far West, the West of the Great American Desert and the Southwest, of the great mountains and the Pacific Coast, they were struck by how different it was from the familiar wooded lands of the Midwest and the bustling cities of New England and New York. Prepped by myths and stories, by the geographic imaginary of the West, they crossed over in anticipation, almost with bated breath, to find out what the West was, what it meant. What they found, as Emily Post put it, was a West that was both geographically and ethnologically different, intriguing, and daunting.

Its great open spaces and intimidating terrain, rugged mountains, gigantic sequoias and the immense rock formations of Yosemite, and dry desert lands prompted ideas of freedom, radiance, and awe. The large scale of the environment and its seeming emptiness encouraged travelers to pause, to reflect on their place in it, to try to make some sense of the natural world in their narratives. The geographic West was a place where men like Francis Parkman, Charles Lummis, Mark Twain, and John Muir could test ideas of masculinity, self-reliance, and independence (and themselves) against the mythic ideals of the West. For the women, Helen Hunt Jackson and Emily Post, genteel women from the East, it provided opportunities to redefine themselves as adventurers, women who rode horses in Yosemite and camped out in Indian Country, who eschewed for a time the comforts they were accustomed to enjoying. The West also prompted narratives that blended nature writing with travel writing, such as Muir and Jackson combining scientific knowledge with a kind of spiritual awe as they described the magnificent features of Yosemite Valley.

The ethnological West, a land of diverse cultures and races, of multiple contact zones, of new settlements and ancient pueblos, likewise challenged travelers' ideas of the West, the nation, and themselves. Spending time with Native Americans and Mexican Americans, travelers like Parkman and Lummis reassessed their understanding of these groups. Despite their differences, Jackson found common ground with Native and Mormon mothers and used her narrative to inveigh against the attack by the Mariposa Battalion against the Indians of Yosemite. Twain broke with his usual parodic, ironic stance to speak out against the injustices the Chinese populations of the mining West faced. Parkman lived for nineteen days with an Oglala Sioux band, recording their practices, rituals, and stories before they faced the violence that would decimate them and the buffalo on which they depended. After spending time with Mexicans and Pueblo Indians on his tramp through the Southwest, Lummis became an advocate for them, recording their histories and cultural practices in his narrative. Going west, these travelers learned a different political ecology that changed their perspectives of the nation and engaged them in continued advocacy for the cultural others they encountered.

Expecting to find cowboys and Indians, expecting to find the West of literature and film, Emily Post found a region changed by time, technological modernization, and the influx of tourism. The West that Francis Parkman had visited in 1846 was vastly different by the time Post journeyed in 1915. The only buffalo she saw was a stuffed one in a museum, the Indians she saw had been conquered and commodified as part of an organized tourist industry, and cities with resort-like hotels were growing up along the railroads and highways. During the course of the nineteenth century, transportation changed dramatically, from the riverboats and horses that took Parkman across the northern plains to the stagecoaches that carried Twain to Nevada, the luxurious Pullman cars on the transcontinental railroad, and finally the individual motor car that took Post over the Lincoln Highway.

As much as the travelers enjoyed the advances in transportation, communication, and the growth of cities with their amenities, and as much as they sensed the spirit of progress that drove the settling of the West, they also used their writing to decry the damage caused by careless progress. They describe scenes of abandoned mines and ravaged landscape, the forest that Twain accidentally burned, the vice that accompanied the mining towns, and the costs of migration evident in the graves and discarded furniture dotting the landscape. The later travelers look for but do not find the buffalo that had spread across the Western plains, and, while they enjoy the benefits of a tourism that allows them to peek without danger at the rituals of the Native Americans, they also sigh for the Indians' lost dignity. Civilization is not without its costs, as these writers understand.

Francis Parkman

Traveler, Tourist, Cultural Voyeur

IN HIS CLASSIC STUDY *The Year of Decision, 1846,* Bernard De Voto complains that instead of writing "a key work of American history," of "one of the greatest national experiences" of the period, Francis Parkman produced "one of the exuberant masterpieces of American literature" in writing about his journey West in the momentous 1846. *The Oregon Trail* is certainly a literary masterpiece, a "record of gentlemanly adventure among our Indian tribes" told with grace and style, according to Herman Melville. But it is more specifically a travel narrative that features its author as a traveler, tourist, ethnographer, and spectator, combining competing modes of writing about travel and competing standpoints about the experiences it relates, often in perplexing ways. While there is some disagreement among scholars of travel about the difference between travel and tourism, generally travel is seen as transformative because the traveler gains knowledge not only about the wider world but also about the self, making the journey a double voyage of discovery. Tourism is thought to be a more superficial activity aimed at recreation and escape from the mundane world.[1] Parkman's narrative evinces both types of journeyer, the traveler marked by the trials of the road and the knowledge he has gained, and the young man simply out to have adventures in the West. We can also think of Parkman as an ethnographer, an earnest scholar intent on learning about Native Americans in order "to gather firsthand experience and knowledge for the ethnographical notes" that would inform his first history *The Conspiracy of Pontiac.* Finally, he is a voyeur, gazing on the diverse peoples of the West and tagging them with superficial stereotypes that fill in for careful analysis and reveal his culture's ideas about civilization and savagism.[2] For many readers the hasty generalizations and reliance on racial stereotypes have marred the book as a whole, but the narrative is, in fact, a complicated document, deploying competing standpoints as well as multiple genres—history, adventure tale, autobiography, geographic description, ethnography, travelogue, and perhaps a bit of fiction—to tell the story of his remarkable journey.

As a book about movement and place, *The Oregon Trail* maps Parkman's travels in the West, allowing readers to follow his circular trek across the prairies and plains from St. Louis to Fort Laramie and beyond and then back to St. Louis and toward "home," the last word in the narrative. The various camps, river crossings, and adventures mark the trajectory of movement across space, locating the narrator on the landscape he traverses. The narrative also charts the travels of the many others Parkman encounters, the migrants whose trail he follows, the Santa Fe traders carrying goods to New Mexico, Mormons in search of a safe space to rebuild their community, US troops moving toward Mexico as war begins, mountain men and fur traders coming and going from the Rocky Mountains, and even migrating buffalo whose traces Parkman follows. Most importantly, the book marks the movements and migrations of the Native Americans across the plains, describing cultures that make their home on the move. Like the imagined West, the narrative is cross-hatched with literal and figurative trails. It is a palimpsest not only of the diverse travelers but also of the ideologies of the West, the frontier, the Native American, and the civilization that Parkman brings with him as surely as he brings the supplies needed to survive a summer's sojourn. These competing modes of travel experiences and standpoints as he moves between perceptual locations as traveler, tourist, ethnographer, and spectator, as well as the "long accumulation of contradictions and ambiguities" about the West, as Jonathan Raban puts it in *Driving Home* (12), contribute to the perplexing quality of the narrative and of Parkman's imagined West.

As a traveler, Parkman describes the going forth, the trails, the terrain, and the environments he encounters as well as the accommodations he makes to the demands of western travel. Just shy of twenty-three years of age when he began the journey in March 1846, Parkman was already an accomplished traveler. Setting out with his cousin Quincy Shaw (who likewise hoped to restore his health), he had the means to spend the greater portion of the year traveling, thanks to the fortune amassed by his grandfather Samuel Parkman. He had already made several excursions to the Old Northwest and Canada in search of material for his histories of the conflicts among the French, English, and Indians. He had also greatly enjoyed a grand tour of Europe in 1843–44, "roaming energetically through Italy, Switzerland, France, and England." Having finished a degree in history at Harvard and studied law, reading much but also breaking his health, Parkman set out to the West to recoup his strength, which he tended to test, to exercise his "restlessness and love of wilds" and gather information for *The Conspiracy of Pontiac*. As he wrote to American bookseller Henry Stevens, "I set out tomorrow for the far West, to see the Indians, glean their traditions, and study their character, for the benefit of 'Pontiac.'"[3] He proposed "to join a village, and make [himself] an inmate of one of their lodges" to gain a closeup view of Indians (*Oregon* 168). Describing not only the Oglala Sioux with whom he lived for nineteen days, Parkman also provides a lively account of his imagined West, its terrain, the trials of the road, and the peoples he encounters.

Like many travelers, Parkman sketches the modes of transportation employed to transport him to his destination and the gear necessary to make the trip. He begins by describing the scene in St. Louis, the steamboats "crowded with passengers on their way to the frontier" and the condition of the steamboat he and Shaw sailed on, the *Radnor*. Loaded with goods "until the water broke alternately over her guards" and with the diversity of peoples traveling to the West—Santa Fe traders, "gamblers, speculators, and adventurers," migrants, mountain men, "negroes, and a party of Kanzas Indians," the boat represents a microcosm of the West in 1846 (*Oregon* 37–38). Having arrived in Westport, Missouri, where they would begin their overland journey, Parkman details the gear, clothes, weapons, horses, and provisions that they would take with them—"a tent, with ammunition, blankets, and presents for the Indians" (48). A decade later, Randolph B. Marcy's handbook *The Prairie Traveler* would recommend the supplies pioneers needed to traverse the Overland Trail, including food, camp supplies, and clothing, and how best to pack them. Parkman was content to provide a simple list since he relied on Henry Chatillon, his guide and an experienced hunter, and Delorier (the muleteer) to advise him about traveling in the West.

Following established routes to Fort Leavenworth and then on the Oregon Trail to Fort Laramie, Parkman plots his narrative geographically and chronologically, across space and through time, recounting as he does the conditions of the camps, environment, weather, and people they meet as markers of the journey. Derived from his notebooks written during the journey, the 1849 edition of the *Oregon Trail* is a more literary and expansive version of typical journal writing by migrants, in which the progress of the journey aligns with the narrative. Sarah Wisner, who crossed the plains in 1866, wrote ledger-like entries that noted dates and miles traveled alongside terse comments:

> May 1 Drove 8 miles and camped to wait for company. Company came up and we drove 20 miles more. The country is beautiful but not all settled. Presume it will be some day. Camped on a creek.

Like other diarists of the Oregon Trail, Wisner was careful to leave a verbal map for others who might follow and to record an important event in history, the journey to the Far West. Her own feelings and interpretations of what she experienced are barely articulated. Another emigrant, Algeline Ashley, who made the journey in 1852, tersely records the costs of travel, counting the number of graves and the people who are ill alongside mention of the weather and conditions of the trail.

> June 2 Thunder shower in the afternoon. Very steep hills to cross—some heavy sand. A flowering bunch bean grows on the hills; it looks exactly like a gilliflower at a little distance. Child has the measles. Breedlove is quite unwell. Passed 11 graves. Two wagons left because they were dissatisfied.[4]

Ashley does not reflect on her own reactions to these events; even so, we can hear the curve of emotion, the personal account, rendered through a geographic code. For Ashley and Wisner the topography becomes a metaphor for the self, a self not consciously or explicitly revealed but one that nonetheless is shaped and identified by movement and the environment. We can also see how they use topography and their place along the trail to locate themselves, to find themselves, as their sense of self is made fluid by movement.

Similarly, Parkman uses his travel narrative to locate himself and to represent a more nuanced and complex self than the surface of the narrative indicates. If place identity is tied to self-identity, as H. M. Proshansky, Theodore Sarbin, and Stefan Hormuth have argued, then for a traveler self-identity is fluid, mobile, changing with almost daily movement across place.[5] We can see this fluid, changing identity in the material, physical changes Parkman relates, his change of appearance and his adaptation to Indian food functioning as ciphers for self-identity change. When he contrasts his attire at the beginning of the journey, which "bore some marks of civilization," with the "shabbiness" of his appearance at the end (*Oregon* 48), "a time-worn suit of leather" (391), he is speaking of more than just clothes. He is signaling that at least for a time his sense of self was changed by the experiences of travel, that he has exchanged the accoutrements and identity of "civilization" for those of the wilds. When he returns to Fort Laramie after his sojourn with the Oglalas, he enjoys bread again after a diet almost exclusively of meat "without salt" and comments, "It seemed like a new phase of existence, to be seated once more on a bench, with a knife and fork, a plate and tea-cup" (350). Like the change of clothes, the dietary shift signals self-identity change. In fact, while he was with the Oglalas he adapted enough to their way of life that he developed a taste for dog. "A dog-feast is the greatest compliment a Dahcotah can offer to his guest" (163). Not only does Parkman give readers a sense of the Dakota culture by relating what he ate, he also indicates his immersion, brief though it may be, in their culture. In many ways appearance and food are intimately connected to self-identity. The persona we present to ourselves and the world is wrapped in appearance, and the food we eat is associated with cultural identity. The bread and salt that Parkman misses are elements of a New England culinary identity.

More importantly, his ideas of what is essential in life were affected by his journey: "We had seen life under a new aspect. . . . Our idea of what is indispensable to human existence and enjoyment had been wonderfully curtailed, and a horse, a rifle and a knife seemed to make up the whole of life's necessities. . . . One other lesson our short prairie experience had taught us; that of profound contentment in the present, and utter contempt for what the future might bring" (*Oregon* 355). The kinds of things that might have been deemed "indispensable" for a Boston Brahmin, money, comfort, a promising career, are reassessed on the road, where life seems to be reduced to its common denominators—movement, protection, and survival. As well, the fragility of life is brought home to him: "A month ago I should have thought it rather a startling affair to have an acquaintance ride out in the morning and lose his scalp before night, but here it seems the most natural thing in the world" (127). These are important things to have learned—the essentials needed to sustain life and an appreciation of the present. It seems that the West, with its challenging terrain, great distances, and different ways of life, prompted reassessments of his previous ideas and values. While he may not have been able to shed the ideologies and prejudices of his time, he did learn much about life, his perspective was changed, and he underwent physical and psychic transformations. In these ways, he fits the description of the traveler who recounts two journeys of discovery—the external and the internal.

As he plots his cognitive map, finding himself in the changing day-to-day locations, Parkman also maps the journey, giving his impressions of the terrain, weather, and wildlife as he moves from camp to camp. Relating his trek from La Bonte's camp forty miles northwest of Fort Laramie to find the village of the Oglala chief Whirlwind, Parkman indicates the interconnectedness between these two modes of charting the journey. Here he tells us that he and Raymond, a man hired to help with the livestock, moved from a country parched by the heat, with ravines "white and raw," to a stream "clear and swift" punctuated by "small birds ... splashing in the shallows," and on to a night camp serenaded by the howl of wolves. Waking up to find the mules and Parkman's horse Pauline "galloping away at full speed," Raymond goes after them, leaving the weak Parkman alone with the mosquitoes and vanishing food supplies for three days. Parkman finally leaves camp in search of game to eat, finding nothing but some curlews, water birds, two of which he shot. Once reunited, Parkman and Raymond continue their way toward the mountains only to be held up by a storm, "a zigzag blinding flash, with terrific crash of thunder, and with a hurricane that howled over the prairie." Having gone from the blazing heat to the deluge of the prairies, facing the possible loss of horses and food, left alone in a region habituated by grizzly bears, wolves, and "dangerous Indians," Parkman ponders, "'Am I,' I thought to myself, 'the same man who, a few months since, was seated, a quiet student of belles-lettres, in a cushioned armchair by a sea-coal fire?'" (*Oregon* 228–34). In short course, this episode illustrates the changing landscape, the vagaries of the weather, the contrariness of the animals, the eminent threats from nature and humans, the ever-present need for food, and their cumulative effect on Parkman's self-identity, his sense of who he is. These experiences, mapped by location and repeated with little variation throughout the narrative, go into transforming the New England "student of belles-lettres" into someone who has faced, and survived, the dangers and trials of the road, a classic traveler.

The geography on which Parkman constructs the self of the narrative is likewise a constructed space, an imaginary that represents his ideas of self and the West. Casting himself alternately as ill and out of place in an alien environment, and as an adventurer, the hero of the tale he spins, Parkman sketches competing terrains on which to act out these rival ideas of self. Although he travels almost two thousand miles across a variety of bioregions—prairies, plains, mountains, river byways, desert—Parkman organizes his geographic descriptions around two divergent views of the terrain: empty or full of life, daunting or picturesque, dangerous or rewarding. The vastness and seeming emptiness of the western prairies present a challenge to the eastern traveler, used, no doubt, to forested trails and lush meadows that frame and constrain space and vision. While open space may connote ideas of freedom, as Yi-Fu Tuan has argued, too much space and too much solitude could be daunting and challenging.[6]

Hence, his depictions of the prairie, what Parkman calls the "great American desert," are studded with images of "barren wastes," "level plains, too wide for the eye to measure," and a "boundless waste." Seemingly too vast and too empty to contain life, the prairie is littered with reminders of death, "the vast antlers of the elk" and the "whitened skulls of the buffalo," which function as geographic codes for a self under pressure by the challenges of the journey. Void of big game that would sustain Parkman and his entourage, the area actually was alive with "varmints," wolves, snakes, "unnumbered mosquitoes," and "tadpoles" swimming in his cup of water (*Oregon* 68–84). While the prairies contain evidence of life, the "varmints" pester and threaten rather than sustain the travelers. Animals out of place in drinking water, long since dead, or inhospitable to the human traveler presage the instability of the weather, which shifts dramatically between thunderstorm and "a sultry, penetrating heat" (70). This not only discomfited the travelers but also had a destabilizing effect on Parkman. His sense of alienation is furthered by the monotonous, unbroken quality of the landscape along the Platte River. The sand hills, he writes, are a "barren, trackless waste." "Before us and behind us, the level monotony of the plain [is] unbroken [except by the bleached remains of the buffalo]" (106). Without recognizable landmarks, Parkman relates that he "rode on for hours, without seeing a tree or a bush" (76), lost without markers by which to orient himself. At one point he describes how he crawled up a mountain ridge on his "hands and knees," arriving totally exhausted. "All around, the black crags, sharp as needles at the top, stood glowing in the sun, without a tree, or a bush, or a blade of grass to cover their precipitous sides. The whole scene seemed parched with a pitiless, insufferable heat" (240). Already ill at this point and exhausted, Parkman witnessed a terrain not only representing his debilitated, "pitiless" body but also testing his endurance and the goals of his adventure. In another episode, after chasing a herd of buffalo and exhilarated in the rush of the hunt, Parkman describes having looked about for "some indications to show [him] where he was." But, as he says, "I might as well have looked for landmarks in the midst of an ocean." Although the area "teemed with life . . . there was nothing in human shape amid all this vast congregation of brute forms" (123–25). Without human contact or recognizable landmarks, he is destabilized, alone. This environment is too immense, too barren, too foreign, too alien; it is a place where he can get lost, lose his bearings cartographically and psychically.

 In an alternate depiction of the environment, Parkman sees a landscape rich with life that encourages him to act out another version of himself. Frank M. Meola contends that *The Oregon Trail* is "one of the best examples of the male Anglo-American ego confronting an environment that threatens to break it apart, but that also gives it a space in which to act out its masculinity."[7] Against the barren landscape that threatens to break him, Parkman sketches a "prairie [that] teemed with life" (*Oregon* 125) on which he can act out a heroic idea of himself. Alone after chasing a herd of buffalo, he writes that he was "at leisure to observe minutely the objects around [him]," focusing on the near rather than the distant view of the natural world. Now he notices "for the first time" the "[g]audy butterflies," "strangely formed beetles," and "multitudes of lizards . . . darting like lightning over the sand." He sees that the prairies are actually a rich biosphere, populated with a variety of species: "countless hundreds of buffalo," numerous antelope that approach him "gazing intently with their great round eyes," "villages of prairie-dogs," and snakes sunning themselves (124–25). He is charmed by the stately procession of a "herd of some two hundred elk . . . their antlers clattering as they walked" (172). As he wanders about in the Black Hills (Laramie Mountains), he pays attention to traces of life, finding himself in "a hunter's paradise" of buffalo, elk, and Rocky Mountain sheep, a landscape sweetened by the wild strawberries of July (317). Here his attention is caught by the large animals he can hunt, particularly the buffalo in this "wildest" of "all American wild sports" (403).

Apparently running the buffalo was the epitome of adventure and male testing in the nineteenth-century West. Even the cosmopolitan Washington Irving relished hunting buffalo during his tour of the prairies in 1832. Providing numerous extended and detailed accounts of buffalo hunts in the narrative, Parkman figures the environment as a space where travelers can participate in ancient rituals alongside practiced hunters and Native Americans, a space where he can act out a version of masculinity. Seeing the environment in these scenes as bountiful, he nonetheless participates in the near elimination of the very animals that define the region, "emblems of Western distinctiveness." Of the last hunt near the end of his sojourn, he speculates, "Thousands of them [bulls] might be slaughtered without causing any detriment to the species" (*Oregon* 418). The count of slaughtered beasts signifies his prowess, but he and his group kill so many buffalo that the carcasses summon hordes of wolves (and the sky above them is "always full of buzzards or black vultures"). He estimates that his party have killed enough buffalo to supply "five hundred pounds of dried meat" and that the California men they joined prepared "some three hundred more" (429–30). Cast in these scenes as a land of plenty, the West was also a scene of death and depletion. The eight hundred pounds of meat taken that day are a prelude to the near destruction of buffalo herds in the decades after Parkman's trip. These elements of his imagined geography, what Jonathan Raban calls an "elsewhere . . . for a life beyond the one we're leading," an elsewhere of barrenness and bounty, comprise a geography of masculine testing for the self (or selves) Parkman constructs.[8]

These descriptions of the journey and the environment and their effects on the author mark *The Oregon Trail* as a piece of travel writing and Parkman as a traveler charting his personal cognitive map across the terrain. As well, the narrative charts the sociopolitical aspirations and transformations of the nation in 1846 as it records the movements of diverse groups across the Western plains. "[A] palimpsest . . . nearly blackened with the cross-hatching" of these multiple journeys, the seemingly empty Western prairie was nonetheless a scene of fluid and dynamic movements of peoples along its trails. As Patricia Limerick describes it, "The American West was an important meeting ground where Indian America, Latin America, Anglo-America, Afro-America, and Asia intersected," bringing a "diversity of languages, religions, and cultures" to the West.[9]

During his sojourn, Parkman witnessed much of this diversity on board the *Radnor,* in the stopping places where travelers, traders, trappers, and Native people converged, and in the movements of peoples across the western prairies. Steamboats had opened the Missouri River to navigation in 1829, Seymour Dunbar reports, making travel inland from St. Louis more accessible for the American Fur Trade Company and subsequent travelers. The "Great Migration" to Oregon had begun in 1843 after Congress established a territorial government and granted land to settlers in the Oregon territory. That spring saw the "first considerable body of organized travelers who crossed the American continent in an overland trip with the purpose of establishing homes on the Pacific coast," and by the time Parkman traveled along the Platte River the Oregon Trail was well established. According to John Mack Faragher in his study of the Overland Trail, there were one thousand people on the trail in 1846. In 1848 gold would be discovered in California, and the numbers of people going to the West would increase—to 55,000 in 1850 alone. In 1846 approximately fifteen thousand Mormons were expelled from Nauvoo, Illinois, and headed west to find a place where they might live as they pleased. Trade routes to Santa Fe and Chihuahua, Mexico, were active, luring the wealthy trader Samuel Magoffin and his young wife Susan to Santa Fe. John C. Frémont had issued a California declaration of independence from Mexican rule as the war with Mexico was unsettling borders and sending US troops to Mexico. The same year that William Cullen Bryant noted the reassignment of soldiers from the garrison at La Pointe, Michigan, to the Mexican frontier, Parkman witnessed the movement of troops as Colonel (later General) Kearney led soldiers to Bent's Fort and then to Santa Fe to face the Mexicans in a war that would cede to the United States great holdings in the

West. In addition to colonization, conquest, and expansionism by Anglo-Americans, the area was also the site of the habitual migrations of the Plains Indians and the buffalo they followed. As Dunbar notes, "They were of necessity nomadic, or semi-nomadic, shaping their yearly routine in harmony with the habits of the living food and fur supply on which their existence so largely depended, and moving their villages, trapping camps and hunting parties periodically, in accord with the changes of the seasons."[10] Despite the open spaces and the challenges to travel, the western plains were being crisscrossed in the spring and summer of 1846 when Parkman was recording his own movements.

Parkman begins his narrative by describing the scene in St. Louis where "an unusual number of travelers were making ready their wagons and outfits" for Oregon, California, and Santa Fe and where "steamboats were leaving the levee with passengers headed for the frontier" (*Oregon* 37). Locations where diverse and divergent groups gathered, St. Louis, Independence, and Fort Laramie were important transportation and trade hubs where travelers came together briefly before departing onto the trails that crossed the "American Desert." In a sense, these places created multiple contact zones or locations of cultural contact, where the diverse peoples came together in momentary respite before resuming their movement for economic, political, military, and personal interests, where would-be conquerors—migrants and American troops—paused for a moment, adjacent to those their movement would displace. A witness to this great impulse to move, Parkman wrote of Independence, Missouri, "We began to see signs of the great western movement that was then taking place." He mentions "parties of emigrants," "slavish-looking Spaniards," "Indians belonging to a remote Mexican tribe," and "one or two French hunters" (39). Later at Fort Laramie, the post established by the American Fur Company, Parkman enumerates the Indians in "white buffalo robes," "squaws, gaily bedizened," "trappers, traders and *engagés*" (148), and migrants, "tall awkward men" and "women with cadaverous faces" (157), who converge in this meeting ground of cultures and peoples. Anticipating postmodern hubs of transport, these sites of confluence not only demonstrate the diversity of peoples in the West in an early version of globalization. They also speak to the meeting, mixing, and mobility of empire and capital that bring strangers together. While elucidating the mix of peoples in the West, dispelling any notion that it was empty, Parkman also illustrates the tangle of motives that lured them to the region.

This mix shapes the geographic imaginary Parkman constructs as he records his impressions of the people he encounters. The narrative is dotted with multiple encounters with the migrants and the Mormons who were headed west over the Rocky Mountains. He notes their conditions and the hardships they endure, the emigrant woman "in the pains of child-birth," the graves of those who died along the way—"Mary Ellis. Died May 7th, 1845. Aged Two Months"—the poor "yellow-visaged Missourians," and the "care-worn, thin-featured matron" peeking out from under the wagon covering. Parkman muses that it "was easy to see that fear and dissension prevailed" among the men in the wagon trains and that the "women were divided between regrets for homes they had left and apprehension of the deserts and the savages before them" (*Oregon* 97–98). Though he does not spend much time thinking about the migrants, what he does say echoes the concerns of Caroline Kirkland and Margaret Fuller for the women who followed their men to the Old Northwest to make a new life in the wilderness. The costs of life, health, and family goods, the "shattered wrecks of ancient claw-footed tables, well waxed and rubbed" that were "soon flung out to scorch and crack upon the hot prairie," speak to Parkman of "the stern privations" brought about by an "infatuation" (133, 97) and restlessness that marks so much of American history. Articulating a theory of westward movement that Frederick Jackson Turner would later refine, Parkman casts the history of the nation in the impulse to move ever farther west and the progressive disappearance of Native Americans. Noting the uncanny meeting of the two groups on the prairies when he witnesses a migrant train passing a temporary encampment of Indians, he fatalistically muses that "in the space of a century" the migrants will sweep the Indians "from the face of the earth" (*Oregon* 141).

Some of the liveliest scenes in the narrative occur when Parkman describes in a swoop of color and motion the movement of whole villages of Indians. At Fort Laramie he witnesses the Smoke's village crossing Laramie Creek "in a mass" (*Oregon* 155). He paints a picture of a flurry of activity, a jumble of household goods, people, and animals crossing the creek, horses and dogs laden with travois, warriors on horseback, dogs yelping, and old women screaming. Within moments the turmoil was over. As the tribe gained the other side of the river, the "crowd melted," and within "the space of half an hour" families had reconstructed their lodges (156). Parkman seems astonished by the order in the seemingly pell-mell splash of movement, but this routine of migration and movement comprises the Indians' way of life, their habit of dwelling-in-traveling. Migrations are part of their culture and way of life; as they move, they take their culture with them, literally defining their lives in travel.

As an observer, an amateur ethnographer, Parkman dwells and travels with the Native Americans when he joins Whirlwind's tribe and participates in their migrations. As earlier, he describes the organized dismantling of the lodges, the tasks of the women, the "shaggy horses" waiting to be loaded, and then the movement of the whole village, "little naked children . . . running along on foot," "numberless dogs . . . scampering among the horses," "young braves" galloping about, and "a rank of sturdy pedestrians stalking along in their buffalo robes" (*Oregon* 264). Parkman writes that after the band had killed enough buffalo to sustain them, they decamped again, this time to the Black Hills (Laramie Mountains) for new lodge poles, "all moving once more, on horseback and on foot, over the plains" (307). Once their lodges were erected, "half the population, men, women, and boys, mounted their horses and set out for the interior of the mountains. . . . at full gallop . . . into the dark opening of the defile beyond" (314). Migratory people, the tribe carried its homes on the backs of their horses, methodically breaking and setting up their village as they followed seasonal migrations in search of the necessities of life. They also demonstrate the dynamic geography of the West. Traveling with them, Parkman muses on this "strange or picturesque cavalcade" (314) and sketched an impressionistic conflation of humans, animals, water, mountains, and movement.

Even as he conflates the human and the nonhuman in a colonizing gaze, the scenes prompt him to contemplate the future of this "wandering democracy," writing, "When the buffalo are extinct, they too must dwindle away" (*Oregon* 264, 199). While he understands the sad future for the Indians, at the time, in 1846, their cultural routine of migration adds another dimension to the movements Parkman records and to his own journeys of discovery. Their migrations also contribute to the dynamic mobility of peoples moving across the prairies on the way to somewhere else, of traders constantly moving back and forth between trade centers, of tourists like him journeying in search of adventures before they return home. Sketching these movements, Parkman demonstrates how "travel . . . denotes a range of material, spatial practices" that signal the diversity and fluidity of the West he encounters.[11]

Living and traveling with Whirlwind's band, Parkman points to the complicated connections between travel and ethnography that James Clifford describes: "Ethnographers, typically, are travelers who like to stay and dig in (for a time), who like to make a second home/workplace. Unlike other travelers who prefer to pass through a series of locations, most anthropologists are homebodies abroad."[12] Parkman is at once a tourist out to "pass through a series of locations" and an amateur ethnographer who digs in. He writes in his narrative, "I had come into the country almost exclusively with a view of observing the Indian character. . . . To accomplish my purpose it was necessary to live in the midst of them, and become, as it were, one of them" (*Oregon* 168). The overriding purpose in his journey was to collect ethnographical data, descriptions of the Indians in their habitats, by embedding himself in their culture, even if just for a short time. He writes, "Having been domesticated for several weeks among one of the wildest of the wild hordes that roam over the remote prairies, I had extraordinary opportunities of observing them, and I flatter myself that a faithful picture of the scenes that passed daily before my eyes may not be devoid of interest and value" (251). Thus, even as he often figures Indian scenes as picturesque and appropriates them into his own story of adventure, Parkman also describes their appearance, their villages, and their stories and beliefs, giving readers a view of the Plains Indians culture at mid-century.

He takes readers inside the lodges of his hosts, noting the animal skins and weapons that hang inside, conveying the rites of hospitality—a smoke of tobacco and *shongsasha* and a "wooden bowl of boiled buffalo-meat" as the men share stories, their "endless stories of war and hunting" (*Oregon* 255–57). He provides details of the dog feast that he gave, how the women prepared the food, and the speeches that followed the repast, giving a view of a communal oral tradition that preserved the history, legends, and beliefs of the band. He also retells some of the stories he heard as a way of suggesting their beliefs and of preserving the stories of a people whose lives were soon to change irrevocably. One of these stories recounts the thunder-fighters who shoot their weapons in the air to frighten the thunder, convinced that it has the power to kill. A story about cosmic forces, it illustrates the anthropomorphic theology of the Sioux. As one of the older men related, "The thunder is bad . . . he killed my brother" (255–56). Parkman relates a story that the elder Mene-Seela told about a time when he "fell into a swoon" while hunting beaver and saw three people, "entirely white." Awakening, Mene-Seela grabbed three beavers and claimed they were the white people he had mysteriously seen. Though Parkman asks Mene-Seela, "the grand depositary of the legends and traditions of the village," to tell him more stories, the old man declines, giving Parkman only "fragments" (284–85), perhaps in a moment of resistance to the ethnographic appropriation of his culture. Like Margaret Fuller and later Charles Lummis, Parkman understands the importance of recording and preserving Native culture and stories before they are lost, even as he interjects his own biases, commenting that his informant was "exceedingly superstitious" (285).

From his perspective as an amateur ethnographer, Parkman also records the routine practices of Whirlwind's village. He sketches one day in the life of the village, beginning with hunters sleeping in their lodges, young men playing a ball game, children tossing each other on a buffalo robe, and women "silently engaged in their heavy tasks." At dusk the horses, "hundreds in number," are brought from their grazing spots to the village and staked out by the hunters. As evening descends, he draws a scene of kettles of food hung over fires, women and children "laughing and talking merrily," and the older men smoking their pipes and conversing, with "not a particle of the gravity and reserve usually ascribed to Indians." The merry sounds of the evening are punctured by the "dismal cries and wailings" of a woman in mourning, "gashing her legs with a knife." Later in the night, Parkman walks to the lodge of his host, Kongra-Tonga, and describes the interior of the structure and the family scene contained, "his squaw, a laughing, broad-faced woman" and "half a dozen children scattered about." Outside, he hears a drum and a chorus of voices while a "grand scene of gambling [is] going forward" (*Oregon* 288–92). Taking readers through a day with the village, Parkman conveys the routines of life and familial arrangements, marriage and divorce practices, entertainments, and Indian child-rearing philosophies. He comments on many of the things anthropologists pay attention to: family life, the organization of the community, rituals of hospitality and feasting, the stories and beliefs that try to make sense of life, death, and their place in the cosmos. Even so, his account lacks "thick description," thoughtful analysis of the things he has observed and recorded and an assessment of his analysis that modern anthropology expects.[13] Writing a half-century before Franz Boas would inaugurate the field of American anthropology and insist on scientific methodology, Parkman focuses on observing and recording Indian culture, and, like many other nineteenth-century travelers in the West, lets his own racial bias drive his few interpretations of their culture.

Early in the adventure he encounters a group of Kanzas and describes them in detail: the old man with his head shaved, painted red and decorated with some eagle feathers dangling from a remaining tuft of hair, "old squaws," "two snake-eyed children," "tall lank young men," and "girls whose native ugliness not all the charms of glass beads and scarlet cloth could disguise." Although he takes time to sketch this "ragamuffin horde" (*Oregon* 51), his descriptions are marred by pejorative language and racist depictions. While he may employ mnemonic shortcuts, consistently calling Indians "snaky-eye" and casting older women as "squaws" "ugly as Macbeth's witches" (141), he still cannot escape the learned racism of his time. Even if we acknowledge the use of set phrases and stereotypes, we cannot escape his racist comments and descriptions. When he praises the noble form of the Indian male, an "Apollo of bronze," he undercuts the comparison by saying, "Yet after all, he was but an Indian" (206). After having lived and moved about with Whirlwind's village, spending time in their lodges and eating with them, and providing careful descriptions of their culture, he still writes, "These men were thorough savages. Neither their manners nor their ideas were in the slightest degree modified by contact with civilization" (251). Here Parkman reiterates the dichotomy between "savagism" and civilization that Roy Harvey Pearce argues pervaded nineteenth-century thinking about Native Americans, even when some Americans were defending them against the greed and violence of white America.

As Pearce points out, when Ralph Waldo Emerson wrote his open letter about the injustice of the removal of the southern tribes, "no one thought to denounce American civilization." Civilization and its opposite seemed to be givens, just as the idea of progress was an accepted good, something that civilizations pursued while "savage" societies were either static or doomed. Even Henry Rowe Schoolcraft, who married a Native woman and studied Algonquin legends, could not escape the idea of Indians' savagery and the hope to civilize them. He could not escape the dichotomy between savagism and civilization and the certainty that, as Pearce puts it, "the Indian must die, since noncivilization is not life." So, when Parkman directs his tourist's gaze on the Indians and describes them as both picturesque and savage, he reveals not just his own attitudes but also those of his society that have been constructed by such artists as George Catlin and James Fenimore Cooper, both of whom he references in the text. In fact, Pearce makes the point that it was Catlin "who first taught Americans to look at their West."[14] Still, as Parkman prepares to return to civilization, to Boston to write up his travel narrative, he reflects, "I cannot recall those savage scenes and savage men without a strong desire again to visit them" (*Oregon* 460), thus demonstrating the prevailing thinking that posited the Indian as the Other that one visits but does not become.

Like his contemporaries, Parkman sees no real future for the Indians. With the extinction of the buffalo, their way of live will vanish. "The Indians will soon be corrupted by the example of the whites, abased by whisky and overawed by military posts" (*Oregon* 252), a life that Bryant and Fuller had already witnessed on the Great Lakes. As Lucy Maddox has argued, "Nineteenth-century analyses of 'the Indian question' almost always end . . . at the virtually impassable stone wall of the choice between civilization and extinction for the Indians."[15] Visiting the West at a turning point, during the year of decision, when the steady incursion of whites was becoming evident to the Indians, Parkman notices the transformation in their lives. The "wonder" that "the earth contained such a multitude of white men" is "giving way to indignation" and the violence that will follow (161). Like other travelers to Indian country in the mid-nineteenth century, Parkman sees this change and foretells a grim future for the Natives. As much as he gets to know the members of Whirlwind's tribe and learn about their culture, they remain in his mind savage or at best picturesque characters in his own story of exploration, his own temporary escape from civilization. While he predicts the transformation of the West, he also bemoans that soon "its danger and its charm will have disappeared together" (252) for adventurer-travelers like him. Although he pauses to comment on the future of the country, he quickly interrupts what might have been an astute sociopolitical commentary by return-ing to his narrative plot: "But to glance at the interior of a lodge..." (161). In doing so, Parkman positions himself as a traveler whose purpose is to describe what he sees and the adventures he has had in the West. When he shifts the direction of his discussion here, Parkman demonstrates a tension between mapping as dynamic, tracing the physical and intellectual mobility of a traveler, and map-ping as static and colonizing, suggesting stereotype and learned attitudes about "savagism" that fix the Native people and the West. Working between different modes of mapping, between vivid description and stereotype, between analy-sis and adventure, the structure of his narrative mimics the contradictions of nineteenth-century thinking about Native Americans and the dilemma of how to handle "the Indian question."

In the end, Parkman is a tourist who will return home and continue the life he had left for a summer's sojourn in the West. Like the experiential tourist Erik Cohen describes, he "observes the authentic life of others" but is not converted to their lifestyle, remaining a stranger even as he "learns to appreciate" ("aestheti-cally") the Other. As a tourist, traveler, and ethnographer, Parkman has related his experiences and the people he has seen. Above all, he has represented the life of an Oglala band at a watershed moment, between their traditional ways of life and a new life inexorably changed by the social and political forces that brought others to the West. In 1846 Parkman understands that the nomadic way of life he has observed will not continue. At the same time, he bemoans the fact that the "danger and charm" (*Oregon* 252) of living with the Indians will also vanish. In 1872, in the preface to the fourth edition of *The Oregon Trail*, he laments the losses he had predicted, the "forms and conditions of life ... which have ceased, in great measure, to exist" and quickly enumerates the changes that have occurred in the quarter century since he first visited. Reuniting with Henry Chatillon a few years before writing this preface, he relates that Chatillon told him that "the Indians with whom I had been domesticated, a band of the hated Sioux, had nearly all been killed in fights with the white men." Though he retains his Brahmin point of view, he describes the West that he saw and experienced, a West that would soon enough be transformed by the social, political, commercial, and transportation forces he witnessed. As Clifford has averred, we should "take travel knowledges seriously" for what they tell us about travel and culture, a particular time and place.[16] That is what *The Oregon Trail* does.

Mark Twain and the
Dialogics of *Roughing It*

IN 1861 SAMUEL CLEMENS unceremoniously left a Confederate militia group to go with his brother, Orion, to the newly created Nevada Territory. Orion had been named secretary of the territory by President Lincoln, who hoped to secure Nevada as a state that would support his agenda, and Sam was to be his secretary, the secretary to the secretary. With the discovery of the Comstock Lode in 1859, investors and miners had rushed to the area, making Virginia City the "second great city of the West" and Nevada a new state by 1864, bolstering the value of the Union's paper money and helping to fund national projects with the great silver lodes. As Rodman Paul points out, the "silver mania" began in 1859 and continued through 1864, after which it began its decline. But during its heyday the population of Virginia City soared from four thousand in 1862 to twenty-five thousand in 1874. The town boasted the only elevator west of Chicago, 110 saloons, several opium dens, and twenty theaters and music halls, signs of the exuberance of the times. The period when the Clemens brothers lived in Nevada, then, was "its most exciting years" of rapid growth and speculation. In a letter to his mother in 1861, Sam wrote of Nevada and the mining West: "The country is fabulously rich in gold, silver, copper, iron, quicksilver, marble, granite, chalk, [and] plaster of Paris." The list describes the wealth of the territory with the kind of exaggeration that Sam, as Mark Twain, would deploy in his travel narrative *Roughing It*.[1]

At the time he journeyed to Nevada, he did not propose to write a book of his travels. As Jerome Loving sketches it, after the success of *Innocents Abroad* (1869) and the literary if not financial success of "The Celebrated Jumping Frog of Calaveras County" (1865), Twain pulled together sketches he had written of his 1866 voyage to Hawaii for the *Sacramento Union* with pieces he had written for newspapers like the *Territorial Enterprise*—and the California papers *Morn-*

ing Call, Californian, Golden Era—to construct *Roughing It*. Having found little
to do as secretary to his brother while in Nevada, Twain had tried his hand at
a number of enterprises, including newspaper reporting. As James Cox claims,
it was during his stint with the *Enterprise* that he discovered his pseudonym.
While in the West, Twain also gained a reputation as a humorist, giving lectures
about his trip to Hawaii and injecting humor into his reporting by spicing them
with expletives like "Humbug" and anecdotes about the locals. Following the
success of *Innocents Abroad*, "the book in which Mark Twain defined himself as
a humorous traveler" and that sold over one hundred thousand copies in three
years, his publisher Elisha Bliss urged him to work up an account of his western
travels. So, with the use of scrapbooks and "help from Orion's notebook about
their journey across the plains in 1861," Twain wrote what would become his
"first major effort as a professional writer, planned as such at the very outset."
Loving remarks, "The market was already flooded with narratives of recent travel
in the West, so that Twain had to carve out his particular approach." For this
he invented "the personality of the storyteller," a voice he had practiced in his
tale of the jumping frog and during his apprenticeship in humor as a reporter in
Nevada and California.[2]

Published in 1872, *Roughing It* recounts travels and adventures almost a
decade old. Historical changes like the joining of the Union and Central Pacific Railways at Promontory Peak in 1869 and the end of the war that split the
nation mark the gap in time between his escapades out west and the account
of them. The lacuna between event and narrative is also signaled by the role of
a temperamental memory and Twain's imaginative re-creation of past events.
Gary Scharnhorst grumbles about "the fictionalization of his experiences" and
the ways *Roughing It* "fudges or obscures" his western adventure,[3] yet it is the
very fudging or blurring of boundaries that creates the interstitial, in-between
space, the dialogic mix of genres and perspectives that opens up the narrative
to do more than report about travel. The temporal gap between the adventure
and the construction of the narrative, between the traveling self and the writer,
opens a cognitive, geographic, and historical space from which Twain casts
an ironic gaze backward on the myths and expectations of the West that had
originally drawn him as a young man to Nevada. More than a mash-up of the
scrapbooks and newspaper articles he relied on and sometimes pasted into
the narrative, *Roughing It* is a dialogic blend of travel writing and humor. As it
maps out the physical journeys of its narrator, it creates a rhetorical space from
which to critique the myths of the West and the materialism, speculation, and
politics on which the West and the nation are based. A sophisticated geographic

imaginary, the narrative simultaneously records the naïve traveler's exploits and humorously undercuts them.

In the tradition of American travel writers, Twain charts his journey by paying attention to the methods of travel, the accommodations along the way, and the route he traveled, providing readers with a glimpse at western travel in 1861. He mentions the steamboat trip on the Missouri River to St. Joseph, where he and Orion purchased their tickets at "a hundred and fifty dollars apiece" on the overland coach to Carson City, Nevada.[4] He relates that travelers were allowed only "twenty-five pounds each" and catalogs what they decided to carry with them: "six pounds of Unabridged Dictionary," some changes of clothes, weapons, blankets, pipes and tobacco, canteens for water, and silver coins (*Roughing* 5–7). Like Francis Parkman, the narrator dresses the part, putting on "a rough, heavy suit of clothing, woolen army shirt and 'stogy' boots" (4), which made him feel "rowdyish and 'bully'" (147). He also details the coach that carried them west. Noting that they "changed horses every ten miles" (7), he begins to map out the journey that would take them from St. Joseph to Fort Kearny in fifty-six hours, at ten to twelve miles a day (26). He provides an account of the way stations, where station-keepers sliced up "last week's bread" and "a piece of bacon for each man . . . condemned army bacon" (24). Giving a sense of the motion and adventure of riding in the stage coach, Twain writes that after the mail was readjusted to form a kind of bed for the passengers, the "stage whirled along at a spanking gait . . . the cradle swayed and swung luxuriously" and "the pattering of the horses' hoofs, the cracking of the driver's whip, and his 'Hi-yi! g'lang' were music [to the dozing men]" (11). As the weather heated up, Twain and his companions would strip down to the essentials and climb "a-top of the flying coach" where, as Twain exuberates, they "dangled our legs over the side." "It thrills me through and through," he writes, "to think of the . . . wild sense of freedom that used to make the blood dance in my veins on those fine overland mornings!" (29). His sense of freedom and speed is reinforced by a Pony Express rider, a "swift phantom of the desert," who, with "a whiz and a hail," was gone before Twain and the other passengers could see him (51).

Sketching an animated picture of travel on the overland stage, Twain records a passing moment in transportation history as he simultaneously points to the historical gap, the space, from which he is writing. Western stagecoach travel had been in operation since the summer of 1850, and the overland California mail line had cut the time from St. Louis to San Francisco to twenty-five days, but the coaches had been supplanted by the railroad by the time Twain sat down to write about his adventure. He acknowledges this gap in time when he notes, "Stage-coaching on the Overland is no more, and stage drivers are a race defunct" (*Roughing* 135). Likewise, the short-lived Pony Express sped out of existence when the transcontinental telegraph was completed on October 24, 1861. Although he details the types of riders, what they carried and wore, the rapid exchange of horses, the distance covered each day, and the weight and cost of the mail they carried, when he writes the narrative he knows that the Pony Express has vanished.

This gap in time opens a rhetorical space in which Twain employs humor to create and satirize an image of himself as a gullible, greenhorn traveler, disrupting the trope of heroic testing that adventurers like Parkman exemplified. Marked by humor, this rhetorical space where the traveling "I" and the writing "I" meet employs exaggeration, irony, parody, and "linguistic vertigo" brought on by dizzying shifts in tone and style. As he begins the narrative, Twain confesses that he "was young and ignorant" when he dreamed of the adventures he and Orion would have in the Far West. Using humorous methods and what Lee Clark Mitchell calls a "glut of conjunctions" to connect the plausible with the implausible, Twain sunders realistic expectations of western travel writing.[5] To poke fun at the young man's expectations, he writes a long sentence listing the sights he will see and the adventures he will have. This sentence uses the word "and" eleven times, lumping expected sights of buffalo, Indians, prairie dogs, and antelope together with "all kinds of adventures," that include the less plausible ones of getting "hanged or scalped." The repeated use of "and" heightens the excitement by breathlessly listing all sorts of things, while it simultaneously flattens the mood by joining disparate activities. The next two sentences begin with "And," adding to the list of anticipated activities: seeing "the gold mines and the silver mines" and picking up "two or three pailfuls of shining slugs, and nuggets of gold and silver on the hillside." These unrealistic expectations shape the image of the naïve traveler who thinks he could easily gather gold and silver as if they were ordinary rocks and "by and by . . . become very rich" (*Roughing* 1–2). By deploying humor, this passage pries open the informative narrative of travel by exposing the unrealistic expectations of the gullible traveler about the riches the West had to offer.

Another way that Twain builds the humor that will undermine serious realism occurs when he stitches opposing, disjointed associations together, such as the possibility of meeting Pawnee Indians without the "swallow-tail coats and white kid gloves" usually associated with formal receptions (*Roughing* 4).

When he lists the gear he carried, he undermines the trite expression "armed to the teeth" when he names the "pitiful little Smith & Wesson seven-shooter" he carried (5). Later, seduced by the romance of adventure, "sitting face to face with it!" across the table from Slade, the "Rocky Mountain desperado," he takes two chapters to describe the man, inserting quotes from Thomas J. Dimsdale's 1866 book *The Vigilantes of Montana,* only to picture Slade as a gentleman concerned with the comfort of the travelers at the stage-station. By emphasizing his own fear at the prospect of meeting Slade ("Never youth stared and shivered as I did") and his relief in escaping "being No. 27" of Slade's victims, he undermines the risk by showing the desperado filling the traveler's coffee cup instead of shooting up the station (60–68).

Ironically juxtaposing fear and manners, Twain pokes fun at himself and his expectations of Wild West adventures in what M. M. Bakhtin calls a "zone of *dialogical contact*" where the hero and the author meet in "potential conversation" that promotes a more "*heteroglot*" version of reality, the informative and the comedic. Twain creates this dialogical contact zone, this humorous, ironic, parodic conversation between Twain the author and Clemens the gullible adventurer, between the two "I's," not simply to poke fun at himself or even to parody the expectations of travel writing. Rather, he creates this rhetorical space to critique the myths of the West and American exceptionalism. Parody (or humor), as Bakhtin discusses, "introduces the permanent corrective of laughter" to language and reality.[6] Similarly, Twain uses humor to introduce a corrective to the lure of the West in episodes that explode the stance of the hero, expose the destruction of the environment, and excoriate the materialism and racism that fueled the mining West.

As the title of Twain's narrative suggests, the young adventurer tried his hand at "roughing it," camping and getting out in nature. Bored and restless as the secretary's secretary, he and his buddies decided to try their hand at tree ranching at Lake Tahoe. The lumber industry at Tahoe was in full swing at the time the men hit on this scheme to get rich. According to the *History of Tahoe National Forest,* "Almost from the time of its discovery the [Comstock] Lode was dependent on the Truckee Basin for mine timbers and also for fuel since no other fuel supply was available. Fuel wood powered the seventy-six ore mills in the area by 1861. Equally important was the need for mining timbers. After 1860, deep mines began to use the square set timbering system, which made a series of cubes from square cut timbers to support mining shafts. The result was

a great increase in the demand for timbers; the increasing population also required lumber for buildings."[7] This demand for timber may have fueled Twain's
scheme as apparently it prompted others to enter the lumber trade during the
heyday of Nevada mining.

Offered as a typical male adventure of tramping, camping, and dreaming in
the West, this episode is infused with humor—exaggeration, tall tale, ironic pos-
turing, and a terrifying twist of dark humor at the end—undercutting not only
the ambitions of the young men but also creating a rhetorical space in which to
critique uses of the western environment. As in the opening chapters of *Roughing
It*, Twain details his gear and the journey, mixing realism with exaggeration as
he provides figures for the miles they traveled and the heights they ascended.
Although the trip was only eleven miles, they also had to climb in altitude, and
the narrator exaggerates outlandishly in claiming that they "toiled laboriously
up a mountain about a thousand miles high" and up another one "three or four
thousand miles high." He quips, deadpan, "We were on foot. The reader will find
it advantageous to go horseback" (*Roughing* 147). Here he pokes fun at himself as
a traveler who was not well prepared for travel in the western mountains. Similarly, he pokes fun at himself as an indolent worker, not willing to do the hard
work of camp life or lumbering. Although he ties the expectation of becoming
wealthy with this venture, the narrator does little to make a go of it, preferring
instead to superintend the others. Counter to the heroic pose of the adventurer,
he positions himself as lazy and idle. Likewise, when the men decide they need
to build a house, they soon settle on building a "brush" house after discovering
that it took too much work to chop and trim logs for a log house. Twain builds
this section by progressively taking readers from the plausible to the absurd,
from the log house to one built of saplings to the laughable brush house. And
even though they fished in the lake every day, they "did not average above one
fish a week" (154), hardly the heroic accomplishment of an outdoorsman. In
these ways he uses humor to defuse the image of the heroic woodsman. More
subtle and complicated is the way he disrupts Romantic attitudes toward the
natural world as he both rehearses the rhetoric of the sublime and undercuts it
with dark humor.

Calling up the rhetoric of the sublime, he echoes the Romantic poets when
he drifts about the lake in the boat, letting the current take him while he day-
dreams. Caught between the sky and the water, he admires the transparency
and "Sabbath stillness" of the lake. Like the youth in William Wordsworth's
poem "The Prelude," Twain seems suspended between states of being, between
the water and the air, between reality and dream, drifting with the current on

his "balloon-voyages" and finding a kind of spirituality in the natural scene (*Roughing* 153). In the Tahoe scenes, he anticipates moments in *Adventures of Huckleberry Finn* when Huck and Jim drift on the raft and enjoy the stillness of the Mississippi River and the spiritual feelings it engenders: "It was kind of solemn, drifting down the big still river, laying on our backs looking up at the stars." At Lake Tahoe, Twain describes the "glory of the sun" (152) and the stars that "spangle the great mirror [of the lake] with jewels," prompting the men to "smoke meditatively in the solemn hush" (148). His description of the lake, with its dazzling and brilliant transparency and "great depths," mirrors the ways Henry David Thoreau describes Walden Pond: "The water is so transparent that the bottom can be easily discerned at the depth of twenty-five or thirty feet" (*Walden* 177).[8] Like Thoreau the surveyor, Twain measures his lake's depth, "one-thousand five hundred and twenty-five feet" at its center (*Roughing* 154). The transparency and depth of the pond and the lake suggest universal truths, deep ideas that might be seen just as one can see the fish swimming at deceptive depths. Like many travelers to the West, Twain is struck by the natural environment and the feelings of religious awe it seems to inspire. While Tahoe's water is too cold for much bathing, the purifying ritual Thoreau enjoyed, the mountain lake country nonetheless has rejuvenating qualities, as evidenced by the man who went to Tahoe to die. As Twain put it, soon this man was "chasing game over three thousand feet high for recreation" (149), a humorous exaggeration of the healing qualities of the air that disrupts the solemn mood he has just created.

The semireligious idyll in nature is further disrupted when the inattentive Twain leaves the campfire to get a frying pan to cook his ordinary camper's dinner of bacon, bread, and coffee. The fire leaves it boundaries and goes "galloping" away, "roaring and popping and crackling," setting the area on fire and turning the lake into a "reflected hell!" The lake, which had encouraged him to see to the bottom of things, to find a spiritual meaning in its depths and its reflections of the night sky, is now turned to a mirror of the terrific fire: "Every feature of the spectacle was repeated in the glowing mirror of the lake! Both pictures were sublime, both were beautiful." This episode, the last horrific joke of the venture, satirizes the misadventures of this expedition to Tahoe. Caused by his carelessness in tending the campfire, the wildfire destroys not only the adventure but also forests "as far as the eye could reach" (154–57). The fire disrupts the semireligious sublimity of the lake with a terrifying picture of destruction, demonstrating in exaggerated fashion the unruly twins in the lexicon of the sublime, reverence and awe. In the interstices of this joke, Twain takes on the careless use of the environment. Not only has the venture to get wealthy by tree ranching been sabotaged by their indolence, the forest itself has been destroyed, just as it will be by the timber industry they hope to join. He pokes fun at himself and the misadventure of harvesting trees as he punctuates their scheme with one last calamity, the storm that soaks them. Implicit in the dark humor of this scene is a critique of a get-rich version of the West that leaves it spoiled because of a disregard for the environment, the fire a metaphor for the industry that devastated the forest, the scars still visible.[9] As he would do in *Huck Finn* with scenes of Sabbath stillness on the river following episodes that expose the hypocrisy and greed of a slaveholding society, so he ties the objectification of nature and environmental destruction to the idyll of camping at the mountain lake.

In the nineteenth century, the geographic imagination of the West represented a space in which one could test oneself, as Parkman did, a place of individualism and masculinity. Its vastness and resources also supported an idea of possibility, of fresh starts and new beginnings. And its natural landscapes inspired travelers to gaze at its wonders. But, as Jeffrey Melton points out, the expectation "to strike it rich" drove much of the imagination about the West: "Paramount to the western myth of possibilities is the desire, or even the expectation, to strike it rich." Caught by this fever, Twain tried his hand at timber farming and then at mining. He arrived in Nevada at the beginning of the really flush times. The output in bullion "increased by more than doubling itself each year in 1861, 1862, and 1863," and in 1864 the output was $16 million. Men like George Hearst were well on the way to making their fortunes, and it is no wonder that young Twain would imagine the possibility of becoming wealthy. Thus, it is not very surprising when he announces rather nonchalantly, "By and by I was smitten with the silver fever" (*Roughing* 174). He goes on to speculate on the fortunes to be made, citing the mines whose values have skyrocketed since he has been there, the "Gould and Curry" going from "three or four hundred dollars a foot" to eight hundred and the previously undervalued "Ophir" mine (the one in which Hearst was a partner) going at "nearly *four thousand dollars a foot*!" (174). Fed by the excitement around him and the reports in the *Daily Territorial Enterprise* enthusiastically announcing the "immense—incalculable" wealth to be had, Twain sets off for Humboldt County, the site of the latest mine to strike it rich (176). The italics and exclamation points punctuate a corollary to the exaggerated claims of the reports and the extravagant fortunes that a few lucky men made. Although Lawrence Berkove claims that the *Enterprise* was "the most reliable source of information about the Comstock mines," the reports Twain inserts in his narrative tend toward a mix of fact and hyperbole, blending realism and fictive speculation.[10]

As a traveler, he details the going forth in what soon becomes a parody of adventurous travel. A group of four men, only one of them with any experience mining, they purchase a wagon, "two miserable old horses," and "eighteen hundred pounds of provisions and mining tools" and head out of Carson City. They soon realize that the old horses are not up to the task of pulling the loaded wagon, and so, one by one, the three companions climb out of the wagon and walk alongside it. Twain tries his hand as driver of the wagon, but the load is not sufficiently lightened, so he too walks. Still the horses cannot pull the load, so finally the men push the wagon from behind for the remainder of the two hundred miles, having resigned themselves to "fate." Not content with this hilarious picture of four men pushing a wagon led by two old, useless horses, Twain inserts a comment by some wags they meet along the way that they should put the horses *in* the wagon. He compounds the humor by relaying the malapropisms of Mr. Ballou, one of the party, who states that the provisions would suffer from the horses being "bituminous from long deprivation" (*Roughing* 179–80).

As scholars like Lee Clark Mitchell have noted, *Roughing It* is built on word-play. Mitchell claims, "The book's radical premise is that the West exists as a direction of thought in far more remarkable ways than it does as a geographical place or historical episode." One example of its "extravagant verbal impulse" comes in the person of Mr. Ballou and Twain's digression about him and his love of long words that diverts the geographic, chronological journey to an exploration of a landscape of language.[11] Twain continues to chronicle the misadventures of the crew, including their "long-legged hound pup" cuddling restlessly with the four shivering men trying to sleep out in the open. As Ballou puts it, the dog was "so meretricious in his movements and so organic in his emotions" that it was hard to sleep (*Roughing* 181). The scene of the four men—a sixty-year-old blacksmith, two young lawyers, and young Twain—with their old, feeble horses, attempting to rush to the mines by pushing the wagon, sleeping unprepared on the frozen ground, and drinking coffee made with alkaline water, compounds the ineptness of the would-be miners, making this a parody of adventure and the lure of mineral riches that drew other underprepared prospectors. This adventure is one ludicrous mishap after another, told in the style of classic southwestern humor, with wordplay, parody of manhood, and exaggeration building on exaggeration, with just enough realism to make some of it plausible.

To top off the venture, Twain relates his discovery of precious metals. He begins by confessing, in hindsight, that he was rather naïve when he began his search for silver: "I expected to see it glittering in the sun [and ready for the taking]." He takes the reader with him—"I crawled about the ground, seizing and examining bits of stone" (*Roughing* 184–85)—as if one could just gather silver by the "pailsful" (2). When he comes to a stream glittering with bits of rock, he scoops them up, thinking he has found a stream of gold. The reader watches as he finds a "bright fragment," which he assumes to be a nugget of gold. At this point the narrative shifts from the exterior adventure to the interior ecstasies of a narrator turned Poe-like in his madness and supposed cleverness in concealing his prize: "Smothered hilarity began to oppress me, presently. It was hard to resist the impulse to burst out with exultation and reveal everything" (185–86). Followed by a long conversation with his buddies about their findings for the day and through a "deferral of expectations," he builds suspense as he holds back revealing what he has found.[12] Satisfied that he has piqued their interest, the self-satisfied narrator tosses his "treasure" before them, only to have it pronounced mica, not the gold he had dreamed of. The long buildup to the reveal is made humorous by the letdown, the ironic twist at the end. The narrator's dream of wealth melted away, he is left with the lesson that "all that glitters is not gold" or that "nothing that glitters is gold." Even so, the narrator confesses, "I still go on underrating men of gold and glorifying men of mica" (188), extending the lesson from metal to men.

Despite using humor, parody, and self-deprecating irony, Twain has nonetheless given readers a sense of the times, the "flush times" (*Roughing* 322) of silver mining in Nevada, when "Virginia had grown to be the 'livest' town [in America]," when the silver nabobs converted the wilderness into a civilization, with all of the benefits and costs associated with progress. One of these costs is the violence that he reports, the twenty-six murder victims in the Virginia City cemetery and the "desperadoism" that "stalked the streets" (318, 322). Another is the preponderance of vice: "Vice flourished luxuriantly during the hey-day of our 'flush times.' The saloons were overburdened with custom; so were the police courts, the gambling dens, the brothels and the jails" (339). In a population made up mostly of men and supported by an ethos of speculation, of boom-and-bust spending, in a town that counted saloons and gambling dens, it is little wonder that vice would thrive. The spendthrift attitude of the miners toward their personal activities made its mark as well on mining activities and their effect on the environment. As Rodman Paul notes, "A willingness to spend lavishly, and to try and then discard expensive equipment, characterized Comstock operation. Always the emphasis was on quick results and larger gross yields."[13] Although Virginia City was still at the height of activity when Twain lived there and he did not witness the aftermath of environmental damage caused by mining, he did see the remains of the California mines. When Twain visits Sacramento Valley, home of the earlier gold rush, he finds it spoiled, ruined, deserted by the mania that had hit it twenty years earlier. Twain writes of the California scene, with "its grassy slopes and levels torn and guttered and disfigured by the avaricious spoilers," its towns deserted, scenes of "lifeless, homeless solitude," the people who populated the region "victims devoted upon the altar of the golden calf—the noblest holocaust that ever wafted its sacrificial incense heavenward" (391–92). After the humor of trying his hand at mining and milling, after the misadventures of the naïve narrator, Twain begins to close the Far West section of *Roughing It* with reflections of the cost of chasing the glitter of gold or mica—the cost on human lives and the landscape. The humor operates in the narrative as a dialogic place from which corrective views emerge. What may have seemed like the inept adventures of an innocent abroad in the West, is also a very serious critique of materialism and greed, of the gilded age, the age of mica, that drove a nation crazy for the sparkle of gold and silver.

Of the groups of people lured to the mining regions of the Far West, among the Irish and Cornwall men and the Englishmen and Americans who gathered in Virginia City, were the Chinese. Paul notes that the California 1860 census counted "34,933 Chinese among the state's 380,000 inhabitants, and of the Chinese three fourths were residents in counties where mining was the principal occupation." These immigrants worked as placer miners, cooks, laundrymen, and servants. With the opening of the Comstock Lode, Chinese workers moved to the Virginia City area and established the first Chinatown in Nevada. By the 1870s, Virginia City had one of the largest concentrations of Chinese in the West. Part of the Far West scene from the 1850s onward, the Chinese presence demonstrates the West as a meeting ground where "minorities and majorities occupied a common ground."[14] Along with the Indians that Twain notices, the "Goshoot" tribe, and the Mormons he visits, the Chinese occupy an important ethnographic space in the West and a dialogic rhetorical space in the narrative. His discussion of the Native Americans swings between description of them as "the wretchedest type of mankind" and a rumination of James Fenimore Cooper's "Noble Red Men" (*Roughing* 127–29). His discussion of the Mormons moves between a tourist's gaze (as he stares "at every creature [they take] to be Mormon," hoping for a look at the "western 'peculiar institution'" of polygamy, a parody of Mormon marriage practices) and a more scholarly explanation of

Mormonism (86–87). As with his sections on Native Americans and the Mormons of Utah, Twain constructs a dialogic space to describe the Chinese that moves between humor, tourism, reporting, and outrage.

When he and his partners were marching up and down the mountains in search of Lake Tahoe, he writes, "We sat down tired and perspiring, and hired a couple of Chinamen to curse those people who had beguiled us" (*Roughing* 148), playing on attitudes about Chinese superstitions. Later he relates a story of Colonel Jim and Colonel Jack, who have struck it rich and gone to New York to see the sights and ride about in grand style. They board an omnibus, delighted by its style but ignorant of the fee system that allows anyone with money to ride. A young lady and other passengers board the bus until finally "a Chinaman [crowds] his way in." The two colonels are taken with the democracy of the transit system, and Colonel Jack declares, "Jimmy, it's the sociablest place I ever saw. The Chinaman waltzed in as comfortable as anybody." He then ruminates that they would have Blacks riding the bus as well (*Roughing* 307). While this episode plays on the rustic ignorance of the two colonels in the big city, it also suggests that racial others are targets of humor even as they participate in the changing demographics of the nation, in making it "sociable." In these two quick episodes, Twain uses the Chinese as part of the joke, the humor, of the narrative. But as he has done with other rhetorical spaces, he follows the jokes with clear critiques of American practices of racism and injustice.

In addition to these quick references, he devotes an entire chapter to the Chinese that is a mix of reporting, tourism (focusing on an exotic other), racially infused humor, and anger at the injustice served the Chinese in California and Nevada. Estimating that there were about a thousand Chinese in Virginia City, he provides a glimpse at the "Chinese quarter" and the lifestyles of the Chinese, their occupations, thriftiness, work ethic, and views on death. Inserting an article he wrote for the *Enterprise*, he continues to describe the lives of the Chinese, paying particular attention to opium smoking, their stores, and their lottery system. He ends the report in tourist fashion by visiting a Chinese restaurant, eating with chopsticks and "dicker[ing] for a pagan god or two" (*Roughing* 374). As he does so, he lapses into racist humor, mimicking the broken English of Tom and reiterating racist stereotypes about them—that they "make good house servants" and are "quick to learn." These attempts at humor nonetheless create a rhetorical space from which Twain offers some of the most scathing remarks of the narrative. He attacks a legal system in which the Chinese have no rights, where "no Chinaman can testify against a white man," and where boys stone "an inoffensive Chinaman to death" before a crowd of people who did nothing to stop the crime (369). Making the point that despite the fact that "all Chinamen can read, write and cipher" (370) but are unable to vote, he sounds as he will in *Huckleberry Finn* when Pap drunkenly rants about the mulatto professor who "could *vote* when he was at home" even though Pap is too illiterate and lazy to exercise his own voting rights.[15] At the end of the chapter, while Twain acknowledges that no "*gentleman or lady*" would mistreat the Chinese, he calls those who do so "scum" and the policemen and politicians who serve them the "dust-licking pimps and slaves of the scum" (375). While he may employ racist humor and reiterate stereotypes about the Chinese, the energy of the chapter comes from his pointed and angry criticism of institutionalized racism. Speaking in his own voice and not that of the adolescent Huck, Twain is blunt and forceful in criticizing the discrimination against the Chinese that has all the marks of the racism African Americans faced in both the ante- and postbellum periods.

The episodes I have looked at about travel, get-rich schemes, and racial others demonstrate the ways that Twain portrays travel and life in the Far West. Readers get a sense of stagecoach travel, of the natural world of Lake Tahoe, of tree ranching and mining, and of the varied peoples who inhabited Nevada in the early 1860s. Indeed, Rodman Paul calls *Roughing It* "the most readable book about Washoe and the mining West." Yet, as Mitchell claims, "reality is always up for grabs in the western world of *Roughing It*." More than obscuring reality, *Roughing It*, I argue, disrupts realism with humor. Larzer Ziff has said, "Twain is . . . able to fulfill the travel narrative's obligation to provide description and information while also carrying on a comic critique of the travel form." In my view, Twain uses humor not simply to comically parody the travel form or the heroic traveler but also more seriously to critique a version of the West and the nation that celebrated materialism, masculinity, and progress despite their costs. Twain's humor disrupts "the mythic framework that constructed and maintained the West as an American Imaginary, articulated core values of individualism, success, industriousness, masculinity, and a possessive attitude to the land, creating a powerful monomyth for identity." By straddling and blending the genres of travel and humor, he writes a fluid text that straddles ideologies and imagines a more complicated, dialogic geography of the West and the nation. Like Caroline Kirkland and Constance Fenimore Woolson, who used irony and humor to point to the foibles of westerners, but in more exaggerated and persistent ways, Twain blurs the lines between reality and humor, between fact and fiction, to create rhetorical spaces, third spaces where binaries are broken down and parody provides a corrective of the mono-myth of the West. Laughter, as Bakhtin has argued, is a corrective to the "one-sided seriousness of the lofty direct word" because it is *"too contradictory and heteroglot"* to be confined in a genre, ideology, or national myth.[16] Just so, Twain has written a text that is not confined, that breaks generic boundaries as it disrupts western and American ideals of masculine individualism and exceptionalism.

INTERLUDE

Before he wrote *Roughing It*, while he was still adventuring in the West, Twain wrote a short story, "The Celebrated Jumping Frog of Calaveras County," that in many ways anticipates the longer travel narrative. First published in the New York *Saturday Press* in 1865 as "Jim Smiley and His Jumping Frog," it introduced him to the American literary scene as a first-rate humorist. Based on a tale he heard at Angel Camp in the Tuolumne Hills, the story crafts the voice of the comic, ironic storyteller that would foreshadow the humorous persona of the traveler in *Roughing It*. In the story the narrator travels to Angel Camp and, at the request of a friend, meets up with the loquacious Simon Wheeler, who tells him about Jim Smiley's addiction to betting and his wonderful jumping frog. The story practices some of the elements of humor that Twain would deploy in *Roughing It*: deadpan deliveries, exaggeration, absurd lists of creatures and events that Smiley bets on, a "glut of conjunctions," the personification of animals like the stuffed frog that "hysted up his shoulders . . . like a Frenchman," and the vernacular that Wheeler uses in his digressive delivery of the story.[17] It ends with a shocking twist and change of mood as Smiley realizes he has been conned by the stranger who filled Daniel Webster with quail shot, and the narrator abruptly escapes Wheeler's endless tale just as he is about to launch on another exploit, "And—." Before he could continue with an anecdote about a "yaller one-eyed cow," the narrator mutters, "Oh, hang Smiley and his afflicted cow," and he walks away to end the story ("Frog" 287–88). In these ways Twain writes an entertaining story that layers narrators and narrative voices to tell a ridiculous tale of a trained jumping frog and a gullible Smiley who is defeated by a cheating stranger.

As he will do in *Roughing It*, Twain uses humor as a corrective not only to the "one-sided seriousness" of "straightforward genres" but also to "force" readers to a "different and contradictory reality" behind the humor. Loving tells us that in 1906 as Twain was looking over an edition of his anthology of humorists, many of whom were no longer part of the "public memory," that Twain "credited his own survival to the fact that humor was only a part of the 'sermon'—a mere fragrance coming from something eternally relevant to readers in every age." Loving identifies that eternal something as "pathos," the sympathy and compassion for others that the story elicits.[18] Certainly, there is pathos because of the way Smiley is compelled to bet "on *anything*" ("Frog" 284), even to the point of absurdity and sympathy for unfortunates he bets on, the asthmatic horse and the preacher's sick wife. Pathos is also elicited when the good-natured Smiley is scammed by the stranger. A political message may lie behind the names he gives the fighting dog and the jumping frog. His references to Andrew Jackson the Indian fighter and tenacious hero of the War of 1812 and to Daniel Webster, the eloquent orator who supported the Fugitive Slave Law, suggest a spoof on two important figures of the nineteenth century. But I think there is more to the "sermon," for Twain also references the conditions of the mining West that he experienced during his travels. Like the speculators and miners of *Roughing It*, Smiley is addicted to the next venture, to the dream of winning and of getting rich. As Wheeler says, "He was always ready and laying for a chance" and would bet on anything "and take any side you please" ("Frog" 283). Even though the terms of his bets are ridiculous and far-fetched, like putting his dog up against a dog that had not the hind legs for Andrew Jackson's signature move, we feel a degree of sympathy for him and the pup. When Smiley is bested at his own game by the stranger who fools not only the man but also the frog, we feel a bit sorry for them.

Even though the characters and events in the story are humorous exaggerations of reality, Smiley and the stranger stand in for characters of the mining camps and the attitudes they attract, the speculation on future fortunes and the addiction to gambling that were endemic to the mining West. In *Roughing It* Twain writes of the "wild cat" mines and the paper "stock" that were puffed by the newspapers and sold at exaggerated prices. "One plan of acquiring sudden wealth," he writes, "was to 'salt' a wild cat claim and sell-out while the excitement was up" (*Roughing* 289–90), duping naïve buyers and playing on the hysteria of the "flush times." To help make his point, Twain employs the literary technique of the hoax, which Berkove argues "was the principal legacy of his Nevada days." Twain has Smiley and the stranger engage in fooling each other as he writes a story that is itself a hoax, a story intended to deceive by claiming "something impossible or highly improbable," like a shot-filled frog, but which does no harm as it entertains readers. Not as innocent were the ways the Nevada papers duped readers with "strong adjectives" and "froth[ing] at the mouth" (287) into buying claims that were not worth the hype attached to them or the ways unscrupulous miners, like the stranger with his quail shot, loaded ore samples into mines to deceive would-be buyers. "Speculation, misrepresentation, and outright thievery," Paul avers, "were all too common" in the mining West. Indeed, the hoax was a part of Nevada business practices and a trademark of the Sagebrush School of authors. This is the "sermon" of the story, the danger of the con man, the hoax, the wildcat schemes to strike it rich that fooled the gullible and the greedy. Like *Roughing It*, "The Celebrated Jumping Frog of Calaveras County" deploys humor not simply for comedy's sake but also to make a point about moral responsibility, about honesty even, or especially, during the flush times of the mining West. As Scharnhorst points out, Twain "always debunked [the] imaginary West by portraying the region as a nest of snares for the unwary, ripe with fraud, and peopled by confidence men and hucksters." In both the travel narrative and the story that came after and before it, Twain creates rhetorical spaces in which to debunk not only an imaginary West and the storytellers like Wheeler who perpetuate it, but also the materialism, greed, and inhumanity that propelled a nation and a people into spending themselves and the natural world in a frenzied compulsion to "win" at all costs. In the interstices of the story, in the dialogic gaps between southwestern humor and the reality of the West, between the said and the implied, between the joke and the sermon, the "intellectual puzzle," Twain constructs a dialogic contact zone from which a corrective to the hoax of American exceptionalism emerges.[19]

Helen Hunt Jackson

Bits of Travel at Home *and What the West Sounds Like*

TRAVELING BY TRAIN ACROSS the western prairies, "unfenced . . . unmeasured, unmarked," Helen Hunt Jackson contemplates the "empty loneliness" of the villages that dot the terrain. "Now we are getting out into the great spaces," she muses. "This is what the word 'West' has sounded like."Just three years after the joining of the Central and Pacific Railroads in 1869 to form the first transcontinental railroad across the United States, Jackson journeyed from Chicago to Utah and California, to the bustling city of San Francisco and then to Yosemite Valley with her friend Sarah Woolsey. In her Pullman car, looking out of the window as the morning spread over the "great spaces" of the prairie, noting the grain, the droves of cattle grazing, the solitary trees ("[they] look like hermits in a wilderness"), and the lonely villages, Jackson thinks about what the word "West" sounds like, what it means.[1] This effort to hear the West, to get at what it looks like and what it means for her shapes the series of travel sketches of her ten-week sojourn in the West that she will send to the *New York Independent*, a Congregationalist newspaper that took stands against slavery and for women's suffrage and published some of the best literary writers of the period. Later she would collect the California essays with pieces on Colorado and New England in *Bits of Travel at Home* (1878). The success of her efforts might be measured by the reviews she received, such as the one in the *Hartford Courant* that asserted, "No writer has given so vividly, brilliantly, and yet without exaggeration, the characteristic features of the great west.'"[2]

As she sits in the fast-moving train from Chicago to Ogden, Utah, looking out the window, the West means the great, unmeasured, lonely spaces, the distant view over the prairies that so evoke the grandeur and timelessness of open spaces and the freedom to move and to think. But Jackson's West is also measured in the intimate, close-up views of the natural world, the built environment, and the people of the West. For Jackson the genteel tourist, the West means travel in the comfort of the Pullman car, complete with sleeping chambers and accommodating Black porters, but it also means walking tours through San Francisco's Chinatown and rigorous journeys on horseback through Yosemite Valley. Moving between the distant and the near, motion and repose, adventure and genteel tourism, Jackson adopts a vision and a writing style, a rhythm, that get at what the word "West" sounds like to her. As Yi-Fu Tuan notes, "Human lives are a dialectical movement between shelter and venture, attachment and freedom," and in many ways, Jackson's travels and narrative demonstrate and mimic this movement.[3]

Jackson's writing about the West is sometimes discussed as an example of regionalist writing because of its attention to local characters and environments and its regionalist ideology, whether that ideology adheres to the anti-imperialist, anti-hegemonic regionalism that Judith Fetterley and Marjorie Pryse describe in *Writing Out of Place: Regionalism, Women, and American Literary Culture* or the touristic appropriation of the local that Richard Brodhead affirms as representative of East Coast travelers. James Weaver argues that her text "constructs a nationalistic perspective that depends . . . upon regional identities and struggles to resist imperialist appropriation," while Christine Holbo argues for a "'modern' perspectivalism" that represents both elite and regionalist viewpoints. In many ways, the competing regionalist ideologies that Holbo and Weaver uncover in her travel writing correspond to the movement between the far and the near and the different lenses through which Jackson looks on her western subject. As she views the peoples of the West—the Mormons, the Chinese, the Native Americans—she both voyeuristically gazes at the exotic Other as if they were tourist attractions and situates them with herself in a community, often a community of women.[4]

Looking out the window of her train car, she describes an Indian woman as "the most abject, loathly living thing I ever saw," evincing not only racist stereotypes about Native Americans but also her own emotional and physical distance from the woman. But when she looks more closely, Jackson sees what she had at first missed, the baby on her back, its "soft baby face, brown as a brown nut." When smug travelers offer to buy her baby, for the first time, Jackson says, "I saw a human look in the India-rubber face." She sees "the face of a woman, of a mother" (*Bits* 9–10) and finds a kinship with her as a mother. Having lost her two children and first husband to death, she no doubt feels a bond of motherhood with this woman. Later, in Utah, looking at the faces of Mormon women for some indication of the moral depravity of polygamy, she finds instead that they are happy mothers "standing on doorsills with laughing babies in their arms . . . just as other women do—apparently" (21–22). Jackson's largely pejorative descriptions of the picturesque, foreign elements of the Chinese in San Francisco are tempered by a sense of their view of her, the sisterhood of women who stare at the outlandish costumes of the Other, whether Chinese or American (64). Even her attempts at local color through the use of dialect in her renditions of western characters like her guide John Murphy are tempered by her appreciation of his skills in woodcraft and trail finding. When she arranged for a guided tour up Indian Canyon, Murphy responds, "I'd like to hev ye see it first rate . . . but I want ye to understand before we set out, that I shan't cross if I think there's any resk" (158). In sketches like these, Jackson moves between regionalism as tourism that deploys an outsider's perspective and regionalism as resistance to hegemonic, patriarchal attitudes, regionalism as a way of finding commonality, if only briefly, with others. Later she would turn her understanding of what constitutes the regional, the characters, landscape, communities, and sociopolitical dynamics of the West into one of the most popular novels about mid-century California, *Ramona* (1884). Written to bring attention to the injustices suffered by Native Americans, the novel stitches a woman's regionalist perspective to a heartfelt romance and political critique as it follows its protagonists further and further into the recessed places of Southern California to escape the brutalities of the Americans.

While we can see the movement in her regionalist's gaze and rhetorical strategies as she journeys between the near and the far view, between stereotype and kinship, *Bits of Travel at Home* is primarily an example of travel writing, of travelogue. It is a narrative that recounts how she traveled and her accommodations, what she saw along the way, and her adventures on the road. At times she maps out her route, as when she locates "the Chinese Empire" at "Kearny, Dupont, Jackson, and Sacramento Streets, in the City of San Francisco" and takes readers with her down Montgomery Street as she peeks into the stores and establishments of the empire (*Bits* 62). Like other travel narratives and travel guidebooks, *Bits of Travel* gives readers a view of tourism that the rail systems opened, the accommodations available to travelers, particularly the sleeping arrangements on board the trains and the hotels that have sprung up to serve the new crop of wilderness tourists. She takes time to describe the interior of such establishments as Gentry's Hotel with its clean and neat rooms, the baths at Mr. Smith's Saloon, and the more rustic accommodations but glorious views at Hutchings's Hotel, one of the first hotels in Yosemite Valley and where John Muir had earlier worked prior to his tour of the Sierras. She describes the system of guided horseback tours of Yosemite Valley and the steamboats and rowboats that take tourists out on Lake Tahoe. Like the guidebooks she references such as *Bancroft's Tourist's Guidebook of San Francisco* (1871), Jackson provides useful information about the routes she takes, what she sees, what implicitly is worthwhile for other travelers to see, and what to expect of the trip. Like *Bancroft's*, she goes so far as to comment on ways that women ride horses into the valley, straddle or side-saddle, with a note about the new fashion of bloomers that some of the women have adopted. All of this would be useful information for the person planning a tour of the West as well as entertaining for the armchair tourist reading her accounts in the *Independent*.

But, more than a travel guide, *Bits of Travel at Home* is a narrative of Jackson's adventures on the road and her observations as she tries to get at what the West sounds like. Like other travel narratives, *Bits of Travel at Home* is organized spatially and chronologically as she takes readers along the journey with her, stopping from time to time from her adventures and descriptive sketches of the local to think about what she has seen and experienced. Like the classic travel writing Paul Fussell describes, she takes the reader on multiple journeys—across the landscape, "into the author's brain, and into [the reader's] own."[5] She also employs persistent motifs and rhetorical strategies that not only bring order to the narrative but also, more interestingly, mimic the West that she encounters. Woven into the tapestry of the narrative, concerns about speed, space, and time give us clues about the West that she hears and give her narrative its own particular "sound."

Gazing from the open-air observation car of the transcontinental train upon an overland migrant party halted by trouble on the road, Jackson muses, "But I envied them. They would see the cañon, know it. To us it would be only a swift and vanishing dream. Even while we are whirling through, it grows unreal." Contemplating the speed with which the train whirled—"flowers ... are flying past, seemingly almost under our wheels" (*Bits* 15), Jackson introduces one of the recurring motifs of the narrative—the speed of travel and how speed affects her views of people and landscapes. Here she experiences what Wolfgang Schivelbusch calls "mobility of vision," by which the train traveler "can only see things in motion" through the apparatus of the moving vehicle.[6] The "unreal," dreamlike speed at which she is traveling is offset by the repose from the observation car where she observes the scene, a scene that directs her eye not only to the close by, the flowers, but also out to the "broader spaces, where there are homesteads and green meadows" (15). Thus, she joins and juxtaposes speed and distance, motion and repose, composing as she does so a dialectics of movement and place. As her style of writing in this episode demonstrates, Jackson moves between the near and the far, deftly draws quick, impressionistic pictures, and uses words like "whirling," "flying," and "suddenly" to rhetorically suggest the experience of speed. Like the motion and speed of travel itself, her impressionistic style moves quickly through landscapes and then pauses so she can reflect on what she has seen. The pacing of other episodes imitates the pace of travel, its great speed and moments of pause and repose.

Known for her "considerable descriptive powers," Jackson, a well-published author by the time she went west, used her talent to draw pictures of the western landscapes and interiors.[7] Doing so, she used an impressionistic style that quickly gives readers a look at the scene as she moves by and through it. Climbing up and down the Sierras in a wagon driven by a Mr. Foss, who was in "the habit of driving six horses at full gallop" (*Bits* 44), she writes: "Gigantic rocks, and gnarled rock, and fallen trees covered with moss, and trickling streams, and foaming cascades, and waving bushes of white blossoms, and great spaces of pink and scarlet and yellow flowers beneath, all seemed to be flying up the hill as fast as we were flying down" (47). Using sparse descriptions for each item ("gigantic," "gnarled," "fallen"), she hurries readers through a description connected throughout by "and," a conjunction that ties together rocks, trees, streams, and flowers, all equally part of the scene. The speed with which we read this passage as it barely pauses at the conjunctions suggests her own hurried impressions as the stagecoach flies down the mountain road. "It was perilous; it was reckless" (47). What can one really see at such speeds? Yet she and we do see, quickly but clearly and amazingly fully.

Even when she is not whirling through the landscape, she infuses her rhetoric with fast-paced descriptions of what she sees. Take this description of the saddle trains at Gentry's Hotel: "Ten, twenty, thirty, horses, mustangs, mules, rusty black, dingy white, streaked red; ungroomed, unfed, untrained; harmless only because they are feeble from hunger . . . bridled with halters, likely enough, or with clumsy Mexican bits, big enough to curb a mastodon, or not bridled . . . gaunt-ribbed, swollen-jointed, knock-kneed, piteous-eyed beasts" (*Bits* 98). Using lists of numbers, colors, and bridle types, and hyphenated adjectival phrases, all joined by semicolons (six in this sentence), Jackson scurries the reader through this highly detailed picture of the state of the horses used to carry tourists into Yosemite, barely pausing to catch her breath with each semicolon before, a half page later, she comes to the end of her sentence.

In another instance, it seems she is too impatient even with the semicolon, substituting dashes in her hurry to describe the brilliant rainbows of the falls of Pohono: "The bright, broad zone of color, arching, and yet seeming to belt and confine the flowing lengths of fleecy white,—expanding and spanning them still when they seemed to seek to be free,—deepening, flashing with brighter color, like renewed jewels, and clasping closer when they seemed to sink and yield,—there was an infinite tenderness of triumphant passion, of mingled compliance and compulsion, surrender and conquest, in the whole expression of the movement of the two as they swung and swayed and shone and melted together in the radiant air" (*Bits* 136). As if impatient with staid, conventional sentences, Jackson strings together phrases, colors, movement, verbs, similes, contrasting pairs of words and ideas, attached to and separated from each other by dashes, to paint her picture of the rainbows. Not only does this passage suggest movement and speed, the speed with which she dashes off the lines and we read them, it also suggests the whole drama of nature and the West, perhaps of the self, of surrender and conquest, of the desire to be free yet to merge with another. As she writes at the end of this passage, "Almost one felt as if he knew more than he should, in watching them" (*Bits* 136). This suggests that she has gained some kind of transcendent knowledge from looking upon the multiple rainbows at play around the falls.

Passages like these fill the travel sketches, providing not only quick, descriptive impressions of the landscape and her experiences. In their speed, the compounding of images and words suggests something essential about the West and travel in it. Certainly, she comments on the recklessness of the western driver and the primitive quality of mountain roads over which they seem to go at breakneck speeds, but there is a persistent interest in motion, whether she describes careening around the mountain turns or speeding over the prairie landscape on the transcontinental railroad. Even when she is stationary, she writes with speed. Her biographer suggests that Jackson did not like to stay put, that she "was known for living intensely, moving and speaking quickly," and that she traveled often for her own "physical and mental health."[8] We can see that personal motive agitation, the desire to live intensely as she quickly and deftly details her experiences, the rainbows that speak sublimely to her of freedom, the surrealistic quality of speed as plants seem to fly past her.

In some ways she anticipates the fascination with speed that will drive Jean Baudrillard through the American desert in search of "*astral* America" and that will send Jack Kerouac racing back and forth across the continent, evincing a national agitation to move and to move quickly. As Baudrillard says, "Speed creates pure objects." [9] To some extent Jackson's sentences are pure objects, uncluttered by the extraneous, but they are also experiments in capturing speed on paper. Like Leland Stanford, one of the great financiers of the transcontinental railroad, and photographer Eadweard Muybridge, whom Stanford commissioned to prove that horses can fly, Jackson was interested in capturing motion, distance, and perspective in her writing. While in San Francisco she visited Muybridge's studio to view his photographs of the California landscape. Describing a series of photographs of "the California vintage," she announces in *Bits of Travel* that what distinguishes Muybridge's work is "stand-point," the stance from which the landscape is observed and captured in the photo, the ways he renders the skies, and a painterly composition that makes the scene come to life through perspective and groupings. Muybridge, she claims, is "an artist by nature" (Bits 85–86). She is interested in the ways he conveys the lived experience in a moment. This he was commissioned by Stanford to do. By using a series of stop-motion photographs of a racing horse, he captured that moment when all four legs are in the air and caught motion in what would be the beginning of motion pictures. This is what Jackson attempts in her writing as she imitates the speed of movement in the quick succession of impressionistic sketches that capture fleetingly the western experience.

I think Jackson is also suggesting something about the West, how it breaks conventions, is reckless in its drive toward the future, is so vast that one must not linger: "Is there any other country except America where such a road and such driving would be permitted?" (*Bits* 47–48). She may also be suggesting how the new technologies of travel, especially the railroad, have changed notions of speed and distance; compared to the walking speed of the emigrant wagon trains (1–2 miles per hour), the speed of the train (possibly up to 65 miles per hour) and the distance it could cover in a day must have been astonishing. In his study *Railroaded: The Transcontinentals and the Making of Modern America*, Richard White discusses the ways that definitions of motion, speed, and distance changed with the transcontinental railroads as "absolute space" was converted by time and cost into "relational space" and the "natural geography" was transformed into "measures of value" as the landscape was converted to commodity. Not only did the new transportation speed up the journey, it also realigned definitions of distance and speed to cohere to a corporate model valuing profit above all else. Jackson may also be suggesting something about the speed with which the West has been transformed. When she rode to California in 1872, it was on the cusp of the great changes that the explosion of transcontinental railroads had a hand in, bringing modernity to the region and the nation in just three quick decades.

The West that Parkman had experienced in 1847 would be vastly different at the end of the century when buffalo would be replaced by cattle, the Indians "conquered" and controlled, mountains blasted to make way for the rails, corn and wheat growing where once the prairie grasses waved, and cities growing up along the edges of the western prairies.[10] These changes and the speed with which they were taking place may have been at the back of Jackson's mind as she journeyed through the West. They may have been part of what it sounded like—motion, speed, activity, transformation, and the future they seemed to promise.

Entering the forests that lead to Yosemite, which Jackson calls Ah-Wah-Ne, she remarks on the size of the trees: "The great sugar-pines were from one hundred to two hundred and twenty feet high, and their lowest branches were sixty to eighty feet from the ground" (*Bits* 94). Here she deploys another of the motifs that shape *Bits of Travel*, the motif of space—its vastness, the size of spatial objects, and the distances between places. At issue are not only the "grandeur of these innumerable colonnades" and the great distances of the West but also the way one sees them, their effect on perspective. Continuing her description of the forest, she writes, "Sometimes, through a break in the tree-tops, will gleam snowy peaks of Sierras, hundreds of miles away." Surrounded by the immense trees, she occasionally gets a glimpse of the distant snowcapped mountains as if space has both expanded (with the giant trees) and shrunk. She explains the effect of seeing such great distances: "Perspective becomes transfiguration, miracle when it deals with such distance, such color, and such giant size." Experiencing a transformation of perspective as she journeys imaginatively from the present back to mythic time, she is transported to "measureless cloisters" where she would not be surprised "to have seen beings of Titanic structure" in "some supernatural worship" (94–95). Moving from objectivity to reverence, Jackson attempts to describe these unprecedented new sights, which prompt her to think about the way she sees, about perspective, and about her stance in such unfamiliar territory. Regarding nineteenth-century efforts to describe the sequoia, one of the great trees of California, Daegan Miller writes, "Gazing upon a sequoia was to see something unprecedented, something impossible, something for which previous experience could only leav[e] one stunningly ill equipped." The challenge for writers, photographers, and painters, Miller explains, was to "frame the view," and so they turned to statistics, comparison, and metaphor to put the giants in perspective.[11] Similarly, Jackson was stunned by what she saw of the great spaces and other features of the West and was challenged to frame the view for readers and for herself. These efforts to put space in perspective run through the narrative that both explains and mimics what she sees.

Earlier, looking out from the comfort of the Pullman car on the way to Ogden, she describes the prairies as unfenced, undivided, unmeasured, and unmarked—in other words, as boundless and open spaces of "empty loneliness" (*Bits* 5–6). The unobstructed views of great swaths of dry spaces prompt her to think of them as lacking the usual markers of size and definition. To describe this space, she turns to a series of words prefixed by "un" to emphasize that lack, the unending sameness of the prairie punctuated by repetition. Trying to account for the new phenomena of western space, she adopts rhetorical strategies that both attempt to put it in perspective and mimic the challenge to viewpoint that space presents. She measures, turns to myth, uses language that suggests the unbounded vastness of the landscape, and moves from distant views to the near and familiar. Looking out on the "unmarked" prairie, her eye catches the lines of the rail tracks until she can bring into focus a more familiar object, the "short, fat" man walking with two trombones (6). After the grandeur of the "measureless cloisters" sculpted by the immense trees (95), she turns to the mundane world of tourist hotels, Mr. Hogdin's wretched hotel with its appalling food. The perspective she gains from these strategies not only helps to frame the view, it also situates her in space, maps her location, and steadies her against the dizzying distances and heights of the West. As Gillian Rose has argued, "When feminists talk about the experience of space, very often they invoke a sense of difficulty. Being in space is not easy." That is why, Rose argues, women turn to metaphor and logic to locate themselves, as Jackson does.[12]

While she consistently takes up the problems of perspective that the great distances and "rarefied" air cause, peaks of the Wasatch Range "thirty miles distant" appearing "near at hand" (*Bits* 20), Yosemite Valley poses the clearest challenge to perspective because of its unprecedented immensity. On one occasion, Jackson waits alone along the trail to Pohono Falls while her guide John Murphy leads the rest of the party onward. Although she does not reveal why she elected not to continue with the group, the Indian tale of the evil spirit of Pohono she recites may have spooked her. Situated among the great granite colossi of Yosemite—Sentinel Rock, El Capitan, the Cathedral, the Spires, and the Three Brothers—she tries to describe them by giving their elevations: "Only between three and four thousand feet high." "[But] the figures had lost their meaning. All sense of estimated distance was swallowed up, obliterated by the feeling of what seemed to be immeasurable height." She explains that some people think "that the eye does not recognize differences of magnitude beyond a certain limit" (111), suggesting the failure of the usual methods of framing the view against the formations and the mythic time of Pohono. On another foray into the valley, to the Sentinel Dome, she contrasts the tiny flowers nearby with a glimpse of the Sierras: "Only by glimpses at first could we bear the grandeur of the sight. We were one thousand feet above the highest fall in Ah-wah-ne.... Mountains seemed piled on mountains." She could see all the way to "the great valley stretches of the San Joaquin and the Sacramento," about one hundred miles away, she writes. "Only one thing except the far Sierras was higher than we" (132). Her perspective from the high places allowed her to see the great distances and space of the West. During her last adventure in the wilderness with her guide, they found themselves on a steep trail. On their left "rose a granite wall"; arising on "the right hand—space! nothing more: radiant, sunny, crisp, clear air." Hemmed in on the one side by the mountain wall and on the other side of the steep trail by empty space, she looked across to the "grand domes and pinnacles of the southern wall" and down "into the depths of the Ah-wah-ne." Overwhelmed, she turned away "dizzy, shuddering." Impatient with her weakness, she returned her gaze "toward the measureless space again" (159–60). For Jackson these great, unimaginable, dizzying spaces defined the West and what it sounds like. Yet they challenged the eye and caused a kind of vertigo, an unsettling of the self that her description mirrors in the ways it breaks her sentences, strings together a chain of adjectives, uses the exclamation point and emotive language, "dizzy, shuddering."

Because these spaces unsettled her and challenged her perspective, in her account Jackson tries to bring them into a "rational framework" by measuring the seemingly immeasurable. While she occasionally mentions how many miles she has traveled or the distances between hotels, most often she measures altitude, the height of trees, and the dimensions of natural formations as a way of locating herself and rhetorically controlling the unbounded spaces. John Sears argues that measurements "function, paradoxically, both as a means of bringing extraordinary phenomena within a rational framework and of certifying that tourists are in the presence of something that transcends their familiar world." He writes that the very scale of Yosemite and the "emphasis on assessing the size of objects at Yosemite appears closely tied to the mapping and measuring activities" of western surveys. Similarly, Jackson uses measurements as a way of mapping her location, of finding herself in the immensity of Yosemite.[13] And so, like John Muir, though without quite the same scientific interest, she records elevation as a way of suggesting size and distance. She notes, for instance, that the South Dome rises "nearly six thousand feet high" (*Bits* 130) and that Yosemite Falls is "two thousand and seven hundred feet up in the air" (103). Viewing the distant San Joaquin, she notes, "We were one thousand feet above the highest fall in Ah-wah-ne" (132). In other examples, she writes that Gentry's Hotel sits at "seven thousand feet above the sea!" (100) and that Yosemite Falls was three thousand feet from her windowsill at Hutchings's Hotel (106). She records vertical distance: "Hundreds or, for aught we could feel, thousands of feet below us thundered the river" (119). By recording altitude and height, she not only suggests the scale and size of the natural world but also locates herself amid the profound and unsettling spaces around her, the "fathomless space" of the abyss (119).

Like other visitors to Northern California, Jackson notes the measurements of the great trees, recording not only their height, "from two to three hundred and twenty-five feet high," but also their girth, writing that it took "twenty-four steps to climb up a ladder set against the side of a fallen tree" and that a tree stump measured "over nine yards in diameter" (*Bits* 146). Clearly these big trees have been laid claim to by tourists, like Ralph Waldo Emerson before her, who have built platforms and nailed shingles with the names of the great on them, Bryant, Grant, and Samoset. To some extent Jackson participates in the imperialist impulse to control by naming and measuring, but she also leaves room for wonder at the trees that have stood for "centuries of royal solitude" (146). In another episode she describes the face of Tu-tock-ah-nu-la, a giant rock formation, by noting the size of the pine tree that makes up the phantom's "ear": "The weird effect of such phantom shapes as these, when seen three thousand feet up in the air and of such great size, cannot be imagined. . . . No doubt the tree was two hundred feet high, but it did not seem in the least out of proportion as an ear on the gigantic head" (137). Here she deploys multiple strategies—statistics, perspective, and wonder—to describe the boundless spaces, the great rock formations, and trees in Yosemite, rhetorically controlling the vastness of the West as she does so.

Along with measuring space and the great trees, she measures and accounts for time, creating as she does another controlling motif of the narrative. When she hears axes as she waits alone for Murphy and the rest of the travelers to return down the trail, she sees that a felled pine tree, "nearly two hundred feet high," has rings that mark its age at four hundred years. She says caustically to the woodsmen who have cut it down, "Four hundred years growing, and cut down in three hours" (*Bits* 113), juxtaposing the time it takes to create such giants with the speed with which they are destroyed. In this same episode she contemplates the legend of the first chieftain who lived in Ah-wah-ne and whose face is supposedly carved in the rock, taking us imaginatively back into legendary time. Then, as she finishes the story of the chief, Murphy reappears and asks her, "has not the time seemed long to you?" referring to the hours she spent alone on the trail (114). In this passage, Jackson connects biological time—the time it took for the giant trees to grow, legendary time, and personal time—the hours she waited and the time it took the woodsmen to chop down the tree. As the great formations suggested the vastness of geologic time to Muir, they suggest to Jackson the great expanses of time and the different ways to measure it. As she has done with her ruminations about space, she has taken us from the immeasurable—the time of legends and myth—to measurable personal, historical time as a way of accounting for the West.

Additionally, Jackson moves from the distant, the immeasurable, the vast, to the close at hand and the familiar as a strategy to manage the immensity of space and time. Thus, after contemplating the great size and age of the big trees, she turns to describe "a tiny striped squirrel" that had fallen from its nest high up in the trees (*Bits* 147). She carefully makes a soft bed of leaves for it, hoping its squirrel parents will rescue it or that it will quietly die. But when she returns from touring the Calaveras Grove, the little squirrel still "lay there, moaning," its short life a comparison to the centuries' old trees. Evoking a kind of pity and fellow feeling from Jackson, the suffering little creature, one of God's "feeble folk," represents the familiar domains of home and family against the wondrous immensity of the trees (147). In another instance, after viewing the great face of Tu-tock-ah-nu-la with its pine tree ear, Jackson takes readers with her to Mr. Smith's saloon, where she finds the accoutrements of tourism—bathtubs, a billiard room, and a reading room complete with California newspapers and stationery. Here she finds comfort in the well-kept tourist establishment that employs a "tall and portly black man" to wait on its guests (138–39). This kind of movement, from awesome space and time to the familiar world, resettles Jackson spatially and psychically as it brings her in from the abyss and also mimics the West's great and intimate spaces and the dialectical movement between "shelter and venture, attachment and freedom" that Tuan claims as part of the human experience.[14] As daunting as its vast spaces are, the West that Jackson discovers is also a location where the small creatures find a home and where civilization and tourism have carved a place of comfort and familiarity.

When she pauses and slows down from her usual quickly paced, impressionistic account of her travels to peer closely at the West, Jackson also takes time to comment on the social issues she witnesses, particularly the negative consequences of expansionism on Native Americans, the environment, women, and other marginalized people. Although the adventures the narrative relates occurred a decade before her seminal works on Native Americans, *A Century of Dishonor* and *Ramona*, and although she still repeats racist stereotypes about them, calling the Digger Indians "loathsome" (*Bits* 91), we can see an emerging appreciation of Native Americans in the narrative. As she leaves Oakland to finally journey to the great valley, she pauses to criticize Lafayette Bunnell, who named the valley Yosemite after he and the Mariposa Battalion had "killed off Indians in the great Merced River Valley" (87). Bunnell was supposedly the first white man to discover the valley and was one of the volunteers who in 1851 attacked the Ahwahneechee people, who had long before fled the pressures of imperialism. A report by one of the volunteers claimed that they "killed three hundred, and [had] taken one hundred and fifty squaws" in an act of genocide. The audacity to then give the valley an *"American"* name, "Yo-sem-i-ty," another form of erasure, angers Jackson to the point that she quotes a paragraph in which Bunnell tries to explain why he did not use the original Indian name, Ah-wah-ne, for the valley.[15] Sarcastically calling his explanation "naïve," Jackson declares that she will call it Ah-wah-ne out of respect for the Indians (87). Indeed, throughout the sections devoted to the valley, she consistently uses the Native names for the natural places, symbolically reclaiming for the Ahwahneechee the territory they have lost.

When she discusses the names of the two great falls of the Merced River, giving the Indian names, Pi-wy-ack and Yo-wi-he, and their meanings, she caustically comments on their renaming by whites: "Then came the white men, liars; they called the upper fall 'Nevada,' and the lower one 'Vernal': and the lies prevailed" (*Bits* 115). In these ways Jackson offers an oblique critique of the massacre that opened the valley to whites and their deliberate violence against the California Indians. She also recites some of the Indian legends that relate to the place, of the evil spirit of Pohono and of the love story of Te-tock-ah-nu-lah, the "first chieftain who ruled the Children of the Sun" (113), as ways, in a gesture reminiscent of Margaret Fuller, to preserve their stories and culture. As a writer, her focus is on names and legends, but beneath this writerly concern is a criticism of the massacre and the expansionist drive that claimed and renamed the Ah-wah-ne. Because she understands the colonizing power of naming and of erasing indigenous histories, she consistently reminds readers of the original names and legends of Ah-wah-ne. Later *A Century of Dishonor* (1881) would more explicitly and forcefully sketch "our nation's record of cruelties and perjuries" against the Indian tribes, and *Ramona* (1884) would attempt "to recall Americans to their original commitment to human equality and justice."[16] But here, in a moment of repose from her travels, she takes time to comment on the injustice and violence of expansionism.

The "greed of gold" (*Bits* 143) that drove the disaster at Ah-wah-ne left other evidence of its destructiveness. Portraying the abandoned mine fields as "grave-yards full of buried monsters," Jackson decries the effects of mining on the land: "The earth has been torn up with pick-axes, and gullied by forced streams; the rocks have been blasted and quarried and piled in confusion" (89). Further on, she takes time to describe hydraulic mining techniques, the perpetual gush of water to extract gold from the land by a "huge, black nozzle" onto the "cliff-like side" of the riverbank. What is left is "an acre or two of sand-quarry" (92). The perpetual roar of the hydraulics eerily accentuates the stillness and loneliness of the place as the mining superintendent's wife sadly remarks, "it's terrible still here, all but that water" (94). Noting the solitary cabin of the wife and the "deserted cabins" (141) of others who were lured by gold, she describes the people who remain as blighted and injured: "Pitiful faces meet you at each turn in these luckless little mining towns,—faces of women hardened and weary and lifeless; faces of little children sick and without joy; faces of men dull, inert, discouraged, and brutal" (144). She sees the Chinese miners who "looked like galvanized mummies" "bent double over the old worn-out gullies and hollows," sadly shaking their pans for gold (142). She even stops her usual descriptive writing to pen a defiant chorus that gives words to the sound of the water gushing over the pebbles in the sluices:

> Over and over and over
> And give up the gold
> The gold, the gold
> And over and over and over,
> Untold, untold, untold! (93)

The repetition of the words "over," "gold," and "untold" along with the repetition of the long "o" drive home the insistent, monotonous, maniacal drive to extract gold while they mimic the grind on the pebbles and the people.

Jackson's critique is not so much about progress or technology, for she has enjoyed the latest in transportation technology, the emerging tourist industry, and the opening of Yosemite Valley to visitors. Rather, it is about the destructiveness of greed. During the same outing in which she calls attention to the blight of mining, she celebrates the quick work that the new "steam-threshers" make on the lush wheat fields of San Joaquin Valley, "finishing in a single hour the work of many days" (*Bits* 89). She also gushes over the conversion of the land to wheat fields, fruit orchards of "pears, figs, apricots, plums, apples," and vineyards that have already produced wine (141) to suggest an idyll of fruitful cultivation and civilization. Her critique is about greed, a crass, violent materialism that ruins lives and the environment. As her biographer points out, Jackson's criticism was not against "expansion per se but what she saw as the wrong sorts" of expansion that did not "respect local environments or the preeminent rights of native residents." Taking a cue from Amy Kaplan's important essay "Manifest Domesticity," James Weaver points to ways that *Bits of Travel* both "concerns itself with the expansion of domesticity into previously 'wild' spaces" even as it "calls into question the value of the process of domestication" when Jackson calls attention to the "very real material costs exacted upon the land and upon marginalized peoples."[17] Like other travelers to the West, Jackson both promotes and participates in its domestication or cultivation and criticizes the damage that unprincipled expansion has caused. A tourist who enjoys some of the privileges of genteel travel, Pullman cars, comfortable hotels, and good food, Jackson is also a traveler whose perspective looks not only out onto the vast, natural spaces of the West but also on the human places and the effects humans have had on the environment and the indigenous people. These places also constitute what the word "West" sounds like.

As she moves from the distant to the near, from motion to repose in the narrative, as she moves between an appreciation of the wild and the benefits of progress, between adventure and comfort, she mimics the experience of travel and tourism to the West in the 1870s. Her narrative's movements indicate, as well, ideas of herself as an independent adventurer and a genteel woman tourist. At a time when travels to the Far West by unaccompanied women were considered of "dubious propriety" because of the "long train rides, difficult terrain, and nights in remote, ramshackle accommodations," she presents herself as a privileged traveler who enjoys the luxuries of the Pullman car. The movements of the narrative also suggest her competing regionalist stances as her ethnocentric, outsider's views of the West's peoples are countered by her sympathy for the women she sees and her critique of dangerous materialism. Yet, even as she critiques the negative effects of expansionism, her travelogue ironically invites touristic incursions into the wild areas of the West as she shows readers the way in. These shifts in focus mimic the complex region that she experiences, its multiple and challenging perspectives, its complex of competing and contradictory landscapes and histories. This is what the word "West" sounds like to her.

INTERLUDE

There is a moment in the novel *Ramona* when Helen Hunt Jackson seems to be responding to Lafayette Bunnell's act of renaming Ah-wah-ne. It comes when Alessandro, the Indian lover of Ramona, gives her a new name, an Indian name. As they flee the tyrannical Señora Moreno, the aunt who raised the mixed Scots-Indian girl, and the greedy, murderous Americans who have violently taken the Indian village of Temecula, Ramona reveals that she has just learned that she is Indian. Out of love for him, she declares that she will live with Alessandro as an Indian. When she asks him to call her Ramona instead of Señorita, as he has done out of deference to her position as a member of the wealthy Moreno family, he tells her that he already thinks of her by an Indian name, Majel, the name of the dove. He tells her, "It is by that name that I have oftenest thought of you since the night I watched all night for you, after you had kissed me, and two wood-doves were calling and answering each other in the dark; and I said to myself, that is what my love is like, the wood-dove."[18] She responds, "Majel is my name, then . . . but I would like it better Majella. Call me Majella." In this moment of naming, Alessandro enacts an anti-imperialist move that reclaims the Indian heritage. He rejects her Spanish name, Ramona, in a gesture against the Spanish and Mexicans who first began the erosion of the indigenous way of life beginning with the missions and continuing with the large ranchos that employed Indians like Alessandro to work the land that had once been theirs. By renaming Ramona, Alessandro also lays claim to Ramona, ironically asserting his patriarchal rights to her gendered space. Then, when Ramona replies that she likes Majella better than Majel, we see an anti-patriarchal move on her part, a compromise between the Indian name and the Spanish suffix "a" that connotes the female. Alessandro accepts the compromise, creating a gendered third-space identity between the Indian and the Spanish that symbolically represents the third space where they hope to live between the pressures of imperialist deterritorialization and the strength of their love. This third space also represents the space between protest and sentiment that Jackson creates in the novel, her last major work and the one in which she hoped to do for Indians "what Uncle Tom's Cabin did for the Negro."[19] Although the two books are not explicitly linked, we can see how her adventures in California prepared her to write *Ramona*, her most famous book, by prompting her to think about the significance of naming in the contest between Americans and American Indians.

John Muir and the Nature of Travel Writing

JOHN MUIR WAS ONE of America's great naturalists and nature writers. He is best known for his vivid descriptions of Yosemite Valley and the natural landscapes of the Far West that combine scientific study with personal, spiritual reveries prompted by his experiences in the wild. He is also known for his advocacy for preserving wild places as a stay against the advances of progress and technology and for maintaining wilderness areas not only for the wild creatures but also for harried tourists in need of recreation and re-creation. Using his many writings to teach readers "how to see," Muir took them with him as he explored the hidden and sometimes dangerous places of the Sierras. As William Frederick Badé wrote, "Thousands and thousands, hereafter, who go to the mountains, streams, and cañons of California will choose to see them through the eyes of John Muir, and they will see more deeply because they see with his eyes." A careful observer of nature, he also made important discoveries about the role of glaciers in forming Yosemite Valley, including the discovery of existing glaciers in the Sierra. Moreover, he was an advocate for the creation of national parks, using his articles for *Century* magazine to convince Congress to create Yosemite National Park in 1890. Then, with two Berkeley professors and a San Francisco lawyer, he created the Sierra Club in 1892. The club's purpose was "to explore, enjoy, and render accessible the mountain regions of the Pacific Coast," to publish information about them, and to work to preserve the "natural features of the Sierra Nevada Mountains." Because of his many efforts to preserve wilderness areas, he is one of our "secular saints" and, as essayist and poet Frank Stewart puts it, is known "not only as the father of the national parks, but also as a hero and a visionary."[1]

Rather than rehearse the facts of his life and his advocacy for natural things, important as they are, I am interested here in thinking about Muir as a traveler and a travel writer, and the confluence between travel writing and nature writing in *My First Summer in the Sierra*. As we have seen, travelers in the nineteenth century noticed and commented on the natural environment. In Bryant's lists of trees, Fuller's learned appreciation of the prairies and the possibility of living in harmony with nature, Woolson's criticism of the conversion of the Cuyahoga River into a stream of fire, and the western adventures recounted by Parkman, Twain, and Jackson we have seen how descriptions of nature and human relationships with the natural world have been important themes in travel writing. Perhaps today when we can escape facing nature as we travel, going from one airport to another, riding in air-conditioned automobiles or camping in recreational vehicles outfitted with modern amenities, we can divorce travel writing from nature writing. But in earlier days, when travel meant riding or walking close to nature, the two forms of writing were interconnected, one sculpting the other as they do in Muir's journal. Here careful observations of the natural environment coincide with rambles through the Sierras, the journal a map where Muir's geographic imaginaries come together—an imaginary of travel, an environmental imaginary, and a geo-spiritual imaginary.

Having arrived in California after tramping a thousand miles to the Gulf of Mexico, Muir managed to spend the summer of 1869 in the "loose employ" of a sheep man, Patrick Delaney, during which time he tramped through the Sierra Nevada of California, studying nature, making sketches, and writing in his journal. Encouraged by his professor at the University of Wisconsin to keep a notebook of his observations, Muir made careful and personal entries about what he observed and experienced. He did not publish this journal, *My First Summer in the Sierra*, until 1911, near the end of the fight to prevent damming Hetch Hetchy Valley. Water-thirsty San Franciscans had been looking at the Hetch Hetchy as a water source, beginning their lobbying of the federal government several years after the creation of Yosemite National Park. A drawn-out battle, it did not end until Woodrow Wilson's presidency in 1913, when the Raker Bill to dam the Hetch Hetchy and the Tuolumne River was passed, a year before Muir would die of pneumonia. During the prolonged debate, he was urged in 1899 by his editors, Walter Hines Page of the *Atlantic Monthly* and Robert Underwood Johnson of *Century*, to write an autobiography. Out of that request came *Story of My Boyhood and Youth* (1913) and *My First Summer*, the latter of which was initially serialized in the *Atlantic* and then published in book form by Houghton Mifflin. Lawrence Buell relates that Johnson arranged for Muir to visit Concord, Massachusetts, in 1893, where he visited the grave of Ralph Waldo Emerson, whom he had hosted in Yosemite in 1871, and Walden Pond, the site of Henry

David Thoreau's hermitage. Perhaps his pilgrimage to Concord also spurred his autobiographical efforts, giving the older Muir a chance to reflect on his youth. Perhaps they were intended to influence the Hetch Hetchy debate, to remind readers of the idealistic young man who spent his life examining and defending the wild. Michael P. Cohen claims that what Muir published is hardly a simple transcription of the forty-year-old journal but rather is organized thematically and carefully crafted. Like Thoreau's *Walden*, Cohen argues, *My First Summer* "telescopes the actual experiences of several summers" into one. Cohen spends some time pointing to the intersections between the young man and the older Muir in the text, arguing that their aims and perspectives conflicted, as the young Muir sought freedom in the wild while the older Muir knew more about the practical realities of life that interfere with and interrupt the spiritual quest.[2] Whatever the case, the motives for bringing the edited journal to press were no doubt complicated.

Like Thoreau's *Walden* and Cooper's *Rural Hours*, *My First Summer* recounts both tramps and observations of the natural world, making it an example of the ways American travel writing intersect with nature writing and spiritual reflection. With dates for each entry, the journal follows Muir on his daily saunters into the Sierra. Doing so, it follows three trajectories of travel: the march with the sheep to summer pastures and back to the home camp, his own rambles in nature, and the passage toward the sacred in an imaginative defiance of gravity and historical time. Engaged by Delaney to go with his shepherd and the flock as it moved to ever higher pastures and to "see that the shepherd did his duty," Muir was otherwise "perfectly free to follow [his] studies," to learn about the plants, animals, and rocks of the Sierra.[3] From the outset, Muir's travels followed complementary physical trajectories, determined by the sheep and spurred by his own curiosity, which intersect and rub against a more spiritual trajectory.

The narrative begins June 3, 1869, as the sheepherders leave the "home ranch" on the Tuolumne River. Like other travel writers, Muir begins with a description of the provisions they carried and the members of the group—Delaney, plus "Billy, the proud shepherd, a Chinaman and a Digger Indian." He notes the pace at which they traveled, "about a mile an hour," and the shape of their entourage, "an irregular triangle . . . with a crooked, ever-changing point made up of the strongest foragers, called the 'leaders,'" with the lambs and older sheep "dawdling in the rear" (*My First* 7–9). From the first camp, where readers get a brief view of the crew's routine, the herd is moved to the "nearest of the green pastures, about twenty or thirty miles" away and on to successive pastures as they eat their way through the grass and follow the summer's warmth up the mountains. Along the way, Muir comments on the mindlessness of the sheep, their trepidation crossing streams, the stampedes, the deprivation by bears who take what mutton on the hoof they desire, and the ways the nibbling sheep destroy the meadows in their path. He comments on the greed of most California sheep men and the occupation of the shepherd, whose life is to mindlessly follow the sheep, the "wool bundles" (76). And he also remarks on the ways the gold miners defaced the landscape, "riddling, stripping every gold gully and flat" (74), the incursion of tourists "winding single file through the solemn woods in gaudy attire" (131), and the presence of Indians, whom he describes as close to nature, instinctual, and dirty "half-happy savages" (277).

He writes of the move on July 8 "toward the topmost mountains" and the way the hungry sheep "rushed wildly ahead, crowding through gaps in the brush, jumping, tumbling like exulting, hurrahing flood-waters escaping through a broken dam" (*My First* 113–14), the verbs in this passage accentuating the movement of the sheep. Following the sheep, he charts their way along the Merced and Tuolumne divide to Tamarack Flat, then to Indian Cañon, Lake Tenaya, and Soda Springs, place names that suggest their spatial movement through the Sierra. They continued up the mountains following good pastures until September 6, when Delaney decided it was time to move the flock back down before the weather turned. In these ways the narrative tracks the movement of the sheep to pastures and then back to the ranch. Along the way, readers are acquainted not only with the peculiarities and perversities of the sheep but also of life at the various camps, how the men arranged sleeping in the open, and what they ate, the bacon and mutton—the "bread famine" (101) that Muir complains about. Readers also meet Muir's companions, including Carlo the dog, and learn about the tasks Muir had in minding the sheep and Billy the sheepherder. The narrative ends on September 22, 1869, with the return of the flock to their headquarters and an accounting of the sheep lost to bears, accidents, and camp dinners.

We do not read Muir to learn about sheepherding or camp life, however, for it is the other trajectory, the rambles he makes as he studies and gets to know the plant, animal, and mineral life of the Sierra, that most interests us. In tandem with the movement following the sheep, the narrative charts a trajectory of discovery that is plotted by the condition of the clouds and the weather, the height of the mountains, the elevation at which Muir stands, and the excursions he makes to investigate the wild. Thursday, June 12, begins, "A slight sprinkle of rain" (*My First* 48). Often the day's entry begins with a scientific notation about the clouds or the weather: June 22—"Unusually cloudy" (82); July 2—"Pearl cumuli over the higher mountains" (98); July 23—"Another midday cloudland" (194); July 28—"No cloud mountains, only curly cirrus wisps" (224); August 22—"Clouds none, cool west wind" (310–11); August 27—"Clouds only .05" (316); September 6—"Still another perfectly cloudless day" (329). When these comments are gathered, they provide a kind of meteorological map that indicates the location of the clouds relative to the mountains and the change in the weather as summer advances and retreats. Sometimes he pauses to describe a mountain thunderstorm, the "silvery zigzag lightning lances" and the "ringing strokes succeeded by deep low tones" (165–66), but most often he records the cloud formation as a way of noting the day. Unlike other travelers who remark on the condition of the weather, particularly the storms they are caught in, as part of their adventure, Muir's meteorological map tracks his journey chronologically, pairing the date with the condition of the clouds and the weather. As the journal and the journey come to an end, he notes the frost in the morning: August 29— "Clouds about .05, slight frost. Bland serene Indian summer weather." August 30— "A few clouds motionless ... Frost enough for crystal building" (318). Just as the return of the sheep to the home camp indicates a return from mountain pasturing, the frost of Indian summer provides another indication of the termination of the mountain sojourn.

Another way that Muir plots the trajectory of discovery is by constructing a vertical chart of elevation, a kind of literary geological map. While most journeyers create a horizontal map by counting the miles traveled across the terrain, Muir tracks elevation as a marker of movement and location. As he locates himself by means of the camps, the place names of rivers, valleys, and mountains, and the changing weather conditions, he also situates himself by a vertical record that includes the height of trees as indicators of location. As the sheep camp moves into the mountains, Muir notes, "We have now reached a height of six thousand feet." At the same time, he measures a manzanita tree, "the bole of which is four feet in diameter and only eighteen inches high from the ground" (*My First* 117). These careful measurements are the mark of a scientist, the objective record of the environment, but they also correlate the size of the trees with the elevation at which they grow. He writes that the higher they went, they more abundant the silver firs, which could be "seven feet in diameter and over two hundred feet in height" (120). On that same day they "climbed a thousand feet or more in a distance of about two miles, the forest growing more dense and the silvery *magnifica* fir forming a still greater portion of the whole" (122). The size and height of the trees not only help locate the trees on the verbal map Muir is constructing, they also mark Muir's location. Plotting his course, he writes for July 11, "We are now about seven thousand feet above the sea" (132); on July 16 he puts the elevation of the mountain meadows at "about eight thousand feet" (161); his July 26 "ramble to the summit of Mt. Hoffman" takes him to eleven thousand feet ("the highest point in life's journey my feet have yet touched") (199). Later he notes that their camp at Lake Tenaya is "about nine thousand feet above the sea" (268); that a ramble on August 13 to Three Brothers took him to "about eight thousand feet above the sea, or four thousand feet above the floor of the valley" (279–80); and that the Cathedral "is said to be about eleven thousand feet above the sea" (334). By recording elevation, he constructs a geological map that overlays the meteorological map of cloud formations and the botanical map of the trees, creating a palimpsest by which to locate himself and to chart his physical journey of discovery.

More importantly, this vertical trajectory charts his ascent to higher, more transcendent places in an "exploration in spiritual geography." Not only do his rambles take him higher in the mountains, they also take Muir into mythic space, a place of religious feeling. Buell declares, "Among all the great American nature writers, he was the most striking case of spontaneous pantheism." Thurman Wilkins calls his spiritual experiences "a mystical pantheism, though often expressed in theistic terms." Regardless of the label for his religious inclination, Muir records his imaginative, spiritual travels along a sacred vector. While he is drawn to see the hand of God and to read divine hieroglyphics in the natural world throughout the Sierras, a clear connection emerges between the vertical ascent in altitude and the vertical vector of the sacred. The careful geological map that tracks elevation also plots his ascent to spiritual locations, what Tuan calls mythic space. Tuan writes, "Mythic space is an intellectual construct . . . a response of feeling and imagination to fundamental human needs." Distinguishing mythic space and time from "historical time and oriented space," he explains that mythic space is commonly indicated by a vertical axis and "may be called cosmic."[4] During his rambles in the mountains, Muir travels not only the "oriented space" of the mountains but also "mythic space," both of which are indicated by the record of altitudinal locations.

Early in the journey, as the sheep herders begin to ascend the mountains going up to "twenty-five hundred feet," Muir describes a moment of transcendence akin to Ralph Waldo Emerson's experience of transparent continuum with nature in which he becomes one with "the blithe air." Making the connection between altitude and spiritual experience, Muir writes, "We are now in the mountains and they are in us, kindling enthusiasm," creating a "glorious . . . conversion" that breaks down the "old bondage" of time and place (*My First* 20–21). As with Emerson's metaphor of the transparent eyeball through which the currents of the Universal Being circulate, Muir describes a moment of oneness with nature that frees him from conventional notions of time and place. Stepping out of historic time, Muir imaginatively enters a zone that links him to origins and the "immortal" history that nature tells (20–21). Tuan delineates three kinds of mythic time: "cosmogonic, astronomic, and human." "Astronomic time" refers to the repetitive time of the seasons. "Human time" refers to the course of human history. Cosmogonic time, he writes, "is the story of origins, including the creation of the universe." As Muir writes about breaking the bondage of time and place and entering "this newness of life" (21), he is describing what Tuan calls mythic, cosmogonic time.

Describing having climbed a "mass of granite about eight feet high," again connecting a vertical axis of height with the sacred, he writes that he felt the boulder was "like an altar": "The place seemed holy, where one might hope to see God" (*My First* 64–65). In another episode, "perched" on Yosemite's North Dome he feels "prostrate before the vast display of God's power" and hopes to learn from "the divine manuscript" of the dome (175). Here we find Muir considering the domes and boulders in the Sierra as not only geologic structures to be sketched and studied but also as altars, signs of God. His ascent of Mount Hoffman illustrates more clearly the intersections between movement up the mountains and movement into mythic, cosmic space and time. Continuing to record elevation, he infuses the entry with a mythic voice encouraging him to another realm: "Ramble to the summit of Mt. Hoffman, eleven thousand feet high, the highest point in life's journey my feet have yet touched. . . . as if nature had wooingly whispered, 'come higher.'" There Muir hoped to learn "the meaning of these divine symbols crowded together on this wondrous page" of nature (199–200). One last example illustrates the intersecting trajectories of his travels when he ventures to the aptly named Cathedral Peak. He begins with measurements of the vertical location: "about eleven thousand feet above the sea, but the height of the building itself above the level of the ridge it stands on is about fifteen hundred feet" (335). Then he stops to describe the space as the location of the mythic, a place that responds to his imaginative, religious need to connect with something larger, higher than himself and mundane human existence. He writes, there is "the Cathedral itself, a temple displaying Nature" in its stones: "This I may say is the first time I have been at church in California. . . . In our best times everything turns into religion, all the world seems a church and the mountains altars" (336). Here on the peak he experiences a spiritual moment that connects him to higher laws, his position at that height suggesting his soul's journey. I do not want to get into the specific theological and philosophical foundations for Muir's thought; others like Michael Cohen and Dennis C. Williams have already done so. What I want to call attention to are the ways his journal charts the multiple trajectories of travel, directionally as he follows the sheep camp and his own explorations to named locations; chronologically by dates and by the conditions of clouds; spatially by noting the elevations he reaches and the height of rock formations and trees; and spiritually as he records moments of transcendence in his travels. These are all markers of location and time and travel—horizontal and vertical, historical and sacred, which for Muir are interconnected in his study of the natural world.

Not only does Muir chart his own trajectories of travel, his descriptions of what he does and what he observes are also infused with the language of movement. To describe his journeying as he goes out to explore, sketch, and study the natural world, he consistently uses the verbs "ramble" and "saunter" to imply the unhurried quality of his hikes. He looks forward to "many a glorious ramble" in the Yosemite region (*My First* 132) where he "sauntered along the river-bank" to "lily gardens" (80) and "sauntered in freedom complete" (210). On August 11 he writes, "Rambling all day getting acquainted with the region north of the river" (272). And he points to the leisurely quality of these walks: "How long I must have lingered, observing, sketching, taking notes" (295). Unlike the pace that the hungry sheep keep, Muir's is slower, allowing him to linger where he wants, to follow whims to examine lilies or trees or rock domes. Postulating on the origins of the term "sauntering" in his essay "Walking," Thoreau suggests that it may have come from the term *Sainte Terre*, someone supposedly in search of the Holy Land; or it may have come from the term *sans terre*, someone "having no particular home, but equally at home everywhere." "No more vagrant than the meandering river," the saunterer meanders at the same time as setting "a course to the sea," the sea being a metaphor for the deep meanings of life. Preferring the first meaning that suggests a holy wanderer, Thoreau pronounces, "For every walk is a sort of crusade . . . to go forth and reconquer this Holy Land from the hands of the Infidels" ("Walking" 185). Like Thoreau's holy saunterer, Muir is at home in the Sierras, meandering in walks of discovery and recovery of holy lands, God's land. Muir writes that he is "free to rove and revel in the wilderness all the big immortal days" (*My First* 174), connecting the ability to move freely with other freedoms. Given the means by Delaney to "be left perfectly free" to pursue his studies (5) when not tending the sheep, Muir enjoys freedom of movement to get off the path, to follow his whim, to think, to be. Tuan writes, "Spaciousness is closely associated with the sense of being free. Freedom implies space; it means having the power and enough room in which to act." Fundamental to the idea of freedom, Tuan continues, is the "elementary power to move."[6] Rambling about the open spaces of the West, of Yosemite Valley, Muir exemplifies the freedoms of the traveler as he saunters and lingers at will, as he studies the natural world and experiences moments of spiritual transcendence in nature. Like the West that Thoreau imagined, a place of wildness, freedom, the future, the Sierra is Muir's Holy Land, a place of "pilgrimage" (137).

In addition to using verbs of motion to describe his own going forth, Muir infuses descriptions of the environment with them, suggesting the dynamic quality of nature. Describing the sun, he focuses on what it does: "Down the long mountain-slopes the sunbeams pour, gilding the awakening pines, cheering every needle, filling every living thing with joy" (*My First* 66). Choosing verbs rather than adjectives in the passage, Muir describes the sunbeams as dynamic, active agents of nature. In another passage, he again selects action verbs: "Warm, sunny day, thrilling plant and animals and rocks alike, making sap and blood flow fast, and making every particle of the crystal mountains throb and swirl and dance . . . in joyful rhythmic motion in the pulses of Nature's big heart" (98). These verbs illustrate that nature is always in process, the rhythm of "Nature's big heart" a metaphor for the cyclic and ongoing processes of nature. Describing streams along the Merced and Tuolumne divide, he again uses verbs: "gliding," "simmering," "uniting," "bouncing," "dancing" (129). In another instance he writes, "Everything is flowing—going somewhere, animals and so-called lifeless rocks as well as water" (316–17). As Muir says, everything in nature is "kept in joyful rhythmic motion," and his verbs punctuate his view of nature as always being in motion, dynamic, in process of becoming and changing. Not only does he tramp about the natural world, that world is itself in constant motion, going somewhere and affecting other objects of the environment.

Moreover, he sees evidence of past movements of the boulders and glaciers that moved down the mountains and sculpted the meadows, moraines, and rock formations. He observes, "These boulders lying so still and deserted . . . were nevertheless brought from a distance . . . quarried and carried and laid down here." This evidence leads him to postulate that the boulders had been "overswept by a glacier . . . grinding down the general mass of the mountains . . . and dropping whatever boulders it chanced to be carrying at the time it was melted at the close of the Glacial Period." Declaring this "a fine discovery" (*My First* 133–34), he postulates the effects of glaciation, the ancient movements that shaped Yosemite Valley.[7] Glaciation describes the movement of an "ancient glacier [that] passed with tremendous pressure," leaving the rocks polished and striated and the moraines pushed by this force. Even the line of treeless areas indicates ancient movements, "where avalanches of snow had descended, sweeping away every tree in their paths" (289–91). As these examples illustrate, Muir sees nature in motion both in the present, with the action of the sun and the streams, and in the distant past when glaciers and avalanches pushed their way around.

As he indicates spatial movements, Muir also takes readers chronologically to the past, to a time of origins, to a mythic time when mastodons roamed the Sierra and "century avalanches" roared down the mountains. "Reading these grand mountain manuscripts," he finds that "everything in Nature called destruction must be creation,—a change from beauty to beauty" (*My First* 308). Just as the days and seasons change and just as the natural world is always in process, so Muir sees the larger cycles of time, the larger motive processes of nature, the "change from beauty to beauty." These cycles of time and ancient movements inflect his narrative, creating a cosmic travel narrative, more than a simple record of the rambles of one man. As he prepares to leave the Sierra for the season, he reflects on what he has learned, "the lessons of unity and inter-relation of all the features of the landscape," a lesson written long ago by the movement of the glaciers and reinforced by the daily processes of the "hardy plants, some of them still in flower" (321) as summer moves toward autumn. As the narrative traces his travels, it also traces the ancient travels of glaciers and avalanches, the continuous motion of plants, animals, minerals, the weather, and the sun. It charts divergent and intersecting trajectories as it maps movement chronologically and spatially through historic and mythic time and space.

As he charts his summer in the Sierra, Muir moves between characteristics of travel writing and nature writing. Nature writing has been described as operating in a middle ground between scientific information and artistic expression, of working in the in-between narrative spaces of fact and art, between "pastoral aesthetics and romanticist natural piety" and "empirical study and scientific interests," between the "pursuit of the seeable and the unseeable." Muir, one of the great American nature writers, writes in these in-between spaces as scientific discourse rubs up against aesthetic and spiritual depictions of nature. As a naturalist, Muir provides the scientific names for plants and arithmetical data when he describes the shrub *Adenostama fasciculata*, a member of the rose family, noting that it measures "about six or eight feet high" and "has small white flowers in racemes eight to twelve inches long" (*My First* 25). He compiles lists of plants, naming, for instance, the various ferns he encounters, "cheilanthes, pellaea, gymnogramme" (52), demonstrating his easy familiarity with botanical science. Trained in geology as well, his discovery of a living glacier and his understanding of glaciation, John Leighly explains, were "solid contributions to the geomorphology of glaciated mountains." He exercised the habits of careful observation and "seems always to have had with him a tape measure, an aneroid barometer for measuring elevation, and frequently a thermometer." We have seen that he was careful to measure elevation and the height of trees and to record meteorological data. Coupled with the more scientific jottings, Muir used literary tools such as personification that make the natural world come alive for his reader, sketching the humanlike characteristics of two species of squirrel, the California gray and the Douglas, their ability to think and scold, to brag and become shy. He writes of the "plant people" and the "other people" of the Sierra, the deer, bears, birds, and insects (207–8), suggesting as he does a "reverence for nature."[8] Deploying simile, he crafts the personality of nature, like the stream that "sings and shines like a happy living creature" (46). As well, he mixes in spiritual language, calling the processes of nature "the Godful work . . . in so holy a wilderness" (22) and sharing his own feelings of rapture as he drifts, "enchanted," his body "all one tingling palate" at the beauty of the Tuolumne (206). In these ways, Muir's writing exemplifies nature writing, the scientific, aesthetic, and spiritual rubbing against each other, creating a middle narrative space. When we add in the conventions of travel writing to our discussion, we see that *My First Summer in the Sierra* also operates in a middle ground between travel writing and nature writing as he takes readers with him on his rambles and sketches the natural world. To sketch the natural world, he must get out in it, and to help us to see nature he must take us with him on his rambles.

Instead of producing a document of jumbled or conflicting purposes and narrative trajectories, as his self-definition to Robert Underwood Johnson would suggest, that he is a "self-styled poetico—trampo—geologist—bot. and ornith—natural, etc!!!," Muir's narrative exemplifies the power and beauty of the cleavage joint. Cleavage joints are the point where geologic forces rub against each other to create what Muir calls a "subtle balanced beauty" (*My First* 341). Near the end of *My First Summer* he writes, "The most telling thing learned in these mountain excursions is the influence of cleavage joints on the features sculptured from the general mass of the range" (341). Cleavage joints, Muir later concluded, "*do not so much mold and shape,* as disinter forms already conceived and ripe" in order to create something new. These spaces, the joints between formations, the in-between spaces, are caused by the forceful meeting of two masses that sculpt new land formations with a power and beauty of their own. Using the metaphor of the cleavage joint, we might suggest that the beauty and power of *My First Summer* derives from the meeting of genres, of nature writing and travel writing, and of times, the historic and the mythic, from infusing the biological and the geological with the spiritual. In this joint, this meeting place, Muir's geographic imaginaries come together—an imaginary of travel, an environmental imaginary, and a geo-spiritual imaginary. And it is from this cleavage joint that his "environmentalist commitment" will derive, motivating him to spend a lifetime advocating for the wild spaces.[9]

Charles Fletcher Lummis

Mapping A Tramp across the Continent

When Charles Fletcher Lummis accepted a position as city editor with the *Los Angeles Times* in 1884, he easily could have taken the train from Chillicothe, Ohio, to Los Angeles. By 1884 the nation was connected by the four main transcontinental railroads, the Northern Pacific, the Central and Union Pacific, the Atlantic and Pacific, and the Southern Pacific, as well as by the many regional lines. The Atchison, Topeka, and Santa Fe line, which was completed to Albuquerque in 1880, along with the Atlantic Pacific and the Southern Pacific forged two southern routes to Southern California through the American Southwest. These lines helped unify and extend national markets to the West Coast and would have been good options for a traveler to Los Angeles.[1] Lummis chose instead to walk.

Secretly married to his first wife, Dorothea Rhodes, a medical student at Boston University, Lummis had left Harvard University just shy of his required mathematics credits to first work on his father-in-law's farm and then as a journalist for the *Scioto Gazette* in Chillicothe. Although the editor of the *Los Angeles Times*, Colonel Harrison Gray Otis, might have preferred that Lummis come immediately to Los Angeles by way of train, he apparently admired Lummis's "gumption" in deciding to go by foot. Lummis's biographer Mark Thompson relates that instead of riding the train, in a gesture of both Thoreauvian self-reliance and self-promotional exuberance, the young man decided to walk from Cincinnati, his jumping off spot, to Los Angeles. He would tramp across the continent and write about his adventures for both the *Times* and the *Chillicothe Leader*, garnering national attention and making a little money on the way, five dollars per letter he sent to the *Leader*. Walking across the continent would provide him with an intimate view of the land and its peoples that he would have missed had he taken the train. Walking also afforded a chance to test his mettle, to prove his self-reliance at a time when technology was staking an ever-increasing claim on the way people traveled. And walking would give the ambitious young man a way of making his mark on the journalistic world. Before he left he had a publicity picture made, featuring a determined Lummis in his unique outfit: a white flannel shirt that tied at the neck, knickerbockers, red knee-high stockings, a felt hat, low-cut Curtis and Wheeler shoes, and a Winchester rifle slung over his shoulder.[2]

Eight years later, in 1892, Lummis collected and edited his letters to the *Los Angeles Times* into book form for Charles Scribner's Sons. James W. Byrkit, who collected his Chillicothe letters, remarks that the Ohio letters were more "freely spoken and spontaneous" than the more "commercial, self-promoting, and politic reporting" he reworked for the *Times*. Even so, both sets of letters as well as the book version tell the same basic story of the tramp across the continent. A "third-generation adaptation" of the two sets of letters he sent to the *Times* and the *Leader, A Tramp Across the Continent* maps not only his itinerary along the rail lines and his adventures but also his changing ideas about the Southwest and its people.[3] Not only did Lummis change his ideas about Mexican Americans and Native Americans the further he plunged into the Southwest. In the eight-year interlude between the tramp and pulling together the book, Lummis matured as an advocate for their rights and revisited some of the scenes of the original journey. In these ways, the narrative recounts two journeys, the original tramp and a second, more intellectual one, as he translates his experience through the act of writing.

Much like autobiography, the travel narrative tells the experiences of the two "I's," the exuberant young man and the public self that Lummis the journalist had crafted by 1892. Or, as Mario Cesareo puts it, the text represents "the conversion of the traveling eye to the writing gaze." Like many autobiographical travel writers, Lummis relies on both his memory and the original notes and dispatches he wrote during the journey: "Unwilling to trust my memory, at this late date, for details of impression, I go back to my letterbook and reproduce what I wrote to friends that night."[4] At times these two "I's" meet in the narrative to demonstrate how Lummis's ideas were changed both by the journey and by subsequent acquaintance with the Southwest. For instance, in chapter 6 he relates, "In Colorado the Mexicans are much in the minority, and are frequently nicknamed 'greasers.'" He corrects that derogatory slur against the Mexicans by pointing to their "hospitality, courtesy, and respect for age," something he learned as he stayed in their homes during the tramp. Then the second "I," the writing "I," interjects into the narrative, "I speak now from years of intimate, but honorable, personal acquaintance with them—an acquaintance which has shamed me out of the silly prejudices against them which I shared with the average Saxon" (*Tramp* 31). Likewise, when he relates his "first introduction to the Pueblo Indians" he juxtaposes his perspective after having "lived for four years among them" with his initial reactions ("[when] they were new to me in every detail"). He writes that he was astonished to see their "excellent houses, with comfortable furniture and clean beds," evidence that they were not savage but rather "as industrious as any class in the country" (38). Lummis then goes on to provide a corrective perspective of the Pueblos, which is missing in the original, more racist letter he wrote for the *Leader*. That letter details how the man who entertained him, Alonzo, "a sort of High Muck-a-Muck," had his "rather handsome squaw" prepare him a lunch of mutton, tortilla, coffee, and "some matchless cheese."⁵ In that early letter his touristic, racialist gaze is on the food, the jewelry the woman wears, and the buckskin Alonzo was making, a contrast to the more writerly, historical perspective of the Pueblos in the 1892 *Tramp*. Looking at these three versions of his introduction to the Pueblos of San Ildefonso and the comments about his initial prejudice about the Mexicans, we can see how the past and present selves meet in moments of reflection as Lummis relates the physical journey across the landscape and the intellectual journeys because of it.

Like many other travel narratives, *A Tramp* deploys multiple and sometimes competing personas and ways of mapping the journey. On the one hand, he presents himself as a self-reliant "vagrant," a "man who got outside the fences of civilization" to go "vagabondizing" (*Tramp* iv). Like Thoreau who answers the question of why he went to live at Walden Pond by saying that he "wished to live deliberately" (*Walden* 90), Lummis poses the question "But why tramp?" Like the earlier Harvard man, Lummis announces that he wished to experience "life in the truer, broader, sweeter sense, . . . to have the physical joy" of walking and thus learn "more of the country and its people." In a gesture to the transcendentalist strain of American manhood, he claims that he wanted "the physical joy" of walking and to "have the mental awakenings of new sights and experiences" (*Tramp* 5). He also travels as an adventurer, like Francis Parkman, another Harvard man, whom he declared "the greatest of American historians." Like Parkman, Lummis is concerned with tracking his physical location and relating the hardships of travel, his hunts, and narrow escapes in the wild, giving readers another example "of the male Anglo-American ego confronting an environment that threatens to break it apart." Then, as an ethnographer, Lummis traces "a new cultural geography of the Southwest," infusing the narrative with the voices of the people he meets, their stories, histories, and cultural practices, even though an underlying imperialism, Tereza M. Szeghi claims, "reinforces Anglo American values." These multiple personas and itineraries complicate the narrative and the stories that the travel book tells. As Martin Padget remarks, *A Tramp across the Continent* is "part travelogue, part regional history, part ethnology, part folklore, and part adventure storytelling," a book that layers multiple journeys.[6]

Most literally, Lummis plots his itinerary, chapter by chapter and almost mile by mile, taking readers along the rail lines that he follows, over the mountains and deserts to Los Angeles, naming the towns and way stations along the route. Byrkit explains that Lummis planned his journey around a "routebook" he compiled of former Chillicotheans whom he might visit along the way and the rail lines that provided a sure route through the West.[7] Sometimes literally walking on the cross ties, he layers the changes that expansion, technology, and the railroad brought to the West on the intimate acts of walking and writing. Early in the narrative Lummis points to the connections between this new infrastructure, his writing, and the journey: "My writing kept me busy till within two hours of sunset next day." He then trekked seventeen miles to the post office ("just in time for the mail"), where he dispatched his letters and decided that rather than carry all thirty-seven pounds of his gear that he would send some "ahead from station to station on the broader shoulders of the express company" (*Tramp* 18). As he travels in tandem with the rail lines, availing himself of the accompanying post offices, telegraph offices, and section houses built to house the rail crews and equipment, Lummis maps the travel, communications technologies, and accommodations available to foot travelers.

Of a section house in Colorado, his "fifth State," he remarks that he had "a supper of rancid bacon, half-raw potatoes, leaden bread flounced with sorghum, and coffee" and that the place was so infested that he spread his sleeping bag outside for the night (*Tramp* 10–11). At Rio Puerco he sleeps on the floor of the rail station, "the only accommodations, nine times out of ten, for the next nine hundred miles" (60). Because there were only six towns from western Arizona to Los Angeles, his lodgings were either the bare ground or a chair tilted beside the stove of some lone telegraph station. On other occasions he describes the humble homes that lodged him, the "poor little Mexican ranch-house" where he was treated with hospitality (*Tramp* 76) and the German household in San Antonito he stumbled into after being caught in a snowstorm. He also writes that he and Shadow, the greyhound he adopted in San Carlos, often had to make a bed in the wild and eat the game he procured. These kinds of comments situate him on the map of the tramp and indicate how it was often sustained by the lonely way stations and homes along the way.

Because Lummis follows the rail lines, he is rarely geographically lost, but as he makes his entrance into the West and burrows into the Southwest, he increasingly finds himself in strange territory that challenges his sense of self. He writes, "We stepped into a civilization that was then new to me—that of swarthy Mexicans and their quaint adobe houses" (*Tramp* 31). Their food, the tortillas and red stew, *chile colorado*, also new to him, was generously flavored with red chili peppers. Although he claims, "I never missed and longed for any other food as I did for chile when I got back to civilization" (54), at the time the food was new and a marker of self-identity change. And so the cartographical map doubles as a cognitive map, a representational map that locates self-identity in conjunction with place. As Eric Leed observes of travel, "The flows of passage not only provide information about the world; they provide information about the self of the passenger."[8] At the same time, then, that Lummis tells us where he is, among the Mexicans, for instance, he also charts a map of himself, a cognitive map by which he plots not only *where* he is but *who* he is, in this case a novice among the Mexicans of the American Southwest. This cognitive map is further complicated by moments when the second "I," the writing "I," comments on identity in transition during the tramp, on the self who would long for chile even after the journey had ended.

As it was for Helen Hunt Jackson, that moment of stepping over into the West was momentous. Jackson signaled it by reflecting, "This is what the word 'West' sounded like" (*Bits* 6). For Lummis, the West bears "a weight of silence," its open spaces "an infinity of nothing" (*Tramp* 9), a seeming void in which he will have to situate himself, find a place for himself, construct an identity that coheres with his imagined geography of the West. Even if the West is no longer "woolly" (*Tramp* 24), populated now by the "cowboy dandy" of the "cattle rancho[s]" (9), it is both an imagined geography crafted by tales of the West and a physical space in which Lummis shapes and tests versions of himself. If, as Krista Comer argues, "traditional western space" is "gendered male," then the West is a place where he can locate a masculine identity.[9] Not only does he dress the part of an adventurer in the West like Parkman and Twain before him, he also maps his identity by measuring feats of endurance and prowess just as surely as he mapped the miles he covered.

Early in the tramp, he boasts that he covered "thirty to forty miles" a day and had "grown robust as a young bison." He brags, "My lungs were growing even larger, my eyes were good for twice their usual range" (*Tramp* 9–10). Because he carried a pedometer with him, he can accurately record how far he travels each day. At the end of the narrative, he proclaims that he had walked "a fraction over 3507 miles" ("I had been out one hundred and forty-three days, and had crossed eight States and Territories") (101). Mark Thompson specifies that he walked 6,523,542 steps.[10] To test his mettle early on, Lummis tries to see how far he can go in twenty-four hours, then boasts that he made "an even seventy-nine miles." Even though he has covered an incredible number of miles, he asserts, "The record would have been better had I not fallen asleep when I sat down to rest, and thus lost three hours" (9). The concern with measuring and counting evinces a competitive need to outdo others, to prove his bravado, his masculinity. But it also provides a way to locate himself, the self he constructs, during the tramp.

At five feet six, Lummis was, as he often mentioned, a "trained athlete" who had practiced wrestling and boxing during his Harvard days to condition his body and mind.[11] Not only does Lummis put himself in situations that test his physical mettle, climbing up Pike's Peak in a November gale or walking seven hundred miles with a broken arm that he set himself and then taking a side trip down into the Grand Canyon, hanging in one precarious moment by his teeth. He also maps and measures to ascertain his hardy masculinity. So, when he recounts his arrival at the Signal Service station at the crest of Pike's Peak, "perhaps the highest inhabited building on earth," he gives the date (November 4), the time (3:30 p.m.), and the elevation (14,147), emphasizing how much higher it is than his readers back home are. While these figures help situate Pike's Peak for readers and locate Lummis on his trek, by emphasizing the extremity of the location, its great heights and dangers, they also point to his own athletic ability and bravado.

Not content with tallying the number of miles traveled and the elevation of mountains, Lummis counts other things as a way of mapping the tramp and himself. Mapping, naming, and measuring not only attest to his prowess. As tools of imperialism, they also bring the "infinity" of the West under narrative control. Early in the journey, in his exuberance to be "really 'out West'" (*Tramp* 9), he enumerates the things he killed, the two antelope that provided him with a dinner of roasted steak, a large hawk, a rattlesnake that he teased before killing, and his first centipede. Throughout the journey, he persists in listing and counting the wild creatures he encounters: the twenty trout he caught in the Rockies, the "flock of bighorns" he tries to shoot, a black-tail deer "whose antlers were six spikes," the "fifty-three and a half pounds" wildcat that he packed some ten miles just to weigh (*Tramp* 25–29), the coyote he poisoned and then stuffed and carried with him. In these ways his adventures chart the journey and the narrative of himself that he promotes, one that emphasizes his endurance, his prowess as an outdoorsman, his ability to meet the challenges of the journey. As place markers, these events locate Lummis in "the geographical ecology," answering for himself the question "where am I?" By also answering the question "who am I?" they locate him on a cognitive, psychic map. As Lummis projects his idea of himself as masculine and authentic on the world that he describes, he creates a kind of psychogeography, "the unconscious construction of the social and physical world" in which he "project[s] psychic contents outward" onto the world.[12] In these ways the map of the tramp and the man taking the tramp overlay and intersect each other.

In his survey of the history of travel, Leed describes the traveler as paradigmatically male and travel as a test: "The fatigues of travel, the suffering of the journey, remain a cause and a measure of the extent to which a traveler is marked and tested by experience."[13] Descriptions of the trials of the road, the moments when things go wrong, when the traveler is faced with unexpected perils, make the narrative part adventure tale. For a male traveler like Lummis (and Parkman before him) these trials test his masculinity, the version of himself as the hero of his own story. In addition to enumerating and measuring as plotting devices, Lummis uses experiences that test his endurance and strength to locate himself. For instance, the story he tells of trekking over the Sandia Mountains takes readers with him over the snow-covered track and the moments when his willpower and endurance are tested. The day he left Golden, New Mexico, on a December morning carrying nearly forty pounds, which included some gold specimens from the mines, was one such case. He writes, "It was the hardest long walk I ever attempted." He and Shadow trudged through the snow, following only the "tracks of a single horse." Stomping through foothills of San Ysidro range, as the snow grew deeper and the elevation higher, he was in a sweat and Shadow in a "perfect lather" from their efforts: "We were in a trackless wilderness, far from help, or food, or warmth. . . . The wind . . . came shrieking savagely." Shadow was worn out. Lummis recalls, "I picked him up and threw him upon my heavy knapsack. . . . It was already several degrees below zero." His sweat-soaked clothes became "frozen stiff": "Nothing but 'bulldog' kept me up." Exhausted, he fell in a burrow and death seemed a reality as night approached. But then seeing two figures in the distance and led by "Hope" and "Will," he made a "fearful struggle" and stumbled into San Antonito. There he "fell fainting across the threshold of the first house" he came to (*Tramp* 49–52). Not content to relate how he survived this harrowing experience, Lummis remarks that the next morning, "thanks to perfect physical training," he was able to go his way because he was anxious to reach a post office (52–53). As he writes the adventure and describes the December mountain scape, Lummis also plots a narrative of the heroic, masculine self who endures the most harrowing adventures.

As Martin Padget observes, Lummis was also "actively engaged in mapping a new cultural geography of the southwest," and he enumerated the miles and adventures, collected animal skins and antlers, and stowed precious stones in his pack just as he collected artifacts and stories of the American Southwest. He constructs a map of himself as an authority on Southwest culture as he draws a cultural map of the region, the cognitive map of the self again interfacing with the geographic map. As with Parkman, there is a clear connection between travel and ethnography, between writing about travel and writing about culture. But Lummis's ethnography, his effort to record the stories, arts, and practices of a people, is complicated by his tourist's urge to collect mementos of an authentic journey and by his masculine urge to prove himself as an authority. James Clifford recognizes that "collecting has long been a strategy for the deployment of a possessive self, culture, and authenticity." By surrounding himself and his narrative with artifacts, Lummis uses his collection of the Southwest to shape an identity as an authority on the region. Just as he loads his pack with agates and gold nuggets, with coyote skins and deer antlers, so he loads his mental pack with stories, mementos of a different kind by which to remember the experience, to prove the authenticity of the experience, and to profit from it through cultural and real capital. As he mentions, he collected enough to construct a "whole museum of curios and mementos" (*Tramp* 6) and to form the basis of numerous books, including the popular *Land of Poco Tiempo* (1893), which he prepared almost simultaneously with the 1892 *Tramp* during an extended stay first at the Chaves family hacienda at San Mateo and then at Pueblo Isleta (1888–1892).[14]

Scholars have critiqued Lummis's ethnography, pointing to his amateurism and ethnocentric outsider's assumptions about the Other.[15] But it is helpful to think of his persona in *Tramp* as tourist/ethnographer, collector of cultural treasures and personal mementos. As an ethnographer he records the lifestyles, ceremonies, domestic arrangements, stories, and rituals of the cultures he visits, retaining as he does so the outsider status of the observer. As a tourist, Lummis mediates this outsider status by collecting artifacts and stories as signs of an authentic experience that validate his travels. He is both outsider and authentic: outsider spokesperson for the cultures he visits but privy to the stories that validate his travel experience. The things he gathers display as well the acumen of his collecting decisions because he buys and collects directly from the source, the culture itself, and not the touristic representation of the culture. As an early Anglo traveler on the cusp of culture tourism to the Southwest, he was in a position to set the standard for later travelers about the value of the region before it became a mecca for artists like Mabel Dodge Luhan, Mary Austin, and Georgia O'Keefe, and tourists who would come to view the ceremonies and buy the artifacts, whether they were authentic or souvenirs manufactured for tourists. Looking back at his collecting, he remarks, "Now some very excellent travelers from the East buy these fantastic images and take them home as 'Indian idols,' whereby they become a laughing-stock." They did not understand the significance of the pottery figures they bought or the ways the astute Pueblos sold the idea of the "'red' men" to unwitting tourists (*Tramp* 43). Lummis, however, had an eye for interesting artifacts and an ear for the stories of the Southwest that he would both preserve and capitalize on for the rest of his career, creating the Museum of the Southwest in 1907 and writing over a dozen books about the region.

At Acoma Pueblo, for instance, he gathered many "interesting trophies"—"moccasins, necklace ornaments of native jet . . . and some superb arrow-heads . . . and many other curios" (*Tramp* 65) that, with other relics, nuggets, and petrified wood, he shipped from Grants, New Mexico, to Los Angeles. While visiting the Navajo Indians, whom he refers to as "among the most savage aborigines of the West" even if they were "the wealthiest nomad Indians in the United States," he acquired a "load" of Navajo treasures. These included "a lot of the barbaric silver bracelets, belt-disks, earrings, etc., and a magnificent blanket." He brags in *Tramp*, "I have in my collection blankets worth $200 apiece" (80, 84). Combining ethnography with collecting, he details how the Navajos crafted their jewelry and blankets, giving a quick survey of the history, significance, and value of their arts. He notes, "Their supply of silver is now drawn almost exclusively from civilized coin," and he describes buttons made of quarters and half-dollars, "worn as simple ornaments," adorning clothes, gun scabbards, saddles, and bridles. He introduces readers to Chit-Chi, "the best silversmith of the Navajos," who turns out work for some American patrons, including Lummis who later receives a ring from him as "a token of affection" (83). The pieces that he describes suggest not just imperialist acquisition but also the connoisseurship of his collecting, his good taste, and knowledge of the arts.[16]

Procuring items like Indian jewelry is part of the tourist experience, enabling Lummis the tourist to bring back something to adorn his person and the Los Angeles home he will build, El Alisal. As well, procuring Indian crafts was part of nineteenth-century ethnographic practice when removing indigenous artifacts and preserving them in museums and private collections was accepted practice. Earlier in the century, Margaret Fuller had called for a "national institute" to house the "remains of the Indians" to preserve their history, even if the Indians themselves seemed doomed (*SL* 143). When Lummis assumed the editorship of *Land of Sunshine* in 1895, he highlighted the impressive Southwest and indigenous collections of Dr. A. Palmer, W. D. Campbell, and Lorenzo Gordin Yates, as he urged the formation of a museum. Likewise, early twentieth-century anthropologists and folklorists sought to preserve the stories of "'exotic' Others" for fear their cultures might disappear under the pressure of "modern industrial culture."[17] And so Lummis the tramp began stocking pieces that would eventually go into his Southwest Museum and extend the experience of cultural tourism for visitors unable to journey to the pueblos themselves.

In addition to the material goods he gathered, Lummis collected stories, that gave voice to the variety of peoples of the Southwest and the desperate lives of some of the men inhabiting the West. He tells the story of Old Monny, a prospector, and his fight with a cinnamon bear that left him a "cripple for life" but owner of the skin of the bear that mauled him, "eleven feet four inches" (*Tramp* 25–26). He relates a story told to him by the Mexican desperado Mariño Lebya with whom he "had many very entertaining talks." One story centered on a "very round eastern man" who attempted to buy a round of drinks for the fellows in a bar in Golden, New Mexico, only to have Lebya pronounce, "I'm Mariño, and I hate fat men. If you're here tomorrow, I'll peg you down out here and light a fire on that big stomach" (49–50). Stories like these, the material of western lore, emphasize the toughness of characters and the dangers of travel, giving readers a flavor of the West as they simultaneously reinforce stereotypes about it. Interspersed with Lummis's own adventures, they contribute to the masculine persona he builds in the narrative.

In another section of the narrative, he quotes letters by two Indian boys at school in Santa Fe. While the brief letters are, as Lummis states, "comically idiomatic," they tell in the boys' own voices the kind of education the Pueblo children were getting in the Indian schools. The education of Indians, as their letters suggest, put an emphasis on work—in the laundry, on the roads, in the fields, in the kitchen, and elsewhere ("working in the new building, we painted the whole building")—and on eastern pedagogies of reading and geography. As one boy writes, "I have learn maps of Aisa and Erop and U S s [*sic*]" (*Tramp*, 42–43). Lummis uses these letters to criticize the "alleged education" that children forced to live apart from their families and homes were receiving. Even if he is patronizing about the letters and the prospect of educating the Indians, the "swart pupils," he later joined the fight against separating children from their families, taking on the Albuquerque Indian School on behalf of Isleta Pueblo in 1891.[18]

Later Lummis lets Patapalo, the "quaint old Mexican" who claims he was bewitched by one of the local *brujas* so "that he scarce can walk," tell the story in "his own words" of an adventure he had with witchcraft. The story relates a strange meeting, on the plain miraculously covered by "10,000 mesquite bushes," of a congregation of men and women. During the dark Mass everyone first kissed a goat that spoke, and then an upright snake went through the gathering and put its tongue in everyone's mouth. When it was Patapalo's turn to receive the snake's tongue, he cried out, "Jesus, Mary, and Joseph, save me!" and was instantly transported alone back to the barren plain (*Tramp* 74–75). Told in the simple words of the *paisano* (with Lummis's translation), the story illustrates the beliefs, "superstitions," of the Mexican folk. Stories like these comprise much of the local color interest of the travel writing, provide a kind of literary quality to the adventures, and give readers an ethnographic view of cultures different from their own.

As well as giving space in his narrative to local voices, Lummis recounts the histories of the Pueblo Indians and the Spanish in the Southwest not only to put his adventures in context but also to provide a corrective to the generally accepted Anglo-based history of the United States. In chapter 7 of *Tramp* he gives a brief history of how the Spanish explored and colonized the Southwest, establishing missions and churches and leaving "their stamp" on the customs, language, and religion of the region. He takes on the Black Legend of Spanish cruelty and conquest in the New World tartly saying that "the Spanish conquests . . . were far less cruel than the Saxon": "The Spaniard never exterminated. He conquered the aborigine and converted and educated him, and preserved him." Lummis also writes about the founding of Santa Fe in 1605 by Juan de Oñate, the Pueblo Revolt of 1680 when twenty-one priests "were butchered by the swarthy insurgents," and the reconquest of Santa Fe by Diego de Vargas in 1693 (*Tramp* 39). Giving this historical sketch, even quickly and superficially, he hopes to let his eastern readers "realize that there is a West, and was one long before there was an East" (38–39).

During his stay with Colonel Mañuel Chaves, near San Mateo in western New Mexico, Lummis had the chance to observe the "home-life" of a well-to-do Mexican family. He mentions the design of their adobe house and the "scrupulously neat" beds covered with Navajo blankets. He lists the food, stews of mutton with rice, roasted beef, frijoles, *chile*, *galletitas* (shortcakes), and the coffee and wine that he was served. And he shares their entertainments, the "sweet Spanish folk-songs," the game Floron (much like the New England game of "Button, Button, Who's Got the Button") and the Día de Los Santos Inocentes, which sounds a bit like April Fool's Day, when "jovial" jokes are played on the unsuspecting (*Tramp* 71). This description of the Chaves household and the folk life of upper-class New Mexican culture is the material of ethnography. Describing these practices and sprinkling his discourse with Spanish words, he establishes himself as an outsider/insider, a "participant observer" who has been privy to the Mexican culture of the United States. Indeed, by the time he writes about the activities of the Chaves household for the book, he has returned and spent the better part of a year with them, more intentionally recording New Mexico folk songs and *dichos* (sayings) that he would recite and translate in The *Land of Poco Tiempo*. "None too soon," he says, "for they are fast changing and disappearing under the new order of things."[19] When he writes about the mysterious Penitentes of San Mateo, he takes readers into a secret society that few Anglos at the time had observed. He describes how they parade through the streets during Lent, "flaying their own bare backs" with scourges and "bearing crosses of crushing weight" or "burdens of cactus" in penance for their sins until on Good Friday one of their own is crucified, "chosen by lot!" Though he gives only a quick description here, he notes, "Afterward I not only witnessed these ghastly scenes, but photographed them all, including the crucifixion" (72), a longer account of which he provides in *The Land of Poco Tiempo*.

Stumbling into Isleta Pueblo, the place where he would later live for four years after leaving the Chaves compound, Lummis describes the pueblo and its hospitable people, its "well-tended farms" and herds of livestock (*Tramp* 55), blending as he does the two "I's"—the traveling I and the writing I, the outsider and insider gaze—to describe the customs of the pueblo. In this case, he writes about the ritual ceremony the Fiesta de los Muertos, the Day of the Dead fiesta. He writes about the three days of preparations for the ceremony, the baking of various breads and cakes in the outdoor "beehives of ovens," the *hornos*, commenting that "there are few better breadmakers than these Pueblos" (57). He describes the preparations of the women in terms of hair, clothes, and boots, noting that on the day of the ceremony "each woman was dressed in her best . . . her costliest corals and turquoise and silver beads [hanging] from her neck" (58). The fiesta seems to be primarily a woman's ceremony, as the men have taken to drinking quantities of wine during the days leading up to the ceremony and are separated from the women in the church. After the three days of preparations, the ceremony itself begins as the sacristan climbs "the crazy staircase to the roof of the church" and rings the great church bell. Lummis follows the procession of women with their baskets of offerings to the church graveyard and on to a Mass, the church lit by flickering candles, the women kneeling inside, the "heaped-up baskets" of food, "contortions in bread and cake, funny little 'turnovers' with a filling of stewed dried peaches" offered to the dead through the intermediary of the priest, who benefits from the generosity of the offerings. Lummis remarks, "The ringing of the church-bell of Isleta is an experience that is worth a long journey to enjoy" (57), suggesting not only the ethnographic value of the ceremony, its combination of Catholic and Native rituals, but also the culture tourism that accompanied the extension of the rail lines into New Mexico. Viewing Native Americans and ethnic Others has long been a part of the American tourist experience, as we have seen when Bryant and Fuller gazed on the Native Americans at Mackinaw. But as transportation modernized, making travel to remote areas easier, "social others [like Native Americans and Mexican Americans] became an extension of the tourist spectacle."[20]

Indeed, the next chapter of Lummis's narrative begins, "At Isleta the Atlantic and Pacific Railroad has its junction with the Atchison, Topeka and Santa Fé, and ... the general line of the former ... gives access to the most wonderful and least-known corners of America" (*Tramp* 59). As Lummis continues his tramp westward, he stops at Laguna Pueblo to watch the Christmas dance, another cultural event in the narrative. But when he remarks, "Laguna is the most picturesque of the pueblos that are easily accessible; and as the railroad runs at the very base of the great dome of rock upon which the quaint houses are huddled, there is no difficulty in reaching it" (62), he indicates how the railroad and the visitors it brings make a curious juxtaposition against the centuries' old pueblos and ancient customs. In fact, Lummis notes that some of the Pueblo dancers carried tomahawks, "though that was never a characteristic weapon of the Pueblo Indians," as well as revolvers and Winchesters, demonstrating the contamination, or hybridity as Laguna writer Leslie Marmon Silko might put it, of ancient traditions by the modern tourist industry that catered to stereotypes about Indians (62).

As the extension of the railroad brought eastern travelers and ideas to the Pueblos, the Pueblos began to market their culture, selling foods and Indian artifacts to tourists who came to gawk at them and their adobe homes. By the next decade, tourists were invading the pueblos of New Mexico to observe their ceremonies and rituals, Emily Post remarking in 1916 that "lots of tourists" were going to Isleta. She points to the theater of tourism promoted by the various Harvey hotels in the Santa Fe system, where the "hotel people, curio-sellers, and

Indians are the actors, the travelers on the in-coming trains are the audience"
(*Motor* 160). In a conflation of travel, ethnography, and tourism, visits to the
pueblos exemplify what is called cultural tourism. Cultural scholar Jennifer
Craik defines cultural tourism as "customized excursions into other cultures and
places to learn about their people, lifestyle, heritage and arts in an informed way
that genuinely represents those cultures and their historical contexts." She also
notes that not only are tourists affected by the cultures they visit, the cultures
are affected by tourism as they learn to market themselves and their wares to
tourists. [21] When Lummis climbed onto the housetops at Laguna, Acoma, and
Isleta to observe the ceremonies, he was an accepted observer, perhaps one of the
early visitors but probably not the first. Others would follow as cultural tourists
to learn about and gawk at the social Others of the Pueblo. Indeed, when I visited
Taos Pueblo in 2018, tours were organized by the tribe, complete with a brief
history, a lesson on making adobe, and opportunities to purchase baked goods
and jewelry, evidence that in this instance the Taos people, like other Native
Americans, have taken control over the presentation and marketing of their
culture. To control and profit from tourism to the tribes, AIANTA, a Native
American–controlled organization, has recently been formed to advance educational tourism about American Indians, Alaska Natives, and Native Hawaiians.

Lummis's access to the Pueblos and Mexicans of New Mexico speaks to more
than his unique personality. It speaks also to a practice of tourism that had taken
off with the extension of the railroad in 1879 and that he promoted in *A Tramp
across the Continent*: "It is a perennial wonder to me that American travellers
care so little to see the wonders of their own land . . . the wonderland of the
Southwest, with its strange landscapes, its noble ruins of a prehistoric past, and
the astounding customs of its present aborigines. A pueblo ceremonial dance is
one of the most remarkable sights to be witnessed anywhere; and there are many
other customs no less worth seeing" (*Tramp* 55). Although Lummis claimed that
the narrative of his travels is "not a guidebook, but the record of a walk and of
. . . the random impressions of them, recounted by the light of later study and
intimate acquaintance" (41), he nonetheless promoted travel to the Southwest in
it and his other narratives, going so far as to claim later that he coined the phrase
"See America First." Marguerite S. Shaffer notes that in his August 1912 editorial
column in *Out West*, "In the Lion's Den," Lummis claimed the phrase as his
own, but she clarifies that "he in fact borrowed the See America First slogan and
linked it to his earlier work."[22] Regardless, in *A Tramp across the Continent* Lummis encourages readers to see America's cultural and natural wonders. He takes
readers with him to view the cultural and folk-life practices of the peoples of the

Southwest and encourages readers to view some of its natural wonders. Of the
Garden of the Gods outside Colorado Springs he writes, "It is something which
every American should see" (20), and of the Grand Canyon he tells readers, "It
is a crying shame that any American who is able to travel at all should fail to see
nature's masterpiece upon this planet before he fads abroad" (92). Despite his
disclaimer, the narrative of his tramp is, in fact, a kind of guidebook to America's
Southwest and an introduction to its unique cultures and landscapes.

Lummis's journey across lands that were, in his words, strange, quaint, and
noble was transformative for him. While he could not escape some of the stereotypes and patronizing attitudes he brought with him on the journey, he
was physically and mentally tested by the journey. His biographer notes, "The
tramp had changed Lummis forever." He would retell the story of the tramp and
return to photograph and record in more detail the cultures and peoples of the
region and become an important advocate for the Mexicans, Indians, and the
environment. Indeed, the Southwest became the overriding theme of his life
and writing afterward. The tramp was not just a journey from which he would
return home. It was also a journey to new places, insights, and the creation of
a new persona, marked by the "trademark ensemble" he came to wear: a Span-
ish-style corduroy suit, red Navajo sash, and Stetson sombrero. His personal
spaces, his very person, and the home that he built himself and decorated with
his collections create a *testimonio* of his travels and the self-identity he created.
The rugs, pictures, and baskets that adorned his space create a kind of visual
poetry of the Southwest that speaks more eloquently of the effects of the region
on his sense of self than the stilted poems he wrote from "the Lion's Den." In
these ways the trek exemplifies what Dean MacCannell calls ethical sightseeing
because Lummis's conscience and character were influenced by the journey, and
he realized "the productive potential" of his travels, even if it was also a journey
of appropriation.[23] Like the outfit he adopted and the rooms he assembled, *A
Tramp across the Continent* is an ensemble of voices and genres. In the narrative
we hear Lummis's own multiple and sometimes competing voices, the voice of
the traveling "I" and the voice of the writing "I." We hear the voice of male bravado and the more measured voice of the amateur ethnographer and historian,
both inflected at times by ethnocentric patronizing. We also hear the voices
of the people he meets on the trek who tell their stories in their own words. A
diverse narrative, *Tramp* weaves personal adventure with cultural exploration,
geographic mapping with cognitive mapping, ethnography with tourism.

Interior view of El Alisal, the home of Charles F. Lummis, circa 1920–1929,
photo by C. C. Pierce

Emily Post in the West

LIKE MANY EASTERNERS TRAVELING to the West, Emily Post kept trying to put her finger on what the West means. Marveling at the expansiveness and radiance of the western landscapes, she claims in *By Motor to the Golden Gate* that the spirit of the West is more "geographical" than "ethnological" (*Motor* 216), as if place more than culture shapes the character of those who live among its prairies, deserts, mountains, and seacoasts. Transplanted residents to the West, like the pampered Mrs. R, the socialite Pauline M., and the "invalids" of Colorado Springs, who live on isolated ranches, drive their own motorcars, ride astride little burros, and camp out, things they would never have done in the East, seem to have undergone a metamorphosis of health and spirit in the West. Shedding their timidity and elite fastidiousness to embrace a more cheerful and energetic spirit, they are proof to Post of a change in character that she ascribes to a change in place. For Post there is something in the air, a "rejuvenating radiance" (225), that lifts the human spirit and makes the West and its inhabitants different, more vital than in the East. Exulting in its effect on herself, she claims at the end of the western section of *By Motor to the Golden Gate*, "I feel as though I had acquired from the great open West a more direct outlook, a simpler, less encumbered view of life" (240). Despite her claim that the spirit of the West is more geographic than ethnological, Post's understanding is mediated by ethnology, myths, legends, stories, and films. Moreover, Post's own experience is shaped by both geography and ethnology, by the terrain and the roads she travels and by a culture of comfort that values interiors, the built environment, and a progress that refines the very openness the geographic West suggests.

Having crossed over into the West along the Lincoln Highway after traveling from New York City to Chicago in comfort and reporting on the journey in her own spirited style, in this second leg of the trip to San Francisco she contemplates what it means to be in the West and what comprises the Western spirit. When she reaches Cedar Rapids, Iowa, she enthusiastically exclaims, "It was the West, the real great, free, open West we had come to see. Ranches, cowboys, Indians" (*Motor* 88). Combining a sense of the geographic and ethnological, she thinks of the West in terms of landscape and culture, a cowboy culture no doubt informed by literature, dime novels, and movies. Even though she was a bit disappointed that Omaha was an "up-to-date and perfectly Eastern city" (99), she sees the "aspiration" to move "forward" (105), the energetic spirit that transforms the rawness of place. In many ways, Iowa, Post's gateway to the region, serves as a cipher for her complicated and at the same time simplistic ideas of the West. Like Iowa, Post's West is a conglomerate of the vast, open landscape, the mythic culture of the West, and material progress, which ironically closes the very frontier it simultaneously represents, illustrating the "Western Paradox" that Donald Worster describes.[1]

Driving out onto the "interminable distance" of the western prairies, the flatness and sameness of the scene, the unobstructed views of great distances, Post has a sense not just of the geography of the West but also of what that vastness represents. Gazing across the prairies, she has an "an impression of the lavish immensity of our own country": "Think of driving on and on and on and yet the scene scarcely changing, the flat road stretching as endlessly in front of you as behind" (*Motor* 114). The geography of the prairies, its open spaces, suggest to her the national spirit, an "American Imaginary" of "something bigger, simpler, worthier," even something "boundless and enchanted" (115) that would characterize the national spirit at its best. The West as Neil Campbell explains is often associated with the core values of "individualism, success, industriousness, masculinity, and a possessive attitude toward the land," as represented by the ranches, cowboys, and Indians Post hopes to see.[2] This is the West that enthusiasts of rugged individualism like Francis Parkman and Charles Lummis experienced as they physically tested themselves against its harsh conditions. For Post, committed to her own comfort instead of testing herself against the terrain, the western landscape suggests "directness of outlook, fearlessness, open-air customs of living, and an unhampered freedom from unimportant trifles" (130), a "more direct outlook, a simpler, less encumbered life" (240), freedom, expansiveness, and spunk, all of which represent her own version of western individualism. The immensity of the western spaces suggests to her not only great possibilities for personal transformation but also a vastness of mind and soul: "If only you could live with such vastness of outlook before you, perhaps your own puny heart and mind and soul might grow into something bigger, simpler, worthier." She writes that out in the endlessness of the prairies, "you feel as though mean little thoughts, petty worries, or skulking gossip whispers, could never come into your wind-swept mind again" (115).

No doubt hers is an idealistic view of life in the open West, informed by her transient experience as a tourist intent on journeying in comfort. But, as we have seen in other paeans to the open spaces of the West, there is a connection between a geography of open spaces and ideas of freedom, character, and potential. Similarly, Post conflates geographic spaciousness and personal freedom with a national ethos that is "bigger, simpler, worthier" (*Motor* 115) because it has the freedom and room in which to act. In the vanguard of the See America First movement that promoted American scenes, tourism, and patriotism, she see the mythic West as emblematic of the national spirit at its best, even as she occasionally forgets the reality of slick muddy roads, tricky stream crossings, and the difficult Raton Pass, to say nothing of the rustic accommodations.

Automobile travel in 1915 retained a more intimate relation to the road, the environment, and the locals than train travel, outside the more rustic choice of tramping. As motorists, the Post entourage could determine when and where to stop and how long to linger; they could meet strangers, picnic, and even car-camp along the way. But in the open-air car they were also at the mercy of the dust, against which they armored themselves with goggles, veils, and dusters, and the vagaries of western weather—the rain, hail, and snow between Trinidad, Colorado, and Las Vegas, New Mexico (*Motor* 142). They were also at the mercy of the roads, which became worse the farther west they went, especially when they turned south off the Lincoln Highway and onto a section of the National Old Trails Road, the old Santa Fe Trail. As part of the Good Roads Movement to assure drivable roads for automobile tourists, the National Old Trails system of historic roads and trails provided another transcontinental road system to unite the nation. Driving that section of the Old Trails Road in 1915 may have given Post an idea of what the road system meant to tell, "the story of American expansion, the story of the old trails, the story of the pioneer." In "Motor Routes to the California Expositions," published in *Motor* in March 1915, A. L. Westgard wrote, "It may be stated here that there is no paved road on the route west of Kansas City before reaching within a day's ride of the Pacific Coast, except short stretches near the larger towns, the improvements being confined to grading the natural soil and building bridges and culverts." Westgard advises that from La Junta to Trinidad, Colorado, recent improvements made the road "at least comfortable," but from Trinidad the going was rougher as the National Old Trials Road ascended "the convict-built scenic road up over Raton Pass" before crossing the New Mexico state line "over a very winding road into Raton."[3] In some ways, Post and her travel companions (her son Ned and cousin Alice) were pioneers of the emerging road system that had recently opened the West to motorcar travel.

Traveling so close to nature and the developing roadscape was daunting. Driving through Iowa, their car suffered three punctured tires and "zigzagged sideways, backwards, every way but forward" (*Motor* 82) as they slogged through mud. In Nebraska the roads encouraged speed even though the speed limit was twenty miles per hour: "You are approaching the race-way of America, and you, too, are going to race!" (112). Once on the southern route, upon making inquiries about the road from Colorado Springs to Albuquerque, they learned, "These people out here talk of being hauled through quicksand streams, or of clinging along shelf roads at the edge of a thousand-foot drop as though it were pleasant afternoon driving." The dip into New Mexico brought inquiries about Raton Pass: "This lady is going down to New Mexico. Do you know anything about Raton Pass?" Despite alarms about the pass, they decided to forge ahead, having been "imbued with the spirit of the West" and focusing more on adventure than comfortable travel (132–34). On the less developed roadways, the group had to ford streams and "ventur[e] into New Mexico ruts" (139). All of this wreaked havoc on the low-slung Mercedes: "Washed out roads, arroyos, rocky stretches, and nubbly hills. We just about smashed everything, cracked and broke the exhaust, lost bolts and screws, and scraped along on the pan all of the way [between Las Vegas, New Mexico, and Santa Fe]" (149). After enough of this kind of travel, the car "was in a seriously crippled condition," so that they shipped it and themselves on the train at Winslow, Arizona, for the rest of the journey to California (184). In these ways the geography of the West was real and personal, messy and inconvenient at times, not the abstract view of her paeans to the West. Rather, it was mediated by Post's mode of travel, by the motorcar and the roads traveled. Photographs that accompany the narrative testify to the condition of the roads and the effect on the vehicle, stuck in the mud and navigating the nearly nonexistent roads of the West, and on the exposed passengers bundled up against the weather.

Likewise, Post's understanding of the West was mediated by the stories of the old West. Despite her claim in *By Motor to the Golden Gate* that the West is

"To See the Sleeping Beauty of the Southwest, the Path Is by No Means a Smooth One to the Motorist," from Emily Post, *By Motor to the Golden Gate* (1916)

more geographic than ethnological, it is also a site of culture and a site shaped imaginatively by culture. Just as she had hoped when she initially crossed into the West, she sees near Pueblo, Colorado, "a cowboy galloping over the plains swinging a lariat," a herd of cattle, and a small caravan of covered wagons. She says of this little "frontier drama" that all that was otherwise needed was "a band of befeathered Indians on the warpath" (*Motor* 136), revealing the hold that culturally shaped stereotypes had on her ideas. The land was not "empty," as Baudrillard would put it.[4] It was inhabited not only by actual people and lifestyles but also by an imaginary shaped by a long history of storytelling and myth. Post did finally meet "two Indians on ponies," but instead of being on "the warpath" as she had imagined, they politely showed the Post entourage the way to Las Vegas, New Mexico, after they had gotten lost in a blizzard (142). Her thrill "at an encounter with a real live cowboy" was likewise punctured when a cowboy who had come roaring over the plains toward them, possibly to hold them up, she imagined, good-naturedly joined them for a picnic of sandwiches and ice cream (143–45). In her narrative she quickly describes the "little Mexican, or Indian, adobe villages" seen on the way into Santa Fe (147), and then writes her own metaphoric version of Santa Fe's founding, of the injustice and cruelty of Spanish conquest. She also notes the multicultural, exotic aspect of the town, "the color and picturesqueness" of its mix of Mexicans, Indians, and cowboys, claiming that "nothing less like the United States could be imagined" (152). After leaving Santa Fe, Post writes, the travelers find themselves in "the middle of an Indian reservation" (173) where they are forced to camp out because there are no hotels or towns nearby. Having heard enough tales about the marauding Navajos to frighten her, Post was not sure that she wanted to "sleep out in the wildest, loneliest country in the world, surrounded by the very Redskins . . . [of those] grewsome stories." But her imagined drama of the West was once again punctured when she was told, "The Indians are as peaceful as house cats now" (172). Fearful of sleeping on the ground because of her "abject terror of snakes," she confesses in her narrative that her fears of "prowling Indians, strange animals, spooks, [and] spirits" vanished as she looked at the night sky and "its sparkling purity" (182). Though vast and magnificent, the geographic West is not empty; full of life, it is also an ethnological location. It is the site both of the actual cultures of Mexicans, Indians, and cowboys and of the cultural imaginary shaped by the stories and myths that frame and mediate Post's experiences, even as she pokes fun at her own naivety.

By the time Emily Post journeyed west, cultural representations of the West, its landscapes, and peoples had long been part of the American imaginary. From George Catlin's famous portraits of Native Americans to Frederic Remington's and Charles Marion Russell's representations of mythic western characters, and Alfred Bierstadt's and Thomas Moran's immense paintings of the awe-inspiring natural formations of Yosemite, Yellowstone, and the Grand Canyon, to surveyors and ordinary folks with Kodak cameras, the West had been portrayed visually in painting, sculpture, and photography. Postcards and tourist pamphlets had crafted an image of the scenic West to support tourism and train travel. Written representations had appeared in travel narratives like the ones I have discussed as well as in novels such as Owen Wister's *The Virginian* (1902), the westerns by Zane Grey that began appearing in 1903, and short stories by Bret Harte and Mark Twain, who captured the gambling, venturous West. The western dime novel series (ca. 1860–1920) and the Deadwood Dick series (1877–1897) featuring archetypal western heroes popularized a mythic, fast-shooting, and rambunctious West. Wild West shows like Buffalo Bill Cody's and Wild Bill Hickock's began in 1872 to reenact the western drama for eastern viewers. And beginning with Thomas Edison's *Cripple Creek Barroom* (1898), followed in 1902 by his *Romance of the Rails* and Edwin S. Porter's 1903 *The Great Train Robbery*, motion pictures began to bring a make-believe, simulated West to viewers. These and other forms of popular culture would have helped shaped Post's geographic imagination, her expectations of what to find on her journey, what she called "the West of Bret Harte's stories, the West depicted in the moving pictures" (*Motor* 99).[5]

In some ways, the West that Post encountered was like a stage on which the American story, the story of the "lavish immensity of our own country" (*Motor* 113), was enacted. When she describes the lariat-swinging cowboy, the caravan of wagons, and the prospect of "befeathered Indians on the warpath," she compares the sight to a "drama" and a "scene in the moving pictures" (136). The "frontier drama" is a continuing reenactment of the drama of the contact zone, "the space of colonial encounters," set in motion by the actors moving across the vista, but the moving vehicle from which Post views the scene also converts the authentic moment into an artistic artifact. According to Andrew Gross, who studied western motor tourism, "the way landscape moves across a film screen mimics the way it slides [past] the windshield," so that it seems that the landscape, not the traveler, is in motion. Post demonstrates the confusing meeting of the authentic experience and the "filmic representation" when she says, about crossing the plains in the "days of the caravans and stagecoaches": "We might have been taking an unconscious part in some vast moving picture production." Actually, as she notes, they traveled on roads, not the trails of the past (135).[6] The imagined past, the reality of the present moment, and the metaphor of motion pictures intersect in this moment.

The West in Post's travel writing is both real and a version of the real, a production manipulated by various layers of art—the narrative, the photograph that accompanies it, and the imagined motion picture. The photograph she took to capture the "moving picture production" demonstrates how the motorcar frames the scene of the caravan they pass on the road, the photographer's view from within the car indicated by the front end that juts into the shot. Interspersing her narrative with photographs, she produces, Gross claims, "a low-tech version of the filmic representation" of her travels. Anticipating Baudrillard who wrote of the "screenplay" of the American desert viewed from the speeding car, Post creates her own version of the simulacrum from scenes that are framed by her moving car, illustrating the ways motion and the structure of the car shape her view and at least momentarily confuse reality and the "screenplay." These motion pictures, *"artificial paradises"* of travel, create an alternate reality framed by the car and popular culture that is juxtaposed against the intimate experience of the road with its mud and creeks that car travel also affords.[7] To drive home the point about the meeting ground between reality and imitation, Post writes of watching the staged reality of moviemaking in California: the façade of the

"A Glimpse of the West of Yesterday," from Emily Post, By Motor to the Golden Gate (1916)

movies, the hollow built set, choreographed action, and actors who both imitate and enact reality. Post writes that the "injured face of the heroine was only red paint" (*Motor* 205) but then notes the actual blood streaming from the head of the daredevil movie star who purposely drove his car into an oncoming train as part of the movie. The uncanny meeting ground in the movies of simulation and reality, of actual blood and red paint, points to the intersections between realism and representation that produce, like Post's narrative, an intimate and framed, staged, and simulated ethnological West.

Post's experience of the geographic and ethnological West is mediated and contained as well by the interiors, hotels, and staged tourism she encounters. Taking time to describe the furnishings and amenities of the various hotels from New York to California, she notes, "If you are a transient tourist, it is the room you are shown into that necessarily colors your impression of that city" (*Motor* 88). As she said, the dingy hotel in Cedar Rapids with its "bottle-green paper," stained carpet, plumbing that did not work, and a "depressing view of a torn-up street" (87) colored her impression of that city and drew the ire of readers when her article first appeared in *Collier's*. Indeed, much of her descriptive power goes to describing the hotels and interiors of buildings she visited, such as rooms at the Hotel Potter in Santa Barbara, with their "white enamel and shadow chintz furnishings" and great bouquets of roses (199), homes and decor throughout Southern California ("[with] combinations of color that fairly set your teeth on edge") (190); and the Mirasol Hotel, "a sort of post-impressionist *ne plus ultra*, in housekeeping," with its groups of bungalows, flowers, bathrooms, "rose-chintz sitting-room," and super-modern furnishings (202–3). In Riverside, the combination of the "beauty of a Spanish palace," the "picturesqueness" of old missions, and "the most perfect modern comfort," makes the Mission Inn "worth traveling" to (192), as if it were the object of travel. Instead of only providing a place along the journey to lay one's head for the night, hotels in 1915 were becoming tourist destinations themselves. The coast between Los Angeles and San Diego, she notes, is "one long succession of big ocean resort hotels" (192), their advertisements vying for travelers as they describe the "imposing hallway" and the "gorgeousness" and luxury of the built space (187–88). The hotel had become such an important part of the travel experience that Los Angeles named herself the "City of Hotels," and its advertisements touted the hotels instead of the other sites of possible interest to tourists (188). Indeed, the hotels frame the tourist experience for guests and contain them within their artificial environment, illustrating the ways the West of nature was being contained as it was promoted as part of the See America First campaign.[8]

If the hotel was a staging ground for tourism, cultural tourism staged the West for travelers as artifice intersected with and confused reality. Just as the hotels were becoming part of the tourist experience, so too were museums, performances, and exhibitions. Excited to see the West she had anticipated, Post finds that Cheyenne, Wyoming, is not the Wild West town she had imagined but rather a city with paved sidewalks, an imposing capitol, and modern buildings. She complains, "The West of yesterday was no longer to be found in Cheyenne!" Instead it has a yearly "Frontier Days" (*Motor* 118). Begun as a one-day cowboy roundup, Cheyenne's Frontier Days Celebration, billed today as the "World's Largest Outdoor Rodeo and Western Celebration," began in 1897. Post missed Frontier Days, the Cheyenne of legend, and the great herds of buffalo that travelers like Parkman had been able to chase. Instead, the only buffalo she sees was stuffed in a Des Moines, Iowa, museum, preserved for visitors who missed the real thing (91). Frontier Days and the stuffed buffalo are ciphers of what she experiences in her tour, a mix of western reality in the early twentieth century, the West of imagination, and the West of museums and staged events that preserve, reenact, stage, and curate western heritage and history.

The simulated, commercial West became obvious in the Southwest, in part because of the influence of the Harvey Hotel franchise. In 1876 an English immigrant, Fred Harvey, had opened a lunchroom at the Santa Fe rail station in Topeka, Kansas. Because of its success (and good food, service, and price), Harvey went into partnership with the Atchison, Topeka, and Santa Fe Railroad and opened more lunchrooms along the line. Harvey devised a system to efficiently serve food to travelers and hired young women as waitresses, the Harvey Girls, who were "a signature component of Harvey's success and one of his most enduring legacies." In conjunction with the Santa Fe line, Harvey built a food, hotel, and tourism empire that promoted the Southwest. Shaffer notes, "By the 1920s Santa Fe/Harvey opened over a dozen major hotels and had established its famous Indian Department for collecting and selling Native American arts and crafts. . . . Through this symbiotic partnership, Santa Fe/Harvey built a systematized tourist infrastructure . . . to market and sell a standardized tourist product: the Southwest." A "pioneer of cultural tourism," Harvey also "employed Native Americans to demonstrate rug weaving, pottery, jewelry making and other crafts at his Southwest hotels. The sales of those items in Harvey's stores influenced the design of native arts." This complicated the relationship between the authentic and the imitation, the simulacrum.[9]

Post writes, "Stopping at the various Harvey hotels of the Santa Fé system, not being travelers on the railroad, is very like being behind the scenes at a theater. The hotel people, curio-sellers, and Indians are the actors, the travelers on the incoming trains are the audience. Other people don't count." In the first instance of her behind-the-scenes look, Post describes the efficient way that lunch is served to a newly arrived train full of people. Hearing the shout "Twenty-six!," she then watches how "with the uniformity of a trained chorus . . . a flurry of white-starched dresses [runs] back and forth," and twenty-six places are set and "slices of toast and soup in cups" appear before the twenty-six train passengers arrive. Then she watches as the "white-aproned chorus [carries] enormous platters of freshly grilled beefsteak, and . . . savory broiled chicken" and pours cups of coffee, tea, and chocolate (*Motor* 160–61). Because she is not one of the twenty-six, Post must wait for lunch as all attention is focused on the train passengers who have to be fed and back on the train in good time. The well-known Harvey efficiency is presented by Post as if it were a choreographed dance in which each one knows her part, a dance of aprons, platters, and cups.

The second scene of the great drama or "comedy" is acted out on the platform of the Albuquerque train station. When a train comes in, "out of nowhere appear dozens of vividly costumed Navajos and Hopis" with blankets, beads, and silver ornaments to sell, crying out "'Tain cent!' 'Tain cent!'" The Native women arrange themselves and their goods in two rows between the train and the station, remaining silent until the first passengers alight when they begin their "chorus" of two words, apparently the only English words they know (*Motor* 162). The reality is that Native peoples had lost much of their traditional ways of sustaining themselves in the face of white encroachment and had taken to making crafts specifically for a market of tourists and posing as picturesque characters for the passing trains of tourists. Participating in a "souvenir market," the Natives had transformed "authentic traditional crafts . . . of use value" and themselves into commodities for the traveling public.[10] They had learned their part as "exotics" in the elaborate tragicomedy of culture tourism and commodity tourism.

"The third Harvey scene," Post writes, "is frankly a vaudeville performance of Indian dancing and singing." The stage is the Indian exhibit room of the Alvarado Hotel in Albuquerque that displays and sells Indian crafts (*Motor* 162–63). After dinner, tourists take their place on benches arranged along the walls to watch the Native Americans dance. Post describes the typical step as "a sort of shuffling hop" accompanied by "a droning chant or . . . a series of sounds not unlike grunts." She also notes the dress of the performers; the women mix American shoes and dresses with traditional blankets while the men are "much more picturesque" with their velvet shirts, silver belts, turquoise jewelry, and red headbands. She acknowledges that, for the "Anglo-Saxon" audience, the dance is very monotonous, but it is otherwise for the Navajos and Hopis: "Dancing to them is a religious ceremony, not merely an informal expression of gayety" (163). This suggests the disjunction between entertainment and ritual. She gushes over the collection in the exhibit room, "probably the most wonderful collection of their crafts that there is." There she meets a collector for the Harvey Company, probably Herman Schweizer, whose conversation is focused on the monetary value of items in the collection and his "business dealings" with Indians, whom he claims have "no idea of credit" (164–65).

Three acts of a managed experience by Harvey, three acts in the vaudevillian variety performance of dancing plates, chanting sellers, and dancing Indians, all set against a background of colorful crafts demonstrate how the tourist experience is efficiently regularized as the authentic is converted into theater and consumables for tourists. An example of imperial nostalgia, "where people mourn the passing of what they themselves have transformed," tourists in the Harvey system are partners in the "commercialization of culture and cultural products" and the restructuring of cultural products into "crafts" for sale as souvenirs of the trip and the past.[11] Even when not organized by Harvey, excursions to the pueblos, to Laguna, Acoma, and Isleta, where "lots of tourists go" (*Motor* 170), participate in the commercialization of culture. Indian guides take tourists up the cliff sides of Acoma, "the skyland citadel of enchantment" and open their village, "a prehistoric Aztec citadel of communal houses" occupied by people living as they did "hundreds of years ago," to transient tourists, "to an average, ignorant tourist" who does not stay to learn their history (178–79). As Post's narrative demonstrates, the tourist's experience of the West, like her own, is mediated by structures of tourism, whether managed by Harvey or the Indians themselves. While she may go up to Acoma and peek into their homes, hers is a temporary and managed experience, part of the cultural tourism of the Southwest.

The California exposition at San Diego and the Pan-American Exposition in San Francisco that inspired Post's journey comprise the most obvious examples of the mediated experience of the West. Both exhibitions were extensive, extravagant built environments to celebrate technological and commercial progress. The San Diego Exhibition celebrated the opening of the Panama Canal and the ambitions of San Diego as the first American port of call for ships coming north from the canal. Built on an architectural theme to suggest Spanish history and the settings of Helen Hunt Jackson's popular novel *Ramona*, the exposition was "designed to show by actual demonstration what could be accomplished in our own land of the West" (*Motor* 193). The exhibits that caught Post's eye included agricultural models of a citrus grove and a grain farm. She was also struck by the Indian exhibits and "a life-size model of the pueblo of Taos" (194). The Pan-American Exposition in San Francisco highlighted the city's grandeur and emergence from the 1906 earthquake that had devastated much of the city. An extravaganza, it brought over eighteen million people to travel through its international pavilions, enjoy its sports and cultural displays, and witness new technologies, including a transcontinental telephone call by President Woodrow Wilson. Post enjoyed viewing the exhibits of the states and nations gathered at the exposition, the camper who tossed flapjacks, the Mexican who made "anchillades and tomales," and those preparing other international foods given away to the visitors. It was a place where you could meet for dinner at the Chinese Pavilion "that had nothing Chinese about it except its Chinese ornamentation" (234). She notes the Samoan village and the scantily clad Samoan queen, who after her performance mingled with the audience, breaking thus through whatever veneer of realism her dance intimated. She also notes the Court of Abundance and exhibits that represent ideas of progress, the replication of a Ford motor assembly line, the Sperry Flour and the Fuller paint company displays, and the feats of an "aeronaut" at Aviation Field. These exhibitions, done on a large scale, allowed cities to promote themselves and visitors to sample cultures, technologies, and industries in a zone of replication, giving them a taste of "anchillades" without having to journey to Mexico. In these ways the exhibitions mediated the travel experience for Post and the other visitors. All was managed, replicated, and commercialized. It was almost like shopping at Gump's, San Francisco's "most celebrated shop" (221), for Japanese and Chinese goods without actually visiting the ethnic enclaves in the city, much less the countries themselves.

Although Post hoped to experience the old West of legend, of cowboys and Indians, what she encountered was a New West mediated by transportation, technological, and commercial progress as well as by an increasingly sophisticated tourist industry. Glancing at the newspapers of the cities she visited, Post saw sentences that shouted "'Enterprise, confidence, civic pride are what make the citizenship of our city!' 'Des Moines is ever moving forward!'" (*Motor* 94) and stories that celebrated "the spirit of the people," unity, harmony, energy, enterprise, civic pride, and devotion (105–6), all signs of progress. She found Colorado Springs to be a blend of western characteristics with eastern "cosmopolitan society" (119) and in the ancient city of Santa Fe noted an odd mix of old and new ("Besides big modern automobiles are Indians leading little burros") (153). Indeed, her car, an emblem of the mix of modernization and "authentic" travel, is the central visual image of the narrative. Poised against the mountains or the stark desert, the ancient geologic, geographic West, the car, a product of human invention, emblematizes the mix of the modern and the ancient in her photographs. By putting the car at the center of photos, she suggests its centrality in the new West. She also suggests the intersection of the geographic with the ethnological, the landscape with the cultural object. Seen through the camera lens, the motor vehicle is both a part of the landscape yet distinct from the landscape that forms the background of the picture. Although Post posed the difference between the geographic and the ethnological West, in fact they intersect in the travels and the record of the travels, the ethnography her text constructs of the culture of travel.

Like these pictures, her experience of the West is a mix of the geographic, the openness of the West, and the ethnological, its diverse cultures; it is a mix of the terrain and the built environment, of adventure and comfort, of the natural and the technological, of the real and the simulated, the past and the future. Through this mix, Post creates a narrative of an authentic experience that she describes as transformative. Even though she claims that she is a "transient tourist" intent on her personal comfort, she also claims that her travels in the West have transformed her: "When we started, I had an idea that ... we would

"Across the Real Desert," from Emily Post, *By Motor to the Golden Gate* (1916)

find it probably difficult, possibly tiring, and surely monotonous—to travel on and on and on over the same American road. . . . Was there ever such variety?" (*Motor* 238). "I suppose the metamorphosis has come little by little all across our wide spirit-awakening country, but I feel as though I had acquired from the great open West a more direct outlook, a simpler, less encumbered view of life" (240). She has done things, such as sleep in the open air, and seen places, like Santa Fe, that she never imagined she would. She has felt the rejuvenating spirit of the western air. Such is the experience that travelers desire, what they hope for—something that puts them in contact with the resources of the self through journeying. By writing about her excursion from New York to San Francisco, Post has given readers an imagined rejuvenation of spirit, a moment of hope on the cusp of national transformation and rediscovery.

The SOUTH

*F*ollowing two main routes, down the Mississippi River and down the eastern seaboard to Florida, northern travelers to the US South chart journeys into a land both lush and troubled, a region of environmental and cultural differences, of "divisions, arguments, and complications."[1] Environmental differences mark travelers' understanding of the South as an exotic landscape, an elsewhere of fecundity that made the South a tourist destination in the nineteenth century, a way to leave home without going abroad. Yet even as the century progressed and transportation technology changed, travel to and around the South continued to be challenging, chaotic, a sign of the intentional incompetency of the South that supports racism and cotton, as Frederick Law Olmsted would put it.

Dating from John James Audubon in search of birds to sketch for his *Birds of America* in 1820, travelers from the North paid attention to the changes in weather and flora—the Spanish moss, the spikey yuccas and swamps of Florida, the flowers of Baton Rouge—that let them know they were in the South. The botanizing John Muir found that the farther south he went, the more unfamiliar the natural environment as he sketched a biocentric ecology that had a place for even the venomous animals and thorny plants.

Travelers also pondered the southern condition to get at an understanding of the persistent racism, the "problem of the color-line" that W. E. B. Du Bois identified, and the ways that history haunted the South. Overlaid with evidence of a violent history and the inescapable racism that propelled so much of it, their narratives recounted visits to monuments to the past, Bryant and Woolson's fictional tourists visiting the Spanish forts of St. Augustine, and Twain recounting a stop in Vicksburg. Most conspicuous to these travelers was race, the institution of slavery, and the humbuggeries of the past that conspired against the technological and commercial progress of the New South. From the economic and sociological examinations of the South and "the cotton kingdom" by Olmsted, Twain, and Du Bois to critiques of the ethics of sightseeing, these travelers noted the tension between the ideals of America and the promises of its natural world against the violence and brutality fed by greed and racism, in what might be called the southern paradox.

John James Audubon

Migrating with the Birds

JOHN JAMES AUDUBON WAS a birder, an ornithologist, a naturalist, a painter, and a writer. He was also a restless traveler. Having suffered financial ruin in the Panic of 1819, his budding mercantile business bankrupt, Audubon decided in 1820 to take a journey to New Orleans, his second one, to continue work toward his great book *Birds of America*. He also went to raise money to support himself and his family, whom he left behind for what he thought would be a seven to eight months' absence. By the time he decided to take this journey, he had moved from Saint-Domingue (Haiti), where he had been born on his father's sugar plantation, the child of an illicit liaison, to France, where he grew up during its period of political turmoil. Leaving France for the United States to avoid conscription in Napoleon's army, he located first in Mill Grove, Pennsylvania, where he met his wife Lucy Green Bakewell in 1804. To secure his father's permission to marry, he returned briefly to France and then went back to the United States. Married, he and Lucy moved to locations in Kentucky and Ohio, while he carried goods for his mercantile business along the Ohio River to St. Genevieve, Missouri, and then tried to find work after the business failure. Restless and energetic, he was no stranger to travel in an era when it could take months to journey across the sea or into the back country of the new nation. Nor would he stay at home after the expedition to New Orleans, continuing to follow the birds and his ambition wherever they took him. Like many of the birds he followed in his many peregrinations, his life's story is one of migration.

The narrative of the expedition to New Orleans, "Mississippi River Journal," charts his journey down the Ohio River to its juncture with the Mississippi River and then down that great river to Natchez and New Orleans. Ostensibly written to his son Victor, the journal not only maps his course for the family to follow, it also gives readers a view of travel and life along the Mississippi River in 1820. Simultaneously it draws a picture of the abundant and varied flora and fauna of the Mississippi basin. Audubon was driven by "an astonishing desire to see much of the World, & particularly to Acquire a true knowledge of the Birds of North America" ("[in order to] finish My Collection"), and he shapes his narrative around intersecting purposes—to record the travel itself, to communicate with the family he left at home, and to gather information about the birds of the Mississippi River region. Seeing, shooting, and drawing birds not only drive the journey, they also shape the travel narrative and the autobiography of Audubon the traveler. The birds are the subjects of intellectual, naturalist study and of artistic representation, but they also additionally operate as metaphors of travel and self, of migration and identity, as the emotional center of the narrative. Danny Heitman notes that "the birds he chronicles became not merely objects of scientific data, but characters in a dramatic narrative." While Heitman is thinking about a novelistic narrative of the life that Audubon charts in his many documents, his observation aids us in understanding the tone and trajectory of the travel narrative, the ways the verbal collections of birds, the lists he makes, provide an order of meaning, a narrative that is implied by and behind the lists.[1]

Audubon begins the journal: "Thursday—Ohio River Oct—12th 1820 / I left Cincinnati this afternoon at half Past 4 'oclock, on Board of Mr Jacob Aumack's flat boat—bound to New Orleans—the feelings of a Husband and a Father, were my Lot When I Kissd My Beloved Wife & Children with an expectation of being absent for Seven Months" ("Journal" 3).[2] In this first entry, he mentions his traveling companion, Joseph Mason (who will help with the drawings), the condition of the river ("Low"), the weather ("fine"), and how many miles they traveled (fourteen). He also notes: "Shot Thirty partridges—1 Wood Cock—27 Grey Squirrels—a Barn Owl—a Young Turkey buzzard and an Autumnal Warbler . . . the young of the Yellow rumped Warbler . . . a Young Male in beautiful plumage . . . and I drew it" (3). Here we can see how the interests of the journey and the narrative intersect, the mundane details of travel cutting across the activities of the naturalist and woodsman, the pull of family against the ornithological purpose of the journey. We also see the ways the organizing principles, the chronological and spatial plot of travel and the collector's lists, shape the narrative. A story of departure from family and home, the journal relates restlessness and discovery as well as finding self on the river and through the activities of seeing, collecting, and drawing birds.

Like many travel narratives, the journal is organized by date, location, and miles traveled. As well, Audubon records the changing weather conditions as an indicator of location in time and space. He writes, for instance, "Sunday 10th December 1820 / We floated down to the *Caledonian point* or *Petit* Landing about 4 Miles above the *real* Mouth of *White River*" ("Journal" 45). And: "Sunday, December 17th 1820 / Raining all day, I finished my Drawing—Landed at *Pointe Chico*" (53). He notes the frost on Monday, October 16, the "Gale" on November 2, and the "Indian Summer" on November 3 (5, 8, 9). This kind of record-keeping charts the journey chronologically and spatially, giving his readers (his son Victor, his wife Lucy, and today's readers) a way to locate him and his progress down the river. The entries also provide a view of the conditions of travel, the changing terrain, and the people he meets or sees along the way, the business of traditional travel narratives.

Traveling on a cargo flatboat captained by Jacob Aumack, Audubon left Cincinnati headed for New Orleans. He signed on as the boat's hunter, giving him the opportunity to take the boat's skiff to explore the local environs in search of game and birds that he would collect and then draw as the boat followed the current first westward to Missouri and then south to New Orleans. Time and again Audubon arranged a dead bird with wires on a mounting board so that the posed creature looked almost alive, and thus he drew the birds as he traveled downriver. The flatboat on which he traveled was a common way of navigating the nation's interior rivers. Flatboats had been a common means of transportation on the Ohio and Mississippi Rivers since at least the passage of the Northwest Ordinance of 1787. During the thirty to forty years of the heyday of flatboat travel, "probably a million people lived in them for weeks at a time, during journeys of from three hundred to two thousand miles." A flatboat was basically a flat-bottomed boat with a cabin on top where people and cargo could be somewhat protected from the weather. Because it lacked locomotion, the "flatboat floated at the mercy of the current," making about 4–5 miles per hour. Audubon's biographer, Richard Rhodes, estimates that he averaged fourteen miles a day from Cincinnati to the Ohio River's juncture with the Mississippi River.[3] The entire journey to New Orleans took just about three months, Audubon arriving in that city on January 7, 1821.

In addition to the flatboat on which he floated, Audubon noted a variety of travelers and boats along the way, providing readers a glimpse of life in the early republic. On November 24 they passed a family of three in two skiffs, "Too Lazy to Make themselves comfortable" ("Journal" 26). Like a flatboat, the skiff was wide and flat-bottomed, but it lacked the protective cabin or hut of the flatboat, hence Audubon's disdain for the skiff travelers who must have ridden exposed to the weather. At the confluence of the Ohio and Mississippi he saw two Indians in a canoe, trappers who "spoke some French" and "Looked so Independent, free, & unconcerned with the World that I Gazed on them, admired their Spirits, & Wished for their Condition" (21). On November 30 they passed nineteen flat-boats (34), and on December 3 they were passed by three "Keel boats" (37). On December 6 as they passed the St. Francis River confluence he saw settlements on its banks as well as a "Tolerable sized Plantation," his "first Mississippi Kite," and the "steam boat Paragon" (40). The *Paragon* was one of the early steamboats that had begun making the journey from Louisville to New Orleans, completing the voyage in just under nineteen days in 1819. On December 10 near the mouth of the White River they met another group of Indians, "2 Canoes of Indians from the *Osage Nation*" (45), with whom they shared a dram of whiskey and traded for two venison hams. The Indians they meet along the river suggest the intermingling of the races and adaptability of Native Americans to the condi-tions of white settlement despite the wars that had been waged against them. Then on December 12 he met the "*Steam Boat* the *Maid* of *Orleans*" ("on board of Which I put a Letter for My Dearest Friend My Wife") (49). As steamboats began to speed travel, the Post Office Department issued contracts for them to carry mail and deliver it, upon docking, to local post offices. "By the 1820s, more than 200 steamboats regularly served river communities," allowing travelers like Audubon to send and receive mail, even though there was often quite a time lag between posting, delivery, and response. As this quick survey illustrates, a mix of craft, from canoes to early steamboats, and a mix of peoples—Indians, settlers, and traders—plied the inland rivers at a time when the young nation balanced for a moment on the cusp of modernity as developing transportation technology began to diminish time and space. By 1828 the time to steam from Louisville to New Orleans was reduced to eight days, and by the 1850s it was down to four days, a far cry from the three months it took Audubon's flatboat to carry him to New Orleans.[4]

Because the flatboat provided shelter for the night and Audubon brought in game for their meals, the group did not interact much with the villages they passed along the way. Even so, Audubon briefly comments on the living con-ditions he observed. The section of the Mississippi River from New Madrid, Missouri, to Natchez, Mississippi, appears to have been poor, underdeveloped, or exhausted. Audubon remarks on the devastation still evident in New Madrid after the 1811 earthquake, calling the town "one of the poorest" on the river ("Journal" 23). He comments that near the White River they came upon a "Setlement Owned by a Frenchman" who helped the travelers find their way to "the only Tavern in the Country," which offered a room with "3 Beds containing 5 Men.'" The mental picture of Audubon trying to get comfortable on a "Homespun Bedstead" adds humor to the scene (45–46). The Arkansas Post, where he stayed for a night, once a flourishing trading post and fort under the French and Spanish and for a brief time in 1819 the capital of the new Arkansas Territory, was "a poor, Nearly deserted Village," Audubon writes, with "Wornout Indian Traders and a few American families" (47). But once Audubon emerged from the poverty of Arkansas into the cotton South, the terrain and the towns seemed to change, to show the effects of a lush terrain, warmer weather, and a long history of settlement by the Spanish, French, and Americans. On Sunday, December 17, 1820, Audubon writes of seeing his first "Spanish Beard" (Spanish moss) as well as cotton, corn, and peach and apple trees. On the next day he watches "immense flocks of Parokeets and Swamp *Blackbirds*" and kills ten of the parakeets for his hunting dog Dash, who had just birthed ten pups (53–54).

The day after Christmas, they arrived at Natchez, which was founded in 1716 by French settlers, then turned over to Spain after France was defeated in the French and Indian War, and finally claimed by the United States after the American Revolution. Before steam-powered boats that could go upstream against the strong currents of the Mississippi, traders from the Ohio Valley would unload the cargo from their flatboats at Natchez and return home overland on the Natchez Trace. Audubon arrived at a time of transition as the first steamboats were appearing on the river, competing with and changing the established methods of travel and trade. Seeing "Large Rafts of Long Logs" set to go downstream to New Orleans, he also writes that the shore was "Lined by Steam Vessels Barges & flat Boats" and says "Hundreds of Carts, Horses and foot travellers Are Constantly, meeting and Crossing" ("Journal" 59), demonstrating the importance of Natchez as a trading center. Natchez was really two cities. The lower town along the shoreline was marked in Audubon's day by "ware Houses, Grogg, Chops, [and] Decayed Boats" and the "carrion crows" (black vultures) that consumed the immense trash of the city. In the other part of the city, on the bluffs, Audubon reports on having found a more cultured society, a theater, "Bales of Cotton," a jail and courthouse, "Two Miserable Looking Churches," a bank, a post office, a public reading room, and two printing offices (60). He proclaims, "Natchez's Hotel is a good House built on the Spanish plan," and he relates his awkwardness at once again handling a fork and plate at dinner after the rougher mealtime conditions on the flatboat (62). Native Americans made part of the scene, providing meat for the Natchez citizens: "Indians are Daily seen here with different sorts of Game—for which they receive high Prices." Racially diverse but not racially equal, the remains of "an Ancient Spanish fort" serving as the burying ground for enslaved people, Natchez was an established port and trading center when Audubon arrived. He lingered about a week, drawing some portraits to raise money. But, in his haste to depart, he left behind his portfolio of birds and the miniature of his wife, much to his dismay (64).

From Natchez to New Orleans he continued to note the boat traffic on the river ("Many flat boats, 3 Steam Boat and 2 Briggs waiting for Cotton") and to remark on the changing terrain ("the Lands are flattening fast—the orange trees are Now and then seen Near the Rich Planter's habitation—and the Verdure Along all the Shore is very Luxuriant and agreeable") ("Journal," 65). The levees along the Mississippi built to protect towns from floods cut his view of the land so that he saw only the upper windows and roofs of buildings and the tops of trees. Passing the plantations that front the river, he notes, "Flat Boats are Landed at nearly every Plantation [to conveniently ship goods]." "Travellers on horse Back or Gigs go by us full Gallop," he writes, suggesting the business of plantation life. Near one plantation they were visited by a group of "french Creoles," who spoke neither "french English nor Spanish correctly" ("[they] have a Jargon composed of the Impure parts of these three"). The white, unpicked cotton still on the boll so that it "Looked Like if a Heavy Snow had fell and frozen on every Bud" contrasts with the dark green of the woods. "The Moss on every [tree] darkens the under growth and affords to the melancholy Mind, a retreat" (65–68). He gives a quick view of plantation life at Monsieur Amand's sugar plantation ("the finest Plantation we have seen"), which produced "about 400 Hogsheads of Sugar" and had about 70 "Negroes" overseen by a Black man who "Spoke roughly to his under servants but had a good indulgent Eye" ("[He] No doubt does what he Can to Accommodate, Master and All"). "The Miserable Wretches at Work begged a Winter Falcon We had killed" (72), Audubon writes, suggesting the poverty of their lives and diets. Audubon does not comment any further on the slave system, perhaps because he had been born on his father's Caribbean plantation and had himself owned about nine slaves before he lost his business to the Panic of 1819. In fact, he had taken two slaves with him on the earlier trip to New Orleans and sold them to fund his return home.[5] Now he turns his eye to the landscape, the treeless sugar plantations and gardens where

"Roses in full bloom revive the Eye of the Traveller who for Eighty Days has been confined to the Smoaky inside of a Dark flat bottomed Boat" (72).

On January 7, 1821, he landed at New Orleans, a city with a cosmopolitan mix of immigrants from Europe and the northern states mingling with the established creole residents and African Americans, both free and enslaved. One of the most important ports in the world because of its location on the Mississippi River and easy access to the Gulf of Mexico, New Orleans traded in cotton, sugar, and slaves, made easier with the advent of the steamboat. It was a commercial, banking, and cultural hub reflecting the old French influences tempered by American and West Indian tastes. Audubon witnessed much of this mix of people and affluence. There he met the famous painter John Vanderlyn and worked for a time for an Italian painter on theater sets. He also met up with some of his friends, such as Nicholas Berthold, showed his pictures to such dignitaries as the British consul, and joined "Mr. Arnauld" for dinner. After having been so long on the flatboat he noticed that the manners of Arnauld's guests rubbed him the wrong way: "We had a good dinner, and great deal of Mirth that I Call *french Gayety*, that really sickened me. I thought myself in Bedlam, every body talkd Loud at once" ("Journal" 73). Disliking the gaiety of the upper classes, he also criticized the hubbub and commotion of the city. While the market displayed a great variety of game—birds such as mallards, teal, geese, robins, and starlings—as well as both local and West Indian vegetables, it was also a place where petty thievery was common. Going out on Sunday, January 14, 1821, he noted, "The Levée early was Crowded by people of all Sorts as well as Colors, the Market, very aboundant, the Church Bells ringing the Billiard Balls knocking, the Guns heard all around." The cacophony of religious and secular noises must have been bewildering to a man who had spent months in the quiet of the river. He goes on to say, "I saw however no handsome Woman and the Citron hüe of almost all is very disgusting to one who Like the rosy Yankee or English Cheeks" (77), illustrating his own prejudices but also the number of mixed-race women parading on a Sunday morning.

Labeled today as Sportsman's Paradise, Louisiana in the early 1820s was the site of great migrations of birds. The passage of an immense flock of golden plovers brought out hunters who "assembled in Parties of from 20 to 100 at Diferent places" ("every gun goes off in Rotation"). Unmindful of the need to conserve nature, these hunters fired until approximately "144,000 must have been destroyed." Audubon relates, "A Man Near Where I Was seated had killed 63 dozens" ("Journal" 87). At a time before game laws, when hunting birds and even using them for target practice was acceptable, the men fired away at the birds unaware of the possibility of hunting them to extinction. As Ludlow Griscom observes in his introduction to the 1950 popular edition of *The Birds of America*, "Audubon has left us accounts of . . . rare and vanished birds." [6] These included the Carolina parakeet, the passenger pigeon, golden plovers, two species of which were on the 2016 North American Bird Conservation Initiative Watch List. Like the birds that have vanished, the New Orleans of 1820 lives only in art and in travel narratives like Audubon's.

Having spent about six months in New Orleans showing his drawings and trying to earn some money by teaching drawing, painting portraits, and picking up other odd jobs, Audubon was offered employment at Bayou Sarah on the Oakley Plantation teaching the teenage daughter, Miss Eliza ("[teaching] all I could in Drawing Music Dancing &c &c") and so found himself "bound for several Months on a Farm in Louisianna" ("Journal" 103). Although he gives an uncomplimentary view of the indulged upper classes of Louisiana plantation life, noting that "Mr. Pirrie" was often in "State of Intoxication," Mrs. Pirrie given to "Violent Passions," and Eliza spoiled and vain (125), Audubon focuses the journal on the natural landscape and the birds. When newly arrived at the Pirrie plantation, he writes, "The Aspect of the Country [is] entirely New to us," noting "the Rich Magnolia covered with its Odoriferous Blossoms," the red clay, and the "thousands of Warblers & thrushes." Impressed by the great difference in the natural world of the plantation, he confesses, "I enjoyd Nature" (104). With that, much of the rest of his journal about the months at the plantation center on his excursions into the woods and swamps looking for animals, sighting alligators, and collecting birds to draw. At times the journal becomes a list of birds he has sighted and short biographies of the birds like the chuck-will's-widow "in full and handsome plumage" that a Choctaw Indian brought him (111), the red-cockaded woodpecker, the "Louisiana warbler" (Louisiana waterthrush), and two species of ibis. Birds are the characters he most responds to during the sojourn at the plantation brought to life in his descriptions here and in his multivolume *Ornithological Biography* and in the paintings that he would publish in the monumental *Birds of America*.

More than simply charting his voyage in conventional ways and providing a view of southern life in 1820, the narrative converges around the activities of seeing, shooting, and drawing the birds, with the two organizing principles of the narrative, the chronological/spatial and the ornithological/natural, overlaid on and intersecting each other. As well, the trajectory of movement alternates with the collector's lists of birds. Christopher Irmscher contends that for early American naturalists "art and taxonomy meet in productive and seductive ways."[7] Likewise, in Audubon's travel writing, journey, art, and taxonomy meet in productive ways. As Audubon maps his journey by noting the date, weather conditions, and miles traveled, he also maps the game killed and the birds identified, collected, and drawn, naming and counting them. Because he had to supply fresh game for the crew on the flatboat and collect birds that he would draw, he pays attention to the natural life, giving it ample space in the journal. From the first entry when he notes the time he left Cincinnati, kissing his wife and children good-bye, and recording the number of miles traveled on that first day, he also lists the game that he and the other members of the boat shot and describes birds he draws, like the "Autumnal Warbler" "in beautifull plumage" ("Journal" 3). Similarly, other entries combine the usual matter of travel with information about local wildlife, counting the kills and sightings almost as one would count the miles and describing the wildlife and birds as one would describe the conditions of the road. Doing so, he crafts another way of tracking where he is and who he is, another kind of cognitive mapping. So on October 14 he locates himself by saying that they passed Laurenceborough and walked to Bellevue, but he also locates himself by counting the Fish Hawk he shot, the "Wild Turkey, 7 Partriges a Tall Tale Gowit and a *Hermit* Thrush [that was too] torn to make a drawing of it" (4). On October 16 he mentions the frost and being stuck on a sandbar, but he also relates that he drew a hermit thrush, giving a quick description and examining the contents of its stomach for scientific purposes (5–6). In the midst of the gale of November 2 as they passed Henderson, Kentucky, his former home, he remarks that he could make only a rough drawing and lists the birds they saw, ending the entry by saying, "extremely Anxious to be doing something in the Drawing Way" (8–9). On November 3, when he mentions Indian summer, he also lists what he killed—"4 Squirels—one Butcher bird—and a Swamp Blackbird"—and what he saw—geese, sandhill cranes, and ducks (9). The entry for November 14 is taken up with lists and quick descriptions of the birds seen and the "Imber Diver" (young red-throated loon) he finished drawing (17). He also gives a quick description of a "fin-tailed duck" (ruddy duck), giving its size (15.5 inches) and coloring: dark blue bill, "Legs & feet L. Blue" (18). On November 24, the day he saw the family on the skiff, he lists the game killed and the birds that he saw—"Carrion Crows" (black vultures), "Turkey Buzzards" (turkey vultures), and ivory-billed woodpeckers—noting as well that he spent "the greater part of the day drawing" ("Journal," 26). His entrance into the cotton South is likewise marked by the Carolina parakeet, the mockingbird, migrants that winter in the South ("our Summer Birds"), the chuck-will's-widow, and ibises. And so it goes, the descriptions of travel intersected by lists of game killed and birds seen, killed, and drawn.

Because the purpose of the journey was to add more birds to his collection of drawings, to provide material for what would become *Birds of America*, the birds provide trajectory and also constitute much of the emotional energy of the narrative. Having recovered the portfolio he left at Natchez, he takes much of the rest of the April 5 entry to list the drawings of birds the portfolio contains and then to relate how painted buntings are often caged and tamed as songbirds. He tells the story of one bunting that escaped its cage but returned within thirty days and remained in the cage for the rest of his life, as if it were his natural habitat. Though the miniature of Audubon's wife had just been returned to him, something he had fretted about, in this entry he takes more time to describe the habits of the bunting than to reminisce about his wife. In the entry for January 1, 1821, as one might expect, he reflects on his life, noting, "What I have seen and felt has brought some very dearly purchased Experience." This entry too is laced with locational markers of place, time, and natural environs, including the orange trees around Baton Rouge and the birds—"Irish Geese" (double-crested cormorants) and mallards ("Journal" 65). The July 4 entry, instead of thinking about the nation's birthday, is devoted to a list and quick description of the birds of Bayou Sarah—blue jay, "Yellow Bird" (goldfinch), Baltimore oriole (northern oriole), and a ruby-throated hummingbird. Moments that seem to call for reflection, for contemplation, are intersected and interrupted by the birds, the story of the caged buntings perhaps a metaphor for Audubon's wandering life and the recovery of the portfolio of drawings like the return of a lost part of the self. Indeed, the lists of birds he compiles in the journal contribute to his identity and become a kind of narrative not only of the journey but also of the self. Irmscher argues that, "gathering plants, birds, rocks, and artifacts," American naturalists not only contributed to knowledge of the natural world but also "in doing so . . . defined themselves," the collection being a reflection of the collector. This is certainly true for Audubon, who is remembered more for his painted collection of birds than for the details of his intimate life. More, the lists of birds and animals, the verbal collection of natural objects in the narrative, operate as plot devices and as a "root metaphor" of the life he relates.[8]

Although he gives a quick biographical sketch of his father for the benefit of his son (November 28, 1820), most of the journal's biographies are of birds, as if his relations with them stand in for human relations. Beyond giving ornithological descriptions, their measurements and colorings, he brings some to life by telling stories about them. Later he would write more extensive bird biographies for his *Ornithological Biography* (five volumes in 1831 and 1839), combining scientific observation with personal experience to describe the habits of birds as an accompaniment to the paintings in *Birds of America*. Anticipating this larger work, in the journal he wrote short biographies of some of the southern birds. This was a practice already established by ornithologist Alexander Wilson, who saw himself as "'the faithful biographer' of his birds, of their manners and dispositions" derived from personal observation.[9] In Audubon's hands these descriptions become more than scientific descriptions; they constitute part of his own life's story.

For instance, on July 29, while employed at the Pirrie plantation, he experienced an episode with some red-cockaded woodpeckers. As if they were human acquaintances, Audubon writes of the "pleasure of meeting" the birds, two males both wounded in the wing and giving off their characteristic cry. He notes that the tall pines are its usual habitat and describes the way they "cunningly" look under loose pieces of bark for insects. Using language that personifies the birds, he refers to them as cunning, shy, courageous, and stubborn. He tells how he put the two woodpeckers in his hat to carry them back to the plantation. When he would periodically check on them, he "found them trying to hide their Heads as if ashamed to have lost their Liberty." By the time he returned to the plantation one of them had died. The survivor he put in a cage, but the clever bird made his way out of the cage, using his "Chisel bill with great adroitness," and began climbing the brick walls, looking for insects in the cracks of the brick. Audubon comments that he "drew him in that Position," arguing as he does so with the drawing done by his rival Wilson, whose *American Ornithology* had recently appeared (1808–1814), saying how Wilson got the coloring of the red-cockaded woodpecker wrong. He ends this anecdote by remembering when he first met this species a few miles from Nashville, as if the woodpecker were indeed an old friend and his story a part of Audubon's life story ("Journal" 113–14).

The respect Audubon has for the bird and the care with which he relates this story indicate that the story of the woodpecker is as much about him as it is about the bird. The qualities of character he finds in the woodpecker might apply to him as well—cunning, stubborn, courageous, clever, and adroit despite hardships thrown in his way. While the biography of the bird is a part of his travel story, it also mirrors the self he shapes in the narrative. Audubon's adventure with the woodpecker, as with other birds, constitutes much of the adventure and plot of the travel narrative, shaping a trajectory that competes with the usual aims of travel writing. Moreover, just as charting the miles and locations of travel locates the journeyer, the "who I am" implicated by the "where I am," so charting the interactions with the birds maps the "Where do I belong?" By placing himself in the story of the woodpeckers, he positions himself as part of the natural ecology and creates an identity as a woodsman that would become his public persona. Part of the ecology, the birds whose stories he tells add a dimension to the ecology of the self he creates and travel translates.

Richard Rhodes surmises, "Studying birds was how he mastered the world, and himself."[10] That may explain why, finally reunited with his family, he began to ponder his next expedition, for more birds. As he writes the "Mississippi River Journal" for his son Victor, occasionally giving him some fatherly advice, Audubon constantly corresponded with his wife. He was anxious to send letters to her and receive letters from her, and he notes at one point that it has been twenty-six days since he has last heard from Lucy ("Journal" 146). Eager to reunite with her after eighteen months of being apart, he nonetheless ends the journal with a copy of a letter he wrote to Representative Henry Clay expressing his desire to "Explore the Territories Southwest of the Mississippi" for more birds for his collection (154). Perhaps like some of the birds he follows, he is a migratory being, restless and compelled to move. He belongs afoot in nature, looking for and drawing birds.

The South that Audubon experienced, the South along the Mississippi River, was one of contrasts, of opulence and poverty, of cultured sophistication and exuberant, abundant nature. It was a South of plantations and commerce, of travel up and down the great river road. It was a place where technological progress and modernization rubbed against a long history of colonization and settlement by the Spanish and French, some of their edifices already in ruins. Systems of slavery and conquest of the Native Americans were living reminders of the past, of a heritage that the modern South inherited and perpetuated. These views are just quickly glimpsed in the "Mississippi River Journal"—Audubon rarely comments on them—but they are present nonetheless. The South that caught Audubon's attention was the natural South: game to be hunted; birds to be counted, collected, and drawn; drooping Spanish moss and opulent magnolia blossoms; cotton and sugarcane. It was a South of natural abundance at a time when little thought was given to conservation and preservation outside of the museums like Peale's Philadelphia Museum and the Western Museum in Cincinnati that had begun collecting examples of nature and culture, stuffed birds and Indian artifacts. It was a time when naturalists, ornithologists like Audubon, sought to catalog, describe, and preserve in words and paint the abundant, diverse bird life of America, partly to describe the natural world and partly to define the United States. Irmscher calls *Birds of America* "one of the last evocations of America as the land of plenty, of vast unencumbered space inhabited by numerous species." Part of Audubon's legacy for us is that we can see in his work some of those vanished species of birds, his journal and his bird books creating textual museums of the past.

William Cullen Bryant and a
Tour of the South

IN THE SPRING OF 1843 William Cullen Bryant and his wife Frances undertook a tour of the South at the invitation of his friend and literary colleague William Gilmore Simms, an influential writer who became a spokesperson for southern literature, culture, and politics. The two had met in 1832 when Simms visited Bryant in his office at the *Evening Post*, inquiring as he did about a good boarding school for his daughter. That was the beginning of a decades-long friendship between the two men and their families. In fact, Simms's daughter would attend the same boarding school as Bryant's daughter Fanny, whom Simms invited in 1840 to spend the winter on his plantation, though Bryant decided against it due to Fanny's precarious health. In his letter to Simms expressing his decision that Fanny should remain home, Bryant wrote, "I have a strong curiosity to visit your part of the country. . . . If I can find the leisure and raise the wind as the saying is I may possibly be tempted to play truant towards spring."[1] Finally finding the leisure to "play truant," Bryant and Frances left New York on February 24, 1843, on a tour that would last six weeks. Sandwiched between his multiple trips to Illinois, Bryant's southern jaunt was documented as a series of six letters sent for publication in the *Evening Post*. The first letter, dated March 2, 1843, marked his arrival at Richmond, Virginia, and the beginning of an itinerary of southern tourism that would take him to some of the major cities of the South, Richmond, Charleston (South Carolina), Savannah, and St. Augustine, and to a three-week interlude at Simms's home, Woodlands, in Barnwell County, South Carolina, then called the Barnwell District.

His letters enabled readers to follow him south, giving them a quick view of the old South even though the letters generally avoided the personal and lacked the cognitive mapping of other narratives. His intent was to quickly present where he went and what he saw to the largely northern readers of the *Post* who hoped to be entertained as they were informed about the strange region of the South. Howard R. Floan describes these letters as "uncritical and affable . . . casual reports of things seen and done." Writing as a tourist, Bryant makes observations about the kinds of things one would expect, the warming climate, the remarkable flora of the South, its cities and monuments, points of interest in a tour that would extend to St. Augustine, Florida. Bryant remarks on the changing weather as they went southward from Washington D.C. as the March snow became "thinner and finally disappeared altogether." After leaving Savannah by steamer he feels he has "stepped into the midst of summer" and notes that the delightful if sultry weather of Florida will make it a place for northerners seeking the healing warmth of the southern climes. Indeed, sickly people and convalescents had already started wintering in St. Augustine because of its "salubrious" climate, making Florida a better and less expensive option than the West Indies for many. The young Ralph Waldo Emerson had wintered there in 1827, finding it a "queer place" offering little to do, even though "the air & sky" were "delicious." By 1860 a correspondent for the New York Times would claim, "Several hundred invalids and pleasure-seekers from the North spend the Winter here."[2]

With the warming climate, Bryant also delights in the array of plants and agriculture flourishing in the South. He maps the journey in part by naming the plants he finds, the "magnolias, their dark, glazed leaves glittering in the March sunshine" ("Tour" 23); the pine forests of North Carolina and the marshes of South Carolina; and the abundance of Florida, where he finds "everything green, fresh, and fragrant," the "wild roses in flower" (34). In St. Augustine he lists the pomegranate, orange trees "fragrant with flowers," the broad-leaved fig, and the flowering Pride of India tree (41). He describes the hummocks, small knolls or mounds rising from the marshes, chosen as sites of plantations because they were "a kind of oasis, a verdant and luxuriant island in the midst of these sterile sands" (35). Viewing the South's agricultural crops—tobacco, sugar cane, and oranges—he also criticizes the ways pine trees are destroyed by the collection of turpentine, which he calls "a work of destruction" (28). With swift brush strokes he also sketches the cities, the piazzas, and the plantations he views—Charleston's "spacious houses . . . surrounded with broad piazzas" and lush gardens (29), the beautifully laid out streets of Savannah, and the odd coquina buildings of old St. Augustine.

Bryant describes the chaotic travel in the South, particularly when he relates the various transfers between Richmond and Charleston, in and out of train cars and steamers: "About two o'clock in the morning we reached Blakely, on the Roanoke, where we were made to get out of the cars, and were marched in a long procession about a quarter of a mile down to the river. A negro walked before us to light our way, bearing a blazing pine torch . . . , and a crowd of ne-groes followed us, bearing our baggage" ("Tour" 27). Railroad building in the South, Seymour Dunbar explains, lagged behind the North in part because it was not as "restless as the North" and was more sparsely populated.[3] As Bryant's narrative demonstrates, travelers had to cobble together various conveyances to travel through the South in the early 1840s. Once he reached Florida, he would be transported by wagon for the eighteen miles between Picolata, where his steam-ship would have landed, and St. Augustine. During the ride, he was regaled by a garrulous driver who told him stories of murders committed by Indians, most likely during the Second Seminole War (1835–1842) which had only recently ended. The fort at Picolata had provided a supply depot, a hospital, and a base of operations during the war, and there a young William Tecumseh Sherman had a small part in dealing with Wild Cat, Chief Coacoochee, one of the Semi-nole leaders. Bryant mentions an episode shared by his driver about a group of Indians, thought by Bryant to be "Wild Cat's gang," who overcame a traveling theatrical troupe and adorned themselves in the "garb of Othello" and Richard the Third and Falstaff (40). In these ways Bryant deftly sketches travels in ways that would have entertained readers, sticking to a scripted itinerary and saying complimentary things about the region and southern manners, remarking on "the hospitality of the planters" (35) and claiming that southerners possess "the most polished and agreeable manners of all Americans" (29).

The South that Bryant toured was also overlaid by the past, its history com-memorated by monuments, ruins, and graveyards that became stops in the touristic itinerary. In Richmond, Bryant visits the oldest Episcopal Church in Virginia and its "burying-ground" "where sleep some of the founders of the col-ony," including the patriot Patrick Henry. As he travels down the James River, a place named Powhatan is pointed out to him as well as the rock where Captain John Smith was supposedly saved by Pocahontas ("Tour" 24). In Charleston, he visits Fort Moultrie, "breathing recollections of the Revolution" (28), anoth-er reminder of a past defined by British settlement and the revolution against English rule. Savannah was already old when Bryant stopped there, its public cemetery dating from before the Revolution and the Bonaventure plantation already abandoned, its ancient oak trees swathed in gray moss. "Of the mansion there are not remains," he writes (38), but he finds the cemetery, now famous for its statue of the bird girl featured on the cover of John Berendt's *Midnight in the Garden of Good and Evil*. In St. Augustine, the "oldest city of the United States," founded in 1565 by the Spanish, Bryant enters a region with a colonial past different from the storied past of New England and Virginia. Here he finds the Spanish influence mixed with English, Native, and Minorcan traditions.

Driving the narrow streets that lead to his hotel, Bryant encounters evidence of this past in the monument that commemorates the Spanish Constitution of 1812, the coquina building material unique to Florida, the old houses in ruins made of a stone that seems "a pure concretion of small shells." Noting the Minorcan population, a mix of Minorcans, Greeks, and Spaniards who speak their own language (a Catalan dialect) and continue to follow some of their old customs, Bryant captures their Palm Sunday rituals and songs. These people comprise "the remains of those who inhabited the country under the Spanish dominion" ("Tour" 41), forced as indentured servants in 1768 to leave Minorca to work on the plantation of Dr. Andrew Turnbull, a Scottish physician. Protesting the harsh conditions, they revolted from the New Smyrna plantation and migrated to St. Augustine in 1777. In St. Augustine, Bryant visits also the "old fort of St. Mark, now called Fort Marion, a foolish change of name" [in honor of Revolutionary War general Francis Marion]." Begun in 1672 to protect Spanish Florida against the British, it is the oldest masonry fort in the continental United States. There he sees evidence of past conflicts, cannonballs imbedded in the shell conglomeration of its walls, the "half-obliterated inscriptions scrawled on the walls long ago by prisoners," and secret cells in which he saw a wooden rack and "a quantity of human bones," possibly the result of the Inquisition in the Americas (42–43). Fort Marion is also the site where Seminole chiefs Wild Cat and Osceola were held prisoner during the Indian wars that spanned the century. With these quick descriptions, Bryant reminds readers that the South has a long history of settlement and conflict, going back at least to Spanish settlement, a past that is kept alive in the faces and speech of the Minorcans, the ongoing conflicts with Native Americans, and the graves and forts that continue as sites of both conflict and tourism.

Haunted not only by the past, the South that Bryant visited was also haunted by race and contemporary slavery. Travel south prompted many northern visitors to contemplate the political and humanitarian dilemma of race relations and slavery at the same time that southern Blacks were objects of the tourist gaze and part of the tourist experience. Indeed, readers expect travelers to the South to pay attention to race, race relations, and, before the Civil War, slavery. Bryant's observations about African Americans in his letters both fit expectations about travel narratives about the South and perplex readers. His comments that "the blacks of this region are a cheerful, careless, dirty race, not hard-worked, and in many cases indulgently treated" ("Tour" 34) and that slavery enacts compromises between master and slave read as naïve, insensitive, and willfully blind to the harsh realities of life for enslaved people.

Bryant was an outspoken critic of slavery, using editorials in the *Post* and his poetry to criticize it. "The African Chief" (1825), a poem that exposed the tragedy of slavery, would resonate as the *Amistad* case was being heard in the courts in 1839–1841. Knowing his reputation as an advocate for democracy and justice, critics are hard-pressed to understand what Bryant is doing in his comments in "Tour in the Old South." Generally, scholars venture that Bryant did not want to alienate his host—Simms—and other distinguished southerners by presenting a harsh picture of slavery. In his biography of Bryant, Gilbert Muller muses that during his tour of the Deep South "Bryant offered little commentary on the institution of slavery." He speculates, "Perhaps the generosity and grace of his hosts induced him to suppress an untoward mention of the South's peculiar institution" and his position as "a guest among the South's aristocracy" prompted him to forego overt criticism of the institution. In his biography of his father-in-law, Parke Godwin similarly explains why Bryant did not indulge in an overt criticism of slavery: "He regarded himself as the guest of the kind people who had opened their houses for his entertainment and comfort, and his sense of propriety would not allow him to return their good-will with unfriendly disclosures of what he had seen or heard." In a letter to a mutual friend, James Lawson, about Bryant's trip, Simms blames the "very wretched weather" during Bryant's stay and the fact that Simms's wife had just given birth for Bryant's circumscribed visits to the surrounding areas: "The consequence has been that he has had few opportunities of seeing either our people or our climate."[4]

If Bryant does not use his public travel letters to the *Post* to overtly criticize slavery, what does he do? How does he represent enslaved people and their lives in the letters? Although Simms lamented that Bryant had few opportunities to see "our people," he did get out for some southern entertainments during his three weeks in the interior of South Carolina: he had "been out on a raccoon hunt, been present at a corn-shucking; listened to negro ballads, negro jokes and the banjo; witnessed negro dances; seen two alligators at least; and eaten bushels of hominy" ("Tour" 30). When Bryant describes some of the activities of the corn-shucking, he resorts to racialized humor to suggest there is something entertaining or comic about the Blacks' rustic society. He describes their dances as "capering, prancing, and drumming with heel and toe upon the floor" and transcribes Toby's speech for "'de majority of Sous Carolina,' on 'de interests of de State,' and 'de honor of ole Ba'nwell district'" as part of the "frolic" the shuckers enjoy (33). At first glance, it seems that by using vernacular humor Bryant adopts a patronizing attitude toward the unschooled workers. But in ways that anticipate Harriet Beecher Stowe's 1850 characterization of Sam and Andy's capers and speechifying in *Uncle Tom's Cabin* when they attempt to delay the slave-catcher Tom Haley from setting out after the escaped Eliza, Bryant subverts the representation of blacks as "cheerful" and "careless" with quiet critiques of their situation. Indeed, concepts of democracy and citizenship lie behind Toby's speech, reminding readers that African Americans could only imitate but not participate in democracy. When Bryant transcribes two of their work songs of "comic character" (32) as interesting cultural artifacts, he also notes that they are "set to a singularly wild and plaintive air," here anticipating Frederick Douglass's claim, "Slaves sing most when they are unhappy. The songs of the slave represent the sorrows of his heart."[5] And when Bryant writes that the celebrants at the shucking "had performed their daily tasks and had worked all the evening [at the shucking], and some had walked from four to seven miles to attend" (33), he undercuts the seemingly easy compromise between the master who "has power of punishment on his side" and the slave who practices "an invincible indolence" that purchases a "imperfect and slovenly obedience" for "good treatment" (34). Quietly calling attention to the plaintive, sorrowful quality of their songs and the long hours atop long hours of toil, Bryant reminds readers of the difficulty of the "compromise" for the enslaved workers and creates a subtle counterpoint to the comedic moments and his apparent silence on slavery.

In other instances, he demonstrates their integrity through the work they do, their religiosity, and leadership. He shows Africans at work in the tobacco factory where "eighty negroes—boys they are called" rolled and cut plugs ("Tour" 25); at a sugarcane factory, "three negroes, well-clad young men" going about their work (46); and in the field sowing cotton with a "young white woman and a boy" (39). In these sketches of enslaved African Americans at work, he draws them as dignified, conscientious, and busy at their work. When he describes the songs the tobacco workers devise to help with the labor, he notes "a murmur of psalmody running through the sable assembly" (25). Commenting on the tunes that come from hymns and sacred music, he quotes his host who points out that "almost all these persons are church members." Bryant here reflects that the Baptist church in Richmond has "a congregation of twenty-seven hundred persons, and the best choir" (26) to indicate the importance of religion in the lives and culture of Black Americans. Rather than painting them as abused or degraded, Bryant shows that they endure their situation with dignity and a spirituality that permeates their lives.

When he visits the public cemetery in Savannah where whites are buried, he ventures "a little distance" to the "burial-place of the black population." Although composed primarily of "hundreds of nameless graves, overgrown with weeds," the graveyard also contains "half a dozen spacious brick tombs" and grave markers, some erected by owners to commemorate a favorite ("Tour" 36–37). Bryant pauses the narrative of his travels to summarize and quote from the "scattered memorials" to deceased slaves. These epitaphs point to the honesty of a young woman who perished in the catastrophe of the steamer *Pulaski*, loved ones departed too soon from life, and the religiosity and leadership of others—a cooper who was a member of the 2nd African Church of Savannah and Andrew Bryan, a "black preacher, of the Baptist persuasion" who was imprisoned and whipped for preaching but lived to the age of ninety-six (37–38). These few epitaphs testify to the dignity, integrity, and religiosity of a population, many of whose lives are unmarked and untold. By calling attention to them, Bryant gives individuality to their stories and lives that counter the silence of the un-marked graves and his own travel letters' silence on slavery. Although he does not overtly criticize slavery or present the harsh realities of the lives of enslaved people in his narrative of a six-week journey through the South, the subtext of his observations counters what seems superficially to be a naïve view of slavery and the lives of enslaved people.

INTERLUDE

A little over twenty years after Bryant and his wife toured the South and after the ending of the Civil War and the death of Abraham Lincoln, whom he elegized in "The Death of Lincoln," Bryant wrote "The Death of Slavery." This was the last poem he read to his dying wife, to which she "added some kind words of commendation." The poem was composed in May 1866 and published in the July 1866 issue of the *Atlantic Monthly*. Muller calls the poem "an extravagant rendition in verse of the nationalistic passion, religious fervor, and moral outrage that had characterized Bryant's editorials during the Civil War." Albert F. McLean Jr. observes that it uses "Gothic terror, religious piety, nationalistic fervor, and moralistic sentimentality in denouncing involuntary servitude." He adds, "In celebrating the demise of Negro slavery, Bryant systematically condemned the cowards, hypocrites, and criminals who had defended it and were still potential enemies." As part of National Poetry Week, on August 18, 2017 the *Atlantic Monthly* chose to reprint "The Death of Slavery" as a reminder of the past and a protest against the racism that had surfaced in Charlottesville, Virginia, just days earlier. The *Atlantic* had decided to reprint poems that had originally appeared on its pages as a way to celebrate poetry. Bryant's poem seemed an obvious choice after efforts to take down the Confederate monuments, specifically one of General Robert E. Lee astride his horse, led to protests by a group of white nationalists and the death of one of the counterprotesters, Heather Heyer. Annika Neklason of the *Atlantic* wrote, "The last stanza of the poem, in which Bryant addresses the physical remnants of slavery, feels particularly resonant at the end of this long and difficult week."[6] This poem's message thus moves back and forth in history, resonating with today's readers as it did with Bryant's original audience of post–Civil War readers in its condemnation of slavery and the racism that rationalized it.

The poem begins by sonorously addressing slavery, "O thou great Wrong," and then proceeds to hold up to slavery its great wrongs, keeping "millions fettered," wielding a "scourge," and turning "a stony gaze on human tears." The poem gives a clear picture of the terrors of slavery, the cruelty and heartlessness of the treatment of the "laborer," the separation of families, the "guilty shame" of the "inner lair," the crimes and sins audaciously committed without fear of "vengeance," all sowing "a harvest of uncounted miseries." While Bryant sees the Civil War that ended slavery as the result of the "wrath of Heaven," he also notes the costs of the "bloody war that thinned the human race." Themes of freedom and liberty and God's vengeance against the greed and corruption of slavery resound. As he approaches the end of the poem, he looks back to the past: "the Black Death . . . / Worship of Moloch, tyrannies that built / The Pyramids." In this way he suggests that human history is haunted by misdeeds, by "foul phantoms" reified in the physical remnants of corruption.[7]

In the last stanza, the poet both looks forward to the future, "better years," and backward to the "shadowy past," the graves, the slave pen, the "grim block" where slaves were sold, the "scourges and engines" of pain as mementos of slavery. These grim reminders of a past of cruelty and greed he imagines will "moulder and rust" from disuse. But the ending couplet of the poem problematizes this hope for the future with "a warning to the coming times." The work of the memorials in the poem, the "symbols that proclaim [slavery's] crimes," is to keep the memory of the past alive, to act as a reminder of the past's misdeeds and as a warning against reenacting the plagues of the past. Although the poem shows all of nature rejoicing in the liberty of the enslaved, the ending presciently understands that the greed and animosity that fueled slavery's reign are not extinguished but continue to haunt the South and the nation. The graves, the "slave-pen," and the auction block are symbols of both the past and the future, a grim foreshadowing of the Jim Crow era and the current rise of racial strife and white nationalism.[8] Like the other memorials he had visited in 1843, the forts, the graves, the ruins and monuments that marked a long history of conflict, the memorials in the poem, indeed the poem itself as a memorial, remind and warn of national sin in ways starkly different from those of the monuments to the defenders of slavery, like the statue of Robert E. Lee, which spurred conflict rather than reflection. Although Bryant may have hesitated about overtly criticizing slavery or looking too closely at the lives of enslaved people in his public letters from the South in 1843, he was not hesitant on other occasions, as when he wrote "The Death of Slavery," in calling out the crimes and terrors of the peculiar institution.

Frederick Law Olmsted in the Cotton South

IN 1853, BEFORE HE became the landscape architect who designed New York's Central Park, before he became an advocate for open spaces for the public, as he was still trying to find himself, Frederick Law Olmsted served a stint as a roving correspondent for the *New-York Daily Times*. Using the pseudonym "Yeoman," suggesting his democratic leanings and a prudent measure for "traveling incognito . . . in the slave states," Olmsted traveled throughout the South, writing up his impressions. He would be paid $300 for the series of letters he posted. Before leaving on the first of two journeys through the South, Olmsted wrote a friend that he wanted a "reliable understanding of the sentiments and hopes & fears" of southerners. His first journey (1852–1853) took him along the seaboard from Maryland to Louisiana. During the second journey (1853–1854) he traveled to the interior of the South, down the Ohio River to the Mississippi and on to Texas. As the young man from New York set off on his first venture, he wrote, "I have thoughts of going south this winter . . . mainly with the idea that I could make a valuable book of observations on Southern Agriculture & general economy as affected by Slavery." He would write three books based on these letters, *A Journey in the Seaboard Slave States* (1856), *A Journey through Texas* (1857), and *A Journey in the Back Country* (1860), and then consolidate them into *The Cotton Kingdom* (1861).[1] Already making connections as a young farmer between the land and the people who work it, Olmsted was primed to make keen observations of life in the South and the effects of slavery on it. Written ten years after William Cullen Bryant's letters about his southern tour, Olmsted's letters about Virginia and the Carolinas provide a view of the South in the decade preceding the great split that plunged the nation into its costly civil war.

If Bryant quickly sketches the South and avoids overt criticism of slavery, Olmsted paints with "tedious prolixity" (*Cotton* 85) the details of a journey both orderly and difficult and a South he finds lacking in cultivation, an economically and morally impoverished South.[2] Developing an ecology and ethics of use—of labor, land, transportation, and cultivation—Olmsted suggests the interconnections and intersections between them: that how you treat one is indicative of how you treat the others. Demonstrating cases of intentional incompetency of the cotton kingdom, the contradictions that are endured for the sake of cotton and capitalism, Olmsted shows how slavery and cotton affect the South as a whole, explaining its general slovenliness, inefficiency, and skewed values. As a traveler he observes and experiences firsthand these contradictions as he travels by way of the chaotic transportation system and observes the layers of life he passes. He comes to understand what people will tolerate in the name of capital, acknowledging like the Caribbean intellectual Eric Williams the economic basis for slavery, that its origin "can be expressed in three words: in the Caribbean, Sugar; on the mainland, Tobacco and Cotton" and that "the cotton industry was the capitalist industry par excellence." Like Williams, Olmsted understood that racism was "the consequence of slavery" and hence of capitalism.[3] He perceived that in the effort to secure cheap labor and to exchange labor for capital, planters and the South accepted and endured the inefficiencies of the poor white class and a brutalized class of enslaved people, weak or nonexistent civic, religious, and educational institutions, and transportation technologies that lagged behind those in the North. And, as his narrative illustrates, he understood that these things were tested on the road, in the transportation systems where identities and ideologies were tried as people, goods, and ideas were moved about.

After a particularly trying journey from Raleigh to Fayetteville, North Carolina, during which he both walked and rode in a stagecoach pulled by horses so "balky" that the driver constantly and ruthlessly beat, cursed, and abused them, along roads that were largely unmarked and pocked by stumps, fallen trees, and mires, after the delays and long hours of travel, Olmsted pronounced, "There is nothing that is more closely connected, both as cause and effect, with the prosperity and wealth of a country, than its means and modes of travelling, and of transportation of the necessities and luxuries of life" (*Cotton* 135). What astounds Olmsted is that even though Raleigh has a "large distributing post-office" and that the road he and the mail traversed was a main highway, travel was still painfully slow, "one day two miles an hour, the next four miles, and on each occasion failing to connect with the conveyances which we pay to scatter further the intelligence and wealth transmitted by it." Not only does the sad state of transportation hinder the circulation of mail and ideas essential to a democracy, it also hinders the movement of important cargo and goods.[4] He notes that a cargo of three thousand barrels of resin was dumped because of the high cost of transportation and that a wagon loaded with sugar, flour, tea, axes, and other necessities was unable to move out of a slough despite the efforts of "six mules, and five negroes." What astounds and troubles Olmsted is that the cruelty to the animals and the gross inefficiencies of the transportation system were "regarded by no one, apparently, as at all unusual" (135–36). This state of affairs was mirrored for Olmsted in the inefficient use of land, one farmer telling him that there was no money to be had in raising a corn crop beyond the mere subsistence needs of the family because "it cost too much to get it to market," even though farmers often had to buy corn and "waggon it home from Raleigh." Instead, they believed cotton was the only cash crop. Ironically, Olmsted confesses that he did not see "a single cotton-field" during the ride to Fayetteville (129).

Although he spent one night during this leg of the trip at a neat and cheerful Quaker-like home and was served a dinner composed of a variety of meats and corncakes, when he later took advantage of a delay along the road to rush into a log cabin to warm up, he found a different scene. Of the two women of the house, one smoked a pipe and the other, a young woman whose "face was as dry and impassive as a dead man's," "was doing nothing, and said but little," though "once in a about a minute . . . [she] spit with perfect precision into the hottest embers of the fire." Their living condition was more "scanty and rude" than any house he had seen "with women living in it, in the United States" (*Cotton* 135), betraying an assumption that women naturally domesticate and civilize the rude conditions of men and that these women represented an aberration. He also remarks on the "listlessness" of several men standing against their log "hovels," men who blinked at him "as if unable to withdraw their hands from their pockets to shade their eyes" to even greet the traveler (130). The sparsely populated region, the rude conditions of their homes, the "listlessness" and passivity of the inhabitants, and the accepted inefficiencies of their transportation system say much to Olmsted about the southern character. He reminds readers, "This is a long-settled country, having been occupied by Anglo-Saxons as early as any part of the Free States," and he says that the road he has described is "the main road between the capital of North Carolina and its chief seaport." Yet it has not advanced culturally or technologically at the same pace as northern regions. He blames the skewed ecology of use he observes on slavery and the attitudes it generates about work and life. As he notes, the two wooden women sitting in their rude cabin "were not so poor but that they had a negro woman cutting and bringing wood for their fire" (135). What he suggests is not only a racial and class hierarchy in which the basest white person can claim to own a black person, but also that slavery enervates the poor white population and stymies the progress and civilization of the South. His exasperation about travel in the South leads him to the conclusion that its systems of life are uncivilized: "Barbarous is too mild a term... The improvidence, if not the cruelty, no sensible barbarian could have been guilty of" (135–36).

If this episode were the only example of the inefficiencies and frustrations of traveling in the American South, we could rationalize that the conditions of stagecoach travel or the particular driver who was so cruel were aberrations or that they exemplify travel in the back country of the Carolinas. But the delays and neglect, the disordered quality of travel seem endemic to the time and place. When he travels from Washington to Richmond by "the regular great southern route," one of the best of routes in the South, he transfers from steamboat to rail and takes nine hours to travel 130 miles (*Cotton* 32). This trip was uneventful and one of the least chaotic, an improvement over Bryant's harried 1843 travel into the South, giving him a chance to observe the plantation mansions, the fields and forests, and the Black and white people who peered out of windows to watch the train pass. Noting an advertisement for a railroad company saying that it would "take coloured people only in second-class trains," Olmsted wryly remarks, "Servants seem to go with their masters everywhere." Thus he indicates racial segregation and its inconsistencies just as he notes the "close cohabitation" of Black and white children who play together but do not go to school together (32–33).

The train ride from Richmond to Petersburg, Virginia, began fairly well, with only a minor delay at a bridge, but then smoke swirled from the truck of a car, the result apparently of "a neglect of sufficient or timely oiling." As he left the station, Olmsted observed a Black man oiling the trucks: "He did not give himself the trouble to elevate the outlet of his oiler, so that a stream of oil, probably costing a dollar and a half a gallon, was poured out upon the ground the whole length of the train" (*Cotton* 44–45). Then, when he traveled from Petersburg to Norfolk, he was rushed through breakfast to get to the train station on time only to be delayed at the wharf where he was to connect with the steamboat that would take him to Norfolk. After waiting an hour for the late boat, finding shelter from the rain in a crowded shed with men chewing tobacco and women scolding children, he was told that the boat was not delayed, just that it was not time for it to arrive. Even after another half-hour of waiting, his fellow travelers did not seem perturbed: "All seemed to take the harrying and waiting process as a regular thing" (106). Apparently, no one expected the trains and steamboats, much less the stagecoaches, to run on time, and no one was surprised when the machinery was not properly maintained or that those called upon to maintain the trains would waste oil in their carelessness. If, as Olmsted says, transportation provides a window into the culture, the culture he presents is one that is passive and careless with its resources, or as Harriet Beecher Stowe's New England character Miss Ophelia puts it, "'shiftless'" (82).

The culture that a focus on transportation portrays is also one that privileges economic capital over human or social capital. Despite the lack of the more civilizing amenities, schools, good roads, up-to-date health care, and regularly meeting churches, even for the wealthy plantation owners, that could be built and sustained by the ready labor force of enslaved and white laborers, slave owners habitually put their human chattel on trains in exchange for cash, selling them to support the cotton kingdom in the Deep South. Olmsted remarks, "For all [the lack of social amenities], labourers are being constantly sent away. I have not been on or seen a railroad train, departing southward, that it did not convey a considerable number of the best of negro labourers, in charge of a trader who was intending to sell them to cotton-planters" (*Cotton* 84). It bewilders Olmsted to see plantation owners putting the modern transportation system in the service of the peculiar institution. Likewise, he is puzzled by the use of labor the scene suggests. Instead of employing labor to better the living conditions of all, Black laborers' real value lies in a market that primarily asks, "What is he worth for cotton?" (11). Their mobility vastly different from Olmsted's and the usual associations between travel, freedom, and social mobility, the trafficked human chattel demonstrates the immobility of enslaved people and the static economy of the South. While transportation is supposed to circulate the ideas, necessities, and goods that contribute to the cultivation of society, in the South that Olmsted observes it also is a vehicle for the transport of enslaved people and the perpetuation of slavery and is meant to keep them in place, bound by the system.

Because the road is a location where things happen, where personal and national identities are forged, where race and class meet in unexpected ways, Olmsted's observations about travel reify the complicated regional and national debates about race and mobility. John Cox reminds us that the road "has long been the space where members of different communities, races, cultures, or classes have most frequently interacted with each other."[5] A public space, the road in Olmsted's South is particularly marked by race and class hierarchies that determine the types of movements that take place on it. Demonstrating how public transportation is a site for enacting the fraught race relations of the antebellum South, Olmsted sketches the complex, contradictory situation of African Americans. Even as he observes companies of Blacks at train stations waiting to be shipped to the cotton South (*Cotton* 121), he also observes white passengers just arrived by steamboat along the James River greeted with "the appearance of enthusiasm" by "well-dressed negro servants," and this suggests to him affection and family feeling ("Black and white met with kisses") (107). Even as these greetings between Black people and white people were expressed, "Field negroes, standing by, looked on with their usual besotted expression, and neither offered nor received greetings" (107). This double vision of affection and "besotted expression" exemplifies the stratification of Blacks in slavery and points to ways that the hard labor and brutal treatment endured by field hands forms a character different from those who experienced more material advantages. Later, in a stagecoach to Gaston, North Carolina, Olmsted remarks about one of the passengers, "a free coloured woman . . . treated in no way differently from the white ladies," alluding to a position of respect despite color. Although he was informed by his travel companion that this treatment "was entirely customary at the South," Olmsted cryptically remarks, "Notwithstanding which, I have known young Southerners to get very angry because negroes were not excluded from the public conveyances . . . at the North" (127). Here the road and public transportation serve as sites where racial contradictions are enacted, where Olmsted can point to both the closeness of the races and the separations that divide them. Some are sold, transported for capital, or denied access to mobility while others are welcomed and afforded some degree of respect.

Traveling through the South, "spying" on it as an outsider, Olmsted was positioned to analyze the complex ways race was enacted in the calculus of labor and freedom.[6] Like other travelers, he criticizes the cruelty of overseers, the way slavery has degraded its workers into "dull, idiotic, and brute-like" beings (*Cotton* 33), the use of enslaved women as breeders, and the callous exchange of enslaved humans for cash (46–47). But as he travels through Virginia and the Carolinas, he also discovers a more complex, nuanced Black society and economy, pointing to contradictions regarding race and labor that undermine any possible rationalizations about slavery or Black Americans. Observing a funeral in Richmond, he notes not only the ways the Black mourners attempted to replicate white funeral and sermonic practices but also the different kinds of clothes worn by the mourners, from cast-off garments and ones made of "negro cloth" to "foppish extravagance" and the stylishness of "many of the coloured ladies," that indicate not simply fashion but also class distinctions in the black community (35–38). Later, as he delineates the poor living and working conditions of enslaved people in Virginia, the meager allowance for food, their houses, the rough clothes furnished by slave owners, and the people doing what they can "to provide for themselves" to supplement their scant conditions (78–79), he also depicts the relative independence of others, like a tobacco peddler he meets on the road (155–58). Earning ten dollars a month, the peddler tells Olmsted that any Black "can get good wages if he's a mind to be industrious, no matter wedder he's slave or free" (158). Pointing to the geographic and economic mobility of some, like the peddler, against the enforced immobility of others, like the enslaved people in Virginia, Olmsted begins to draw a more nuanced view of Black lives. When the peddler indicates differences in the ways Black people are treated in North Carolina, where he is from, and South Carolina, where blacks are "not so well clothed and . . . don't appear so bright" (157), he points to regional differences in the practice of slavery and the effects on the character of those who are enslaved.

Contrasting the situation of Blacks who are degraded by field work and driven by a whip-carrying overseer with those who hire out their own time, Olmsted notes the effects of labor on character, the moral exchange of labor on human lives. Describing the work of enslaved men who dive into the coastal waters of the Carolinas to remove submerged cypress stumps, for which they receive whiskey, money, and respect from the bosses, Olmsted exclaims, "What! Slaves eager to work, and working cheerfully, earnestly, and skillfully? Even so. Being for the time managed as freemen, their ambition stimulated by wages, suddenly they, too, reveal sterling manhood, and honour their Creator" (*Cotton* 115). In another instance, Olmsted remarks on the gangs of enslaved men employed to work for months at a time in the Great Dismal Swamp cutting lumber and splitting shingles: "The slave lumberman then lives measurably as a free man; hunts, fishes, eats, drinks, smokes and sleeps . . . as much as he pleases" (110). Because the men in these two examples are able to earn a little money and are given some latitude in what they do with their spare time, they are "more sprightly and straightforward in their manner and conversation than any field-hand plantation negroes" (111), the freedom and trust afforded these men the cause of their more positive character.

In contrast, plantation manual labor managed by a whip-wielding overseer on a horse resulted in people he describes as "clumsy, awkward, gross, elephantine in all their movements; pouting, grinning, and leering at us; sly, sensual, and shameless." He observed as well that when the overseer went to one end of the

line of labor, "the hands at the other end would discontinue work," demonstrating the "compromise" between power and subversive indolence that Bryant
had described.[7] Olmsted declares that he had never witnessed "anything more
revolting than the whole scene" (*Cotton* 154), postulating that if treated similarly
their progeny would likewise bear the stamp of character on their faces. The
difference in demeanor seems to be attributed not only to the kind of work that
is done, though it is all difficult, but also, more importantly, to the degree of
freedom and respect given by employers and overseers. As Olmsted suggests,
the conditions of work, of production, shape the character of the worker and
ethos of the region and nation.

Considering the work done by the "negroes employed in the turpentine
business" who seem "to be unusually intelligent and cheerful," he compares
them to the "white people inhabiting the turpentine forest" who are "entirely
uneducated, poverty-stricken vagabonds" (*Cotton* 140). The whites of the region,
Olmsted is told, make unreliable workers not only because they work only spo-
radically but also "because, being white men, [overseers] cannot 'drive' them.
That is to say, their labour is even more inefficient and unmanageable than that
of slaves" (141). As he was told by a plantation owner, "You never could depend
on white men, and you couldn't drive them any; they wouldn't stand it. Slaves
[are] the only reliable labourers" (63). They were reliable because they could be
commanded. Moreover, some jobs were racially marked, making them undesir-
able for whites despite the money they could make. While Blacks were able to ask
"high wages" to work on railroads or in tobacco factories, whites were unwilling
to do the same work. As Olmsted's acquaintance told him, "If you should ask a
white man you had hired, to do such things, he would get mad and tell you he
wasn't a nigger" (63). This statement points to the racialization of labor and the
inefficiencies that were endured for the sake of maintaining racial distinctions.
As an outsider, Olmsted understands an important irony about labor in the
South, that Blacks are the better workers (for whatever reasons), whites won't
work at jobs labeled "black," yet the best Black workers are sold to work cotton
elsewhere, their value as capital more important than their ability to enhance
the workforce and life of the community (85–88). In the introduction to *The
Cotton Kingdom*, Olmsted writes, "My own observation of the real condition
of the people of our Slave States, gave me . . . an impression that the cotton
monopoly in some way did them more harm than good" (10). He understands
that "the slave work ethic infects the entire community," as John Cox puts it.[8]
The inconsistencies regarding race and labor and the willingness to put up with
inefficiencies in order to maintain racial difference indicate to him that freedom

and self-autonomy are better factors for a productive economy and better human character than the South's ecology of use.

Like the transportation system, the systems of labor in the South provide windows into the values of the culture, making *The Cotton Kingdom* "an invaluable source for the occupational differentiation and variations in life style among slaves." As an outsider, a traveler on the public roads, Olmsted's observations and analyses of the South remind us of the complicated history of race relations in the United States and the effects of racism on labor, the economy, and human relations. Perhaps what he learned in his travels south convinced him of the need to establish places where people could come together in democratic ways, to enjoy the open spaces of the natural world against the barbarism of racism and materialism. In an 1866 essay proposing what would become Prospect Park in Brooklyn he stated, "A sense of enlarged freedom is to all, at all times, the most certain and the most valuable gratification afforded by a park.'"[9] Like the ideal of the open, democratic road, the parks he designed ideally would foster not only a love of nature and a reprieve from the mechanization of society but also the mobility, freedom, and equality of a democratic society.

John Muir's Botanizing Tramp
through the South

SETTING OFF WHEN HE was twenty-nine years old on a jaunt through the South, after having walked about Wisconsin, Canada, and the Upper Midwest, after having been temporarily blinded in his right eye by a mechanical accident, John Muir struck out to "see something of the vegetation of the warm end of the country." Leaving Indianapolis on September 1, 1867, he went first by train to Jeffersonville, Indiana, just across the Ohio River from Louisville, Kentucky, where he began his botanizing tramp through the South. He recorded the walk in a journal that maps the jaunt geographically, biologically, and cognitively, noting dates, places, and the distance traveled in a day, listing and describing the changing plants he met, and recording his reflections about what he observed and experienced. Like the layered journeys recorded in it, the published travel narrative *A Thousand-Mile Walk to the Gulf* (1916) is an assemblage of the original journal written hastily during the trek, revisions, additions, and pages from other journals and sketchbooks gathered as he was dictating his autobiography from 1908 to 1910. Although it was published after his death, it "records Muir's intellectual coming of age and his developing sense of the moral meaning in natural phenomena" and gives readers a firsthand view of the postbellum South just two years after the official ending of the Civil War.[1]

Like other travelers to the South, Muir finds it to be beautiful and strange, haunted by conflict and violence as well as graced by beauty and kindness. Coming to the South on the heels of the Civil War, he saw reminders of the destruction and ravages of the war on the land and the people, but he also received simple kindnesses and hospitality. Traveling afoot, he enjoyed an intimate relation with the road, the folks he met, and the plant life he observed and collected on this botanizing trip. His brief meetings with locals are genuine, and his time in the open, including nights spent outdoors, led him to feel at one with nature.

So intimate was his relation to the natural world that at the end of the narrative he writes of being bathed in "spirit-beams," of forgetting the self: "You lose consciousness of your own separate existence: you blend with the landscape, and become part and parcel of nature."[2]

In this passage Muir alludes to the famous statement by Ralph Waldo Emerson in *Nature* (1836) in which the self, like a transparent eyeball, loses all "mean egotism": "The currents of the Universal Being circulate through me; I am part or parcel of God." Here Emerson relates the "perfect exhilaration" he felt "on crossing a bare common, in snow puddles, at twilight, under a clouded sky," a transcendentalist epiphany about his oneness with the landscape. While both Emerson and Muir relate moments of losing oneself in the landscape, they also connect those transcendental moments with walking—over the common and through the South—and with seeing—Emerson's transparent eyeball and Muir's careful observations in his journal. In *The Ecological Approach to Visual Perception* James J. Gibson makes the connections between mobility and seeing: "One sees the environment not just with the eyes but with the eyes in the head on the shoulders of a body that gets about. We look at details with the eyes, but we also look around with the mobile head, and we go-and-look with the mobile body."[3] As Muir walks through the South, he is also looking at, seeing, the environment and the people who inhabit the region as if he were a walking eyeball, making his perception kinetic rather than static and the objects of his view mobile, part of his experience of moving through the landscape.

Travel connects him to the landscape. By walking and exploring, botanizing and sleeping out in nature, he experiences a physical oneness with nature. Likewise, perception connects him to the landscape. According to Gibson, "the supposedly separate realms of the subjective and the objective are actually only poles of attention. The dualism of observer and environment is unnecessary.... Self-perception and environment perception go together." A mobile observer of nature, Muir disrupts the dualism between himself and the environment. Moreover, his movement through the South disrupts preconceived notions about the region and its environment as he interacts with people and confronts the strange forms of tropical flora and fauna. These moments of strangeness prompt him to theorize about what he has experienced, that object and subject, life and death, savage and civilized are only "poles of attention" in the larger scheme of creation and the environment. As his mobility, his "visual kinesthesis," displaces him, sets him in unfamiliar locations, it also prompts him to new awareness about nature and the "moral meaning" of what he has seen. As relocation to new environments leads to self-concept change, to restructuring "the ecology of the self," so Muir's

mobility and perception of the new and strange lead him to restructure an ecological point of view, one that is increasingly biocentric.[4] As he moves through
the South, he shapes a theory that emphasizes unity, harmony, and interdependence. The narrative, then, traces not only his geographic journey but also the
ways he achieves an intellectual, moral oneness with nature that complements
his physical closeness to the landscape.

On the first day of September 1867, a young John Muir set forth on a journey
to the South that would take him through Kentucky and the mountains of Tennessee to the Georgia port city of Savannah and then across Florida to the Cedar
Keys. Once out of Louisville, he used a pocket map ("to rough-hew a plan for
my journey"), following a "southward direction" ("by the wildest, leafiest and
least trodden way I could find") through the rural South (*Gulf* 1, 2). Generally,
he followed marked roads, though a few times he went off road to try to find
his way across mountains, beside rivers, and through the swamps of Florida.
Along the way, Muir keeps track of the journey by noting dates in his journal
entries, the towns he passed or stayed in for a night or two, and sometimes the
miles he made on a particular day. He also maps the journey by recounting the
accommodations along the way, the taverns, homes, and outdoor spaces where
he laid his head for the night. He mentions the food offered to him, the bacon
and corn products shared by rural folk. Along with his customary diet of bread
and crackers, they were mainstays for Muir during his southern jaunt. Muir also
describes some of the people he met along the way, the hospitable farmers who
gave him a place to sleep, the charitable African Americans recently "freed" by
the Civil War, the hostile bands of Civil War guerrillas still patrolling the roads,
and desperate folks impoverished and unsettled by the ruinous war. Because he
traveled afoot and relied on the casual hospitality of people he met along the way,
he was able to sketch intimate if brief views of southerners and their way of life.
As he mapped his journey on roads that seemed themselves to wander and get
lost, Muir mapped the South at a turning point in its history as it tried to regroup
after the destruction of the Civil War. As Lewis Perry has argued, "To travel,
or to read about travel, was, after all, the appropriate way to learn about and to
present knowledge about a nation on the move." As a "sign of civilization," the
southern roads, as they had for Olmsted, suggested to Muir a place that lacked
clear direction and had not yet defined itself anew after the war.[5]

On the first day out from Louisville, Muir notes that he "walked twenty
miles, mostly on river bottom, and found shelter in a rickety tavern" (*Gulf* 2).

The next day, he writes, he followed "farmers' paths, but soon wandered away from the roads," encountering not only "a tribe of twisted vines" but also a tumbling stream that must have been running high. An African American woman called out to him that she would get the "men folks" to help him cross the stream and enlisted a ferry horse and a "little sable" boy to ferry him across (3–4). Thus begins the tramp—walks along the paths, off-road rambles, and the quick meetings with folks along the way setting the pattern for much that follows in his narrative. During his Kentucky rambles he meets the surveyor Munford who grills him on his botanical knowledge (8), an old Black man who pointed to places where the "Rebs" and Yankees had met in conflict during the Civil War (9), and others who journeyed on the Kentucky roads, all of whom, "white and black, male and female, travel on horseback" (13). As was the custom for travel through rural America, Muir relies when possible on local households for a place to sleep and a shared dinner, like the meager meal of "string beans, buttermilk, and corn bread" a family of African Americans shared with him (29), evidence of both the kindness and desperation of so many inhabitants of the rural South. Had he stayed a night at the hotel at Mammoth Cave, with its "fashionable hotel grounds in exact parlor taste" (11), he might have enjoyed more sumptuous fare such as Franklin Gorin enjoyed in 1876: venison, beef, quail, ham and eggs, brandy, and honey.[6] As it was, he avoided tourist attractions as he tramped through the South, instead sharing the road and rustic accommodations with the regional population. Though Muir does not take the time to ponder race relations in the postwar South and still traffics in racialized descriptions of the Blacks he encounters, calling the boy who helps him across the stream "a queer specimen, puffy and jet as an India rubber doll" (4), he nonetheless presents a racially mixed South in which Blacks share the public road and participate in traditions of rural hospitality.

While the people he meets on the Kentucky roads are generally accommodating and friendly, the farther south he goes the more obvious is the poverty and the evidence of war. In the Cumberland Mountains he meets a harder set of people—a young man who tries to rob him but gives it up when he discovers Muir is carrying nothing he deems of value, just some books, toiletries, and a plant press (*Gulf* 17–18); an illiterate man who prophesies a looming international war; the "motherly" but cautious woman who has to weigh whether she can afford to keep him for the night (21); and "wild, unshorn" men coming out of the mountain recesses to grind their bag of corn at the grist mill (36). Like these desperate people, the houses he sees, set "far apart and uninhabited," and "orchards and fences in ruins" are all "sad marks of war" (27). Sharing a "frugal

meal" of cornbread and bacon, one host, who was at first critical of a man spending his time "picking up blossoms" (23–24), urges Muir to turn back from his
walk since the Cumberland Mountains are patrolled by gangs of guerrillas
looking to plunder unwary travelers. As Muir notes, "The seal of war is on all
things. The roads never seem to proceed with any fixed purpose, but wander as if
lost." Seeking directions to the next town on his itinerary, Philadelphia, Tennessee, he takes the advice of a Tennessee "gal" who has suggested an alternate
route over the hills, but he becomes lost until stopping at the home of a "negro
driver" who gives him "a good deal of knowledge" about the teamster trade
(32–33). The haphazard directions, the roads that are themselves lost, speak to
Muir of the mountain South: "This is the most primitive country I have ever
seen, primitive in everything" (37). Like the three mountaineers in the "shackly
wagon" he meets on the road, the south seems to "slide . . . in slippery obedience
to the law of gravitation" (44–45), accommodating itself to the vicissitudes of
life without really progressing forward.

His impressions of Georgia are a bit more positive as he walks to Athens,
the site of plantations where cotton is "merrily" being picked: "The negroes are
easy-going and merry, making a great deal of noise and doing little work." He remarks that the African Americans in Athens are "well trained and are extremely
polite" and that the old plantations are worked by the "same negroes who worked
them before the war," now for seven to eight dollars a month (*Gulf*, 52). Although
Muir does not comment, as Olmsted would have, on the economic situation of
the cotton kingdom or the uneasy compromises that Bryant had observed between planters and laborers that extended into the post-slavery South, he does
complain about the never-changing topics of conversation among his southern
hosts: "long recitals of war happenings, discussion of the slave question, and
Northern politics" (59). When he approaches the home of a wealthy planter to
ask for food and lodging, he is at first turned down, but when he explains that he
is a wandering botanist, the man and his wife reluctantly extend their hospitality,
explaining that so many people traveling the country are not to be relied on and
that a recent guest had absconded with some of their silver (62). Their suspicion
and the numbers of people on the road, "perhaps fewer than one in a hundred"
who could be trusted, speak to the changed tenor of the road caused by the war
and its aftermath. Sherman's march through Georgia, like the ghosts of the men
killed in a nearby train wreck (59), haunts the South as northern "carpetbaggers"
hoping to profit from the South's loss foretell a new future. Throughout Georgia,
Muir observed traces of the war "apparent on the broken fields, burnt fences,
mills, and woods ruthlessly slaughtered" as well as "on the aged, half-consumed,

and fallen parents, who bear in a sad measure" the marks of the "most infernal of all civilized calamities" (84). The new South will have to be rebuilt, in part by the newcomers, but it will continue to bear the scars of the war.

Arriving in Savannah almost penniless and receiving no word from home or the money he had ordered to be sent by express, Muir confesses to "feeling dreadfully lonesome and poor" (*Gulf* 65). As he waits for his money, he makes a "nest" for himself at Bonaventure Cemetery, "the weird and beautiful abode of the dead" (76, 74). His daily inquiry at Adams Express Company, a transport company that carried newspapers, mail, and money, is finally rewarded on the fifth or sixth day of his stay. Faint with hunger, down to eating only a cracker a day, he asks about his package. The clerk puts him off, requiring identification since Muir is a stranger to Savannah and has no one to vouch for him. During the mid-nineteenth century the way money was transferred was changing. Transport companies like Adams competed with the postal system that was moving from the use of registered mail to the postal money order as safe ways to transfer small amounts. On May 17, 1864, "An Act to Establish a Postal Money Order System," sponsored by Postmaster General Montgomery Blair, initiated the postal money order system for soldiers and civilians and an itinerant population who needed easy and safe ways to send and receive money.[7] Part of the process required proper identification of the receiver, as Muir indicates when he is quizzed by the clerk to prove that he is John Muir the botanist (79–80). After he finally pockets his money, the famished Muir buys a piece of gingerbread, a "jubilee of bread," from "a very large negro woman" he encounters on the street just outside the express office (82, 81). Like Benjamin Franklin newly arrived in Philadelphia and stuffing his pockets with great loaves of bread, Muir pictures himself walking and "munching along the street" in his own version of "marching through Georgia" (81–82).

From Savannah, one of the great seaports of the nineteenth century, Muir took the steamship *Sylvan Shore* to Fernandina, Florida, at the mouth of the St. Johns River. "Florida is so watery and vine-tied," he writes, "that pathless wanderings are not easily possible in any direction" (*Gulf* 89). "Little grading is required for roads, but much bridging, and boring of many tunnels through forests" (103). He decided to follow a gap in the overgrowth made by the railroad, "stepping from tie to tie" (90). In 1861 businessman and politician David Levy Yulee had built, with slave labor, the Florida Central Railroad that crossed Florida from Fernandina, through Gainesville, to the Cedar Keys on the Gulf Coast. Yulee's line reduced the time and costs of transportation by cutting across rather than sailing around the foot of Florida. This is the route that Muir elected to follow, with short excursions into the "vastness and unapproachableness of the great guarded sea of sunny plants" (90) when a particular plant or flower caught his attention. On October 16 he found himself in the "trackless woods" looking for a dry place to spend the night amid "all manner of night sounds" from strange insects and beasts, until he finally found a "little hillock dry enough to lie down on." Here he spent a lonely and rather gloomy night, with only a bit of bread and some "brown water" to sustain him (94). The next day, his bread gone, he came upon a shanty where loggers were busy at work, "the wildest of all the white savages I have met." Nonetheless, these barbarians shared their meal with him, "yellow pork and hominy" (95). Later in the day he shared "liver pie, mixed with sweet potatoes and fat duff" with another group, three men with three dogs that viciously attacked him (96). Though rough, these men shared what they had with the traveler, demonstrating the hospitality often afforded the foot traveler. In another instance, however, Muir encountered a "brawny young negro" with glaring and wild eyes who may have intended to rob him (104). Then, just outside of Gainesville, he came upon a Black man and wife sitting around a roaring fire, their child who looked like a "black lump" lying in the ashes (106). The couple offered him some water, and when they called to their child, "Come, honey, eat yo' hominy," he emerged "from the earth naked as to the earth he came," causing Muir to muse, "surely I am coming to the tropics" (107). Once arrived in Gainesville, on the cusp of the growth that would make it an education center, he obtained food and lodging at a tavern. James B. Hunt explains, "Having little understanding of the legacies of slavery, race relations, postwar dislocations, and personal loss, Muir gave cursory attention to the human plights to which he bore passing witness." But Muir's encounters along the Florida road nonetheless illustrate the desperate situations of the people, the extreme poverty and filth of one family ("evidently desperately chronic and hereditary") a sign of the place and time (109).[8]

After spending a few days with "Captain Simmons," one of the few "scholarly, intelligent men" in Florida, joining him on a deer hunt and plunging into the Florida country in search of a palmetto grove along a trail swallowed by a swamp and through the "thorny, watery Southern tangles," Muir finally pushed through toward the Cedar Keys on the Gulf of Mexico (*Gulf* 111, 119). Cedar Key was the terminus of the Florida Central Railroad, chosen for its accessible harbor and most likely for its proximity to Yulee's plantation Margarita. There the botanist succumbed to the malaria he had no doubt contracted while sleeping with the dead in Bonaventure Cemetery and aggravated by the nights out in the damp Florida air. Of one such night in the Florida wetlands, he wrote, "Slept in the barrens at the side of a log. Suffered from cold and was drenched with dew. What a comfort a companion would be in the dark loneliness of such nights!" (110). After being nursed for three months by Richard W. B. Hodgson, part-owner of a nearby lumber mill, and his wife, who had agreed to lodge him when he first arrived in Cedar Key, and regaining some of his strength, he was able at last to do a little exploring. Finally, in early January 1868 he booked passage on a Yankee schooner loaded with lumber to Havana, Cuba.[9] Thus, his trek across the US South came to an end.

Traveling afoot, following established roads and paths and the rail line that cut across Florida, and wandering about on his own, Muir completed his thousand-mile walk to the Gulf of Mexico in fifty-three days. His journal gives readers a glimpse of the postwar South and the roads that ran through it. By sketching the various people he meets along the way, even if quickly, Muir catches its tenor. If we think about the road as a location where things happen and identities are tested, a place that gauges the movement and ethos of an era, then the southern road Muir tramped represents not only the uneasy changes in the rural South but also the possibility of democracy as diverse peoples took to the road. Despite the reality of racism or Muir's own lack of understanding of the legacy of slavery, the South he saw, experienced, and recorded points to the road as a place where both white and black and both male and female on the road conduct business as teamsters and loggers or search for work, where the unsettled find a temporary home, or where people simply travel from one place to another. Muir's road also points to the fraught ethos of the time, to the southern paradox of danger and kindness as strangers on the road might be accosted and robbed or hosted in the system of hospitality. For Muir the road was also a place of discovery, and his adventures would inspire others to follow in his footsteps in search of America in the South, the theme of an issue of the *Sierra Club Newsletter*, "Re-tracing John Muir's Famous Walks."

In addition to mapping his route through the South, Muir also charts its natural life, listing and describing the plants he sees. In this way he draws a kind of botanical map, a biogeography, that overlays the traveler's map and situates him as a participant in the intellectual, scientific conversation about the nation. As Perry Lewis argues, the road is a location where knowledge is gathered and disseminated, where "literary and intellectual vocations" are discovered and forged. The road, that strange, exotic, and dangerous avenue through the South, becomes a location where Muir discovers not only plants and animal life new to him but also his vocation as a peripatetic nature writer. Hunt claims that Muir's walk transformed him and shaped his "environmental thought, ethics, and worldview" and convinced him to find his life's work tramping and describing the natural world.[10] Finding a home in the environment, he relates early in the narrative how he was awakened by "the alarm notes of birds" in a hazel thicket that had served as his bed. Looking up he saw "several beautiful plants" ("strangers to me") right at his face (*Gulf* 6). Calling this "the first botanical discovery in bed!," he points to two motifs that run through the botanical map of his tramp, the strangeness of the southern environment and his desire to experience a closeness or oneness with nature that is both visceral and moral. Indeed, at the end of the narrative, after he has tramped through the South, voyaged to Cuba, and then ventured on to California the year before his first summer in the Sierras, he proclaims as Emerson had in *Nature*, "You blend with the landscape, and become part and parcel of nature" (212). This first botanical discovery illustrates just such a moment as he makes of nature a bed and finds the strange plants at his face when he awakens. The birds seem to be "scolding or asking angry questions," the kind that as the journey progresses will prompt Muir to also ask questions about the natural order of things. While this particular moment prompted feelings of delight and pleasure as Muir lingers, enjoying the "trees and soft lights and music" (6) of the impromptu campground, other experiences will prove to be more threatening to his philosophical, cognitive equilibrium. The cumulative effect of journeying south and encountering new landscapes will generate a new ethos of ecology that he sketches as the narrative and the tramp come to an end.

Although it may seem an oxymoron, Muir finds the oneness he seeks not only by close physical proximity with nature and delight in nature's "music" but also in moments that startle and threaten. These moments prompt him to question an anthropocentric view of the world and to shape a more biocentric, ecocentric ecology that positions humans as "part and parcel" of the natural world rather than as superior to it. Discourse theorist James Kinneavy explains that exploratory discourse, such as we see in moments when Muir is confronted with the newness of the southern environment, is grounded first "in fact and accepted notions," represented by the familiar aesthetic, religious, and scientific books that Muir carries with him—Robert Burns's poems, John Milton's *Paradise Lost*, the New Testament, and Alphonso Wood's *Class-book of Botany*. When new facts or observations do not fit with the accepted system of thought, like the "strange land" where Muir knows "hardly any of the plants" (*Gulf* 58), Kinneavy explains, the writer experiences a "stage of cognitive dissonance" that may "converge into a crisis" of thought. Confronted with the strange and in a sense psychically unhomed by the different, a writer like Muir figures a "new theory, model, or paradigm" that replaces the familiar philosophy, in this case an ethos of ecology that situates the human in the natural order of things.[11] While at times the word "strange" simply refers to the new and different, as when he remarks that he met "a strange oak with willow-looking leaves" (6), at other times "strange" suggests the dissonance and disorientation of discovery that uncovers not only a new organism but also a new way of thinking. Muir writes, "Since the commencement of my floral pilgrimage I have seen much that is not only new, but altogether unallied, unacquainted with the plants of my former life" (85). In doing so he signals an emerging cognitive map that is layered with the botanical map of the natural world of the South, which in turn is layered on the geographic map of travel.

As he journeys south by foot, wandering off-road and living in the natural world, he is confronted with new plants that suggest to him an Eden of both luxurious beauty and snares, tangible and philosophical.[12] The paradox of the South, that it is a place of great beauty but also great danger, prompts him to think about celestial and ecological meanings, particularly humans' place in the ecosystem. As a botanizing traveler, he lists the plants he finds, often giving the Latin and familiar terms for them, "*Ericacae* [heathworts]," and describes their botanical features as he does of the sensitive *Schrankia*, "a long, prickly, leguminous vine, with dense heads of small, yellow fragrant flowers" (*Gulf* 18). But following the *Schrankia* vines to a backwoods schoolhouse, he moves beyond simple description to muse on what the young scholars might learn from it and exclaims, "How little we know as yet of the life of plants—their hopes and fears, pains and enjoyments!" (19). For Muir, the natural world is not simply a site of scientific study but also a place inhabited by sentient fellow beings, a place that speaks of greater creative forces and his fellowship with its beings.

This fellow-feeling is easy to come by when the natural world is familiar. He figures Kentucky as an "Eden, the paradise of oaks" and the "most favored province of bird and flower" (*Gulf* 15, 14). And from the heights of the Cumberland Mountains, the "first real" mountains he had climbed, he looks out on the valley below, claiming it to be the "most sublime and comprehensive picture" of nature (16). Descending the mountains, he crossed a cool stream, about which he writes, "there is nothing more eloquent in Nature than a mountain stream, and this is the first I ever saw." Its banks, "peopled with rare and lovely flowers and overarching trees," resemble a sanctuary, a sacred place where he can feel the "presence of the great Creator" (30). In an enthusiastic moment he can proclaim the benevolent presence of God, the Creator, in nature. But as he notes, the path was "strewn with flowers" but also with thorns clawing and catching the pedestrian, causing one to become entangled, physically and philosophically.

As he says, "The south has plant fly-catchers. It also has plant man-catchers" (27). This realization prompts him to move from the familiar task of botanizing to constructing a new moral ecology. As he moves south, the young man from Wisconsin will encounter more and more "strange plants" that will provoke "even deeper and more profound reflections" about the meaning of nature.[13]

Walking the river country of Georgia along the Chattahoochee River ("the first truly southern stream I have met") (*Gulf* 48), he enters a region that not only mixes the luxurious with the dangerous, the thick muscadine vines and rattlesnakes on the move, but is also strange to him. On September 28 he notes the familiar oak and grasses but finds the flowers unfamiliar: "Strange plants are crowding around me now. Scarce a familiar face appears among all the flowers of the day's walk" (54). As he approaches Savannah, nestled between the Savannah River and the Atlantic Ocean, the Spanish moss and cypress swamp, the wall-like thickets and vines, seem to enclose him in a mysterious natural bower that makes him feel out of place: "Am made to feel that I am now in a strange land. I know hardly any of the plants, but few of the birds, and I am unable to see the country for the solemn, dark, mysterious cypress woods." Instead of feeling one with nature, instead of finding himself in a sacred place, he feels alone and out of place. "The winds are full of strange sounds . . . and I am filled with indescribable loneliness." In a moment of cognitive dissonance, of existential loneliness, he feels as if he were the stranger, unhomed and "far from the people and plants and fruitful fields of home" (58). Contrary to the notion that enclosed spaces as opposed to the great open spaces connote home and shelter, here the suffocating enclosures pose a threat to Muir's "established human meaning." Although this incident was just a moment in the narrative, a moment before he refreshed himself with a dip in the "black, silent stream" and found his way to a planter's house for the night, it presages the ways the strangeness of the South haunted him and pushed him to new considerations. His mobility has made things and himself seem out of place.[14]

At Bonaventure Cemetery in Savannah, he gazed "awe-stricken" at the row of majestic live oaks strewn with Spanish moss "as one new-arrived from another world" (*Gulf* 69). Yet here in this home of the dead, which ironically also contained "one of the most impressive assemblages of animal and plant creatures," he felt at home in its "friendly union of life and death."[15] Although the moss gave the place a "funereal effect," the graveyard, he writes, seemed "like a center of life. The dead do not reign there alone." "One of the Lord's most favored abodes of life and light," Bonaventure would be an uncanny home to him for a week as he awaited the arrival of his packet of money. "Part and parcel" with the world of Bonaventure, he thinks about the lessons of harmony and unity, of the cycle of life and death, how in the midst of death, nature and life are "at work everywhere." Looking at the iron railings that enclose some of the graves, tributes to the dead, he remarks that Nature "corrodes the iron and marble, and gradually levels the hill" of earth made by the grave (68–71). He sees that life undoes death, that all is part of the harmony or cycle of being. Sleeping in his moss nest, physically a part of the natural world of the cemetery, he becomes accepted by his "bird neighbors in this blessed wilderness" (78), becoming a member of this unique environment. His sojourn with the dead must have been one of the strangest stays during his journey, but the proximity to them and the life that abounded caused him to reflect on a holistic, unified ecology that included the dead with the living.

Once he received his money, he continued to Florida, the "Land of Flowers" that he had imagined as draped "by luxuriant, bright-blooming vines" in a "flood of bright sunshine." What he found instead were salt marshes and "strangeness" (*Gulf* 87–88). Taking a moment to eat his "bread breakfast" after having skipped a land-based trek across southern Georgia to arrive at the coastal town of Fernandina by steamboat, he uses the language of strangeness, negation, and loneliness to describe the spot: "Everything in earth and sky had an impression of strangeness; not a mark of friendly recognition, not a breath, not a spirit whisper of sympathy came from anything about me, and of course I was lonely." A location of lack, of a lack of the familiar and the friendly, it causes him to contemplate tropical danger as he imagines an alligator set to spring on him with its "big jaws and rows of teeth" (89). Although the sound that spurred the fearful specter was made by "a tall white crane," and although he blamed his overactive mind on the fatigue and hunger of the Bonaventure sojourn, we can also see that suddenly landing in a location so unlike home contributed to feelings of loneliness and fear, of being, in a sense, lost.

Florida, with its new plants and soggy terrain, was not what he had expected, and the newness of it affected his equilibrium. Unsure of making his way through the tangled morass of the Florida lowlands, he opted to follow the path hewn out for the central Florida railroad as a way of finding his way geographically and cognitively through the "unfathomable" plant life and "unapproachableness" of the Florida landscape. Indeed, he relates how when he left the railroad path to collect a new plant specimen, he became "tangled" or sank into the muck (*Gulf* 90), a cipher for the cognitive challenges derived from the new terrain. Yet it was on one of these side excursions that he made his "grandest discovery" of the day, the palmetto, the entanglements a prelude to the discovery that would lead to his new ecological theory. Describing the size of the palmetto and the way light pours between its leaves, he says that the specimen was "indescribably impressive and told me grander things than I ever got from human priest," causing him to question the truths "they" (scientists and priests) proclaimed—that "plants are perishable, soulless creatures" (92). As he contemplates his presence in the "hot gardens of the sun" he often visited in dreams, lonely amid a "multitude of strangers," strange plants and "strange winds" ("whispering, cooing, in a language I never learned"), he thanks the Lord for "admission to this magnificent realm." His language, poetical and spiritual, intimates meanings and "influences that [he] never before felt" (93). On the verge of revelations that he does not yet articulate, Muir feels the influence of the strange on his way of thinking about nature's beings and his relation to them.[16]

The weirdness and danger of the Florida-scape become more pronounced as he spots an alligator and hears stories of their ferocity. Although he never saw "more than one," the reports about their savage attacks prompted him to muse that even though creatures like alligators and snakes repel us, "they are not mysterious evils" but rather "part of God's family" and part of God's plan of "balanced repulsion and attraction," much like his realization in Bonaventure of the unity and harmony between life and death, of the reciprocity of polar opposites. Critiquing the self-centered view of most people, he claims that we are "blind to the rights of all the rest of creation!" (*Gulf* 97–98). Just because humans may be repelled by the ugly and the dangerous does not mean that they do not have a place in the religio-biocentric ecology he begins to construct. Even when confronted with the dangerous, "Muir understood God to be always active in creation."[17]

Later, at Cedar Key, after he had recuperated from the bout with malaria and was once more able to go about botanizing, he encountered the Spanish bayonet, a yucca with sharp, stabbing leaves. Thinking about the ways that the thorny vines, dwarf palmettos, and yucca bayonets attack humans "without the smallest consideration of Lord Man," he satirizes pompous assumptions that humans are the dominant creature (*Gulf* 133). As well, Donald Worster explains, he "rejected the old Christian notion that the economy of nature had been designed for man's exclusive benefit." Muir sneers at assumptions that all of nature is meant for human use, the whale a mere storehouse of oil and cotton only made to become clothing. Instead, he understands that humans are just a part of the great natural design: "Why should man value himself as more than a small part of the one great unit of creation?" Indeed, "venomous beasts, thorny plants, and deadly diseases of certain parts of the earth prove that the whole world was not made for him," and the ages that created and destroyed "whole kingdoms of creatures" may also destroy human creatures (139–41). Situating humans as only a part of creation and not the reason for it, Muir articulates a biocentric, ecocentric view of nature that counters the traditional human-centered view. Developed in the strange landscapes of the South, his "shift from anthropocentric to the biocentric vision," Thurman Wilkins explains, "would remain the core development of Muir's thinking."[18] He regards other natural forms, not only animals but also plants and minerals, as sentient beings, capable of "sensation," "earth-born companions and our fellow mortals" (140, 139). Having contemplated the strangeness and danger of the southern plants and animals, even the air, he understands not only that "the whole world was not made for [humans]" but also that the nonhuman beings are "people" (134) who share a fellowship of sensation and being with him. Understanding this basic fellowship with other natural forms, he realizes that he is indeed "part and parcel of nature" (212), a member of the ecological community of humans and all other species.

Confronted by the strange, the new, and the dangerous, experiencing moments of great loneliness, out of the familiar abodes of place and mind, finding himself a stranger in a strange land, Muir was at once "delighted, astonished, confounded" (*Gulf* 176)—not only by the strange "language of the winds" but also by a new language of ecology that he was articulating. Out of the separate moments of strangeness and the cumulative effect of leaving familiar plants and winds as he went farther south, he sketches a new paradigm in the narrative, of a land ethic, as Worster explains, that blends spiritual and ecological understandings of the interdependence, unity, and "essential love, overlying, underlying, pervading all things." As so often occurs in Muir's narrative, discovering the strange and unknown in the botanical world leads him to scientific, philosophical, religious, personal revelations that signal the transformative quality of his journey. Michael Cohen notes that in *A Thousand-Mile Walk to the Gulf*, "Muir began consciously and categorically to deny, point by point, many nineteenth-century assumptions about God, Man, and Nature." That is why he inscribed the journal, "John Muir, Earth-planet, Universe." Had he remained in the familiar territory of Wisconsin and not ventured to the tropical South, one wonders if he would have arrived at the same theoretical and personal locations or led others to them as well. As Larzer Ziff has observed, "The power of great travel writing resides . . . in the author's capacity to present his heightened self-awareness in a manner that serves to move readers to question the unexamined familiarities of their own lives."[19]

Constance Fenimore Woolson

Tourism and "The Ancient City"

LIKE "ROUND BY PROPELLER," her narrative about travel around the Great Lakes, Constance Fenimore Woolson's travel narrative of St. Augustine, Florida, "The Ancient City," published two years after the Great Lakes piece, uses a fictional narrator and a group of tourists to take readers on a literary excursion in the oldest city in the United States. Published in December 1874 by *Harper's New Monthly Magazine*, which enjoyed a wide readership in part because of its emphasis on travel writing, the story layers different modes of storytelling that mimic the layers of history and voice. Told from the perspective of Woolson's female narrator, Martha, the narrative listens to the voices of others, attends to their nuances, and challenges complacent claims about place, history, race, and gender. From the historian Professor Macquoid, who went on the journey in part for the "pleasure of imparting information," to the wistful asides by Sara St. John and the words of local inhabitants who often contradict the expectations of the northern sightseers, Woolson challenges easy assumptions about the South.[1] By recasting the gaze and complicating voice and genre, Woolson "throw[s] new light on the structure of historical reality and historical knowledge" that María Cotera calls for. Meditating on the ways minority women's voices are heard in her book *Native Speakers*, Cotera questions assumptions about "history, agency, and marginalization" that Woolson exposed over a century earlier.[2] Following eight northern tourists as they go on sightseeing excursions around the city, her narrative crafts an imaginary geography that represents the meeting ground between the past and the present, an ancient city overlaid with history and monuments to the dead that meet the modern tourist and the modernizing tourist industry.

Layering textual modes—the poetic, the historic, travel reportage, short story, and romantic love plot—that simultaneously satisfy and confound reader expectations, Woolson uses the multiple voices of the tourists to expose the long history memorialized in the monuments and to satirize the tourists' careless, patronizing attitudes toward history, place, and the Other. Confronted with evidence of three hundred years of conflict in Florida, the winter sojourners often disregard the memories the monuments are meant to preserve, including the recent Civil War, as they pursue their own intrigues. While shaping the characters and fictional subplots of the narrative, Woolson shrewdly exposes what Dennis Berthold calls "the superficiality of travelers" who lack the responsibility and productive potential of ethical sightseeing that Dean MacCannell outlines. MacCannell claims, "The ultimate ethical test for tourists is whether they can realize the productive potential of their travel desires" in the ways they "grasp and make sense of the world" and understand "the *gap* that separates them from the *other-as-attraction*."[3] As she takes readers on an armchair tour of the city, Woolson reveals this gap when she turns their focus from the locals to the sightseers in a kind of reverse ethnography as both readers and locals focus on the gazers.

Arriving by steamer in "balmy" Florida after leaving New York in a January snowstorm ("Ancient City" 1), the band of travelers settles in for a winter's interlude in St. Augustine, which was emerging as a major resort location for sickly people, convalescents, and northern tourists from the increasingly elite classes. Hoping to escape the cruel winters of the North to find relief from, if not a cure for, such ailments as tuberculosis, people had been coming to St. Augustine at least since Ralph Waldo Emerson's stay in 1827, just six years after the United States acquired Florida from Spain. Of the climate Emerson wrote, "The air & sky of this ancient fortified dilapidated sandbank of a town are delicious." Later, its "unrivaled salubrity" that attracted "several hundred invalids and pleasure-seekers from the North" was touted in a *New York Times* story of April 28, 1860. According to Woolson's biographer Anne Boyd Rioux, Florida's mild climate attracted Woolson and her widowed mother Hannah, who suffered from rheumatism and shingles, just as it attracted characters in her story. With an eye toward elite northern visitors—"the gold-bearing Northern tourist" ("Ancient City" 3)—the growing tourist industry was on the cusp of really taking off, with magnificent resort hotels like Henry Flagler's Ponce de Leon, which welcomed its first guests in 1888, and the attendant modernization of the city. Instead of staying at the St. Augustine Hotel, one of the three large hotels in the city when they visited, Woolson's tourists, much like Woolson and her mother in 1873, decide on the more familiar boardinghouse where John Hoffman, one of the eight tourists, has stayed for several seasons. Historian Thomas Graham notes, "Renting rooms to invalid northern 'strangers' during the winter season had long been one of the primary ways of infusing outside money into the rickety St. Augustine economy." Such a windfall would have been particularly important, Graham observes, after the desolation of federal occupation during the Civil War, Reconstruction, and the economic depression of the 1870s. Woolson's sojourners, then, were part of a growing industry that was transforming coastal Florida.[4]

Getting to St. Augustine was a complicated matter for northerners. Much like the chaotic condition of other travels through the South, Woolson's group takes passage on a steamer from New York to Jacksonville, Florida, transfers to a smaller steamer bound for St. Augustine, and then takes a mule train from Tocoi on the St. Johns River to a rail depot shed, where an omnibus carries them "through the ever-present and never-mended mud hole" and over the causeway to St. Augustine ("Ancient City" 5). A railroad from Tocoi to the city had been built before the Civil War, but at this point the line depended on mule power instead of steam locomotives. Building railroads to connect the resort cities and the rest of Florida to the North would become a major endeavor for such financiers as Flagler as they built the state as a luxury tourist destination. But when Woolson's group visits, transportation is still complicated and uncomfortable. Having crossed the San Sebastian River, Miss Sharp, Iris Carew's governess, reads from her guidebook, "After three hours and one-half of this torture the exhausted tourist finds himself at the San Sebastian River, where a miserable ferry conveys him, more dead than alive, to the city of St. Augustine" (5). Although Woolson's travelers do not take the ferry, they are exhausted because even as late as the 1880s travel to Florida "remained a primitive ordeal."[5]

After a night's rest, with the sound of the surf lulling them to sleep, the group is ready to see the city, and thus they begin the real action of the travel story. Equipped with a guidebook and accompanied by Professor Macquoid, who is a walking encyclopedia, the group makes its way around the city, enabling Woolson to infuse her sketch with important historical facts for her readers. When "The Ancient City" was published in 1874, several guidebooks, some subsidized by the hotels, railroads, or land developers, guided tourists and satisfied their curiosity about Florida. *Sketches of St. Augustine* by Rufus Sewell had appeared in 1848, and a charming book, *Petals Plucked from Sunny Climes* (1880), would describe Florida and the Caribbean in lively fashion. Itself a kind of guide to St. Augustine, "The Ancient City" participates in the sight sacralization of more formal guidebooks, the social consensus of just what sights the tourist must see that MacCannell describes in his study of the leisure class.[6] Following the tourists as they visit the usual sights and providing historical information about them, the story also follows the whims and personalities of its characters.

Like most visitors to the city, like William Cullen Bryant before them, they visit Fort Marion, formerly Castillo de San Marco, built in 1565 by the Spanish and more recently occupied by the Fourth New Hampshire Infantry Regiment during the Civil War. Its "secret dungeon" and the "walled-up entrance" are reminders of the imprisonment of non-Catholics and of the Seminole chief who was held there before he made his daring escape ("Ancient City" 12). Along with the US barracks at St. Francis, a former Franciscan monastery, these ancient forts testify to the three hundred years of struggle between the Spanish, French, British, and Native Americans, in addition to the Union and Confederate armies, for control of the land. The travelers peer at the quaint coquina buildings and narrow streets of "Minorca Town," noting the mutiny of the Greek, Corsican, and Minorcan laborers who had been brought as indentured servants by the Englishman Andrew Turnbull in 1767 and subsequently mutinied against the "tyranny of their governor" (7). They visit the Mantanzas River, where the Spanish massacred "three hundred and fifty Huguenots," French Protestants who had fled Catholic Europe. Though the bones of the dead lie beneath the water, the name of the river, "Mantanzas, or slaughter," keeps the memory of the horrific deed alive, leading Sara to ask, "Is there any place about here where there were no massacres?" (16–17). The group also visits a plantation in ruins, its white chimney "a monument to the past," reaching back "more than a century before Plymouth or Jamestown," causing John Hoffman to moan, "Poor Florida! She is full of deserted plantations" (17). These monuments are sober reminders of St. Augustine's long history of violence, colonialism, and tyranny, from 1565—when Pedro Menéndez de Avila first claimed possession of the region from the Native Americans—through the American Civil War. The latter is commemorated by a simple memorial erected in 1872 by the Ladies Memorial Association of St. Augustine for the Confederate dead, "a broken shaft carved in coquina" (13). In this way, Woolson sketches a South that is haunted by the past, daily reminders of history built into the landscape and architecture of St. Augustine.[7]

Yet even as Woolson builds a text in which the past haunts and intersects with the present, she satirizes the tourists' more usual carelessness about history and the sites they visit. As she takes her group of travelers and her readers to the usual locations and rehearses the accepted history of place, she demonstrates her visitors' corruption of the sacredness of the sights with their antics and attitudes. Satirizing their personalities and actions, Woolson draws attention to them, complicating the gaze by turning it on the tourists and the society they represent. John Urry argues that because the tourist gaze is socially constructed, it "is a good way of getting at just what is happening in the 'normal society.'" That "normal society" in Woolson's hands is self-absorbed, unmindful of the costs of colonization as they enjoy themselves during a winter's retreat, figuratively dancing on the ruins of history. Quibbling about words, getting historical facts mixed up, engaging in casual flirtation, and smugly repeating a white male reading of history, the group of eight represents not only "the superficiality of travelers" but also the superficiality of "normal" America society and the ideologies it supports. Shrewdly turning the gazing eye back on the traveling and reading tourist, Woolson "manages," as Rioux argues, "to decenter her text . . . in ways that challenge her northern readers' presumed cultural superiority" and to situate them and her tourists at the margins of local knowledge.[8] Deploying satire, Woolson shifts the attention of the reader and unsettles expectations about sightseeing, travel narratives, and knowledge.

One conversation that illustrates how Woolson unsettles the travel sketch as a genre occurs when the group gets into a discussion about the 1837 escape of "Coochy," the Seminole chief Coacoochee, who was held prisoner in Fort Marion during the Second Seminole War. Aunt Diana confuses the chief's nickname, Wild Cat, for an actual cat. Sara confuses the chief with Osceola, with whom Coacoochee had escaped. When Captain Carlyle explains that Coacoochee was the son of "King Philip," Iris confuses his father with the King Philip of the New England Wampanoags. Sara references "the immortal Pontiac of the West" and "something about the Caloosahatchee," which leads John to primly ask whether she is thinking about "the distinguished chieftains Holatoochee and Taholooche, and the river Chattahoochee." That reminds the captain of the song line "with a hoochee-koochee-koochee," and that reminds Iris of her brother who plays the song on his banjo ("Ancient City" 11–12). Such banter may be entertaining, but it also exposes the historical ignorance and apparent delight of some of the travelers. Considering the captain, whose job it is to protect and represent the country, Woolson's tale prompts disconcerted readers to turn their focus on the thoughtless travelers.

In between these linguistic feats, the captain and Iris keep disappearing together in flirtatious rendezvous around the fort, Iris proposing that they "dance on the top" of the fort ("Ancient City" 9), as the narrative's love plots intersect with and disrupt the informative travel narrative and the history it recounts.

As the group explores the various locales of St. Augustine, Iris flirts not only with the handsome Captain but also with Mr. Mokes, whose money seems to qualify him as a better choice from Aunt Diana's point of view, and with Mr. Hoffman, who gives her roses to wear in her hair. At times it seems as if Iris is playing the three men against each other, perhaps for her own entertainment or self-gratification. Miss Sharp, Iris's governess, pairs up with both the professor, whose arm she grasps aboard the *Oceola*, and Mokes, who gives her history lessons under the Florida trees. At almost every location, couples pair up and wander off figuratively and literally from the historical narrative. At the end of part 1, as everyone is settling in for bed, Aunt Diana informs the others that Iris has disappeared. After speculating on the whereabouts of Mokes and Hoffman, the other women decide that Iris has eloped with the young captain, leaving readers until part 2 to find out what happens to Iris and the love plot. Although *Harper's* readers may have expected a conventional romantic ending, Woolson's love plot exposes the superficiality of the tourist class and its lack of real interest in others outside their circle and mimics the confused and competing layers of Florida's historical story.[9]

Although the professor and Hoffman provide some needed information about St. Augustine and its history for the travel narrative, their racist and sexist attitudes mar fact and open them up to Woolson's quiet satire. For instance, after Hoffman has given a quick historical account of the Minorcans, he comments on their physical appearance, noting the "dark almond-shaped eyes, now and then a classical nose, often a mass of Oriental black hair" that unfortunately do not meet his standards of unified beauty, leaving them metaphorically dismembered. When he remarks that the Minorcan girls remind him of Greece and Italy, Sara, who had been eager to make comparisons to Sappho, comments that she has never been to Italy. Though he does not say anything to her about this lack, the "reflection of an inward smile" that crossed his face suggests his condescension toward the less-traveled Sara ("Ancient City" 7). Woolson also makes a swipe at what we may refer to as "mansplaining," a sexist mannerism employed by some men to demean and discount women's knowledge and intellect.[10] For instance, when the group is discussing the coquina seawall built in 1842, the professor cites facts about it but does not understand as Martha does that the growing town may need the wall's protection. To her statement, he replies, "It will never be anything more than a winter resort, Miss Martha" (9), disregarding her understanding of St. Augustine's future. In these instances, Woolson satirizes the sexist attitudes and microaggressions of men like the professor and Hoffman. These instances demonstrate that, as a woman, Woolson can appreciate the need to hear alternative histories and knowledge, to give voice to the silenced and voiceless. As she satirizes the patriarchal, smug tourists who, superficial guidebooks in hand, assume their own superiority over the gendered and racial Other, she opens spaces between tourist and attraction so that the Other can be heard by the attentive reader.

When most of the group go over to North Beach on the *Osceola*, Miss Sharp taking the professor's arm, the narrator visits the St. Francis barracks and then comes across a monument for the Confederate dead. As she gazes upon "a broken shaft carved in coquina," "an old Negro" leaning on a cane pauses nearby. She engages in conversation with him, asking if he knew any of the forty-four men whose names are inscribed. He answers that he knew them and that his "ole woman" used to take care of some of them when they were babies, suggesting a familial relationship between white and black. When Martha comments on the changes for Blacks with the Civil War, he straightens and says, "Yas, we's free now. . . . I breave anoder breff effer sense, mistis, dat I do'" ("Ancient City" 13–14). While the material circumstances of the elder man's life may not have changed much, and he may not have much time to enjoy it, his sense of freedom is real. By contrast, one of the other visitors at the boardinghouse announces later that evening, "They do not quite know how to take their freedom yet," as if one has to be educated to breathe free air or that freedom is somehow reserved for those who deserve it (14). By complicating the meanings associated with the monument as a memorial to both the Confederacy and emancipation, Woolson undercuts simplistic ideas about slavery, the relations between master and enslaved, and the meaning of freedom that her readers and some of Florida's tourists may have.

Despite this tourist's assertion that "the colored people of St. Augustine" were isolated and "well cared for, and led easy lives," the African Americans the narrator encounters are proud of their freedom in ways that the northern visitor does not understand. The woman thinks "their ideas take the oddest shapes" ("Ancient City" 14). However, when the boardinghouse's Black employee, "The Sabre," "insists upon going and coming through the front door," and Aunt Viny names her daughter Victoria Linkum after Abraham Lincoln, they are asserting their mobility and citizenship in quiet acts of defiance and equality. By contrast, Sara hopes to look across the vast ocean to Africa without any obstructions, like the Canary Islands, eliding the harsh obstructions of the slave trade that made up the history of Black America. When Sara looks wistfully to the Nile for a "breath" of Africa, Martha understands that Africa is here, in St. Augustine's Black section of town. Appropriately called Little Africa before it was named Lincolnville in the 1880s, it signals the residents' connection to the ancestral home and their own sense of community. It is also a place to which Martha must be guided, lacking not only knowledge of the streets along the route but also Aunt Viny's intimate, cognitive map of place. When Viny says, "whenebber *I* wants to go dar, I jes *goes*," emphasizing the "I," she insinuates she has something that Martha lacks, an intuitive knowledge of place (14). When Martha cannot find her way to Little Africa, Woolson positions her as the outsider and Aunt Viny as the insider; when Sara desires an unobstructed view over the ocean to Africa, Woolson positions her a someone who ignores the realities of a past that haunts the racial memory of St. Augustine's Black community. Doing so, "The Ancient City" reveals the gaps in knowledge and perception that characterize her tourists. As feminist theorist Sandra Harding helps us understand, Woolson exposes the gaps in "dominant conceptual schemes" between insider and outsider, tourist and attraction, and text and subtext that lie in the spaces between what is said and what is known.[11]

Having visited the ruins of an old Florida plantation and imagining the story of the place, Sara and Martha find some modern "Arcadians," "who enjoy life as Nature intended." A young family living with very little in the way of material comforts is an example, perhaps, of James Cox's formulation of the South "as a coalescing 'negative identity.'" Their home lacks the comforts and dimensions of middle-class abodes: the house is more like an outbuilding, the dining room is situated out of doors, and there is "no window of any kind, no floor save the sand, and for a door only an old coverlet." At first readers are drawn to what the Arcadians lack, but then, catching the tenor of the place, Sara ventures, "They seem happy enough." The young parents do not work much, living primarily off the land, and they do not intend to send their young boy to school—"None of us-uns goes to school, my lady." Readers can see that Sara and Martha judge the family for what they lack—a nice home, steady work, education, and ambition. But then the young mother turns the scorn on the tourists. She does not want to be like the women who visit the South, and she calls the men "wimpsy," as if they lack some kind of vigor. Pondering the meaning of "wimpsy," Sara sees Mr. Mokes giving Miss Sharp a lesson on St. Augustine and observes, "He is certainly limpsy; then why not wimpsy?" ("Ancient City" 19–20). Reminiscent of Jeannette of Mackinaw who rejected the Bostonian doctor, Rodney Prescott, for her Native lover, Baptiste, in Woolson's Great Lakes story, the Arcadian Anita rejects northern definitions of manhood for her more virile Gaspar. As she does so, Woolson shifts the gaze from the Arcadians to the northern tourists as Anita and the narrative question assumptions about progress, knowledge, and northern consumerism. In this way Woolson poses an ethics of sightseeing that both critiques the careless tourists and demonstrates a more nuanced understanding of the relations between sightseer and attraction, here the local residents like Anita, the elderly Black man, and Aunt Viny.[12]

Deploying multiple layers of storytelling, perspective, and voice, Woolson constructs an ethics of sightseeing as she models a revisionist history of place. When she pauses the plot to listen to the people who populate her story, the travelers with their microaggressions and the locals who form part of their tourist experience, readers hear the personalities of both her travelers and the "attractions." Giving voice to the Arcadians and African Americans, Woolson casts them as subjects with their own experiences and perspectives rather than as objects of the tour in ways that counter reader and tourist expectations. By listening carefully to the multiple voices of place, Woolson demonstrates what Henry James noted about the stories in *Rodman the Keeper*: "As the fruit of a remarkable minuteness of observation and tenderness of feeling on the part of one who evidently did not glance and pass, but lingered and analysed, they have a high value, especially when regarded in the light of the *voicelessness* of the conquered and reconstructed South."[13] Attending to the nuances of her subjects and letting them talk back to the northern travelers, she points to alternative experiences of place and history and to an ethics of inclusion and empathy that extends beyond the usual activity of sightseeing.

This ethics is evident as well when Woolson redirects readers' gaze from the tourist attractions to the fictional travelers and the "normal society" they represent. Doing so, as Anne Boyd Rioux remarked about her short story "Felipa," she "turns the tables on the northern reader and reverses the direction of the imperial gaze, modeling empathy rather than objectification." Both Woolson and her narrator are outsiders glimpsing the lives of the locals, the Blacks, the Minorcans, and the Arcadian couple. They do not get to know their cultures, nor do they attempt to dig in and find out about their way of life or establish a rapport with them.[24] After all, they are sightseers, casual cultural "colonizers" bearing northern money and northern attitudes. Yet even as she participates in promoting tourism to Florida, Woolson obliquely, subtly turns the focus from the locals to the sightseers in these brief cultural encounters, turning what Zora Neale Hurston calls the "spy-glass of Anthropology" back on the visitors. She does this in part by letting the indigenous talk back, not only so they may be heard but also to satirize and critique the outsider, the northerner who thinks she represents knowledge and "ethnographic authority."[14] By deploying and then subverting the tourist's gaze, by juxtaposing outsider, touristic accounts of history and place alongside alternate, corrective insider accounts, Woolson demonstrates an ethics of sightseeing that exposes the smugness of the visitors and their nearsighted ignorance about the complex locations and peoples they visit and then will leave. Implying an alternate method of sightseeing in the narrative's multimodal, polyvocal format, Woolson models a more complex, nuanced, ethical approach to seeing the South that reckons with a history of slaughter, the breath of freedom, and an Arcadia whose "sights" talk back.

Mark Twain's South in
Life on the Mississippi

Geographies of Travel

TRACING THE HISTORY OF the Mississippi River and his own history with it in *Life on the Mississippi* (1883), Mark Twain probes the geographies of the South—specifically the geographic, technological, and social geographies of 1882 when he revisited the great river and the locations of his youth. As the epigraph to the book he employs an 1863 editorial from *Harper's Magazine*, in which "the basin of the Mississippi" is identified as "the body of the nation," pointing to the river basin's great extent and capability of "supporting a dense population." The last line of the epigraph, "As a dwelling-place for civilized man it is by far the first upon our globe," connects civilization to the river and what it stands for. Like the river he describes, the best of civilization is characterized by change and transformation, by movement. In contrast, he will satirize the "sham civilization" of materialism, greed, and hypocrisy that retards the progress of the South in *Adventures of Huckleberry Finn*. After all that Huck, his youthful narrator, has seen and experienced on the river, at the end of the novel he declares that he is going to "light out for the Territory," saying, "Aunt Sally she's going to adopt me and sivilize me, and I can't stand it. I been there before."[1] For Huck, civilization is uncomfortable, static, confining, something that grates against his innate sense of right. But in *Life on the Mississippi*, written as Twain was thinking through the adventures of Huck and Jim, civilization is figured as progress, movement, and the river as the great scene and symbol of the transformation of the nation at the end of the nineteenth century.

Jerome Loving remarks, "It was always Mark Twain's destiny to write about the Mississippi River." Having grown up in Hannibal, Missouri, Twain like other boys nursed an ambition to be a "steamboatman" (*LoM* 21). He had considered writing a book about the river as early as 1866 and had written to his wife Olivia in 1871, "When I come to write the Mississippi book, *then* look out! I will spend 2 months on the river & take notes, & I bet you I will make a standard work." Later he sent seven articles on the river to William Dean Howells, editor of the *Atlantic Monthly*, who ran them from January to August in 1875. These pieces would form the first twenty chapters of *Life on the Mississippi*, describing the "science" of piloting and Twain's apprenticeship as a cub pilot under Horace Bixby. As Loving affirms, "[The 1878 book *Old Times on the Mississippi*] was clearly a dress rehearsal for the adventures of Tom [Sawyer] and Huck [Finn]." It was also a dress rehearsal for *Life on the Mississippi*. Twain returned to the river in 1882 to write a history of it and to refresh his mind during an interlude in the composition of *Adventures of Huckleberry Finn*, which he had put aside in 1876 after completing the first fifteen chapters and again in 1880 after bringing in the Duke and the King and staging Colonel Sherburn's killing of the drunken Boggs. After Twain's return to the river, he was finally able to push the novel to completion for 1885 publication by Harper's. In the meantime, proposing to write a "'standard work'" of the Mississippi, he took along James Osgood, his Boston publisher, and a stenographer to record his reminiscences and observations as he traveled the river of his youth and the river that it had become in the interim. What he composed was "a shaggy conglomeration of genres—journal, autobiography, history, fiction, and travel" that takes readers with him as he maps the geographies of the river.[2]

Having stitched in the sections from *Old Times* and a quick history of European discovery of the river to form the first twenty chapters of *Life on the Mississippi*, Twain announces, "After twenty-one years' absence I felt a very strong desire to see the river again, and the steamboats, and such of the boys as might be left" (*LoM* 110). He is immediately struck by how the glory of the bygone days "had dissolved and vanished away in these twenty-one years" because of changes that had occurred during his absence (112). Beginning his journey at St. Louis, he relates the "absence of the river-man" in the billiards room of the Southern Hotel, the grandest hotel in St. Louis, the growth and refinement of the city, and the "woeful" changes to the levee and riverfront where floated only "half a dozen sound-asleep steamboats" ("I used to see a solid mile of wide-awake ones!") (114). As a nexus of travel on the river, St. Louis is a harbinger of the kinds of transformations Twain will witness as he travels down the river, the past that Twain remembers giving way to the present and the future. The rivermen and the mass of steamboats they used to captain have been exchanged for new types of men and craft, and the old romance of the river has been refined by "progress, energy, prosperity" (114). These are the kinds of changes the narrative will map, the technological, commercial, physical, and cultural changes that the celebrity who must now travel incognito describes as he revisits the locations of the past when he was a cub pilot just learning to read the river.

As the brief sketch of St. Louis illustrates, what those changes meant to Twain and how we are to read them is a bit unresolved. A tension between past and present, between nostalgia and realism runs through the narrative. Focusing on the conjunction between Twain the tourist and Twain the returning local resident, Jeffrey Melton writes, "Twain's problem throughout the narrative has been the overwhelming change he has been forced to encounter, if not reconcile." Similarly, Todd Goddard sees the tension between nostalgia for the old home and an appreciation for progress: "Twain repeatedly invokes the familiar narrative of returning home as a time-altering act of nostalgic performance, only to subvert this act by emphasizing the ever-changing nature of place." Larzer Ziff contends, "While adhering to his belief that there never was and never could be anything so colorful and pleasurable as steamboating, Twain nevertheless accepted the railroad and barge traffic that replaced the paddle-wheelers as improvements in time, money, and safety." James Cox calls the Twain of *Life on the Mississippi*, "the apostle of progress": "In his downward journey to New Orleans, Mark Twain, the apostle of progress, sees the false pasts which society has erected to defend itself from the ruins of time; at the same moment, he laments the lost glory of the steamboating epoch." Because *Life* recounts two journeys, the physical journey down and then back up the Mississippi River, and the emotional, personal journey back in time to his youth, readers note that Twain's reactions to change at times are at variance. As Melton claims, he is both returning home and a tourist of the meeting ground between the present and his old familiarity with the river and the South to which it flows. Memory for Twain, as Todd Goddard observes, is overlaid by "the changed and changing face of the present." Thomas Ruys Smith finds that Twain's "organizing approach" to the narrative was to "reminisce, revisit, and research," making this mosaic of a narrative complexly layered and fluid, much like the river it describes.[3]

For the aspiring steamboat pilot, the river was challenging to learn. Bixby, the pilot who tutored the young Samuel Clemens, told him, "There's only one way to be a pilot, and that is to get this entire river by heart. You have to know it just like A B C" (*LoM* 32). After much effort, the emerging pilot comes to think of the river as "a wonderful book" that he could read, but, while the book of the river divulges some of the river's secrets, he also came to understand that the river was always changing, that it "had a new story to tell every day" (47). The river he describes is fluid, changing its course and disrupting boundaries, requiring the pilot and his apprentice continually to reread it. They must learn "a new vocabulary" and search for "subtle signs," to chart and re-chart their way with each journey.[4] Like the river itself, knowledge, Twain comes to learn, is fluid, unfixed, subject to change.

When he began his career as a cub pilot, he had a notebook that "fairly bristled" with the names of towns and the minute features of the river to help him memorize its "twelve or thirteen hundred miles," "to get this entire river by heart," to learn its "*shape*" (*LoM* 28, 32, 39). But as he discovers, the river defies absolute learning because of its propensity to change its shape and length. In the first chapter of the book, as he introduces the river, its history, and what makes it remarkable, he points to the ways it changes course and breaks down boundaries. He describes "its disposition to make prodigious jumps by cutting through narrow necks of land, and thus straightening and shortening itself" as well as "moving bodily *sidewise*!" (2). In chapter 17 he details how the river shortens itself by cutting "a little gutter" across a narrow neck of land, calculating that the Mississippi between Cairo and New Orleans was 1,215 miles long 176 years earlier, that in 1722 it was 1,040 miles long, and that it had lost 67 miles since then, making its length at the time of writing 973 miles (93). Indeed, one of the first things that he learns from Horace Bixby is that the river is ever changing. The landmarks that guide the pilot down the river must always be tested and reaffirmed or amended. Goddard claims that Twain learns from Bixby "that the value of the Mississippi lies in its changeability"; one might say the same for the "body of the nation" (*LoM* v).[5]

Changeable too is memory, which the old ABCs of the river test. Just south of Memphis on his return journey to the river, Twain sees the ruins of an old warehouse and some houses, prompting him to muse: "I wondered if I had forgotten the river, for I had no recollection whatever of this place; the shape of the river, too, was unfamiliar" (*LoM* 117). He relates: "I couldn't remember that town; I couldn't place it, couldn't call its name. So I lost part of my temper" (118). But as he watches a family go ashore at what seems an unlikely place, there being no town in sight, he realizes that "the eccentric river" had cut off the former river town by building a towhead (sandbar) between it and the river, transforming the French river town of St. Genevieve into a US country town. Then, near Cairo, he laments, "No vestige of Hat Island is left now; every shred of it is washed away. I do not even remember what part of the river it used to be in" (126). He goes on to list the changes in this section of the river: Beaver Dam Rock is now in the middle of the river, Jacket Pattern Island is "whittled down to a wedge," one of the "islands formerly called the Two Sisters" is completely gone, and the other is now on the Missouri side of the river but still a part of Illinois. As these examples illustrate, the shifting river changed the geographic and political shape of the nation and challenged Twain's memory of it and the past. Hoping to disembark at the town of Napoleon, Arkansas, he learns that it is completely gone: "The Arkansas River burst through it, tore it all to rags, and emptied it into the Mississippi!" (169). He muses that it was astonishing to see "the Mississippi rolling between unpeopled shores and straight over the spot where I used to see a good big self-complacent town twenty years ago." It was here, he remembers, that he first had printed news of the *Pennsylvania*'s "mournful disaster" that killed his brother Henry when its boilers blew up (169). The wreck itself, which would have memorialized his brother and the other passengers who were killed, has likewise vanished: "No signs left of the wreck of the *Pennsylvania*" (150).

More than simply changing the geographic shape of the body of the nation as it cuts through and devours land, the moving river is a cipher for a nation that too is ever-changing, in process, forging new meanings, testing the signs of the past, and challenging the stasis of memory. Twain repeatedly joins the shifting river to memory, not only the work of memorization but also to memory of the past and memorials to it, like the wreck that has disappeared beneath the surface. Like the river, memories cross boundaries, are fluid and generate new spaces—geographic, cultural, and psychological—that will lead Twain to and through the undercurrents of the great river and the meanings of civilization. Writing of the South almost twenty years after the Civil War, Twain, Goddard argues, envisions "a space that is radically open, relational, in process, and interconnected."[6]

Not only has the shape of the river changed during his twenty-one-year absence, so too have activity on it and the towns that front it. As Twain remembers, during "the heyday of the steamboating prosperity, the river from end to end was flaked with coal fleets and timber rafts" and the "hosts of the rough characters" who manned them (*LoM* 11). In the old days, the pilot "was the only unfettered and entirely independent human being that lived in the earth" (71). There was a glory in steamboating and good money to be made by pilots and crew when Twain first took to the river, even if it took about twenty-five days to transport cargo from St. Louis to New Orleans and back, including loading and unloading (72). To illustrate the improvements in steamboat technology since the early days, Twain provides a table of some of the famous steamboat trips: for example, the run from New Orleans to Natchez (268 miles) was shortened from 6 days, 6 hours, 40 minutes in 1814 to just 17 hours, 11 minutes in 1870 (89–91). He explains: "The railroads have killed the steamboat passenger traffic by doing in two or three days what the steamboats consumed a week in doing: and the towing fleets have killed the through-freight traffic by dragging six or seven steamer-loads of stuff down the river at a time, at an expense so trivial that steamboat competition was out of the question" (115).

Beginning with St. Louis, Twain describes a geography of the "interplay between the physical and the social" as the South was beginning to transform after the Civil War.[7] Moaning that "a glory that once was had dissolved and vanished away in these twenty-one years" (*LoM* 112), he nonetheless notes the positive changes in St. Louis, which had doubled in size. "Fine new homes" grace the outskirts of the "domed and steepled metropolis"; Forest Park, Tower Park, and the Botanical Gardens demonstrate the city's interest in civic "improvements"; and the narrow streets, although still "ill-paved," are now well-lighted. These details suggest an improved quality of life for the people of St. Louis. He remarks, "St. Louis is a great and prosperous and advancing city; but the river-edge of it seems dead past resurrection" (115). Listing the things that are gone—the "throngs of men, and mountains of freight," the "foul doggeries," and the "poison-swilling Irishmen," replaced by "handfuls of ragged Negroes"—he points to changes in the workforce caused by the new technologies. Along with the towboat and railroad, he blames the "mighty bridge, stretching along over our heads," the Eads Bridge, for the "slaughter and spoliation" of the river edge and its former life (115).

With the expansion of the railroads at midcentury, James Buchanan Eads had understood that a sturdy bridge across the river at St. Louis was needed to ensure the efficient transportation of goods. The bridge he designed, known as the Eads Bridge, was the world's first steel arch bridge and the longest bridge up to that time. Participating in the changes in commerce and transportation after the Civil War, the Eads Bridge joined others that were linking the East and the West. In 1856, just two years after Catharine Maria Sedgwick and the excursionists celebrated the extension of the railroad to the Mississippi River, the first railroad bridge across the Mississippi joined Rock Island, Illinois, to Davenport, Iowa. Thirteen years later, in 1869, the first transcontinental railroad united the nation and changed the ways travelers like Helen Hunt Jackson and the author of *Roughing It* toured the West. Among other improvements Twain witnesses as he continues down the river, are changes in navigating the river, some of which had been initiated by the government to improve safety. Lighting along the river, he quips, has turned it into "a sort of two-thousand-mile torch-light procession" of kerosene lamps dotting the riverbanks.[8] Other improvement like "snag-boats," barge-like structures with cranes and hoists for removing snags and other obstructions, reliable charts developed and patented by Horace Bixby, and wing dams and dikes developed by the US River Commission to deflect the currents and confine the river all contributed to making travel on the river safer. Though he grouses that these improvements have "knocked the romance out of piloting," he acknowledges that travel on the river is "nearly as safe and simple as driving a stage" (138).

Just as navigation on the river and transportation technologies were chang-ing, the economic and civic life of the South was undergoing transformation. Mapping the social geography of the New South during what Broadus Mitchell in 1928 would refer to as the Industrial Revolution of the South, Twain charts the changes in the towns and cities along the river. For instance, he remarks on the new sewage system in Memphis to combat the "desolating visitation of the yellow fever" (*LoM* 147). At Helena, Arkansas, he credits the cottonseed oil mill, a foundry, and other manufacturing businesses, two railways, and a booming cotton trade with transforming the town into the second-most-important city of the state (154). At Natchez he notes the ice factory that manufactures so much that now everyone, not just the rich, can have ice. The first commercial ice manufacturing plant had opened in New Orleans in 1868, and the plant in Natchez began operation in the late 1870s. Natchez, the great cotton and slave port, boasted the Rosalie Yarn Mill and the Natchez Cotton Mill that togeth-er employed over 350 persons. Seeking to take advantage of a good supply of cotton and cheap labor, Mississippi had embarked on a program of cotton mill expansion, going from eight mills to twenty-two mills between 1880 and 1906.[9] These kinds of changes helped convert Natchez and the other river towns into "manufacturing strongholds and railway centers" (192).

Although Twain finds that New Orleans "had not changed—to the eye," the gutters flushed two or three times daily have improved sanitation in a city his-torically plagued by yellow fever. As in Natchez, ice is available for everybody. Twain asserts that it is the "best-lighted city in the Union," having just turned on electric lights in 1882, and "the telephone is everywhere," having been patented by Alexander Graham Bell in 1876. The city had also made "notable advances in journalism," with the extensive business reporting in the *Times-Democrat* and the solid reputation of the *Picayune* as one America's best newspapers. With its good clubs and resorts, New Orleans, he writes, "is a driving place commercially, and has a great river, ocean, and railway business" (*LoM* 200), evincing the ways the South was transforming from a predominately agricultural region into an industrial, commercial, and transportation hub. The glory of the old steamboating days may be gone, but the South that Twain visits is in the middle of an industrial revolution that would transform it, at least economically and technically, into the New South.

According to Twain, the third great factor in the changed South is the Civil War, which, twenty years after its close, continues to haunt and stymie the emergence of the New South. All along the Lower Mississippi he sees evidence of the war, battle scenes and ruins that chart a geography of memory and violence. One of the sites he mentions is Fort Pillow, "memorable because of the massacre perpetrated there during the war," almost the only massacre, he claims, "that can be found in American history" (*LoM* 143). On April 12, 1864, Confederate general Nathan Bedford Forrest surrounded the fort on the Tennessee side of the river, and, even though the six hundred Union troops there surrendered, his troops massacred the three hundred African American soldiers among them in a horrific display of racism. Next, Twain mentions the June 6, 1862, river battle at Memphis, noting that Horace Bixby and James E. Montgomery, both of whom he had served during his steamboating days, had taken part in the fight (147). Then, as he approaches Baton Rouge, he passes Port Hudson, "scene of two of the most terrific episodes of the war" –the "night battle between Farragut's fleet and Confederate land batteries" on April 14, 1863 (194). The forty-eight-day siege that followed soon after resulted in the loss of 12,208 lives and the loss of control of the Mississippi by the Confederates.[10]

At Vicksburg Twain pauses to re-create the scene of the siege and bombardment of the city. He notes how the three thousand noncombatants were "utterly cut off from the world," how the formerly bustling river city went quiet and prices on goods exploded, flour going for "two hundred dollars a barrel." He relates how the "ground-shaking thunder-crashes of artillery" and the "rain of iron fragments" sent residents scurrying to their "cave refuges in the clay precipices," and how finally residents "got used to being bombshelled out of home and into the ground" during the six weeks' bombardment that lasted from May 18 to July

4, 1863. He writes, "Signs and scars still remain, as reminders of Vicksburg's tremendous war experiences." While the "signs and scars" point to the suffering of the South, other Vicksburg memorials signal Union victory. The national cemetery there commemorates the dead Union soldiers (the "16,600 WHO DIED FOR THEIR COUNTRY"), a new metal monument stands at the location of the surrender of Vicksburg to General Grant, and a common memento of the war, an unexploded bombshell ("[that] an aged colored man showed us, with pride") (*LoM* 175–79) also marks the end of slavery. These mementos and monuments preserve and shape an imaginary of the past that continues to shape the present. Like other postbellum visitors to the South, Twain observes, "The war is the great chief topic of conversation." He explains that in the South "every man you meet was in the war; and every lady you meet saw the war" (212). Southerners cannot escape the war even after it is over because it was so much a part of their intimate lives and because the "signs and scars" remain visible and palpable. It seems as if everyone dates events by the war, Twain humorously quoting an old African American woman speaking to a young New Yorker to make his point about the ubiquity of it in the lives, conversation, and thinking of southerners: "Ah, bless yo' heart, honey, you ought to seen dat moon befo' de waw!" (213).

According to Twain, Sir Walter Scott and "Walter Scott disease" were "in great measure responsible for the war" because of the romanticized view of society his novels supported (*LoM* 219, 220). Scott's tales of medieval romance and chivalry, Twain contends, "created rank and caste down there" and the reverence for them that marked antebellum southern culture. He complains that Scott set "the world in love with dreams and phantoms," with decayed and sham institutions and values: "sham grandeurs, sham gauds, and sham chivalries." "Admiration of his fantastic heroes and their grotesque 'chivalry'" created a bogus civilization that Twain argues led to the war and continued to undermine progress in the South. Southern writers, he says, were writing "for the past, not the present" (*LoM* 220). More, "The South has not yet recovered from the debilitating influence of [Scott's] books," as traces of "inflated language and other windy humbuggeries" rubbed up against "the wholesome and practical nineteenth-century smell of cotton factories and locomotives" (195). "And so you have practical common sense, progressive ideas, and progressive works, mixed up with the duel, the inflated speech, and the jejune romanticism of an absurd past" (219). Even as the South was transforming under pressure from industrialization, some of the old forms of thinking and social relations persisted. Part of the conundrum of the South, with its natural resources and luxuriant flora, was the pull of the old habits of chivalry, rank, and racism against the progressivism of the New South. Although Vicksburg had signs of "a promising future of prosperity and importance," Twain opines that "if one may judge from the past, the river towns will manage to find and use a chance, here and there, to cripple and retard their progress" (179–80).

One of the conundrums *Life on the Mississippi* uncovers is the effect on African Americans of the Civil War. Twain comments that he sees a new mobility by which Blacks take advantage of the freedom to travel, but he also gives a picture of the sharecropping system that attempts to keep Black laborers bound in debt peonage and by the persistent racism, what Carol Anderson calls "white rage" against "black advancement." Remarking on the new mobility of some former slaves, Twain notes, "These poor people could never travel when they were slaves; so they make up for the privation now. They stay on a plantation till the desire to travel seizes them; then they pack up, hail a steamboat, and clear out" (*LoM* 150). After being subjected to the immobility of slavery, Blacks in "the migrating Negro region" would go as far as their money would take them. "They only want to be moving," Twain writes (150). Intuiting the connections between freedom, movement, and citizenship, these still impoverished new citizens exercised their freedom by traveling. As Eric Leed has explained, "the right to travel" marks "the status of 'free' man." This was an indicator of the national ethos, as Jack Kerouac would write: "We were all . . . performing our noble function of the time, *move*."[11] Their mobility positions them as US citizens, a point that Gretchen Sorin has made in her study of the correlation between automobile travel and civil rights for African Americans, *Driving while Black*.

But this mobility belies the persistent racism and the neo-slavery of share-cropping. After the Civil War a system of sharecropping was instituted to assure agricultural production: laborers raised crops for the landowner and then shared in the profits. Because the laborer had to purchase supplies and goods from the plantation store, after profits and costs were assessed he often found himself in debt to the store. As Twain points out, the racism, and the "grouty," sullen attitude of the planter toward the black laborer, prevented him from having anything but a "chill business relation with him," opening the door for an outsider, "some thrifty Israelite" to run the store. Pointing to Jewish merchants and their role in the sharecropping regime and the resulting debt slavery, Twain claims, "[The] Israelite . . . encourages the thoughtless negro and wife to buy all sorts of things which they could do without—buy on credit, at big prices, month after month, credit based on the Negro's share of the growing crop; and at the end of the season, the negro's share belongs to the Israelite" (*LoM* 172).

He made the same point later in an article for *Harper's Magazine*, "Concerning the Jews" (1898), about the ways the Jewish merchant manipulated debt so that at "the end of the season [he] was proprietor of the negro's share of the present crop," thus allowing him to secure land.[12] Discouraged and disgruntled by the system that kept him perpetually in debt, the laborer, Twain explains, "will take a steamboat and migrate," leaving the planter with having to get "a stranger in his place who does not know him, does not care for him, will fatten the Israelite for a season, and follow his predecessor per steamboat" (172). In Twain's accounting of sharecropping, the "grouty" attitude of the planter contributes to new systems of slavery under the sharecropping model. Further, echoing what Olmsted had written about antebellum slavery, Twain complains that it also retards the planter and the South as a whole from prospering. Anticipating the difficult ending of *Huckleberry Finn*, Twain figures travel by African Americans as both a means of escape from a difficult situation and as a representation of freedom. He also sketches a racist South that persists in keeping the emancipated laborer in virtual slavery just as the freed Jim was held prisoner to Tom Sawyer's outmoded ideas of heroism and adventure.

INTERLUDE

Returning to the Mississippi in 1882 to escape the difficulties of writing the boys' book turned serious critique of American materialism and hypocrisy, Twain found a South that was both altered and the same, a South energized by new technologies but enervated by persistent racism and social, ideological humbuggeries. Afforded the chance to revisit scenes of his past and gather new material for *Adventures of Huckleberry Finn*, he gathers material that will go into the chapters concerning the feuding Grangerford and Shepherdson families and the scoundrels of the Royal Nonesuch. At the border of Kentucky and Tennessee, Twain hears the story of the Darnell-Watson feud that had been going on for so long that no one remembered what started it. Like the feuding families of *Huck Finn*, these families attend the same church, sitting on different sides and bringing their guns with them. As in the novel, Twain relates in *Life on the Mississippi* how a feud led to the death of "a young man of nineteen." Pursued by "a whole gang of the enemy," he "jumped down behind a wood-pile" while his pursuers "were "galloping and cavorting and yelling and banging away." The young man was chased into a river and tried to escape by swimming downstream. The men kept shooting at him, and—like young Buck Grangerford in *Huck Finn*— "when he struck shore he was dead" (*LoM*, 129–30). In the novel, Huck is "so sick" at what he has seen that all he can do is bring Buck's body to shore and cover it before making his own escape.

In other *Life on the Mississippi* episodes, Twain describes characters that prefigure the King and Duke, their scams, and the Royal Nonesuch. Having mentioned the manufacturing enterprises along the river, he pauses to share a conversation between two drummers in the oleomargarine business and cottonseed and olive oil business, which they reveal to be sham businesses with fake products. Concerned only with "doing a ripping trade," these two drummers prefigure the various schemes the King and Duke hit upon in *Huck Finn* to dupe and defraud people along the river (*LoM* 194). One of the efforts of the King and Duke is the Royal Nonesuch, in which they put on a heavily bowdlerized version of a conglomeration of Shakespearean plays. On his way back up the river in *Life on the Mississippi*, Twain recalls a couple of young Englishmen who had come to Hannibal, arraying themselves in "cheap royal finery" and practicing the sword fight from *Richard III* (237). Unfortunately, a Hannibal villager was taken by what he saw, "and the histrionic poison entered his bones." He left his blacksmith apprenticeship and went to St. Louis to try an acting career, "imagining himself to be *Othello*." Not gifted as an actor, this aspirant finally is cast as the second to last Roman soldier on the night that Twain went to the theater to see him in *Julius Caesar* (237–38). The poor man was duped by the traveling Englishmen and the promise of theatrical glory just as the citizens of Bricksville will be duped by the show that the King and the Duke stage in *Huck Finn*. At least the townspeople wise up to the scam, unlike the hapless apprentice, and are prepared to enact frontier justice.

It is easy for the reader to see how Twain's experiences on the river made their way into the episodes, characters, and social satire of the latter half of the novel. But perhaps the most telling thing Twain came to understand was how the ideologies promoted by Walter Scottism kept the South from truly becoming "a dwelling-place for civilized man" (*LoM* v). In his last desperate scam of the novel, the King sells Jim, a slave he did not own, a man who was already emancipated, and then drinks up the proceeds from the illegal sale. Captured as a runaway slave, Jim is held at Silas Phelps's place while Huck assists Tom Sawyer in his elaborate plans to help the imprisoned freeman escape. Unmindful of the distress Jim may be in, the adolescent Tom keeps the grown man a prisoner to his machinations as he reenacts, as Twain puts it in *Life on the Mississippi*, the "sham grandeurs, sham gauds, and sham chivalries" of "fantastic heroes and their grotesque 'chivalry'" for the sake of his own adventure, his own benefit (195).

These are the very ideas that Twain has claimed in *Life on the Mississippi* led to the Civil War and retarded true progress in the South after the war. The ideas of caste and rank supported by southern ideology kept the emancipated Jim enslaved and imprisoned and also contributed to the disenfranchisement of African Americans after the war. Indeed, Twain argues that the South remains subservient to a worn-out ideology of "a long-vanished society" even as it tries to forge a New South of commerce and technology (*LoM* 219). By crafting the long, bizarre ending to his novel, marked by one ridiculous scheme after another to free a free man, Twain mimics the humbuggeries of the South and drives home the sheer inanity of an ideology based not on progress but on the past, one that "cripples and retards" meaningful change (180). Just as the past and the present meet in uncanny ways in *Life on the Mississippi*, so in *Adventures of Huckleberry Finn* they meet, this time on the figure of Jim, the emancipated African American held prisoner by racism. In many ways, this is the work of *Life on the Mississippi*; more than a standard work or history of the river, it is a map of the deep undercurrents that enabled Twain to reimagine the direction of his great novel and the past it recounts.

Mobility and Immobility in
The Souls of Black Folk

IN 1903 W. E. B. DU BOIS pulled together fourteen essays in the groundbreaking book *The Souls of Black Folk*, acclaimed by Henry James in 1907 as "the only 'Southern' book of any distinction published for many a year." *Souls*, according to Du Bois biographer David Levering Lewis, "redefined the terms of a three-hundred-year interaction between black and white people" in an "electrifying manifesto mobilizing a people" for the work still to be done to "win a place in history." Organized around spirituals, sorrow songs, *Souls* sketches a counter history in which "the voices of the dark submerged and unheard" are heard. The fourteen chapters take up different topics: a biographical sketch of Black minister Alexander Crummell, a "polemical centerpiece" on Booker T. Washington, autobiographical sketches, and critiques of materialism, progress, and the New South. The stunning "Forethought" announces that the problem of the twentieth century is "the problem of the color-line" and introduces the metaphor of the Veil. Du Bois describes how the "two worlds within and without the Veil" create the double-consciousness of African American identity, "this sense of always looking at one's self through the eyes of others." Extending Emerson's notion of the double-consciousness in "The Transcendentalist," the tension between "the two lives, of the understanding and of the soul," to describe the racial twoness of the African American, Du Bois locates identity in the hyphen in "African-American," the in-between spaces of identity that have been hidden from white America by the Veil of racism. One of the daring achievements of the book is to lift the Veil for readers to reveal a realistic, curative, multivalent analysis of the Black community, to pry open assumptions and stereotypes about African Americans.[1]

In some ways, *The Souls of Black Folk* is also a travel book about Du Bois's personal journeys of identity and his exploration of the situation of Black Americans at the turn of the century. Indeed, Anne Raine situates *Souls* in the Thoreauvian tradition that joins travel, self-discovery, and ecocriticism as Du Bois plots a "poetics of race and place" on the southern terrain. Like the best of travel books, it invites readers to three tours: "abroad, into the author's brain, and into [the reader's] own." As Norman Douglas puts it, "the writer should ... possess a brain worth exploring; some philosophy of life ... and the courage to proclaim it and put it to the test.'" These characteristics are evident in *Souls*, particularly in two key essays, "Of the Meaning of Progress" and "Of the Black Belt," which relate the intranational travel south of an astute observer of the human condition, a trained philosopher and sociologist. Organized geographically and spatially, these essays take readers with Du Bois on the road as he goes into the Tennessee hills looking for a school to teach and traces the boundaries of the Georgia Black Belt. "Roaming forlorn counties and peering into crowded cabins, describing people in misery and misery in people," Lewis claims, Du Bois maps the lives of the Black folk as he maps his journeys. Not only does he provide quick glimpses of travel for an African American, he also tells readers what he sees from the road, whom he meets, and the stories their lives tell, exposing the southern social environment and how it shapes and limits people's lives spatially, "materially and psychologically."[2] Using what he sees from the road, he gets at a description of not only the souls of black folk but the soul of place, the geographies of travel, place, and immobility that shape the identities of those who "live within the Veil" (*Souls* 2). Juxtaposing his own mobility against the forms of immobility of the people he describes, he also exposes the paradoxes of the South, a land of "mingled hope and pain" (103), of progress and regression, especially for those who live behind the Veil.

"Of the Meaning of Progress" relates two trips to rural Tennessee, an initial journey to its backwoods and a return ten years later. As a student at Fisk University, Du Bois, a northerner come south, sets out like many of the other students to find a school where he might teach in the summers. Established first as the Fisk Free Colored School in Nashville in 1866 and renamed in 1867 as Fisk University, it was "the most famous college for the uplift" of African Americans by the time Du Bois entered as a sophomore in 1885. The goal of educating African Americans after emancipation had led to the proliferation of teachers and schools, and Du Bois was part of the "mission of educational uplift in the backward South" that drew both Black and white teachers. Setting off in 1886 on the Lebanon Pike east out of Nashville, Du Bois traveled "no more than

fifty miles from Nashville" to Wilson County, where he found his school and a
community that would remain in his memory, prompting him ten years later
to retrace his steps.[3]

Recounting that initial summer trek, he writes, "I see now the white, hot roads
lazily rise and fall and wind before me under the burning July sun: I feel the deep
weariness of heart and limb as ten, eight, six miles stretch relentlessly ahead. . . .
So I walk on and on—horses were too expensive—until I had wandered beyond
railways, beyond stage lines, to a land of 'varmints' and rattlesnakes, where the
coming of a stranger was an event, and men lived and died in the shadow of one
blue hill" (*Souls* 52). If he had the money, he could have taken the Tennessee and
Pacific Railroad that connected Nashville to Lebanon, but, since he did not, he
walked. One can imagine the dusty loneliness of the road as he went farther and
farther from Nashville, past Lebanon and into a region marked by the wild. The
little community Du Bois finds, isolated by the difficulty of travel, by ties to the
land, and the "awful shadow of the Veil," almost seems stuck in time as well as
place, its immobility enforced by the barriers of caste, youth, and life (57).

Arrived in Watertown, he meets Josie, "resting on her way to town," who ea-
gerly guides him to a school where she hopes to be one of the summer scholars
(*Souls* 52). Lewis says that Josie sprang into the road with a barrage of questions
for the stranger, her action figuring the road as a place, a meeting ground where
things happen and not just an avenue "from *here* to *there*." The next morning, he
crossed "the tall round hill . . . then plunged into the wood, and came out at Josie's
home" (52–53). Using the road as an organizing strategy to move the narrative
into the community, Du Bois takes readers with him to Josie's family, to the
school, and then to the other homes and families who lived in that country of
forests and rolling hills. Not only does the road move the narrative, as the "root
metaphor" it also propels themes of movement, mobility, and immobility that
run through the narrative.[4]

Ten years later, when he was once again at Fisk, Du Bois writes that he had "a
sudden longing to pass again beyond the blue hill" (*Souls* 58) and see the homes
and school of those two summers when he taught the youth of the scattered village. He does not relate the return journey, but as before he takes readers with
him as he visits the families of that little world. After recounting the changes
to them and the community, after musing on the effects of progress, of life and
death, he ends the chapter with one sentence to take us out of the valley: "Thus
sadly musing, I rode to Nashville in the Jim Crow car" (62). Instead of walking
the fifty miles between Nashville and the valley, now Du Bois, the "academic
celebrity," takes the train, indicating his enhanced mobility since those early

days.[5] At the same time, by naming the Jim Crow car, he points to the immobility of racism, the isolation that contrives to keep him in place just as surely as it isolates and immobilizes the little community.

"Of the Black Belt" similarly uses travel, the road, as an organizing strategy and "root metaphor" for the actions and social environment the narrative describes. In this essay, Du Bois takes readers on a tour of Dougherty County in southern Georgia. When he and a colleague journey through the Georgia Black Belt, they go first to Albany, the county seat, and then along the boundaries of the long, rectangular county as he gathers information about the lives of Black folk. Interspersed between descriptions of his tour, he traces past journeys of other people into and out of the region, of Hernando de Soto looking for gold, the Africans that "poured in" legally and illegally (*Souls* 92), the Creeks and Cherokees who were removed, the settlers who "poured into these coveted lands" (94), the ruined plantation owners who left and were replaced by "Russian Jews" and capitalists, suggesting a history of movement for the county that at one time was hailed the "Egypt of the Confederacy" (102). If "recorded history" is "a story of mobilities, migrations, settlements," as Eric Leed claims, then the history of Dougherty County that movement tells is one of conquest, trafficking, and violence.[6] Against this history of movement, Du Bois juxtaposes the immobility of the Blacks who populate the region, the folk who are fixed to place symbolized by the abandoned plantations, ruins of the past where "only the black tenant remains" (96).

He begins the essay by mapping the journey to the South: "Out of the North the train thundered, and we woke to see the crimson soil of Georgia stretching away bare and monotonous right and left" (*Souls* 91). While "Of the Meaning of Progress" ends by simply announcing that he rode in the Jim Crow car, here he invites his reader, presumably a white reader, into the car with him. He assures the imagined reader, "There will be no objection,—already four other white men, and a little white girl with her nurse are there. Usually the races are mixed in there; but the white coach is all white" (93). He points to the lopsided racial segregation of the Jim Crow car; evidently, whites may ride wherever they want but Blacks are confined to the Jim Crow car. One guesses that the nurse accompanying the girl is Black and that is why they are in the car, but what has prompted the four white men to ride in the Jim Crow car? Then Du Bois observes, "Of course this car is not so good as the other, but it is fairly clean and comfortable. The discomfort lies chiefly in the hearts of those four black men yonder—and in mine" (93). As they "rumble south," Du Bois writes, "Below Macon the world grows darker; for now we approach the Black Belt." (The region was so named for the richness of the soil and the predominate color of its residents.) "The 'Jim Crow Car' grows larger and a shade better; three rough field-hands and two or three white loafers accompany us" (93). Perhaps the Jim Crow car was cheaper, or perhaps it was the case that laborers and "loafers" of both colors were used to occupying the same spaces. Whatever the case, Du Bois and the "four black men" on the car felt the discomfort of enforced segregation in their "hearts" (93), the humiliation of it, of the blatant reminder of their second-class citizenship.

After a few days in Albany, a placid, segregated southern town that comes to life on Saturdays when "a perfect flood of black peasantry pours through the streets," Du Bois and his companion "venture out on the long country roads" ("that we might see this unknown world"). They first head "leisurely southward" from Albany, which sits near the northeastern corner of the county, and Du Bois notices "a dark comely face . . . staring at the strangers; for passing carriages are not every-day occurrences here" (*Souls* 94–96). Most likely they rode in an open-air two-person carriage pulled by one or two horses during their tour of the county. Organized by the twists and turns of the journey around the county, south and west, then north, the chapter takes readers on a virtual tour of it. By mapping the chapter along county boundaries, Du Bois metaphorically also maps the boundaries of the lives of the people who live in it and the social geometries of power at play. The chapter ends as Du Bois rides into Gillonsville and stops at the preacher's door and hears one last story of the ways Blacks were legally cheated of their land and goods in the post-Reconstruction South, the period of Redemption, "when the former Confederate states," as Henry Louis Gates Jr. puts it, "'redeemed' themselves at the expense of black rights." One of the listeners on the porch, a "ragged misfortune," tells the group that he was promised to be paid in cardboard checks for some work he had done, only to be cheated of the money and then have his mule, corn, and furniture confiscated by the sheriff. The stories told on the preacher's porch illustrate the uneven relations of power in the county, where whites may arbitrarily refuse to pay for work done and confiscate furniture even if it is "exempt from seizure by law" (110). This anecdote illustrates the ways "social change and spatial change are integral to each other," how legal and geographic boundaries are tied together.[7] The sheriff's illegal use of power to suppress Black economic change is obviously condoned in the spatial location of Dougherty County.

Through a "blend of detailed observation and generalization," Du Bois describes what he sees from the road, deftly sketching the people he meets to get at the conditions of life for Blacks in the rural South at the turn of the century.[8] In "Of the Meaning of Progress" he introduces us to his students and the families that comprise the little world of his school: Josie with her great desire for learning; Doc Burke, "ever working" and trying to buy the seventy acres of land where he lived; Fat Reuben and his chubby daughter. He tells us about their homes, the "two very dirty rooms" of Mun Eddings and the Burkes' "scrupulously neat" one-and-a-half-room cabin. He tells us about the food they shared with him—fried chicken, corn pone, beans, and berries. He writes of the churches in the neighboring village and the "soft melody and mighty cadences of Negro song [that] fluttered and thundered." When he revisits after ten years, he makes the rounds of these families, reporting on the changes: the schoolgirls now young mothers with "babies a-plenty"; the troubles the Dowell boys face; Josie—overworked and her dreams of school and love crushed—now dead; new buildings and the debt that came with them; the young people gone to cities; the successes and failures, the inevitable cycle of life, love, and death that define a community. Surveying the deleterious changes to her own family, the older boys run away by their troubles and her daughter dead before her time, Josie's mother sighs, "We've had a heap of trouble since you've been away" (*Souls* 55–58).

Lamenting that his log schoolhouse with its crude comforts was gone, Du Bois notes, "In its place stood Progress; and Progress, I understand, is necessarily ugly." While he may be referring to the aesthetic ugliness of the new "board house" with glass windows, some now broken, more importantly he points to the ways that materialistic progress disfigures human lives. The sketch ends on a sad note. The progress that should have promised hope brought instead "a heap of trouble," prompting him to ask, "How shall a man measure Progress there where the dark-faced Josie lies" (*Souls* 58–62). Although progress is often associated with improvement, at the beginning of the twentieth century Du Bois understands that America has been seduced by other definitions of progress, the "deification of Bread," of money and Mammon, over the "ideal of Freedom" (67). Du Bois also perceives that both bread and freedom have eluded the African American. In fact, real economic, social, and political progress for African Americans regressed as the South was remaking itself into the New South, a region of technological and commercial innovation. At the same time as the old southern ideologies were being redeemed, as the old humbuggeries of slavery and cotton were being revived, the headway Blacks had made after emancipation was violently pushed back, undone.

Perhaps it is fitting that this regression of rights and freedoms was confirmed in a legal decision raised by issues of transportation and movement, *Plessy v.*

Ferguson (1896). Homer Plessy, a mixed-race man who looked white, was asked to leave a whites-only rail car when it was revealed that he was one-eighth black. When he refused, he was jailed and subsequently filed suit against the railroad. The Supreme Court dismissed his claims to equal protection under the Fourteenth Amendment which had granted citizenship, with all its rights, to all people born in the United States and naturalized citizens. Instead, by upholding the enforced segregation of the races, the court set boundaries to how and where African Americans could travel, live, and work. Doing so, it illustrated the connections between travel and freedom, between mobility and civil rights, or the lack thereof. Looking at the differences between the founding Articles of Confederation and the Constitution, John Cox draws attention to these connections, pointing out that the freedom to travel was not extended to all classes of citizens in the Constitution. He notes that while the freedom to travel connotes other freedoms, it also connotes a threat to those in power, for it also has the "potential for subversion." By ruling on "the physical separation of black people from the white population" in the spaces of mobility, *Plessy*, Gretchen Sorin explains, also "excluded African Americans from quality education, housing, and employment," maintaining white supremacy against the challenges to hegemonic order that a mobile Black population seemed to represent.[9]

Writing about his tour the Black Belt as part of his series of studies for the Bureau of Labor Statistics, Du Bois paints a panorama of place that illustrates the diversity of land and people. He sketches "the remnants of the vast plantations," the "neat cottage" and little store of a father who has been able to send two children away to school, the churches where "five hundred persons . . . gather . . . and talk and eat and sing," the houses of prostitution, the unfenced properties and "ugly one-room cabins" of the western edge of Dougherty County, the "well-tended acres" amid the burden of debt, the old man who told "hunting-tales of the swamp," the reminders of the kingdom that cotton built and the land it destroyed. As he says, "It is a land of rapid contrasts and of curiously mingled hope and pain." Although he sees evidence of improvement ("the Negro is rising"), he also understands that over all the diversity and hope "a pall of debt hangs," prompting the African American to ask "why [he should] strive" against the barriers of race and class and law (*Souls* 96–107).

Thinking about the neo-slavery of debt peonage, Du Bois understands, "Only black tenants can stand such a system, and they only because they must" ("ten miles we have ridden to-day and have seen no white face") (*Souls* 96). Although he sees that whites have generally been able to recover from the devastation of civil war, the Blacks have been caught, immobilized by the new systems of oppression, the debt system, sharecropping, convict farms, and laws that work against their economic mobility in the Black Belt. He describes how the old plantation owners have left the county and how "Russian Jews" and outside capitalists have bought up nearly all the land, yet how so many black people are stuck in place, static or, worse, regressing. He sees signs of "modern land-grabbing and money getting," of capitalistic progress in the Black Belt, yet he sees that for Black people "It is a keen, hard struggle for living" (108–9).

Over and over, he points to the debt, the rent, and the systems of forced labor that keep them from progressing and thriving. He tells the story of a young man who had good luck renting, but, when the price of cotton fell, a sheriff seized all that he had, compelling him to move to a place "where the rent [was] higher, the land poorer, and the owner inflexible." "Poor lad!" Du Bois moans, "slave at twenty-two" (*Souls* 104). Of another man who had labored on a farm for forty-five years, "beginning with nothing, and still having nothing," he comments: "He is hopelessly in debt, disappointed, and embittered [by the struggle and the violence]." This man's prosperity was affected by the new fence law in western Georgia that prevented him fencing in his property so that he could raise a "little stock" instead of letting them range free (106). He writes of the convict farm, a "depressing place" where men are forced to toil, "now, then, and before the war" (105), reenacting a history of violence and labor that has persisted since before the war, a system that feeds the need for cheap labor and racist strategies to keep African Americans from moving onward and upward.

In these ways he draws a picture of the forms of immobility of African Americans in the Black Belt, in the broader South, and in the nation. If the freedom to move, to travel, signals and symbolizes citizenship and the other freedoms associated with it, then the systems that contrived to keep the African American in place, immobilized, bound by laws and boundary lines also contrived to deny freedom and citizenship for the African Americans Du Bois describes. Organizing these two chapters around his own mobility, his ability to tour and then leave the Tennessee valley and the Black Belt, he highlights the immobility of place and race that confines so many African Americans, that keeps them stuck and stationary. To drive home the point that this sessility is tied to race rather than class, when he takes the reader with him into the Jim Crow car he illustrates how *Plessy*'s limits on the freedom of movement and access to place struck at "basic civil rights and American democracy," even for members of the "talented tenth" like Du Bois.[10] He knows firsthand how these boundaries, the social geometries of power, and enforced stasis limited the mental horizon of so many people as they became maddened and thwarted by the regression of progress and hope. If the road is a potent metaphor for the nation, a place where debates about the nation occur, a place where knowledge about the self and others is acquired, a sign of civilization and progress, its limited access is a striking metaphor for the uneven racial geometries of power.

This is what Du Bois shows readers when he lifts "the Veil" and takes us on journeys through the post-Reconstruction South. By connecting the freedom to travel with "the problem of the twentieth century," the color line, he invites an understanding of the relations between space and mobility that could lead to possibilities for social and spatial justice. As Jen Jack Gieseking asserts, the geographic imagination can function as "a tool to describe and analyze the power within the literal and metaphorical ways people imagine and render space," including the space of the road and the vehicles that traverse it.[11] By prying open these geographies of travels, Du Bois hopes to redefine the sociological and geographic imaginaries that would envision African Americans on the open road, exercising their citizenship, and participating in debates about the American identity and their place in it.

The last chapter of *The Souls of Black Folk*, "The Sorrow Songs," intones the songs "in which the souls of the black slave spoke to men" (*Souls* 204). These songs, Du Bois explains, "are the music of an unhappy people, of the children of disappointment; they tell of death and suffering and unvoiced longing toward a truer world, of misty wanderings and hidden ways" (207). To tell these stories, many of the spirituals he cites employ the motif of journeying to describe exile from home, imagine a return to Africa, look toward death and heaven for relief from earthly trials, and move forward to opportunities of freedom and justice. They sing of the "sweet chariot" that will take them to the promised land; they call out "Roll, Jordan, roll" and "My way's cloudy"; they rejoice that "the Lord shall bear [their] spirit home" and that Michael will "haul the boat ashore" to gain safe passage to heaven and the ultimate freedom from earthly strife (212–13, 208). They conjure the actual journey to freedom when they sing out "March On" and "Steal Away" (*Souls*, 209), songs of escape and pilgrimage. Du Bois ends the chapter with the words and music to the hymn "Let Us Cheer the Weary Traveller," which supports the theme of journey to "the heavenly way" (214–15). By repeatedly singing "Let us cheer the weary traveller," the choir, the community, insistently encourages a life journey that coheres with Christian principles and that leads toward a better day, whether in the human or spiritual realm.

Over and over, these spirituals, these sorrow songs, conjure up the journey to imagine cosmic and human trajectories, the vertical trajectory of uplift and spirituality and the forward-moving trajectory toward freedom and justice. In many ways these paths are joined as uplift and freedom, spirituality and justice are linked in the travels of the weary traveler who "sets his face toward the Morning" (*Souls* 216). A powerful metaphor in these spirituals, the road and the journeys on it, opens meanings that speak to more than a traveler's adventures. Set against the immobility of racism and slavery, they speak of freedom, justice, and the range of mobility available along its routes that the weary traveler hopes to see.

Henry James

The American Scene *and the Geographic Imagination*

WHEN HENRY JAMES VOYAGED to the United States after "nearly a quarter of a century" of living abroad, he came as both "an inquiring stranger" and "an initiated native." Famous for the international themes of his novels and an experienced traveler throughout Europe, James determined that it was time to return to America to visit old haunts, gather with colleagues, and explore the changes the intervening years had wrought since his departure. Struck with a feeling of nostalgia for his native country, James wrote to his brother, the philosopher William James, "I must go before I'm too old, and, above all, before I mind being older." Anticipating the play on his imagination of a return, he wrote to his friend Grace Norton, "The idea of *seeing* American life again and tasting American air, that is a vision, a possibility, an impossibility, positively romantic." Even before booking passage for the States, James was constructing an imagined geography of what he would find, a geography of possibility and impossibility, of the familiar but also of the romantically alien and exotic. Arranging with his publisher Harper and Brothers to serialize his American impressions in the *North American Review* and then to pull them together in a book, he found a way to finance the journey. After having finished *The Golden Bowl*, he boarded the *Kaiser Wilhelm II* at Southampton, England, on August 24, 1904, for America. Eager and nervous at the same time to "return to the landscapes of his childhood and youth," James set out on an uncanny voyage that would take him to a homeland that was both familiar and strange.[1] After almost a year touring the country, he would return to England and write up his travel narrative, *The American Scene*, which is both a treatise on seeing, the imagination, and meaning making and a powerful example of how the geographic imagination works.

According to scholars, the geographic imagination exists "alongside and in dialogue with" the real and is "a tool to describe and analyze the power within the literal and metaphorical ways people imagine and render space." The geographic imagination helps us recognize how humans understand place and space, but it also helps us think about how travel writers like James render place in their narratives. As Tuan has argued, the ways humans view geographic space tells us about their psychological, social, and spiritual orientations and the mythical, pragmatic, and abstract meanings they impose on the geography. For Tuan the geographic imagination is a primal way that humans locate themselves in the world and the cosmos. For travelers abroad in the world who encounter new places, the imaginative geography, as Edward Said has put it, provides a vocabulary, a rhetoric, for orienting the traveler and representing the Other. Under Said's scrutiny, the geographic imagination reveals unequal, colonizing power relations with others as it constructs "social, ethnic and cultural" boundaries between journeyer and native. More than simply being a "spell" or the work of raw imagination, then, the geographic imagination is the result of "the complex of culturally and historically situated geographic knowledge and understanding that characterizes a certain social group" and connotes social and spatial relations of power. Indeed, Graham Huggan postulates that "the attributed experience of place is mediated, even conditioned, by previous knowledge." While James refers to himself as the "restless analyst" intent at getting at the meaning of the American scene, he also brings with him a geographic imagination that is "a more or less unconscious and unreflective construction," the possibility of the "romantic" vision. James's descriptions of the terrains, spaces, and peoples evince the effects of the geographic imagination, the unconscious expectations of what he will find in dialogue with the facts, the literal, in ways that also suggest the social geometry of power, the ways social relations are worked out spatially.[2]

As he visited sites of his youth, New York, Boston, New England, Newport, and then ventured South to new territory, he commented on the impressions they made on him after the lapse of time, the twenty years of rapid industrialization and technological change of the Gilded Age, a period marked by the rise of capitalism and what Alan Trachtenberg called "the incorporation of America." Recording "a train of associations" (*AS* 5) of the "social conditions, the material [conditions]" (263), he finds a "continuity" in the American scene, in the American character, claiming that "for the restless analyst, there is no such thing as an unrelated fact" (231). Trying to answer the question "continuity of what?" (225), James understands that the manners of a society reveal the "social mystery, the lurking human secret" (29) that holds the key to a culture's ethos. Asking of his era, "The *manners*, the manners: where and what are they, and what do they tell?" (29), he looks to the social geographies of the built environment and to geographies of travel. Interrogating these material phenomena, James deploys the geographic imagination to question assumptions about American identity, about the continuities that define the American character.

When Henry James returned to New England, to places that he had frequented in the past, New Hampshire, Boston, Newport, Concord and Salem in Massachusetts, and then New York City, he brought a geographic imagination shaped by memory and past associations of place that will be tested by the changes he perceives, not just in the individual sites and regions but also in the nation. Rather than rely on conversations with the locals or sketches of regional characters, he lets architectural structures represent the cultures and manners of the region. This tendency in his writing, especially his travel writing, has been noted by several scholars. Looking at James's descriptions of landscapes in *The American Scene*, William Stowe argues that they are "cultural readings of the scenes before him." Leon Edel connects his "eye for the architecture . . . by which man has asserted himself" with his interest in manners and the human drama. David L. Furth and Ross Posnock follow the chain of association from architecture to "the aesthetic—and, therefore, moral—values of a society" and to "political practice," suggesting that for James, or his "restless analyst," built structures are complex sites of meaning by which to interrogate the moral, social, and political meanings they signify. And Lisi Schoenbach asserts that his "search for democratic institutions takes James to locations that offer the concrete, tangible forms," buildings and monuments, each of which "offers up its own concrete, physical mass as the representation of a wide range of abstract, symbolic meanings."[3] Part of the geography, the edifices he examines are both shaped by the geographic imagination he brings to bear in his descriptions and demonstrate how power, knowledge, and culture are deployed in space.

Overlaid by memory, history, and cultural production, sites, like the objects that commemorate the Revolutionary War at Concord, create an imaginative space where the past and the present, the ideal and the actual, and the remembered past and the present meet in uncanny, unsettling ways. As cultural productions, architectural sites bring together original significations with constructed, constituted meaning, whether by Concord officials, the "summer people" of the New Hampshire villages, tourism promoters, or the keepers and shapers of knowledge in universities, libraries, and museums. Although some of the places James visits may seem mere tourist sites, as cultural productions, MacCannell argues, they "are not merely repositories of models for social life; they organize the attitudes we have toward the models and life." They are "powerful agents in defining the scope, force and direction of a civilization" at both the personal and the communal levels. This may be why James pays such attention to them; they constitute models of society, shape attitudes, and define the moral, social, and political climate, making them ripe objects for interrogation. They give him "ways to pry open the power in assumptions, stereotypes, and expectations associated with space and place" and "to describe and analyze power" relations.[4]

What he finds in many of the sites he examines is a social geography characterized by an ugliness and moral blankness generated by the worship of business and the power of possession. This social blankness will leave him at the end of the Salem section staring down "the end of the lane" for the illusory Gable House of Nathaniel Hawthorne's novel and at the end of the book gazing out the window of his Pullman car at the "criminal continuity" of "the general conquest of nature and space" (AS 201, 342, 340). Relaying a sense of displacement at realizing that the Gable House, the signature emblem of Hawthorne's novel *The House of the Seven Gables*, does not now exist and may not have existed in the past that he remembers, he unpacks or ironizes the sight sacralization of the house to get at what has been lost and what has replaced it. Sight sacralization, MacCannell explains, occurs when a place has been identified and framed as being worthy of preservation, as something that has a "moral claim on the tourist," like Hawthorne's house would have had on one of his keenest readers. MacCannell also claims that these kinds of sights incorporate "natural, social, historical and cultural domains." Looking for the house, then, James, who had written five evaluations of Hawthorne's achievement, associated it and Hawthorne with the idea of "American innocence" that had resonated in James's ideas of the country's past. In the centenary essay to celebrate Hawthorne's birth he argues that Hawthorne's genius arose from his "vital relationship to the New England environment" and the ways that he was able to see "the quaintness or the weirdness, the interest *behind* the interest, of things." When James discovers that there was not an original seven-gable house and that there is nothing behind the façade of his imagined geography, he feels a sense of displacement, as if a ladder has been "kicked back from the top of a wall" (201). The house as a sign, sacralized in his imagination, was just a "shapeless object," much like the realities, the cultural, aesthetic values, its appearance suggested (201). Were the values he attached to the house and to New England, after all, only in his imagination and not shared realities? Or was there a reality of value and meaning that has been lost to modernization, to the incursion of industry and immigrants, and to a tourism industry that would reshape the past as it converted the old homes into museums? These are questions that James will ponder as he interrogates some of the constructed sights of New England and then of New York City.[5]

Intent on gathering "impressions" that would reveal a social geography of "the human scene" (*AS* 3–4), James takes readers with him to revisit the villages of New Hampshire. Alongside the picturesque landscapes of the New Hampshire mountains bathed in autumnal light, he finds "the classic abandoned farm of the rude forefather . . . scenes of old, hard, New England effort, defeated by the soil and the climate and reclaimed by nature and time." (15). The reality of "agricultural failure and defeat" (19) is at odds not only with memory but also with the appearance of the *new* New England village refreshed for the "summer people" (20). James is describing the situation that Dona Brown reports on in *Inventing New England: Regional Tourism in the Nineteenth Century.* At the end of the nineteenth century, rural northern New England suffered the effects of deindustrialization, with the loss of local factories and mills, the "centralization of population and work" out of rural areas, and an agricultural "generation of decline." A "pattern of migration" out of the area accompanied these economic changes and left the specter of the "abandoned farm" that struck many people as evidence of "social and moral 'degeneration.'" Much as James does in *The American Scene*, regional writers, Brown reports, warned of local "'decadence' and 'decline.'"[6]

One way out of the economic depression was a new kind of tourism based on "a pastoral, nostalgic vision of rural life" that would entail not only patronizing hotels and resorts and buying summer homes but also "summer boarding on farms" where farm families catered to their seasonal guests from the cities.[7] As James notes, the summer people, "the nonrural, the intensely urban class . . . throwing itself upon the land for reasons of its own," for their own "aesthetic enrichment," may have refreshed the surface appearance of the villages. As they did so, however, they replaced James's desired dynamic of the English "squire and the parson" with one of possession and the "wage-standard" inherent in the business of boarding that upends standards of "sensibility and propriety" both by the boarders and the local "hired" people. Despite the "idea of appearance," James detects the "so complete abolition of *forms*" (*AS* 20–23), the social manners that reach beyond the surface appearances and give depth and meaning to human interaction, the human drama. Even as James exposes his own class when he snarks about the rustic who goes to the front door to deliver a message to the washerwoman, he suggests that the manners he observes lack the substance of true forms. More than cultural formalities, forms are the instruments of thought and meaning. They help preserve and carry forward the manners and meanings of a culture. For him the lack of forms, "the eliminated thing *par excellence* . . . the thing most absent to sight" (22), converts what could have been charming landscapes into locations of social ugliness and moral shallowness. That is why the absence of forms, cultural rituals, and mores for James is so disconcerting. Although the summer people may be aesthetically enriched by the "consoling background" of rural New England and the "little white wooden village," there remains "a sordid ugliness and shabbiness . . . about the wayside 'farms'" (21).

James goes on to ask whether the "outward blankness, the quantity of absence" he detects in the New England village has "its inward equivalent." Positioning the "high, thin church" of a New England village next to the "level railway-crossing" (*AS* 36), he points to the machine in the garden and the uneasy meeting of theology and technology. Their proximity suggests "a kind of monotony of acquiescence" and "abeyance" to the "bullying railway" of the modern era and the "absence" of thought, of a sense of history that leaves him asking "Is this *all*'" (26). He moves from the pretty but "thin" steeple and the rail line that skims the surface to probe questions of thought, class, and democracy. Imagining "the huge democratic broom" that is "brandished in the empty sky" (44), he suggests they have been swept away. Surely there must be more depth to the New England scene, more to the "paradise" of New England than unthinking abeyance to "any traditions but theirs" (36). He notes the "strong patches of surface-embroidery" that interest him, but, even with their display of impressionistic paintings, the new, composed communities lack substance and awareness. Despite their efforts to add a "smutch of imputation" of understanding, there remained a "thinness of their mantle," "crudity and levity," but mostly "flatness" (38). Peeling back the layers of meaning around these pretty little New England villages, James reveals a social geography similarly composed of absence and shallowness.

If the villages suggested something about the common man, the villas of Newport, Rhode Island, had something to say about the monied class. Reminiscing about his own youthful days when Newport was "a quiet seaside" resort with a colony of artists and "old-fashioned streets" and where he forged friendships with artists John La Farge and Thomas Sergeant Perry, James reads into the shift from the "cottages" of his youth to the "villas and palaces" a "social revolution." Signaling more than a change in architectural taste, the "social, local" "drama . . . of a real American period" (*AS* 156, 159) registered a change from a kind of leisured innocence to a sterility driven by the "god of business" (165). Remembering the Newport of his youth as a period of innocence and beauty, "the *pure* Newport time" when "ocean-drives engineered by landscape artists and literally macadamized all the way" heralded "chariots and cavaliers" (165), he is distraught by what he finds when he revisits. This "most socially exclusive and fashionable resort" since its "discovery" by wealthy New Yorkers in the 1860s, Brown tells us, had become "exclusively the home of millionaires" and "synonymous with the vice and idleness of the rich" by the end of the nineteenth century.[8] Replacing the signs of his youth, the new mansions line the seaside drives like "white elephants" (166). Conjuring the image of huge, white creatures that despite their expense and prestige are a burden to keep, James asks us to think of the mansions' bulk and uselessness. Using such words as "sterile," "waste," "vast," and "blank," James metonymically transfers the characteristics of these "lumpish" villas to their witless owners, thereby linking the white elephants to the people who owned the "grotesque" structures. The social revolution he writes of, instead of bringing reforms for the betterment of society, is perpetrated by the very rich in their monstrous "vengeances of affronted proportion and discretion" (167), their revenge against accepted forms and manners in a show of enormous but ineffectual wealth. Announcing at the beginning of the chapter that going back to Newport "threatened" him, James anticipates the distress he feels at finding the Newport of his memory so transformed by "these monuments of pecuniary power" (156, 158).

Similarly, the recently built palatial homes of uptown New York, already marked for removal, evoke a "touching vision of waste" (*AS* 119) in the dizzy project of rebuilding for the sake of rebuilding. In the rush to wealth, cities succumbed, Trachtenberg explains, to a furious "cycle of construction, destruction, construction."[9] Lacking a sense of history or tradition or even who "to curtsey to," the monied powers sitting in their opulent homes testify to the moral and social questions James raises. As he puts it, "The whole costly uptown demonstration was a record, in the last analysis, of individual loneliness: whence came, precisely, its insistent testimony to waste—waste of the still wider sort than the mere game of rebuilding." Alone with their money, living in the present "between an absent future and an absent past," the new aristocracies of New York, "*grope*" for wealth in a "squandered effort" to construct themselves as if they were material edifices (119–24).

Locating social relations in specific geographic, spatial locations such as the summer homes, Newport villas, and Fifth Avenue palaces, James calls attention to the "spatial organization of society" that gets worked out in geographic spaces. Doreen Massey argues that the spatial is "constructed out of the multiplicity of social relations across all spatial scales" and can be thought of in terms of the "ever-shifting geometry of social/power relations." We see the shift in the geometry of power when the farmhouse owners cater to the summer visitors and when the "quiet seaside resort" of James's youth and the new palaces of Fifth Avenue are transformed into behemoths by the big-money people. When James describes these architectural structures, he also depicts a social politics shaped by the "unseen economic and social relations" that reveal the inner emptiness of relations based on money.[10]

Perhaps more distressing to the returning James was the "sight of upheaval" as old landmarks were destroyed and new structures "hoisted in their place" under the pressure of modernity and materialism. One evidence of this upheaval is the "gaping void" left when the house at Ashburton Place in Boston (where James had spent two years during the Civil War trying to build a literary career) was leveled. Instead of being a memento to "the whole precious past," its "obliteration" left him with a dizzying "sense of rupture": "It was as if the bottom had fallen out of one's own biography, and one plunged backward into space without meeting anything" (AS 170–71). This sense of rupture with the past, with memory, pervaded his musings about Boston from his imagined perch on Beacon Hill as he surveys the city's signature buildings. Peering down on the city, with its representations of the "multiplicities of space-time," he sees not only the familiar buildings and the ways they are being overshadowed by the new "detestable 'tall buildings'" (173) but also the ways the dynamics of power have shifted over time. One of the oldest and most prestigious libraries in the United States, a center of intellectual inquiry that had included among its members Ralph Waldo Emerson, the Athenaeum, "honoured haunt of all the most civilized" (172), is being pushed aside by sites of economic prowess. Peering down Park Street, with its church spire that points its spiritual moral to the statehouse as it had in 1829 when William Lloyd Garrison delivered his address against slavery, James finds that the commercial buildings now hold the key to the American social order. Unprotected by zoning laws, the Park Street Church is threatened by a scheme to erect a "business block" at its location. "[The church] mocks assuredly," James writes, "above all, our money and our impatience" (177). The old educated Puritanism finally is just "business." James understood as well as Max Weber that "the Protestant ethic fathered the spirit of capitalism."[11] He realizes that business, trade, and commerce lie at the heart of the city's (and the nation's) institutions and culture.

Similarly, he complains about the way Trinity Church in New York City, at one time the city's tallest building, has been overshadowed by signs of a brash modernity, its spire "so cruelly overtopped and so barely distinguishable" by the new skyscrapers, "extravagant pins in a cushion already overplanted," "triumphant payers of dividends" (*AS* 61, 60). Assaults on memory, changes like those at Washington Square, where he had roamed as a boy, now with its "lamentable little Arch of Triumph" (70), the razing of the house where he had been born, and the original Metropolitan Museum on West Fourteenth Street now "a thing of the past" (142) make him feel as if half his history had been "amputated" (71). The Waldorf-Astoria, a familiar place of comfort and repose, now sits timidly amid the clangor of the new electric cars and the rush of traffic (77–78). More than attacks on James's memory and safety, these changes signal something about the "social question," the role of property and how it tunes the "human note in the huge American rattle of gold" (87–88).

Even so, there is something energizing about the new city for this restless, mobile analyst. Returning to New York after his initial landing, sitting in his Pullman car as it was carried by barge around Manhattan and on to Harlem, he paints a picture of "the restless freedom of the Bay" and the "bigness and bravery and insolence . . . of everything that rushed and shrieked." Alert to both the natural beauty of the bay and the energy of the "ferries and tugs" and bridges, like the Brooklyn Bridge, that carry people about and lace them together, James writes a paean to the energy and power of the city. In Whitmanesque style, he laces together a catalog of verbs and perfect little phrases in "staccato rhythm" to describe the "great frenzied dance," the "half merry, half desperate, or at least half-defiant" scene. Verbs connoting action and liveliness move the passage along rapidly as they integrate the sights and sounds of the harbor: "floating," "hurrying," and "panting"; "throb," "plash," and "play"; "shrieked." Dynamic, alive with motion and activity to catch "the pitch of the vision of energy," the scene suggests the energy and power of nature and the transportation machine, the "enormous system of steam-shuttles or electric bobbins" that transports people and joins them in the "complexity of a web." Both monstrous and democratizing, a vision of power, energy, and audacity, the complex of boats, tugs, ferries, bridges, and skyscrapers signals something "impudently new" and terrible about America, its "potential and possibility" at odds with the stultifying effects of property (*AS* 58–60).[12]

James will go on to disparage the skyscrapers that began poking up in 1860s, displacing or overshadowing the old buildings of New York, and connect them to the power of the market. But for a moment they also represent beauty, like the "'American Beauty,' the rose of interminable stem," as they rise slender and shining yet susceptible to being "picked" by the next fad (*AS* 60). And while he represents the transportation complex as a monster and criticizes the danger of the streets, the electric cars and the traffic running before the Waldorf-Astoria, he also writes of the people strolling through Central Park, "the polyglot Hebraic crowd of pedestrians" that represent something democratizing about the streets, the park, even the electric cars, "a foreign carful" of people now at home in America (95). Central Park, that sylvan retreat Frederick Law Olmsted imagined in his 1870 essay "Public Parks and the Enlargement of Towns," was a place "to which people may easily go after their day's work is done, and where they may stroll for an hour." James found during his ramble there that the park was true to its purpose, "The number of persons in circulation was enormous." He writes of people with "the air of hard prosperity," the common man and woman enjoying the park and children at play, frisking over the green, grouping together. For James this shared experience "was seeing New York at its best; for if ever one could feel at one's ease about the 'social question,' it would be surely, somehow, on such a question" (132–34). Sites of meaning, the park, the bay, and the city streets illustrate a social geometry of power that is a more democratic web of interaction than the isolation of the urban palaces. Like the peregrinations of peoples around the park, James sees the movement of peoples into and around the city and nation as contributing to "the cauldron of the 'American' character" (92). At a time when immigrants comprised about a third of the city's population, James asks of a country historically peopled by migrations, "which is not the alien?" (95). Listening to the polyglot voices as he walks about the city and into the East Side cafés and the Yiddish theaters of the Bowery, James hears the "Accent of the Future . . . the very music of humanity" in their tones (106). Underneath his criticisms of a modernized, materialistic New York runs a thread of hope and possibility for the American scene. Like Margaret Fuller who had hoped for a new poetry drawn from the multiple voices of the Midwest, James hears a new poetry in the "huge looseness of New York" and the dynamic fusion of identities and voices (89). Surveying the social geographies of the built environment and the geographies of travel, James's restless analyst finds continuities of energy and power and materialism that shape the manners of the nation. Tested by the displays of materialism in the social geographies of the North, James's hope for "active democratic citizenship," as Ross Posnock puts it, will be tried by the conundrum of the South's geographies.[13]

When Henry James ventured south, going to new territory, the play of his geographic imagination was different, informed not so much by personal memory of place as by historical and cultural expectations. He had visited Washington in

1882, staying then as in 1905 with Henry Adams. But this "City of Conversation" was as far south as he had gone. He could not take memories and nostalgia with him as he crossed over the Potomac. What he did take was "a vision, a possibility, an impossibility, positively romantic" of the South. Charles R. Anderson reminds us of the surprising "number of Southern characters" in James's fiction, particularly in two novelettes from the 1880s, *Pandora* and *The Reverberator*, which featured an expatriate Carolina family in Europe. What Anderson finds curious is that when James finally visited the South of the Carolinas, his "preconceptions from his reading [about the South] colored his vision" and that he was unable to offer anything fresh about the region. Likewise, John H. Pearson claims that James figured the South as a romantic destination: "James worked deductively [in describing the South in *The American Scene*] with his long-held beliefs about the character of the South . . . a romantic vision of the Confederate States . . . based largely on his own antebellum notions." James admitted as much when he wrote in *The American Scene*, "I was to recognize how much I had staked on my theory of the latent poetry of the South" (*AS* 271). In other words, James's imagined geography of the South—shaped by his family's attitudes toward the South and the Civil War, memorialized by Augustus Saint-Gaudens's bas-relief of the Massachusetts Fifty-Fourth Regiment in which his brother Wilkie (Garth Wilkinson James) had served as an officer, the reading James had done about the South, and the romance of the plantations and the Confederacy—contributed to his theory of the South.[14] Like the nostalgia and memories he brought to the North, this theory of the "latent poetry of the South" created an imagined geography.

James's description and commentary on Mount Vernon, the famous home of George Washington on the banks of the Potomac River, lay out the components of the geographic imagination. Trying to account for the charm of the house, he outlines the pull between the imagined, the "spell" that touches the "sensibilities" and emotions, and the literal, the "little hard facts, facts of form, of substance, of scale" that "look us straight in the face" (*AS* 248). Here he weighs the imaginative against the literal ways of knowing, both components of the geographic imagination. Forming "the rich interference of association," the metaphorical and the factual not only constitute the basis for James's description and analysis of the place but also lead him to associations of meaning, the metonymic logic of his writing, to speculate on the cultural meanings associated with Mount Vernon and how they speak to the larger American scene. The metonymic association between Mount Vernon and the nation prompts him to an analysis of place as he declares that they are both haunted by the "bleeding

Past" (AS 249). Very quickly, then, he outlines and demonstrates the process of the geographic imagination, the interplay between the metaphorical and the literal that creates meaning for the "restless analyst."

Another episode illustrates the processes of the geographic imagination as James comes to grips with his preconceived ideas of the South. Traveling to the South forty years after the Civil War, caught by the lure of the past, James comes with expectations of seeing signs not only of the war but also of the Confederacy that preceded it. What he finds is a new South haunted by the past yet still trying to live out the past regime, the "old Southern idea," in the present. Writing about his entrance into Richmond in the February winter, he describes the process of the geographic imagination, that moment when he realizes the juncture between his imagined ideas of the South and the actual South—the "shock of that question" that "in the presence of the presented appearances . . . the needful perceptions were in fact at play" in his analysis of place (AS 272). He begins by relating how Richmond represented "a potent idea" about the South, how this idea was charged by the "outbreak of the Civil War," and how in his "young imagination the Confederate capital had grown lurid, fuliginous, vividly tragic," replete with images of "the supreme holocaust, the final massacres, the blood, the flames, the tears" (272). Venturing to the scenes of the war, he expects to find evidence of the "haunted scene" lingering in the city. But wandering about the city he realizes that "the sense of actual aspects was to disengage itself" from the imagined Richmond, and it came as a "shock" when he realized that the imagined city of hospitality and holocaust was "simply blank and void" (272). The "Southern character" was "nowhere," and the "mystic virtue" he had attached to Virginia and the "old Southern mansions" gave way to a view of the cheapness of the scene. In a moment he felt his "inquiry . . . turn to clearness" as he saw the "sad poorness" of Richmond, when he realized that "the very essence of the old Southern idea" was "the hugest fallacy . . . for which hundreds of thousands of men . . . [lay] down their lives." Gone were any lingering ideas of glory. Expecting to find a Richmond haunted by scenes of the war and the old mansions, he finds instead something "extravagant, fantastic, and . . . pathetic in its folly, of a vast Slave State." Richmond and the South are in fact "*weak*" and sad (274). What he calls the "incurable after-taste of the original vanity" persists, however, in the "complete intellectual, moral and economic reconsecration of slavery" and the concerted efforts to rewrite history through bowdlerization, propaganda, and the reorganization of the institutions of learning and law to project the "Confederate dream" into the future in a massive act of self-deception (275). In the Richmond section of *The American Scene* we see that moment of shock, that jolt of recognition when James realizes that the metaphoric geographic imagination must resee the present-day South for what it is. Even so, the hold of the "culturally and historically situated geographical knowledge and understanding" persists as he sees the South primarily in terms of slavery and the Confederacy or their absence, its emptiness and poverty of imagination.[15]

We can also see the geographic imagination at work in James's descriptions of the natural South. For him, the South is an exotic landscape as different from the North as theist is from pagan. His journey southward represents not only geographic travel in comfortable Pullman cars, but also a journey into the soul and back through time to a more primitive period. Deploying what John Lowe calls the tropical sublime, James constructs a version of the natural South that reveals the "spell" the idea of the South has on him: descriptions of "enchanting beauty," "the awe and terror evoked by protean, often menacing nature," and the unmapped "avenues into the primeval." Contemplating his passage from the snowy North to the South, "the land where the citron blooms," James thinks about the "conversion" from the North to the South in metaphoric terms that imply elements of the tropical sublime: "This conversion, . . . has always struck me, on any southward course, as a return, on the part of that soul, from a comparatively grim Theistic faith to the ineradicable principle of Paganism" (*AS* 225). Conjuring up images of pagan rites perfumed with citron, James takes readers to an ancient land both beautiful and potentially philosophically dangerous. Thinking about the journey south as going back in time, he reflects that his "progress, under the expanding sun, resembled a little less a journey through space than a retracing of the course of the ages" (225), much like fellow novelist Joseph Conrad's protagonist Marlowe remarks about his expedition into the heart of the African darkness: "We were travelling in the night of first ages, of those ages that are gone, leaving hardly a sign—and no memories."[16] Conflating travel through space with travel in time, James evokes a fear that going to the South will take him to an unmapped time before paganism was converted to theism.

Though he travels to Baltimore, Richmond, and Charleston, it is Florida, rich in "oranges, grapefruit and velvet air" but lacking "everything else" that calls up the tropical imagination. It is for him the "great empty peninsula, of weakness," a "sweet frustrated Florida" (*AS* 303). Visiting a citrus "ranch," musing on the royal palms "as so many rows of puzzled philosophers, disheveled, shock-pated, with the riddle of the universe," he realizes that they may be the true philosophers of Florida, as if human thinkers who would make sense of the order of things were missing. He speaks of the "strange peninsular spell" that Florida casts, the "scantiness and sweetness and sadness" that tempt one to give in to the divine softness of "sub-tropical Florida" and never puzzle more than the palms about the riddles of the universe or "ever come back" (332). Although he warns of the "spikey sub-tropical things that show how the South can be stiff as nothing else is stiff," the softness, the velvet air, and the hope that "the breast of Nature would open" are more dangerous (320, 332). The danger of Florida is the lure of its divine softness, the elixir it seems to promise, the temptation to get lost in the pagan and the primeval and never come back. This is James's tropical sublime, the exotic, sensual beauty of the South suggesting the danger of erasure, of becoming subsumed by the natural and the pagan.

Not only does the geographic imagination rely on the play between metaphoric and literal conceptions of place, it also depends on the act of seeing, on vision. Indeed, the geographic imagination is itself "a visual practice of presenting space and place." As well as being a historical and cultural construct, the geographic imagination demonstrates the ways meaning and place are visually constructed. Tuan claims that "the organization of human space is uniquely dependent on sight" and that "mythical space," which he claims aligns along the vertical axis of vision, is "an intellectual construct" that emerges from the patterns of imagination and geography as "a response of feeling and imagination to fundamental human needs." Here Tuan connects the line of vision with intellectual and imaginative ways of orienting the self geographically. Thinking about the roles of vision and visibility in the geographic imagination, Derek Gregory notes that the late nineteenth-century European way of knowing was "to render things as objects to be viewed" and to "set the up the world as a picture" to be arranged, displayed, viewed. One consequence of the visual orientation to knowledge and the world is to render the geographic space as an aesthetic object, something picturesque or sublime and framed by the viewer's line of sight and orientation. As Tuan notes in *Topophilia*, "The visitor's evaluation of environment is essentially aesthetic. It is an outsider's view." In other words, the observer views the environment as a picture that coheres to available aesthetic standards. For the traveler, seeing— sightseeing—is one of the primary activities of the journey. John Urry reminds us that part of the experience of traveling is "to gaze upon or view a set of different scenes, of landscapes or townscapes which are out of the ordinary." He also claims that the gaze is a social construct that reveals the shape not only of what is seen but also of the "normal society" of the gazer—the cultural and historical baggage a sightseer like James brings to the journey. As well, the gaze reveals the social and political relations between gazer and the people being viewed, illustrating the ways geometries of power are spatially constructed.[17] For a visually perceptive visitor like James, recording what he sees and thinking about what he sees are primary activities that demonstrate important aspects of the geographic imagination.

In the preface to *The American Scene*, James announces that he approaches America "with much of the freshness of eye, outward and inward" as he "gathered impressions" (*AS* 3). Relying on "the agent of perception," James will shape what he has seen into impressions, into scenes of meaning. From the first, James casts himself as one who sees, giving sharp descriptions of the visual details of New York, "the glazed, disglazed, gallery dedicated to the array of small spread tables" (7). But he also contemplates the ways that preconceived notions influence what he sees and the ways that he makes sense of the visual. Arriving in Baltimore, he contemplates the ways that the geographic imagination, the ideas the traveler brings with him, cause one to be "betrayed . . . in the very act of vision." The objects one sees, he understands, are already overlaid with "representational value," and it is the task of the "lone visionary" to decipher the imagined or represented from the real. This task is difficult because the existence of the representation looms "in some distressful shape" before "a traveler, an observer, a reporter" who is "'bound' from the first" by the "stirred impression" (227). Understanding the hold of the geographic imagination on what he sees, James calls into question the "very act of vision" as untainted even as he positions himself as a "restless analyst" who must go out and see the city for himself. Demonstrating what he means, James approaches the city with the idea that Baltimore will be interesting, that he will find something sympathetic about it. Walking about "the dear little city," he realizes how his "impression was fixing itself by a wild logic of its own." Anticipating that he will find "the huge shadow of the War" about the city, he finds instead a kind of "historic peace" in the "repeated vistas of little brick-faced and protrusively door-stepped houses, which . . . suggested rows of quiet old ladies seated, with their toes tucked-up on uniform footstools, under the shaded candlesticks of old-fashioned tea-parties" (227–30). Finding just the right metaphor in the rows of little ladies, James charmingly conveys what he has seen, the Baltimore houses, and interprets his impression of the city as genteelly at peace rather than still haunted by the war. Casting himself as "the expatriated observer," "the palpitating pilgrim" with an "appetite for sharp impressions" (270), James understands the importance of really seeing: "If one doesn't know *how* to look and to see, one should keep out of it altogether. But if one does, if one *can* see straight, one takes in the whole

piece at a series of points that are after all comparatively few" (271). Seeing is
more than an act of recording the sights; for James it is also an act of arranging
and making sense of things, of really seeing the meaning revealed in the look.

As the Baltimore section demonstrates, *The American Scene* is both a highly
visual book and a treatise on seeing. It also demonstrates the social and political implications of seeing and James's comprehension of the relation between
himself as observer and the objects of his gaze. Traveling in a Pullman car to
George Vanderbilt's grand estate in North Carolina, and then to Charleston,
James reflects on his position as seer even as he disrupts the social dichotomy
he represents. Looking out the car window, his views of the mountain landscape
and the "shabby and sordid" social scene enacted at the small train stations
along the way are contained within the parameters of the window (*AS* 292). He
does not see all, just a portion of the scenes before and below him, spatially and
socially, from his position in the train. James is a member of the traveling elite,
riding in rail cars lavishly decorated and appointed with toilets, washrooms, and
kitchens. Indeed, he writes of "the spectator enjoying from his supreme seat of
ease his extraordinary, his awful modern privilege of this detached yet concen-
trated stare at the misery of subject populations" (293). Looking out from "this
superiority of . . . bought convenience" as a tourist, James stares at the array of
people on the railway platform whom he classifies as "forlorn and depressed,"
enacting as he does so a colonizing gaze that aestheticizes and dehumanizes
the human scene. At almost the same time that he seems to marginalize the
"subject populations," James disrupts the easy dichotomy between margin and
center that the scene and his view of it seem to imply. Instead, he stops a moment to reflect on his position and gaze: "It was a monstrous thing, doubtless,
to sit there in a cushioned and kitchened Pullman and deny to so many groups
of one's fellow-creatures any claim to a 'personality'; but this was in truth what
one was perpetually doing" (293). Even as he frames the human scene before
him and falls back on stereotypes about African Americans, whom he describes
as "sinister," lusty, and careless, he also recognizes his own privilege and how
it shapes his view. Moreover, when the train has to stop at a junction and he
must detrain, wait at the station, and then board a new train, James realizes
not just the inconveniences of American train travel but also its suppositions
of independence, that if "your luggage, in America, is 'looked after,' . . . you are
not." In this "unservanted state," James becomes "a perfectly isolated traveler,
with nobody to warn or comfort [him], with nobody even to command"—a
gesture that points to his recognition that he is marginalized by the American
rail system and that illuminates to him that he has only touched the margins
of "the total of American life" (294–95). He realizes that his view, as astute as it

may be, is constrained by his failures to see and fathom all. And so, just as the geographic imagination asks us to think about the connections between space, knowledge, and power, James questions those very equations even as he seems to exemplify them.

His position on the train also demonstrates the ways social and political relations are figured spatially. Many of his encounters with the American scene occur in spatial configurations of trains, cars, museums, and hotels. Complicating the geographic imagination, Massey understands that social relations are experienced differently by "those holding different positions" spatially. In Washington, while waiting in his cab at the railway station for his luggage, James looks out at a group of "tatterdemalion darkies" who "lounged and sunned themselves within range" (*AS* 276). Neatly confined in the space of the cab, James looks out at the African Americans lounging about the platform in ways that indicate the social relations he anticipates—the superior researcher gazing at the raced lower class who seems to fit representations of "the Southern black." He is inside, and they are outside of the cab and society. Looking at them, he thinks he understands why Blacks had been "intensely 'on the nerves of the South'" (277). But as he contemplates the scene further, he realizes not only his position as "non-resident" but also the "'false position' of the afflicted South" that disregarded the pride of these "ragged and rudimentary" men who were members of their own community and "in possession of [their] rights" (276). While the scene at first situates James inside the cab and society, it also locates him as an outsider, outside the community of Blacks about whom he is tempted to pass judgment. James understands here that the multiple "social relations of space are experienced differently" and that the observer and observed both shape the meaning of space.[18]

James's visit to the Museum of Confederacy in Richmond provides another example of the ways social relations are spatially constituted. Although he comes as a visitor, he is both subject to and defies the interpretive power of the museum. Opened as the Confederate Museum in 1896 by the all-female Confederate Memorial Literary Society, the museum's mission was to positively shape the public's opinion of the South and the reasons it went to war. As a visitor, James is welcomed by a "little old lady" in the anteroom of the museum as if she were the very gatekeeper to the meaning of the South. With her "social tone of the South" and "patriotic unction" to the "sorry objects" on display, she ushers James into the narrative the museum promotes. An arrangement of rooms and exhibit spaces, together with the woman and the only other visitor, a young southern man who tells of his father's adventures in the war, the museum's story promotes the Lost Cause. At this juncture, the museum and its supporters exhibit "a configuration of social relations . . . imbued with power and meaning and symbolism." But at the end of the section, the configuration of power and meaning shifts as James regains control of the narrative when he announces that while this amiable "son of the new South" would not hurt a northern fly, he would hurt a southern Negro. Although James may be the outsider, the visitor to the domain of the museum and the history it houses, in the end he creates his own history and ethos of the South. He understands the pathetic patriotism grounded on violence and racism and the ways that the larger social relations of the South are played out. Not only does the episode point to shifting social geometries as James wanders the museum, it also points to the social powers of propaganda, patriotism, and racism that James the outsider comprehends better than insiders like the young man who is deluded by pride—"That's the kind of Southerner I am!" (282–86). As well, it presages the geographic aspects of social justice that the ending of the book will tackle.[19]

Like the museum, the American hotel was another space in which identity and social relations were manufactured and manipulated. Traveling to the South, James comments on the hotel as a social space where waiters attend diners, salesmen stop on their routes, and socialites display their wealth, where history and taste are fabricated (with the magnificent Ponce de Leon of St. Augustine, Florida, for example). These spatial, social locations construct the sociological and geographic imagination that James labels the "hotel-spirit" (*AS* 323), by which "the American scene is lighted" (299). More than simply places where travelers stop for the night or the holiday season, James's hotels tell us how the larger sociological American scene or imaginary is constructed. In a prescient note that anticipates the great artificialities of Las Vegas hotels, James notes the "general painted scene" the hotel creates and how for some people it is "the richest form of existence." Having to depend on them for the first time during his American travels, James realizes that the hotels and "the hotel-like chain of Pullman cars" constitute "the supreme social expression" and carry "almost *all* the facts of American life" with them (299). A site of transit like the hotel-like train cars, the train-like hotels gather people from different strata of American life to live out for a time fantasies created by the hotel. Here are gathered the zealous "negro waiter" whose incompetence causes James to sadly "reflect . . . that it was for *this* [southerners] had fought and fallen," lusty drummers, salesmen with their "air of commercial truculence," women and children, and the "carnivorous coffee-drinking ogre" (312–13).

The large Florida resorts built by the likes of Henry Flagler gather the "affluent class," "Vanity Fair in full blast," the "business-block" and the "indulged ladies of such lords" in social spaces where their uniformity of expression leads James to ponder whether they had invented the hotel spirit or it had invented them (*AS* 327, 330, 334, 335). As he had in Newport and New York City, James understands how the hotel guests succumb to the artificial, the practiced, and the expensive (324–27). He understands the sociological aspect of the geographic imagination: the great tourist hotels play a hand, like the mansions of the North, in constructing an American imaginary supported by the great commercial "glittering, costly caravansary" (324).

Looking for the meaning of the American scene through the framework first of northern spaces and then of southern spaces, James demonstrates how a critical geographic and social imaginary questions assumptions and promotes ideas of justice. Indeed, the geographic imagination "plays a central role in envisioning and enacting just possible futures" in order to "produce social and spatial justice." James may sometimes fall into the traps laid by imagination, racial stereotypes, and privilege, but he also creates a critical geographic imagination to address the social geometries of power and knowledge he observes. Although the American edition of *The American Scene* ends with a view of "a Florida adorable," supposedly to appease an American audience, this appealing view of Florida is prefaced by a harsh assessment of the ways American writers have supplied "an 'intellectual' pablum" to a "body of readers at once more numerous and less critical than any other in the world" (*AS* 337, 336). Cutting through the veneer of American letters, romance, and sentiment, James calls out the uncritical public that "goes upon its knees to be humbuggingly humbugged" by such institutions as the Ponce de Leon Hotel that have produced the romantic illusions of the past, in this case by adopting the "Moorish style" of architecture to mask the realities of the Spanish occupation (337–38). After thus skewering the American public and the institutions, writers, and painters that serve it, James turns to the warm, bright, sweet, but weak vagueness of Florida that does not quite know what to say about itself. This charming, inarticulate ingenuousness is what he finds adorable about Florida, like one might find the shy ingénue adorable.

The more critical section 7 in the English edition published in 1907 by Chapman and Hall was not included in the first American edition published at the time. Rather than leaving readers with a vague note about an adorable Florida, he ends with a sad, bitter tone. Here, in the last section, he sharply criticizes how the "hugeness" of America is "a ground for complacency" in the "general conquest of nature and space" and the pretension of making something from the "large and noble sanities" (340–42). It is as if the very size of the continent shaped an American imaginary of invincibility and exceptionalism that became excuses for conquest and destruction. At once imagining the reactions of Native Americans to the land grab and desecration of the land in the name of progress and positioning himself as an observer aboard the "missionary Pullman . . . the great symbolic agent" (342), James offers his most searing criticism of progress in the narrative. Since the early northern chapters, he has made jabs at progress and materialism, showing the continuity of the "vast crude democracy of trade" (53). Here, at the end of the journey, he imagines America as the "missionary Pullman" of technological and social progress, freighted with meanings of conquest and colonization, chugging over and over, "see what I'm making, what I'm making" (340). In a jeremiad against a destructive materialism, what Haviland calls his "latter-day jeremiad-cum-travelogue," James notes that if he were an Indian, "one of the painted savages," he would look at the "solitude [whites have] ravaged," the disfigurement and violation that "caused the face of the land to bleed."[20] Pointing to the environmental harm that the "vast general unconsciousness" and complacency have caused, James criticizes the symbolic Pullman "for all the irresponsibility behind it" and the "trap" laid for the "lone observer" who may be complacent enough to sit "by the great square of plate glass" and peer out at the land. Hoping for some great chasm or abyss or rupture in the "triumph of the superficial," the narrator, the lone observer, knows he will groan at the "portentous truth" of the "criminal continuity" of the American scene (340–42). Thus, the English edition ends not with a glimpse at the appealing Florida or of the promises of a people joined by modern modes of transport. Rather, it ends with a groan at what the geography has revealed, the "criminal" continuities of materialism and greed that bind the nation.

More than the record of a year-long jaunt through America, Henry James's travel narrative reveals the workings of his geographic imagination and the geographic imagination of the nation. Doing so, it exposes the way the national vision complacently imagines a vast national space, clings to the sad history of the South, and perpetuates racism and the materialism of "Vanity Fair." Calling out the humbuggery that manipulates the national geographic imagination, James writes a text that illustrates the social justice of really seeing "straight" (AS 271). Beverly Haviland posits that The American Scene "plays a transformative role in James's own understanding of how to make sense of the past," but it is also an important text in the ways a critical geographic imagination interrogates the past and imagines the future.[21]

INTERLUDE

After Henry James returned from his trip to the United States and after *The American Scene* was published, he wrote a short story, "The Jolly Corner," a tale in which the protagonist, Spencer Brydon, returns to New York, to his old home, after more than thirty years abroad. Like James he encounters a modern, bustling, commercial city, marked by skyscrapers and electric streetcars, the "'swagger' things, the modern, the monstrous things."[22] Returning, he both steps into the mood of the city, turning one of his properties into apartments and discovering that he has a kind of architectural flair, and resists the modern city, retaining his other property, the house on the jolly corner, for himself. He does not live there or rent it out; instead, he maintains it as if it were a museum of his past, a relic and symbol of the country he left. Toggling between these two houses, these two moods, Brydon wonders what he would have been like had he stayed in America. He tells his friend Miss Staverton, "I might have lived here . . . Then everything would have been different enough." He might have gone into architecture and become a "billionaire," as Miss Staverton imagines. But he is not so sure. Returning to America, getting out of the comfort zone of his discreet, European life, "he found all things come back to the question of what he personally might have been, how he might have led his life and 'turned out' [if he had remained]" ("Jolly" 319–21). This question, the possibilities for his life and his quest to confront his imagined alter ego, drives the story.

Part international tale of manners, part ghost story, and part cerebral adventure story, "The Jolly Corner" follows Brydon as he revisits his old home over a series of nights looking for the incarnation of his alter ego. Exploring the house as James had explored the nation, peeking into its rooms and corners, to find what his imagination had created, Brydon finally comes upon an open door. In this threshold to an eerie space, he confronts the specter of the self he might have become, a being "spectral yet human" ("Jolly" 334). On that spectral self he sees the damage caused by the rough and tumble, materialistic life of America, the damaged right hand, two fingers reduced to stumps, and the poor, ruined sight. Used to a controlled life of discretion, Brydon is so horrified by the vision of his other self that he passes out, loses consciousness. When he comes to, he is resting on Miss Staverton's lap, as she tells him that the specter of his alter ego, his possible other self, has visited her in her dreams. The story ends with Miss Staverton confessing that she likes both the possible and the real versions of Brydon, the version that would have him become a billionaire and the version that would make him the discreet writer of tales and travels.

This is a story of haunting, the haunting of the what ifs and the possible past. Having revisited the United States and been both repelled and charmed by it, by the hustle of modernity and the remembrances of times past, James writes a suspenseful story about the uncanny meeting of the two possibilities for the self and the nation. One is materially successful yet damaged, the other discreet, enervated, living in the comfort of the past. Like *The American Scene*, "The Jolly Corner" recounts an uncanny journey through the imagined geography of the self, of disparate possibilities that are both familiar and strange.

Epilogue

DURING THE LABOR DAY weekend of 2018, I helped my daughter move from Colorado to Georgia, a cross-country drive that we did in a little over two days. How we did it demonstrates the changes in technologies of travel since Emily Post made her transcontinental drive in 1915 and the hold that the geographic imagination continues to have on our perceptions of place and travel. First, I flew from Corpus Christi, Texas, to Denver, and then took a shuttle to Fort Collins to help Cameron finish packing for the move. Leaving Fort Collins, we made a caravan of two vehicles, Cameron in her car (with Google Maps, a dog, and two cats) and me handling the twenty-foot U-Haul van we rented. We drove on multiple-lane interstate highways all the way to Georgia, briefly stopping at gas stations for pit stops. We drove through fast food places for breakfast and lunch—McDonald's, Taco Bell, Subway. My husband, who had to stay home, used his Orbitz app to reserve motel rooms for us so that all we had to do was check in and unload ourselves and the animals. Once in our pet-friendly room, our box of wine handy, we ate our carry-out dinner from Chili's and then slept soundly for the next day's venture. At the end of the road trip, I took an Uber ride-share from my son's home in the North Atlanta area to the Atlanta Hartsfield-Jackson Airport, flew back to Corpus Christi, and then drove the remaining forty-five miles to my home, in time to get back to the university and my students. All in a long weekend, the months' long trek across prairies and hills reduced to twenty-three hours of driving time.

As we drove from Fort Collins, headed east toward the Mississippi, I watched the sun retreating behind the Rocky Mountains in my rearview mirror, thinking of the lines from "America the Beautiful," of "amber waves of grain" and "purple mountain majesties." I do not know if it was wheat, but the great, open land was golden, the land gently rolling. Dotting the gold were the black forms of cattle grazing in the evening. The scene made me think of those great buffalo herds that must have changed the landscape from yellow to black, their great hulks moving across the land. We passed a sign for a town named Kiowa, which put me in mind of Scott Momaday's comment that the Kiowa Indians who had so much space, had so much sun in which to imagine themselves. I also thought of adventurers like Francis Parkman, who loved the buffalo chase but could easily get separated from the rest of his group on the rolling plains without landscape markers to orient himself. Herman Melville's Pip also came to mind, the boy lost in the great sea and losing his mind in the vastness of the same "nothingness." I carried with me cultural baggage, the books I had read and the songs of America, my geographic imagination that tinged the way I looked at the landscape. The western plains were and were not new to me.

Perhaps to compensate for the apparent emptiness of Kansas, roadside signs along I-70 announced such sites as the Prairie Museum that remembers the old soddies, the Czech museum with the largest Czech Egg in the world, and the Buffalo Soldier monument at Fort Leavenworth. Historical notices called attention to Kit Carson, Dwight Eisenhower, Robert Dole, and Harry Truman, pointed out the cattle trails to Abilene, and labeled Lawrence, Kansas, the birthplace of the Civil War. And, of course, advertisements like a sign for Toto's Tacoz played on associations to Dorothy and Toto of *The Wizard of Oz*. When we crossed over the Ohio River, I thought about Harriet Beecher Stowe's Eliza hopping across the ice flows. Then, as we raced through Illinois, I noticed neat farm compounds, often white and highlighted with red paint, nestled between the crops and a stand of forest, reminding me of Margaret Fuller's hope that settlers could live in harmony with nature. I was seeing America from the road at seventy miles per hour, my perspective shaped by my geographic imagination and manipulated by local boards of tourism, and it was shaped by speed, the quotient that so intrigued Helen Hunt Jackson. My quick trip across half of America prompted me to ponder the value of this kind of travel. When we whisk across the nation or hopscotch across it in airplanes, how can we see the particulars of place? Do we just rely on glimpses and generalizations, on a geographic imagination that has been already framed? Is there any value in these mad dashes other than getting there? Is there anything to learn at seventy miles per hour?

At the end of this book, at the end of examining nineteenth-century narratives of travel across America, what is the value of this other, readerly enterprise? How does it help us think about the ways geographies and technologies of travel shape not only the ways we travel but also our traveler's view, our understanding of the road, the particulars of character and environment and nation? Thinking about the relation between environmentalism and literature, Scott Slovic writes, "Literary scholarship and literature itself are, on the most fundamental level, associated with human values and attitudes [that prompt readers] to decide what in the world is meaningful/important to them." In other words, literature engages us in questions of ethics, whether of the environment or of travel across it, in pondering the *whys* of what we do and how we think. Reading these travel narratives prods us to consider our ethical responsibility as travelers, as sight-seers, as analysts of the American scene. They ask us to think about some of the same things that troubled nineteenth-century travelers and that we continue to grapple with. Issues such as the meaning and value of progress in the face of multinational corporations, powerful tech billionaires, and the wealth gap that widens other gaps in the lives of some citizens. The authenticity of travel when vacationers journey only to exotic all-inclusive vacation retreats. The effects of industrialization and suburban sprawl on the environment. The makeup of the national character and the place of immigrants and diverse cultures in it. Access to travel and the citizenship that it seems to promise. These are some of the questions that lurked among the nineteenth-century narratives of travel and that continue to plague us. To cite Slovic once more, "Literature is a lens through which we're able to sharpen our understanding of the world's vital problems—and literary criticism the mechanism for articulating what we come to understand." Prying into the narratives to reveal the meaning of their journeys, I have tried to do the work of literary criticism, to articulate what they tell us about the travel writer, the changing technologies of travel, and the ways the geographic imagination shaped perceptions of the nation.

Reading about the literature of travel takes us imaginatively to new places and invites us to vicariously share the adventures of the journey. It also prompts us to "sharpen our understanding of the [nation's] vital problems." Attending to the literature of travel suggests paradigms for interrogating problems that persist, for listening to the dialogics of travel and contemplating the ethos of place. Henry James demonstrates how to unravel the geographic imagination and test it against the realities of place, how to stand back and examine the way one understands them and the geometries of power at play in travel. Constance Fenimore Woolson exposes the ethics of sightseeing and tourism when she turns the reader's gaze on superficial tourists who are representatives of "normal" society. Francis Parkman and Charles Fletcher Lummis provide ways of thinking, or not thinking, about the cultural Other, the connections between tourism and ethnography, and the responsibility the traveler has in representing other cultures in the age of global tourism. Writers to the contact zones of the West and

South challenge the ways we understand racism as they interrogate its causes and effects and the great hypocrisy of a nation dedicated to freedom and equality. And Margaret Fuller demonstrates ways to convert the experiences of travel to advocate for social justice and the preservation of the country's multiple stories, for the creation of a new American poetry. Travelers like John Muir, Helen Hunt Jackson, and Susan Fenimore Cooper help us understand that the natural world is not there just for us to use but also has meaning and value of its own.

These stories of journeying ask readers to think about the ethics of travel, travel writing, and literary criticism, how to "make them mean something."[1] At their most basic level, travel writing and this book about it ask us to pay attention, to see things anew, and to see straight, even at seventy miles per hour. That, in and of itself, is ethical practice.

NOTES

Introduction

1. Walt Whitman, "Song of Myself," in *Leaves of Grass*, ed. Harold W. Blodgett and Sculley Bradley (New York: W. W. Norton, 1965), 83; Ralph Waldo Emerson, "Experience," in *The Collected Works of Ralph Waldo Emerson*, vol. 3, ed. Alfred R. Ferguson, Joseph Slater, and Douglas Emory Wilson (Cambridge, Mass: Harvard University Press, 1959–1972), 36; Alfred Bendixen and Judith Hamera, "Introduction: New Worlds and Old Lands—The Travel Book and the Construction of American Identity," in *The Cambridge Companion to American Travel Writing*, ed. Alfred Bendixen and Judith Hamera (Cambridge: Cambridge University Press, 2009), 1; Deborah Paes de Barros, *Fast Cars and Bad Girls: Nomadic Subjects and Women's Road Stories* (New York: Peter Lang, 2004), 2; Edward Said, *Orientalism* (New York: Vintage Books, 1979), 55; Michel Chevalier, *Society, Manners and Politics in the United States: Letters on North America*, translated from the 3rd Paris ed. (1839; repr., New York: Burt Franklin, 1969), 309.

2. George Pierson, "The M-Factor in American History," in *The Character of Americans*, rev. ed., ed. Michael McGiffert (Homewood, Ill.: Dorsey Press, 1970), 121; Virginia Whatley Smith, "African American Travel Literature," in *The Cambridge Companion to American Travel Writing*, ed. Alfred Bendixen and Judith Hamera (Cambridge: Cambridge University Press, 2009), 213.

3. Jeffrey Alan Melton, *Mark Twain, Travel Books, and Tourism: The Tide of a Great Popular Movement* (Tuscaloosa: University of Alabama Press, 2002), 16–18 (Tuckerman quote); David M. Wrobel, *Global West, American Frontier: Travel, Empire, and Exceptionalism from Manifest Destiny to the Great Depression* (Albuquerque: University of New Mexico Press, 2013), 198; Larzer Ziff, *Return Passages: Great American Travel Writing, 1780–1910* (New Haven: Yale University Press, 2000), 8. Many of these types of American travel writing have been treated elsewhere. For an overview of American travel writing, see Bendixen and Hamera, *The Cambridge Companion to American Travel Writing*. See also my *Women, America, and Movement: Narratives of Relocation*

(Columbia: University of Missouri Press, 1998); *Antebellum American Women Writers and The Road: American Mobilities* (New York: Routledge, 2011); and "Caribbean Conversations: Travel, Slavery and Empire," in *Essays Exploring the Global Caribbean* (Newcastle upon Tyne, UK: Cambridge Scholars Press, 2013), 136–56.

4. Robin Jarvis, "Travel Writing: Reception and Readership," in *The Routledge Companion to Travel Writing*, ed. Carl Thompson (London: Routledge, 2016), 89; Alan Nevins, *The Evening Post: A Century of Journalism* (New York: Boni & Liveright, 1922), 182; Melton, *Mark Twain, Travel Books, and Tourism*, 17; Bendixen and Hamera, "Introduction," 2.

5. Jen Jack Gieseking, "Geographical Imagination," in *International Encyclopedia of Geography: People, the Earth, Environment, and Technology*, ed. D. Richardson, N. Castree, M. Goodchild, A. Jaffrey, W. Liu, A. Kobayashi, and R. Marston (New York: Wiley-Blackwell and the Association of American Geographers, 2017), 2–3; Henry James, *The American Scene* (1907; repr., New York: Penguin, 1994), 271, 2, 9; W. E. B. DuBois, *The Souls of Black Folk* (1903; repr., New York: Penguin, 1989), 1; Jimmy L. Bryan, Jr., "Introduction: 'Everybody Needs Some Elbow Room': Culture and Contradiction in the Study of US Expansion," in *Inventing Destiny: Cultural Explorations of US Expansionism*, ed. Jimmy L. Bryan Jr. (Lawrence: University of Kansas Press, 2019), 12; Ziff, *Return Passages*, 9; Scott Slovic, *Going Away to Think: Engagement, Retreat, and Ecocritical Responsibility* (Reno: University of Nevada Press, 2008), 131.

6. William Cullen Bryant, *Prose Writings of William Cullen Bryant*, vol. 2, *Travels, Addresses, and Comments*, ed. Parke Godwin (New York: D. Appleton, 1884), 30; Constance Fenimore Woolson, "The Ancient City, Part I," *Harper's New Monthly Magazine*. December 1874, 1–25. www.gutenberg.org/, 17; James, *American Scene*, 320.

7. Seymour Dunbar, *A History of Travel in America* (New York: Tudor Publishing, 1937), 1105, 1091; Lewis Perry, *Boats against the Current: American Culture between Revolution and Modernity, 1820–1860* (New York: Oxford University Press, 1993), 129, 135; Catharine Maria Sedgwick, "The Great Excursion to the Falls of St. Anthony," *Putnam's Monthly Magazine of American Literature, Science and Art*, September 1854, 320; Frederick Law Olmsted, *The Cotton Kingdom: A Traveller's Observations on Cotton and Slavery in the American Slave States, 1853–1861* (New York: Mason Brothers, 1861), 135; Mark Twain, *Life on the Mississippi* (1896; repr., New York: Harper and Row, 1981), 114.

8. Bendixen and Hamera, "Introduction," 1.

9. Mark Twain, *Roughing It* (1872), 5. Mark Twain Project Online, https://www.marktwainproject.org/landing_writings.shtml.

10. James, *American Scene*, 3, 272; Tony Horwitz, *Spying on the South: An Odyssey Across the American Divide* (New York: Penguin, 2019); Margaret Fuller, *Summer on the Lakes, in 1843* (1843), ed. Susan Belasco Smith (Urbana: University of Illinois Press, 1991), 153; Francis Parkman, *The Oregon Trail* (1849), ed. David Levin (New York: Penguin, 1982), 355.

11. Whitman, "Song of Myself," 83; Perry, *Boats against the Current*, 129; James, *American Scene*, 92; Cecelia Tichi, *High Lonesome: The American Culture of Country Music* (Chapel Hill: University of North Carolina Press, 1994), 4.

12. Alison Blunt and Robyn Dowling, *Home*, 2nd ed. (London: Routledge, 2022), 9.

13. Emily Post, *By Motor to the Golden Gate* (New York: D. Appleton, 1916), vii.

14. Charles Fletcher Lummis, *A Tramp across the Continent* (1893; repr., San Bernadino, Calif.: Adansonia Publishing, 2018), 31; Post, *By Motor to the Golden Gate*, 118.

15. James, *American Scene*, 271.

16. Bendixen and Hamera, "Introduction," 1.

The Northeast

1. Blunt and Dowling, *Home*, 9; Henry David Thoreau, *Walden*, ed. J. Lyndon Shanley (Princeton University Press, 1971), 320; Lawrence Buell, *The Environmental Imagination: Thoreau, Nature Writing, and the Formation of American Culture* (Cambridge, Mass.: Belknap Press of Harvard University Press, 1995), 420.

Home Travels in Susan Fenimore Cooper's Rural Hours

1. Susan Fenimore Cooper, *Rural Hours*, ed. Rochelle Johnson and Daniel Patterson (1850; repr., Athens: University of Georgia Press, 1998), 3. Hereafter cited parenthetically in text as *RH*.

2. James Fenimore Cooper quoted in Rochelle Johnson and Daniel Patterson, introduction to *Rural Hours: Susan Fenimore Cooper* (Athens: University of Georgia Press, 1998), xii, xv, ix; Buell, *Environmental Imagination*, 406; Vera Norwood, *Made from This Earth: American Women and Nature* (Chapel Hill: University of North Carolina Press, 1993), 26.

3. Norwood, *Made from This Earth*, 31; Nina Baym, *American Women of Letters and the Nineteenth-Century: Styles of Affiliation* (New Brunswick: Rutgers University Press, 2002), 73; Lawrence Buell, foreword to *Susan Fennimore Cooper: New Essays on Rural Hours and Other Works*, ed. Rochelle Johnson and Daniel Patterson (Athens: University of Georgia Press, 2001), vii. See also Rosaly Torna Kurth, *Susan Fenimore Cooper: New Perspectives on her Works, with an Introduction to Her Life* (Bloomington, Ind.: iUniverse, 2016); and the essays in Johnson and Johnson and Patterson, *Susan Fenimore Cooper.*

4. Baym, *American Women*, 73; Norwood, *Made from This Earth*, 73; Buell, *Environmental Imagination*, 405–6, 421.

5. Baym, *American Women*, 75; Gieseking, "Geographical Imagination," 1.

6. Thoreau, *Walden*, 320; Emily Dickinson, *The Complete Poems of Emily Dickinson*, ed. Thomas H. Johnson (Boston: Little, Brown, 1960), 131–32; Buell, *Environmental Imagination*, 420; Ralph Waldo Emerson, *Nature* (1836), in *Transcendentalism: A Reader*, ed. Joel Myerson (Oxford: Oxford University Press, 2000), 152; Annie Dillard, *Pilgrim at Tinker Creek* (Toronto: Bantam Books, 1974), 273.

7. Bendixen and Hamera, "Introduction," 2; Mary Louise Pratt, *Imperial Eyes: Travel Writing and Transculturation* (London: Routledge, 1992), 157–59; Michel De Certeau, *The Practice of Everyday Life*, translated by Steven F. Rendell (Berkeley: University of California Press, 1984), 115.

8. Norwood, *Made from This Earth*, 31; Susan L. Roberson, *Antebellum American Women Writers and the Road: American Mobilities* (New York: Routledge, 2011), 115–16.

9. Norwood, *Made from This Earth*, 42.

10. Ibid., 31; Dillard, *Pilgrim from Tinker Creek*, 12.

11. Quoted in Roberson, *Antebellum American Women Writers*, 47.

12. Shane O'Mara, *In Praise of Walking: A New Scientific Exploration* (New York: W. W. Norton, 2019), 13, 63; James J. Gibson, *The Ecological Approach to Visual Perception* (Boston: Houghton Mifflin, 1979), 222–23.

13. Eric J. Leed, *The Mind of the Traveler: From Gilgamesh to Global Tourism* (New York: Basic Books, 1991), 72, 13–14; Jessie A. Ravage, "The Home Book of the Picturesque: Father and Daughter," presented at Cooper Seminar, SUNY Oneonta, 1999; Michel Foucault, *Power/Knowledge: Selected Interviews and Other Writings, 1972–1977*, ed. Colin Gordon (New York: Pantheon, 1980), 69; Buell, *Environmental Imagination*, 220; O'Mara, *In Praise of Walking*, 145, 150, 148; Baym, *American Women*, 75–76.

14. Buell, *Environmental Imagination*, 266; O'Mara, *In Praise of Walking*, 148–51.

15. "Our social lives": O'Mara, *In Praise of Walking*, 146, 148.

16. Wai Chee Dimock, *Through Other Continents: American Literature across Deep Time* (Princeton: Princeton University Press, 2006), 3; O'Mara, *In Praise of Walking*, 148.

17. Dimock, *Through Other Continents*, 3.

18. Buell, *Environmental Imagination*, 265.

19. Ibid., 266.

20. Blunt and Dowling, *Home*, 9, 28, 30; Dimock, *Through Other Continents*, 5.

21. Blunt and Dowling, *Home*, 9.

22. Ibid., 28; Tina Gianquitto, "The Noble Designs of Nature: God, Science, and the Picturesque in Susan Fenimore Cooper's Rural Hours," in *Susan Fenimore Cooper: New Essays on* Rural Hours *and Other Works*, ed. Rochelle Johnson and Daniel Patterson (Athens: University of Georgia Press, 2001), 181.

23. Dimock, *Through Other Continents*, 3–4; Yi-Fu Tuan, *Space and Place: The Perspective of Experience* (Minneapolis: University of Minnesota Press, 1977), 88.

24. Donald Worster, *Nature's Economy: A History of Ecological Ideas*, 2nd ed. (Cambridge: Cambridge University Press, 1994), 82. See also Johnson and Patterson, "Introduction," xx, arguing that for Cooper descriptive writing about nature can contribute to the "moral and intellectual progress" of culture.

25. Joanne Dobson, "Reclaiming Sentimental Literature," *American Literature* 69, no. 2 (June 1997): 266–67.

Metaphoric Traveling with Henry David Thoreau

1. Henry David Thoreau, "Life without Principle," in *Reform Papers*, ed. Wendell Glick (Princeton: Princeton University Press, 1973), 156. I use the Princeton editions of Thoreau's writings, indicated parenthetically within the text; "Walking" is in *Excursions*, ed. Joseph J. Moldenhuaer (Princeton: Princeton University Press, 2007), 185–222.

2. Laura Dassow Walls, *Henry David Thoreau: A Life* (University of Chicago Press, 2017), xx, xv. Among scholars who have discussed Thoreau's nature writing, Lawrence Buell in *The Environmental Imagination: Thoreau, Nature Writing, and the Formation of American Culture* situates Thoreau in the center of his wide-ranging analysis. Donald Worster, *Nature's Economy: A History of Ecological Ideas*, 2nd ed., devotes its part 2 to Thoreau. For a quick overview of Thoreau's environmentalism, see Buell's essay "Thoreau and the Natural Environment" in *The Cambridge Companion to Henry David Thoreau*, ed. Joel Myerson (New York: Cambridge University Press, 1995), 71–193.

3. Barbara Packer, "Travel Literature," in *The Oxford Handbook of Transcendentalism*, ed. Joel Myerson, Sandra Harbert Petrulionis, and Laura Dassow Walls (Oxford: Oxford University Press, 2010), 397; William Stowe, "The Literature of Travel," in *Henry David Thoreau in Context*, ed. James S. Finley (Cambridge: Cambridge University Press, 2017), 120–21; Mario Cesareo, "Anthropology and Literature: Of Bedfellows and Illegitimate Offspring," in *Between Anthropology and Literature: Interdisciplinary Discourse*, ed. Rose De Angelis (London: Routledge, 2002), 169.

4. Georges Van den Abbeele, *Travel as Metaphor: From Montaigne to Rousseau* (Minneapolis: University of Minnesota Press, 1992), xxii, xiii; Ilan Stavans and Joshua Ellison, *Reclaiming Travel* (Duke University Press, 2015), 29; Leed, *The Mind of the Traveler*, 72, 13–14; William Stowe, "'Property in the Horizon': Landscape and American Travel Writing," in *The Cambridge Companion to American Travel Writing*, ed. Alfred Bendixen and Judith Hamera (Cambridge: Cambridge University Press, 2009), 36.

5. Tolman quoted in O'Mara, *In Praise of Walking*, 82–83; O'Mara, *In Praise of Walking*, 82, 84.

6. Rick Van Noy, "Surveying the Sublime: Literary Cartographers and the Spirit of Place," in *The Greening of Literary Scholarship: Literature, Theory, and the Environment*, ed. Steven Rosendale (Iowa City: University of Iowa Press, 2002), 184, 187; Harold Proshansky et al., "Place-Identity: Physical World Socialization of the Self," *Journal of Environmental Psychology* 3, no. 1 (March 1983): 59.

7. Thomas Lynch, "The 'Domestic Air' of Wilderness: Henry David Thoreau and Joe Polis in the Maine Woods," in *Weber Studies: An Interdisciplinary Humanities Journal* 14, no. 3 (Fall 1997), 41. Lynch makes the case that the Native Americans were at home in the woods and cites an anthropologist of the Penobscot culture, Frank Speck, who explains how the extensive forests were divided into hunting territories by different bands and navigated by trails, markers, and signs to guide their way.

8. Dimock, *Through Other Continents*, 3; Dunbar, *History of Travel*, 18–20.

9. Henry David Thoreau, *I to Myself: An Annotated Selection from the Journal of Henry D. Thoreau*, ed. Jeffrey S. Cramer (New Haven: Yale University Press, 2007), 274. Hereafter cited parenthetically in the text.

10. Walls, *Henry David Thoreau*, 437.

11. Tuan, *Space and Place*, 131.

12. Ibid., 99.

13. Thoreau quoted in Scott Slovic, *Seeking Awareness in American Nature Writing: Henry David Thoreau, Annie Dillard, Edward Abbey, Wendell Berry, Barry Lopez* (Salt Lake City: University of Utah Press, 1992), 52.

14. Linck Johnson, "A Week on the Concord and Merrimack Rivers," in *The Cambridge Companion to Henry David Thoreau*, ed. Joel Myerson (Cambridge University Press, 1995), 42; Paul Fussell, "Travel and the British Literary Imagination of the Twenties and Thirties," in *Temperamental Journeys: Essays on the Modern Literature of Travel*, ed. Michael Kowalewski. (Athens: University of Georgia Press, 1992), 81.

15. Gieseking, "Geographical Imagination," 3; Graham Huggan, "Ultima Thule/The North," in *The Routledge Companion to Travel Writing*, ed. Carl Thompson (London: Routledge, 2016), 332.

16. Carl Bode, ed., *The Portable Thoreau* (New York: Viking, 1947), 138; Johnson, "A Week on the Concord and Merrimack Rivers," 51–52, also reads Thoreau's "excursions into colonial history" and the history of Western literature as important aspects of the travel narrative.

17. William James, "The Stream of Thought," in *The Writings of William James: A Comprehensive Edition*, ed. John J. McDermott (Chicago: University of Chicago Press, 1977), 38–40.

18. Gaston Bachelard, *The Poetics of Reverie: Childhood, Language, and the Cosmos*, trans. by Daniel Russell (Boston: Beacon, 1960), 14, 8, 102, 122, 150; Johnson, "A Week on the Concord and Merrimack Rivers," 53; John Kucich, introduction to *Rediscovering "The Maine Woods": Thoreau's Legacy in an Unsettled Land*, ed. John Kucich and James Francis (Amherst: University of Massachusetts Press, 2019), 4.

19. Bachelard, *Poetics of Reverie*, 182, 15; O'Mara, *In Praise of Walking*, 82–83, 148, 153, 150, 149; Leed, *Mind of the Traveler*, 13–14. Johnson, "A Week on the Concord and Merrimack Rivers," 42–43, observes that "Thoreau was less interested in their destination than in the journey itself, which provided an occasion for the kind of inward exploration that most fully engaged him," connecting that inner exploration to the passages from Western literature that he inserts in the narrative.

20. Walls, *Henry David Thoreau*, 419.

21. O'Mara, *In Praise of Walking*, 150; Len Gougeon, "Thoreau and Reform," in *The Cambridge Companion to Henry David Thoreau*, ed. Joel Myerson (Cambridge: Cambridge University Press, 1995), 196; Gieseking, "Geographical Imagination," 7; Tuan, *Place and Space*, 52; Len Gougeon, *Virtue's Hero: Emerson, Antislavery, and Reform* (Athens: University of Georgia Press, 1990).

William Cullen Bryant's Summers on the Lakes

1. Jack Vespa, "The Unsurveyed Interior: William Cullen Bryant and the Prairie State," *American Transcendental Quarterly* 11, no. 4 (December 1997): 7; David J. Baxter, "William Cullen Bryant: Illinois Landowner," *Western Illinois Regional Studies* 1 (Spring 1978): 1–3.

2. David J. Baxter, "The Dilemma of Progress: Bryant's Continental Vision," in *William Cullen Bryant and His America: Centennial Conference Proceedings 1878–1978*, ed. Stanley Brodwin and Michael D'Innocenzo (New York: AMS Press, 1983), 14; Allan Nevins, *The Evening Post: A Century of Journalism* (New York: Russell & Russell, 1922), 9, 134; Michael P. Branch, "William Cullen Bryant: The Nature Poet as Environmental Journalist," *American Transcendental Quarterly* 12, no. 3 (September 1998): 3; James Boylan, "William Cullen Bryant," in *Dictionary of Literary Biography*, vol. 43, *American Newspaper Journalists, 1690–1872*, ed. Perry J. Ashley (Detroit: Gale, 1986), 85.

3. Nevins, *Evening Post*, 207, 210–14, 182, 209, 223; Keith Fynaardt, "The Spirit of Place as a Usable Past in William Cullen Bryant's 'The Prairies,'" *Midamerica: The Yearbook of the Society for the Study of Midwestern Literature* 21 (1994): 50.

4. Said, *Orientalism*, 55.

5. William Cullen Bryant, "Illinois Fifty Years Ago," in *Prose Writings of William Cullen Bryant*, vol. 2, *Travels, Addresses, and Comments*, ed. Parke Godwin (New York: Appleton, 1884). Hereafter cited parenthetically in text as "Illinois."

6. Anne Baker, *Heartless Immensity: Literature, Culture, and Geography in Antebellum America* (Ann Arbor: University of Michigan Press, 2006), 1, 48; Perry, *Boats against the Current*, 129, 132, 135; Dunbar, *History of Travel*, 1091, 1105.

7. "Railroad History (USA): Facts, Timeline, Definition," accessed March 19, 2024, www.american-rails.com/railroad-history.html; Dunbar, *History of Travel*, 1009–10.

8. Quoted in Etta M. Madden and Martha L. Fitch, *Eating in Eden: Food and American Utopias* (Lincoln: University of Nebraska Press, 2006), 16.

9. Caroline Kirkland, *A New Home, Who'll Follow?* (1839; repr., New Brunswick: Rutgers University Press, 1990), 33, 44; Raymond Williams, *The Country and the City* (New York: Oxford University Press, 1973), 1.

10. Frederick Jackson Turner, *The Significance of the Frontier in American History* (Chicago: American Historical Association, 1893), 5, 3; Baxter, "William Cullen Bryant," 4–7; William Cullen Bryant, "The Early Northwest," in *Prose Writings of William Cullen Bryant, vol. 2, Travels, Addresses, and Comments*, ed. Parke Godwin (New York: Appleton, 1884), 67. Hereafter cited parenthetically in text as "Early Northwest."

11. Dunbar, *History of Travel*, 1162, 459–60, 462, 468.

12. "Life of Ma-ka-tai-me-she-kia-kiak, or Black Hawk," edited by J. B. Patterson (1833) in *Native American Autobiography: An Anthology*, ed. Arnold Krupat (Madison: University of Wisconsin Press, 1994), 159, 165–69; Ronald N. Satz, *American Indian Policy in the Jacksonian Era* (Lincoln: University of Nebraska Press, 1975), 112–13.

13. Dodge quoted in Dunbar, *History of Travel*, 461; *St. Louis Times*, quoted in Dunbar, *History of Travel*, 465; "Indian War," *Connecticut Courant*, July 24, 1832; Lucy Maddox, *Removals: Nineteenth-Century American Literature and the Politics of Indian Affairs* (New York: Oxford University Press, 1991), 29.

14. Carl Ostrowski, "'I Stand upon Their Ashes in Thy Beam': The Indian and Bryant's Literary Removals," *American Transcendental Quarterly* 9, no. 4 (December

1995): 1–13; Baxter, "Dilemma of Progress," 18; William Cullen Bryant, "The *North American* on the Indian Question," *New York Evening Post*, January 9, 1830; Lewis Cass, "Removal of the Indians," in *The Cherokee Removal: A Brief History with Documents*, ed. Theda Perdue and Michael D. Green (Boston: Bedford Books of St. Martin's Press, 1995), 107.

15. Bryant, "*The North American* on the Indian Question"; Monroe quoted in Susan Scheckel, *The Insistence of the Indian: Race and Nationalism in Nineteenth-Century American Culture* (Princeton: Princeton University Press, 1998), 91; Gilbert H. Muller, *William Cullen Bryant: Author of America* (Albany: State University of New York Press, 2008), 88–92; L. Maddox, *Removals*, 8.

16. Bryant, *Prose Writings*, vol. 2, 402; Bryant quoted in Muller, *William Cullen Bryant*, 4.

17. Baxter, "William Cullen Bryant," 1; Leo Marx, *The Machine in the Garden: Technology and the Pastoral Ideal in America* (London: Oxford University Press, 1964), 4.

18. Henry David Thoreau, "Walking," in *Excursions*, ed. Joseph J. Moldenhauer (Princeton: Princeton University Press, 2007), 196, 202, 206.

19. Donald Worster, *Under Western Skies: Nature and History in the American West* (New York: Oxford University Press, 1992), 81; O'Sullivan quoted in Baker, *Heartless Immensity*, 105; Buell, *Environmental Imagination*, 3; Sedgwick, "The Great Excursion," 321; John O'Sullivan, "Annexation," *United States Democratic Review*, July–August 1845, 5; John O'Sullivan, "The Great Nation of Futurity," *United States Democratic Review*, November 1839, 429.

20. O'Sullivan, "Great Nation of Futurity", 427; William Ellery Channing, "Self-Culture," in *William Ellery Channing: Selected Writings*, ed. David Robinson (New York: Paulist Press, 1985), 226, 240, 228, 263, 264; Ralph Waldo Emerson, *The Complete Sermons of Ralph Waldo Emerson*, vol. 4, ed. Albert J. von Frank et al. (Columbia: University of Missouri Press, 1992), 85, 87, 88; Roy Harvey Pearce, *Savagism and Civilization: A Study of the Indian and the American Mind* (Baltimore: Johns Hopkins University Press, 1953), 64.

21. Buell, *Environmental Imagination*, 78; William Cullen Bryant, "The Prairies," in *William Cullen Bryant: Complete Poetical Works* (1876), Library of Early American Literature (Seattle: Kindle Direct Publishing, 2020), 104–6.

22. Baxter, "Dilemma of Progress,"18.

23. Buell, *Environmental Imagination*, 78. Ostrowski, "I Stand upon Their Ashes," reviews Bryant's representation of the Native Americans in "The Prairies" and speculation by nineteenth-century archaeologists about the mound builders, 9–10.

24. Worster, *Under Western Skies*, 81.

25. Donald A. Ringe, "William Cullen Bryant's Account of Michigan in 1846," *Michigan History Mind* 40 (1956): 321.

26. Dunbar, *History of Travel*, 468; Satz, *American Indian Policy*, 97.

27. Satz, *American Indian Policy*, 246–48.

Margaret Fuller's "Wests"

1. Margaret Fuller, *The Letters of Margaret Fuller*, vol. 3, ed. by Robert N. Hudspeth (Cornell: Cornell University Press, 1983), 83; Susan Belasco Smith, introduction to *Summer on the Lakes, in 1843* (1843; repr., Urbana: University of Illinois Press, 1991) vii, viii.

2. Higginson quoted in Charles Capper, *Margaret Fuller: An American Romantic Life: The Public Years* (Oxford: Oxford University Press, 2007), 141; Nicole Tonkovich, "Traveling in the West, Writing in the Library: Margaret Fuller's Summer on the Lakes," *Legacy* 10, no. 2 (1993): 82; Smith, introduction to *Summer on the Lakes*, vii.

3. Lance Newman, "Margaret Fuller's Summer on the Lakes, in 1843 and the Condition of America," *Transatlantic Romanticism* 38–39 (May 2005): 7; Margaret Fuller, *Summer on the Lakes, in 1843*, ed. Susan Belasco Smith (1843; repr., Urbana: University of Illinois Press, 1991), 75. Hereafter cited parenthetically in text as *SL*.

4. Kirkland, *A New Home*, 4.

5. Dunbar, *History of Travel*, 1109.

6. John Urry, *The Tourist Gaze*, 2nd ed. (London: Sage, 2002), 1–2.

7. Ken Egan Jr., "Poetic Travelers: Figuring the Wild in Parkman, Fuller, and Kirkland," *Western American Literature* 44, no. 1 (Spring 2009): 51.

8. Dobson, "Reclaiming Sentimental Literature," 279.

9. Brigitte Georgi-Findley, *The Frontiers of Women's Writing: Women's Narratives and the Rhetoric of Westward Expansion* (Tucson: University of Arizona Press, 1996), 44; Stavans and Ellison, *Reclaiming Travel*, 44.

10. Newman, "Margaret Fuller's Summer on the Lakes," 2.

11. Ralph Waldo Emerson, "Letter to Martin Van Buren, 23 April 1838," in *Transcendentalism: A Reader*, ed. Joel Myerson (New York: Oxford University Press, 2000), 228–29.

12. Michaela Bruckner Cooper, "Textual Wandering and Anxiety in *Summer on the Lakes*," in *Margaret Fuller's Cultural Critique: Her Age and Legacy*, ed. Fritz Fleischmann (New York: Peter Lang, 2000), 182; Dean MacCannell, *The Ethics of Sightseeing* (Berkeley: University of California Press, 2011), 6–7.

13. "Conform to the institution" and "disappear": L Maddox, *Removals*, 26.

14. Pearce, *Savagism and Civilization*, 129; Georgi-Findley, *Frontiers of Women's Writing*, 60.

15. Kirkland, *A New Home*, 146.

16. Margaret Fuller, "The Great Lawsuit: Man versus Men, Woman versus Women" (1843), in *Transcendentalism: A Reader*, ed. Joel Myerson (Oxford: Oxford University Press, 2000), 393–94; Annette Kolodny, *The Land before Her: Fantasy and Experience of the American Frontiers, 1630–1860* (Chapel Hill: University of North Carolina Press, 1984), 129; Susan Rosowksi, "Margaret Fuller, an Endangered West, and Summer on the Lakes," *Western American Literature* 25 (1990): 125; Anne Baker, "'A Commanding

View': Vision and the Problem of Nationality in Fuller's *Summer on the Lakes*," *Emerson Society Quarterly* 44 (1st and 2nd Quarters 1998): 67, 91.

17. Fritz Fleischmann, "Cultural Translation as Cultural Critique," in *Margaret Fuller's Cultural Critique: Her Age and Legacy*, ed. Fritz Fleischmann (New York: Peter Lang, 2000), 5.

Catharine Maria Sedgwick's Great Excursion

1. William J. Peterson, "The Rock Island Railroad Excursion of 1854," *Minnesota History* 15, no. 4 (December 1934): 404, 410; Chase quoted in Dunbar, *History of Travel*, 1092.

2. Catharine Maria Sedgwick, "The Great Excursion to the Falls of St. Anthony," hereafter cited parenthetically in text as "Great Excursion"; Mrs. E[mma] C. Embry, "Essay on American Literature," in *Catharine Maria Sedgwick: Critical Perspectives*, ed. Lucinda L. Damon-Bach and Victoria Clements (Boston: Northeastern University Press, 2003), 18.

3. Mary Kelley, foreword to Damon-Bach and Clements, *Catharine Maria Sedgwick*, xvii; Carolyn L. Karcher, "Catharine Maria Sedgwick in Literary History," in Damon-Bach and Clements, *Catharine Maria Sedgwick*, 8; Patricia Larson Kalayjian, "Disinterest as Moral Corrective in Clarence's Cultural Critique," in Damon-Bach and Clements, *Catharine Maria Sedgwick*, 107, 106; "Excerpts from Reviews of *Clarence*," in Damon-Bach and Clements, *Catharine Maria Sedgwick*, 103; Brigette Bailey, "Tourism and Visual Subjection in Letters from Abroad and "An Incident at Rome," in Damon-Bach and Clements, *Catharine Maria Sedgwick*, 217; Lucinda Damon-Bach, "'My Readers Will Thank Me': J.-C. L. Simonde de Sismonde, Civil Liberty, and Transatlantic Sympathy in Catharine Sedgwick's Letters from Abroad to Kindred at Home (1841)," in *Transatlantic Conversations: Nineteenth-Century American Women's Encounters with Italy and the Atlantic World*, ed. Beth L. Lueck, Sirpa Salenius, and Nancy Lusignan Schultz (Durham: University of New Hampshire Press, 2017), 3–22, 36, 39; Terry Caesar, *Forgiving the Boundaries: Home as Abroad in American Travel Writing* (Athens: University of Georgia Press, 1995), 8.

4. Notley Maddox, "Literary Nationalism in Putnam's Magazine, 1853–1857," *American Literature* 14, no. 2 (May 1942): 118, 121, 123.

5. Peterson, "Rock Island Railroad Excursion," 412.

6. Charles F. Babcock, "Rails West: The Rock Island Excursion of 1854," *Minnesota History* (Winter 1954): 143.

7. John Austin, "The Collection as Literary Form: Sedgwick's Tales and Sketches of 1835," in Damon-Bach and Clements, *Catharine Maria Sedgwick*, 165; introduction to Damon-Bach and Clements, xxii; Deborah Gussman, "'Equal to Either Fortune': Sedgwick's Married or Single? And Feminism," in Damon-Bach and Clements, *Catharine Maria Sedgwick*, 256.

8. Judith Fetterley, "'My Sister! My Sister!': The Rhetoric of Catharine Sedgwick's Hope Leslie," in Damon-Bach and Clements, *Catharine Maria Sedgwick*, 79.

9. Lydia Maria Child, "A Legend of the Falls of St. Anthony," in *Hobomok and Other Writings on Indians*, ed. Carolyn Karcher (New Brunswick: Rutgers University Press, 1992), 211; Fetterley, "My Sister! My Sister!," 97.

10. "The Great Chicago Fire and the Web of Memory: Tremont House," accessed April 5, 2024. http://www.greatchicagofire.org/landmarks/tremont-house.

11. Babcock, "Rails West," 142; Peterson, "Rock Island Railroad Excursion," 419, 420; J. Philip Gruen, *Manifest Destinations: Cities and Tourists in the Nineteenth-Century American West* (Norman: University of Oklahoma Press, 2014), 7.

12. Fussell quoted in James Buzard, *The Beaten Track: European Tourism, Literature, and the Ways to Culture, 1800–1918* (Oxford: Clarendon Press, 1993), 3; Kelley, foreword to Damon-Bach and Clements, *Catharine Maria Sedgwick*, xvii.

Constance Fenimore Woolson: Nostalgia on the Lakes

1. Constance Fenimore Woolson, "Detroit River," in *Constance Fenimore Woolson: Selected Stories and Travel Narratives*, ed. Victoria Brehm and Sharon L. Dean (Knoxville: University of Tennessee Press, 2004), 6–7.

2. Woolson, "Detroit River," 7; Anne Boyd Rioux, *Constance Fenimore Woolson: Portrait of a Lady Novelist* (New York: W. W. Norton, 2016), 59, 75; Brehm and Dean, *Constance Fenimore Woolson: Selected Stories and Travel Narratives*, 7.

3. Rioux, *Constance Fenimore Woolson*, 14; Post, *By Motor to the Golden Gate*, 33; "Cuyahoga River Fire," Ohio History Central, https://web.archive.org/web/20190213041556/www.ohiohistorycentral.org/w/Cuyahoga_River_Fire; Renato Rosaldo, *Culture and Truth: The Remaking of Social Analysis* (Boston: Beacon Press, 1989), 69–70.

4. Victoria Brehm, "Castle Somewhere: Constance Fenimore Woolson's Reconstructed Great Lakes," in *Constance Fenimore Woolson's Nineteenth Century: Essays* (Detroit: Wayne State University Press, 2001), 101; Sacvan Bercovitch, *The American Jeremiad* (Madison: University of Wisconsin Press, 1978), xiv.

5. Constance Fenimore Woolson, "Round by Propeller," in Brehm and Dean, *Constance Fenimore Woolson*, 11. Hereafter cited parenthetically in text as "Round."

6. Brehm and Dean, *Constance Fenimore Woolson*, 31n25, 31n36; "centrality of physical environment": Lawrence Buell, *Writing for an Endangered World: Literature, Culture, and Environment in the U.S. and Beyond* (Cambridge, Mass.: Harvard University Press, 2001), 18.

7. Dean MacCannell, *The Tourist: A New Theory of the Leisure Class* (New York: Schocken), 143–45.

8. Dennis Berthold, "Miss Martha and Ms. Woolson: Persona in the Travel Sketches" in *Constance Fenimore Woolson's Nineteenth Century*, ed. Victoria Brehm (Detroit: Wayne State University Press, 2001), 112; Barbara Welter, "The Cult of True Womanhood: 1824–1860," in *The American Family in Social-Historical Perspective*, 2nd ed., ed. Michael Gordon (New York: St. Martin's Press, 1978), 94, defines the tenets of "True Womanhood" as piety, purity, domesticity, and submissiveness.

9. Will B. Mackinstosh, *Selling the Sights: The Invention of the Tourist in American Culture* (New York: New York University Press, 2019), 119, 6.

10. MacCannell, *The Tourist*, 1. David Treuer, *The Heartbeat of Wounded Knee: Native America from 1890 to the Present* (New York: Riverhead Books, 2019), 114, notes that some of the atrocities against Native Americans in 1870 against the Blackfeet, in 1871 against the Yahi Indians, and in 1872 against the Yavapai Indians were covered in regional newspapers and picked up in the eastern papers.

11. Constance Fenimore Woolson, "Jeannette," in Brehm and Dean, *Constance Fenimore Woolson*, 49, 50.

Emily Post's Transcontinental Motor Tour, New York to the Mississippi

1. Jane Lancaster, introduction to *By Motor to the Golden Gate*, by Emily Post (Jefferson, N.C.: McFarland, 2004), 3; Andrew S. Gross, "Cars, Postcards, and Patriotism: Tourism and National Politics in the United States, 1893–1929," *Pacific Coast Philology* 40, no.1 (2005): 81; Emily Post, *By Motor to the Golden Gate* (New York, D. Appleton, 1916), 32. Hereafter cited parenthetically in text as *Motor*.

2. Marguerite S. Shaffer, *See America First: Tourism and National Identity, 1880–1940* (Washington, D.C.: Smithsonian Books, 2001), 175, 42, 52, 181.

3. Richard Weingroff, "The Lincoln Highway," *Highway History*, accessed August 3, 2017, highways.dot.gov/highway-history/general-highway-history/lincoln-highway, 1, 2; Shaffer, *See America First*, 137, 161, 140; Effie Price Gladding, preface to *Across the Continent by The Lincoln Highway* (New York: Brentano's, 1915).

4. Quoted in Helen Clemens, "The Rebellious Life of Emily Post," *Biography Magazine*, December 2000, 93; Jennifer Warner, *Minding Her Manners: The Life and Times of Emily Post* (Life Caps, 2014), Kindle, loc. 380–83, 364–65; Lancaster, introduction to *By Motor to the Golden Gate*, 2. For details about the car, see E. M. Post Jr., "To the Man Who Drives," in Post, *By Motor to the Golden Gate*, 243–51.

5. Weingroff, "Lincoln Highway," 3; Lancaster, introduction to *By Motor to the Golden Gate*, 6.

6. Kris Lackey, *Road Frames: The American Highway Narrative* (Lincoln: University of Nebraska Press, 1997), 6.

Francis Parkman: Traveler, Tourist, Cultural Voyeur

1. Bernard De Voto, *The Year of Decision, 1846* (Boston: Little, Brown, 1943), 115; Herman Melville, "'Mr. Parkman's Tour': The Text of Melville's 1849 Review," *Melvilliana*, March 24, 2012, accessed September 1, 2017, http://melvilliana.blogspot.com/2012/03/mr-parkmans-tour-text-of-melvilles-1849.html; E. N. Feltskog, "Editor's Introduction," in *The Oregon Trail*, by Francis Parkman (Madison: University of Wisconsin Press, 1969), 30a. For discussion about tourists and travelers, see also Buzard, *The Beaten Track*, 1–2; MacCannell, *The Tourist*, 13–15; and Urry, *Tourist Gaze*, 2nd ed., 2–3.

2. Frank M. Meola, "A Passage through 'Indians': Masculinity and Violence in Francis Parkman's the Oregon Trail" *American Transcendentalism Quarterly* 13 (1999):

21; James Clifford, "Traveling Cultures," in *Cultural Studies*, ed. Lawrence Grossberg, Cary Nelson, and Paula Treicher (New York: Routledge, 1992), 108; Jonathan Raban, *Driving Home: An American Journey* (Seattle: Sasquatch Books), 8–9, 12, Kindle.

3. Sally A. Hawthorne, "Francis Parkman," *Dictionary of Literary Biography*, vol. 235, *The American Renaissance in New England*, 3rd series, ed. Wesley T. Mott (Detroit: Gale, 2001), 324; Feltskog, "Editor's Introduction," 31a; Francis Parkman, *The Oregon Trail*, ed. David Levin (1849; repr., New York: Penguin, 1982), 46. Hereafter cited parenthetically as *Oregon*.

4. Diaries quoted in Susan Roberson, *Antebellum American Women Writers*, 36, 37.

5. See Roberson, *Antebellum American Women Writers*, for a brief discussion of place identity, 36–37.

6. Tuan, *Space and Place*, 59.

7. Meola, "A Passage through 'Indians,'" 5.

8. Patricia Nelson Limerick, *The Legacy of Conquest: The Unbroken Past of the American West* (New York: W. W. Norton, 1987), 314; Raban, *Driving Home*, 108.

9. Raban, *Driving Home*, 8–9; Limerick, *Legacy of Conquest*, 27.

10. Dunbar, *History of Travel*, 1146, 1203, 1212, 1162; John Mack Faragher, *Women and Men on the Overland Trail* (New Haven: Yale University Press, 1979), 195.

11. Clifford, "Traveling Cultures," 108.

12. Ibid., 99.

13. Clifford Geertz, *The Interpretation of Cultures* (New York: Harper Collins, 1973), 20.

14. Pearce, *Savagism and Civilization*, 64, 127, 111.

15. L. Maddox, *Removals*, 8.

16. Erik Cohen, "Phenomenology of Tourist Experiences" in *Defining Travel: Diverse Visions*, ed. Susan L. Roberson (Jackson: University Press of Mississippi, 2001), 40; Francis Parkman, "Preface to the Fourth Edition," in *The Oregon Trail*, ed. E. N. Feltskog (Madison: University of Wisconsin Press, 1969), xi–xiii; Clifford, "Traveling Cultures," 105.

Mark Twain and The Dialogics of *Roughing It*

1. James M. Cox, *Mark Twain: The Fate of Humor* (Princeton: Princeton University Press, 1966), 6; Rodman Wilson Paul, introduction to *Roughing It*, by Mark Twain (New York: Holt, Rinehart and Wilson, 1953), vi–viii; Encyclopaedia Britannica, "Comstock Lode," accessed May 31, 2018, https://www.britannica.com/place/Comstock-Lode.

2. Jerome Loving, *Mark Twain: The Adventures of Samuel L. Clemens* (Berkeley: University of California Press, 2010), 100–109, 188–89, 121, 173; Cox, *Mark Twain*, 3, 35, 14–15; Melton, *Mark Twain, Travel Books, and Tourism*, 1; Ziff, *Return Passages*, 193.

3. Gary Scharnhorst, "Mark Twain and the Literary Construction of the American West," in *A Companion to Mark Twain*, ed. Peter Messent and Louis J. Budd (Oxford: Blackwell, 2005), 312.

4. Mark Twain, *Roughing It*, ed. Harriet Elinore Smith and Edgar Marquess Branch (1872; repr., University of California Press, 1993), 3–4. Hereafter cited parenthetically as *Roughing*.

5. Drewey Wayne Gunn, "The Monomythic Structure of *Roughing It*," *American Literature* 61, no. 4 (December 1989): 564; Melton, *Mark Twain, Travel Books, and Tourism*, 83; Cesareo, "Anthropology and Literature," 169; Lee Clark Mitchell, "Verbally Roughing It: The West of Words," *Nineteenth-Century Literature* 44, no. 1 (June 1989): 68.

6. M. M. Bakhtin, *The Dialogic Imagination: Four Essays*, ed. Michael Holquist, trans. Caryl Emerson and Michael Holquist (Austin: University of Texas Press, 1981), 45, 55.

7. W. Turrentine Jackson, Rand F. Herbert, and Stephen R. Wee, *History of Tahoe National Forest, 1840–1940: A Cultural Resources Overview History* (Nevada City, Calif.: Forest Archaeologist, Tahoe National Forest, 1982), Cultural Resource Report 15, 120.

8. Mark Twain, *Adventures of Huckleberry Finn* (1885), ed. Victor Fischer and Lin Salamo, with Walter Blair (1995; repr., University of California Press 2003), 78.

9. "Lake Tahoe History," accessed May 31, 2018, http://www.jobmonkey.com /casino/lake_tahoe_history.

10. Melton, *Mark Twain, Travel Books, and Tourism*, 109; Rodman Wilson Paul, *Mining Frontiers of the Far West, 1848–1880* (New York: Holt, Rinehart and Winston, 1963), 74; Lawrence Berkove, "Nevada Influences," in *A Companion to Mark Twain*, ed. Peter Messent and Louis J. Budd (Oxford: Blackwell, 2005), 160.

11. Mitchell, "Verbally Roughing It," 69, 81.

12. "Deferral of expectations": ibid., 69.

13. Paul, *Mining Frontiers*, 68.

14. Ibid., 35; Ron James, "Chinese in Nineteenth-Century Nevada," accessed August 30, 2023, https://www.eventsnevada.com/ChineseInNevada.html; Limerick, *Legacy of Conquest*, 27.

15. Twain, *Adventures of Huckleberry Finn*, 50.

16. Paul, *Mining Frontiers*, 71; Mitchell, "Verbally Roughing It," 85; Ziff, *Return Passages*, 179; Neil Campbell, *The Cultures of the American West* (Edinburgh: Edinburgh University Press, 2000), 9–10, 19; Bahktin, *Dialogic Imagination*, 55.

17. Loving, *Mark Twain*, 102; Mitchell, "Verbally Roughing It," 68; Mark Twain, "Jim Smiley and His Jumping Frog," in *The Works of Mark Twain: Early Tales and Sketches*, vol. 2, *1864–1867*, ed. Edgar Marquess Branch and Robert H. Hirst (Berkeley: University of California Press, 1979), 287. Hereafter cited parenthetically in text as "Frog."

18. Bahktin, *Dialogic Imagination*, 55, 59; Loving, *Mark Twain*, 109.

19. Berkove, "Nevada Influences," 163–64; Paul, *Mining Frontiers*, 8; Scharnhorst, "Mark Twain and the Literary Construction of the American West," 309; David E. E. Sloane, "Mark Twain and the American Comic Short Story," in *A Companion to the American Short Story*, ed. Alfred Bendixen and James Nagel (Oxford: Wiley-Blackwell, 2010), 86.

Helen Hunt Jackson: Bits of Travel at Home and What the West Sounds Like

1. Helen Hunt Jackson, *Bits of Travel at Home* (Boston: Roberts Brothers, 1890), 5–6. Hereafter cited parenthetically in text as *Bits*.

2. Quoted in Kate Phillips, *Helen Hunt Jackson: A Literary Life* (Berkeley: University of California Press, 2003), 173.

3. Tuan, *Space and Place*, 54.

4. James Weaver, "Being In and Not Among: The Anti-Imperial Impulses of Helen Hunt Jackson's *Bits of Travel at Home*," *Legacy: A Journal of American Women Writers* 32, no. 2 (2015): 216; Christine Holbo, "'Industrial & Picturesque Narrative': Helen Hunt Jackson's California Travel Writing for the *Century*," *American Literary Realism* 42, no. 3 (Spring 2010): 245. Shaffer, *See America First*, 280, notes that "elite tourist diaries reveal that Chinese, Indians, and Mormons emerged as standard tourist attractions embodying exotic social others" for travelers to the Far West after the Civil War.

5. Paul Fussell, "Travel Books as Literary Phenomena," in *Defining Travel: Diverse Visions*, ed. Susan L. Roberson (Jackson: University Press of Mississippi, 2001), 106.

6. Wolfgang Schivelbusch, *The Railway Journey: Trains and Travel in the 19th Century*, trans. Anselm Hollo (New York: Urizen Books, 1979), 66.

7. Phillips, *Helen Hunt Jackson*, 24.

8. Ibid., 17, 19.

9. Jean Baudrillard, "America," in *Defining Travel: Diverse Visions*, ed. Susan L. Roberson (Jackson: University Press of Mississippi, 2001), 56–57.

10. For an estimate of speeds of various nineteenth-century conveyances, see dldance post, December 1, 2005, in "How Fast Did Civil War Steam Engines Go?" discussion thread, Trains.com, http://cs.trains.com/trn/f/111/p/51027/646681.aspx; Richard White, *Railroaded: The Transcontinentals and the Making of Modern America* (New York: W. W. Norton, 2011), 146–47, 507, 455.

11. Daegan Miller, *This Radical Land: A Natural History of American Dissent* (Chicago: University of Chicago Press, 2018), 171, 173.

12. Rose quoted in Krista Comer, *Landscapes of the New West: Gender and Geography in Contemporary Women's Writing* (Chapel Hill: University of North Carolina Press, 1999), 28.

13. John Sears, *Sacred Places: American Tourist Attractions in the Nineteenth Century* (New York: Oxford University Press, 1989), 137; Anne Baker, *Heartless Immensity: Literature, Culture, and Geography in Antebellum America* (Ann Arbor: University of Michigan Press, 2006), 46–48, argues that "measurement was also the primary tool for what might be called the formalization of geographical space on the American continent," tying measurement to mapping and surveying activities.

14. Tuan, *Space and Place*, 54.

15. D. Miller, *This Radical Land*, 168–69.

16. Helen Hunt Jackson, *A Century of Dishonor: A Sketch of the United States Government's Dealings with Some of the Indian Tribes* (1881; repr., Minneapolis: Ross & Haines, 1964), 31; Phillips, *Helen Hunt Jackson*, 259. See also Truer, *The Heartbeat of Wounded*

Knee, for genocidal policies against California Indians and Jackson's advocacy for Indian rights, 67–68, 130.

17. Phillips, *Helen Hunt Jackson,* 154–55; Weaver, "Being In and Not Among," 216.

18. Phillips, *Helen Hunt Jackson,* 153.

19. Helen Hunt Jackson, *Ramona* (New York: Grosset & Dunlap, 1884, 1912), 229–30, 206, 207; Jackson quoted in Phillips, *Helen Hunt Jackson,* 252.

John Muir and the Nature of Travel Writing

1. Michael P. Cohen, *The Pathless Way: John Muir and American Wilderness* (Madison: University of Wisconsin Press, 1984), 207; Bade quoted in John Leighly, "John Muir's Image of the West," *Annals of the Association of American Geographers* 48, no. 4 (December 1958): 309; James W. Shores, "A Win-Lose Situation: Historical Context, Ethos, and Rhetorical Choices in John Muir's 1908 'Hetch Hetchy Valley' Article," *Journal of American Culture* 29, no. 2 (2006): 192; "Sierra Club"; Frank Stewart, *A Natural History of Nature Writing* (Washington D.C.: Island Books/Shearwater Books, 1995), 129.

2. Mike Davis, introduction to *My First Summer in the Sierra* (1911; repr., New York: Modern Library, 2003), xxiv; Shores, "A Win-Lose Situation," 199; Buell, *Environmental Imagination,* 316–18; M. Cohen, *Pathless Way,* 350–57.

3. John Muir, *My First Summer in the Sierra* (1911; repr., New York: Modern Library, 2003), 5. Hereafter cited parenthetically in text as *My First.*

4. Dennis C. Williams, *God's Wilds: John Muir's Vision of Nature* (College Station: Texas A&M University Press, 2002), 63; Buell, *Environmental Imagination,* 192; Thurman Wilkins, *John Muir: Apostle of Nature* (Norman: University of Oklahoma Press, 1995), 61; Tuan, *Space and Place,* 99, 131.

5. Ralph Waldo Emerson, *Nature* (1836), in *Transcendentalism: A Reader,* ed. Joel Meyerson (Oxford: Oxford University Press, 2000), 127; Tuan, *Space and Place,* 131.

6. Tuan, *Space and Place,* 52.

7. M. Cohen, *Pathless Way,* 103, also points to Muir's discussion of glaciers and the motif of movement.

8. William C. Stephenson, "A New Type of Nature Writing?," *Midwest Quarterly* 36, no. 2 (Winter 1995): 172; Buell, *Environmental Imagination,* 138, 193; Stewart, *Natural History of Nature Writing,* xvi; Leighly, "John Muir's Image of the West," 3, 9.

9. Muir quoted in Stewart, *Natural History of Nature Writing,* 128; Muir quoted in Leighly, "John Muir's Image of the West," 3; "environmental commitment": Buell, *Environmental Imagination,* 138.

Charles Fletcher Lummis: Mapping A Tramp across the Continent

1. White, *Railroaded,* xxxvii; Martin Padget, "Travel, Exoticism, and the Writing of Region: Charles Fletcher Lummis and the 'Creation' of the Southwest," *Journal of the Southwest* 37, no. 3 (Autumn 1995): 80; James W. Byrkit, introduction to *Charles*

Lummis: Letters from the Southwest: September 20, 1884, to March 14, 1885 (Tucson: University of Arizona Press, 1989), xvii.

2. Mark Thompson, *American Character: The Curious Life of Charles Fletcher Lummis and the Rediscovery of the Southwest* (New York: Arcade Publishing, 2001), 18–19.

3. Byrkit, introduction to *Charles Lummis*, xii–xiii.

4. Cesareo, "Anthropology and Literature," 169; Charles F. Lummis, *A Tramp across the Continent* (1893; repr., San Bernadino, Calif.: Adansonia Publishing, 2018), 45. Hereafter cited parenthetically in text as *Tramp*.

5. Byrkit, introduction to *Charles Lummis*, 120.

6. Charles Fletcher Lummis, *The Land of Poco Tiempo* (1893; repr., Albuquerque: University of New Mexico Press, 1952), 23; Meola, "A Passage through 'Indians,'" 5; Tereza M. Szeghi, "Scientific Racism and Masculine Recuperation: Charles Lummis and the Search for 'Home,'" *Intertexts* 17, nos. 1–2: 101; Padget, "Travel, Exoticism, and the Writing of Region," 423, 433.

7. Brykit, introduction to *Charles Lummis*, xxix.

8. Leed, *Mind of the Traveler*, 72.

9. Comer, *Landscapes of the New West*, 27.

10. Thompson, *American Character*, 47.

11. Ibid., 11.

12. Theodore R. Sarbin, "Place Identity as a Component of Self: An Addendum," *Journal of Environmental Psychology* 3 (1983): 338–39; Howard F. Stein, "The Influence of Psychogeography upon the Conduct of International Relations: Clinical and Metapsychological Considerations," in *Maps from the Mind: Readings in Psychogeography*, ed. Howard F. Stein and William G. Niederland (Norman: University of Oklahoma Press, 1989), 182.

13. Leed, *Mind of the Traveler*, 8, 10.

14. Padget, "Travel, Exoticism, and the Writing of Region," 423; James Clifford, "On Collecting Art and Culture," in *The Predicament of Culture: Twentieth-Century Ethnography, Literature, and Art* (Cambridge, Mass.: Harvard University Press, 1988), 96.

15. See Szeghi, "Scientific Racism and Masculine Recuperation"; Dominika Ferens, "Native Americans, Chinese, and White Progressivists in the *Land of Sunshine*, 1895–1909," *American Transcendental Quarterly* 15, no. 4 (December 2001): 305–16; Padget, "Travel, Exoticism, and the Writing of Region."

16. Shaffer, *See America First*, 270.

17. María Eugenia Cotera, *Native Speakers: Ella Deloria, Zora Neale Hurston, Jovita González and the Poetics of Culture* (Austin: University of Texas Press, 2008), 37.

18. Thompson, *American Character*, 141–71; Szeghi, "Scientific Racism and Masculine Recuperation," 105.

19. Cotera, *Native Speakers*, 29–30; Lummis, *Land of Poco Tiempo*, 166.

20. Shaffer, *See America First*, 280.

21. Thompson, *American Character*, 117; Jennifer Craik, "The Culture of Tourism," in *Touring Cultures: Transformations of Travel and Theory*, edited by Chris Rojek and John Urry (London: Routledge, 1997), 121, 113.

22. Shaffer, *See America First*, 32–33.

23. Thompson, *American Character*, 47; MacCannell, *Ethics of Sightseeing*, 7.

Emily Post in the West

1. Worster, *Under Western Skies*, 81.

2. Campbell, *The Cultures of the American New West*, 9.

3. Shaffer, *See America First*, 141; Westgard quoted in Richard F. Weingroff, "The National Old Trails Road Part 2," *Highway History*, accessed May 8, 2019, https://www.fhwa.dot.gov/infrastructure/not2.cfm.

4. Baudrillard, "America," 56.

5. Andrew S. Gross, "Cars, Postcards, and Patriotism: Tourism and National Politics in the United States, 1893–1929," *Pacific Coast Philology* 40, no. 1 (2005): 79; Shaffer, *See America First*, 267–68. See also Dee Brown, *The American West* (New York: Simon & Schuster, 1994); and Jane Tompkins, *West of Everything: The Inner Life of Westerns* (New York: Oxford University Press, 1992).

6. "Filmic representation": Pratt, *Imperial Eyes*, 6; Gross, "Cars, Postcards, and Patriotism," 91.

7. "Artificial paradises": Gross, "Cars, Postcards, and Patriotism," 91; Baudrillard, "America," 56, 58.

8. For more on the role of hotels in western travel, see Gruen, *Manifest Destinations*, 30, 113.

9. "Who Were the Harvey Girls?," Xanterra Travel Collection, accessed March 18, 2024, https://www.xanterra.com/stories/culture-lifestyle/who-were-the-harvey-girls-and-why-do-they-matter; Shaffer, *See America First*, 52–53; Richard Flint and Shirley Cushing Flint, "Fred Harvey: Civilizer of the West," *New Mexico History*, accessed March 17, 2024, http://newmexicohistory.org/people/fred-harvey-civilizer-of-the-west.

10. Susan Stewart, *On Longing: Narratives of the Miniature, the Gigantic, the Souvenir, the Collection* (Baltimore: Johns Hopkins University Press, 1984), 140, 143.

11. Rosaldo, *Culture and Truth*, 69; Craik, "The Culture of Tourism," 113.

The South

1. John Cox, *Traveling South: Travel Narratives and the Construction of American Identity* (Athens: University of Georgia Press, 2005), 13.

John James Audubon: Migrating with the Birds

1. John James Audubon, "Mississippi River Journal," in *John James Audubon: Writings and Drawings*, ed. Christopher Irmscher (New York: Library of America, 1999), 32, 50, hereafter cited parenthetically in text as "Journal"; Danny Heitman, "Audubon

the Writer," *Humanities* 32 no. 6 (November/December 2011): 24. See also Hayden White, "The Value of Narrativity in the Representation of Reality," *Critical Inquiry* 7, no. 1 (Autumn 1980): 5–27.

2. Following Irmscher's edition of Audubon's "Mississippi River Journal," I quote Audubon's journal verbatim. It exemplifies the loose grammar and orthography of the time, with occasional spellings like "head Hake" (headache) (73) that illustrate that English was a second language to him. See Irmscher, "Notes on the Texts," in Audubon, *John James Audubon: Writings and Drawings*, 870–71.

3. Richard Rhodes, *John James Audubon: The Making of an American* (New York: Alfred A. Knopf, 2004), 153, 14–15, 160; Dunbar, *History of Travel*, 271, 286–87.

4. Dunbar, *History of Travel*, 281, 392–96; "Moving the Mail," US Postal Service, accessed March 19, 2024, https://about.usps.com/who/profile/history/moving-mail. htm.

5. Rhodes, *John James Audubon*, 115, 140.

6. Ludlow Griscom, introduction to *Audubon's Birds of America*, popular ed. (New York: Macmillan, 1950), 20–21.

7. Christopher Irmscher, *The Poetics of Natural History: From John Bartram to William James* (New Brunswick, N.J.: Rutgers University Press, 1999), loc. 844, Kindle.

8. Ibid., loc. 137; Theodore R. Sarbin, "The Narrative as a Root Metaphor for Psychology," in *Narrative Psychology: The Storied Nature of Human Conduct*, ed. Theodore R. Sarbin (New York: Praeger, 1986), 4; White, "Value of Narrativity in the Representation of Reality," 13.

9. Irmscher, *Poetics of Natural History*, loc. 2939.

10. Rhodes, *John James Audubon*, 3.

11. Irmscher, *Poetics of Natural History*, loc. 166.

William Cullen Bryant and a Tour of the South

1. Muller, *William Cullen Bryant*, 137; William Cullent Bryant, *The Letters of William Cullen Bryant*, vol. 2, ed. William Cullen Bryant II and Thomas G. Voss (New York: Fordham University Press, 1977), 139.

2. Howard R. Floan, "The New York *Evening Post* and the Ante-bellum South," *American Quarterly* 8, no. 3 (Autumn 1956): 246; William Cullen Bryant, "Tour in the Old South," in *Prose Writings of William Cullen Bryant*, vol. 2., *Travels, Addresses, and Comments*, ed. Parke Godwin (New York: D. Appleton, 1884), 23, 34, 44–45, here-after cited parenthetically in text as "Tour"; Ralph Waldo Emerson, *Letters of Ralph Waldo Emerson*, 6 vols., ed. Ralph L. Rusk (New York: Columbia University Press, 1939), 1:189; "Florida.: Strange Aspect of St. Augustine—Climate and Productions—Its Unequaled Salubrity—Florida Winters—Summer in St. Augustine—Hotels Crowded—St. Augustine the Resort of Invalids—The Town Three Hundred Years Old—Inducements for Emigration to Florida," *New York Times*, April 28, 1860.

3. Dunbar, *History of Travel*, 1083–84.

4. Muller, *William Cullen Bryant*, 115, 157–59; Godwin quoted in Max L. Griffin, "Bryant and the South," *Tulane Studies in English* 1 (1949): 56; Simms quoted in John C. Guilds, "Bryant in the South: A New Letter to Simms," *Georgia Historical Quarterly* 37 (1953): 142–43.

5. Frederick Douglass, *Narrative of the Life of Frederick Douglass, an American Slave, Written by Himself* (1845), in *The Classic Slave Narrative*, ed. Henry Louis Gates Jr. (New York: New American Library, 1987), 263.

6. Muller, *William Cullen Bryant*, 294; Albert F. McLean Jr., *William Cullen Bryant* (New York: Twayne, 1964), 107; Annika Neklason, "Poem of the Week: 'The Death of Slavery' by William Cullen Bryant," *Atlantic*, August 18, 2017, accessed March 19, 2024, https://www.theatlantic.com/culture/archive/2017/08/poem-of-the-week-the-death-of-slavery-by-william-cullen-bryant/622335.

7. William Cullen Bryant, "The Death of Slavery," in *William Cullen Bryant: Complete Poetical Works* (1876), Library of Early American Literature (Seattle: Kindle Direct Publishing, 2020), 238–39.

8. Ibid.

Frederick Law Olmsted in the Cotton South

1. Horwitz, *Spying on the South*, 3, 19; Olmsted quoted in ibid., 4, 18. See also John Cox, *Traveling South*, 142, 145–46; and Dana F. White, "A Connecticut Yankee in Cotton's Kingdom," in *Olmsted South, Old South Critic, New South Planner*, ed. Dana F. White and Victor A. Kramer (Westport, Conn.: Greenwood Press, 1979), 13–15. Cox claims that *The Cotton Kingdom* is "perhaps the single most widely known narrative of travel through the antebellum South" (145). White details some of the arrangements with Henry J. Raymond and the *New-York Daily Times*, where his travel letters were originally published.

2. Frederick Law Olmsted, *The Cotton Kingdom: A Traveller's Observations on Cotton and Slavery in the American Slave States, 1853—1861* (1861; repr., New York: Mason Brothers, 2017), 65. Hereafter cited parenthetically in text as *Cotton*.

3. Eric Williams, *Capitalism and Slavery* (New York: Capricorn Books, 1966), 3, 127, 7.

4. John Cox, *Traveling South*, 157.

5. Ibid.

6. Horwitz, *Spying on the South*.

7. Bryant, "Tour in the Old South," in *Prose Writings of William Cullen Bryant*, vol. 2., *Travels, Addresses, and Comments*, ed. Parke Godwin (New York: D. Appleton, 1884), 34.

8. John Cox, *Traveling South*, 154.

9. Karla J. Spurlock-Evans, "'Old' Sources for a 'New' History: Frederick Law Olmsted's Journeys in the Slave South," in *Olmsted South, Old South Critic, New South Planner*, ed. Dana F. White and Victor A. Kramer (Westport, Conn.: Greenwood Press, 1979), 54–55; Olmsted quoted in Horwitz, *Spying on the South*, 413.

John Muir's Botanizing Tramp through the South

1. Muir quoted in William Frederic Badé, introduction to *A Thousand-Mile Walk to the Gulf*, by John Muir (Boston: Houghton Mifflin, 1916), xxi; Badé, bid., xxix; James B. Hunt, *Restless Fires: Young John Muir's Thousand-Mile Walk to the Gulf in 1867–68* (Macon, Ga.: Mercer University Press), x; Stewart, *Natural History of Nature Writing*, 113.

2. John Muir, *A Thousand-Mile Walk to the Gulf*, ed. William Frederic Badé (Boston: Houghton Mifflin, 1916), 212. Hereafter cited parenthetically in text as *Gulf*.

3. Emerson, *Nature*, 127–28; Gibson, *Ecological Approach to Visual Perception*, 222.

4. Gibson, *Ecological Approach to Visual Perception*, 116, 125; Stewart, *Natural History of Nature Writing*, 113; Stefan E. Hormuth, *The Ecology of the Self: Relocation and Self-Concept Change* (Cambridge: Cambridge University Press, 1990), 3.

5. Perry, *Boats against the Current*, 129, 135.

6. Margaret Bridwell; *The Story of Mammoth Cave National Park Kentucky: A Brief History* (Mammoth Cave, Ky.: n.p., [1952], 30.

7. Hunt, *Restless Fires*, 111; "Adams Funds," Wikipedia, accessed April 30, 2024, https://en.wikipedia.org/wiki/Adams_Express_Company; Terence M. Hines and Thomas Velk, "The United States Post Office Domestic Postal Money Order System in the 19th Century," accessed March 18, 2024, www.researchgate.net/publication /46475194_The_United_States_Post_Office_Domestic_Postal_Money_Order _System_In_The_19th_Century_A_Nascient_Banking_System.

8. Hunt, *Restless Fires*, 118–19, 130, 134.

9. Ibid., 139, 142.

10. Perry, *Boats against the Current*, 184; Hunt, *Restless Fires*, 2–3.

11. James L. Kinneavy, *A Theory of Discourse: The Aims of Discourse* (New York: W. W. Norton, 1980), 102–3.

12. See Hunt, *Restless Fires*, 86–87.

13. Ibid., 90.

14. Tuan, *Space and Place*, 54.

15. See Hunt, *Restless Fire*, 105, 100.

16. See John Lowe, "Nineteenth-Century Southern Writers and the Tropical Sublime," *Southern Quarterly* 48, no. 3 (Spring 2011): 90–113.

17. Williams, *God's Wilds*, 42.

18. Worster, *Nature's Economy*, 2nd ed., 185; Wilkins, *John Muir*, 56.

19. Worster, *Nature's Economy*, 2nd ed., 17; M. Cohen, *Pathless Way*, 5; Ziff, *Return Passages*, 7.

Constance Fenimore Woolson: Tourism and "The Ancient City"

1. Sharon D. Kennedy-Nolle, *Writing Reconstruction: Race, Gender, and Citizenship in the Postwar South* (Chapel Hill: University of North Carolina Press, 2015), 30; Constance Fenimore Woolson, "The Ancient City, Part I," *Harper's New Monthly Magazine*, December 1874, 1. Hereafter cited parenthetically in text as "Ancient City."

2. Cotera, *Native Speakers*, 140.

3. Berthold, "Miss Martha and Miss Woolson," 112; MacCannell, *Ethics of Sightseeing*, 6–7.

4. Emerson, *Letters of Ralph Waldo Emerson*, 1:189; "Florida: Strange Aspect of St. Augustine"; Rioux, *Constance Fenimore Woolson*, 84, 85; Thomas Graham, *Mr. Flagler's St. Augustine* (Gainesville: University Press of Florida, 2014), 12, 6, 5.

5. "St. Johns Railway Terminus—Tocoi, Florida," Florida Memory, accessed December 11, 2020, https://www.floridamemory.com/items/show/35717; Graham, *Mr. Flagler's St. Augustine*, 34.

6. MacCannell, *The Tourist*, 42. See the University of Florida Digital Collections site for digitalized versions of *Petals Plucked from Sunny Climes*, by A. M. Brooks (http://ufdc.ufl.edu/AA00061997/00001), and *Sketches of St. Augustine*, by Rufus Sewell (https://ufdcimages.uflib.ufl.edu/AA/00/06/13/91/00001/AA00061391_00001.pdf).

7. See Elizabethada A. Wright, "Keeping Memory: The Cemetery and Rhetorical Memory in Constance Fenimore Woolson's 'Rodman the Keeper,'" *Studies in the Literary Imagination* 39, no.1 (Spring 2006): 29–54.

8. Urry, *Tourist Gaze*, 2nd ed., 2; Berthold, "Miss Martha and Miss Woolson," 112; Anne E. Boyd, "Tourism, Imperialism, and Hybridity in the Reconstruction South: Constance Fenimore Woolson's *Rodman the Keeper: Southern Sketches*," *Southern Literary Journal* 43, no. 2 (Spring 2011): 13.

9. The editors of *Constance Fenimore Woolson: Selected Stories and Travel Narratives*, Victoria Brehm and Sharon L. Dean, explain what happened in part 2 to Iris and her possible partners as well as the reconciliation between Sara and John Hoffman, "satisfying the public expectation for a fulfilled romance, but at the expense of a woman's art" (124n58).

10. Webster-Merriam defines "mansplain": "to explain something to a woman in a condescending way that assumes she has no knowledge about the topic."

11. Sandra Harding, *Whose Science? Whose Knowledge? Thinking from Women's Lives* (Ithaca: Cornell University Press, 1991), 70–71.

12. James Cox, "Regionalism: A Diminished Thing," in *Columbia Literary History of the United States*, ed. Emory Elliott (New York: Columbia University Press, 1988), 778; MacCannell, *Ethics of Sightseeing*, 6.

13. Henry James quoted in Boyd, "Tourism, Imperialism, and Hybridity in the Reconstruction South," 18.

14. Boyd, "Tourism, Imperialism, and Hybridity in the Reconstruction South," 22; Cotera, *Native Speakers*, 61, 139; Zora Neale Hurston, *Mules and Men* (Philadelphia: J. B. Lippincott, 1935), 1.

Mark Twain's South in Life on the Mississippi: Geographies of Travel

1. Mark Twain, *Life on the Mississippi* (1896; repr., New York: Harper and Row, 1981), v, hereafter cited parenthetically in text as *LoM*; Melton, *Mark Twain, Travel Books, and Tourism*, 123–24; Twain, *Adventures of Huckleberry Finn*, 366.

2. Loving, *Mark Twain*, 210, 260; Twain quoted in Melton, *Mark Twain, Travel Books, and Tourism*, 125; Ziff, *Return Passages*, 206–7.

3. Melton, *Mark Twain, Travel Books, and Tourism*, 136, 97; Todd Goddard, "Mark Twain's Geographic Imagination in Life on the Mississippi," *Journal of the Utah Academy of Sciences, Arts and Letters* 95 (2018): 187; Ziff, *Return Passages*, 207; James Cox, *Mark Twain*, 164, 187; Thomas Ruys Smith, "The Mississippi River as Site and Symbol," in *The Cambridge Companion to American Travel Writing*, ed. Alfred Bendixen and Judith Hamera (Cambridge: Cambridge University Press, 2009), 71.

4. Goddard, "Mark Twain's Geographic Imagination," 186.

5. Ibid., 200.

6. Ibid., 186.

7. Ibid., 197.

8. "James B. Eads and His Amazing Bridge at St. Louis," *History Gazette* (National Park Service), accessed January 16, 2020, https://www.nps.gov/jeff/learn/historyculture/upload/eads.pdf; David A. Pfeifer, "Bridging the Mississippi," *Prologue Magazine* (National Archives), accessed January 12, 2020, https://www.archives.gov/publications/prologue/2004/summer/bridge.html; "Light the River," National Park Service, accessed January 6, 202, https://www.nps.gov/miss/learn/historyculture/rsongsligh.htm. The Eads Bridge is still used today.

9. Elli Morris, "Making Ice in Mississippi," *Mississippi History Now*, accessed May 1, 2024, https://web.archive.org/web/20170323051824/http://mshistorynow.mdah.state.ms.us/articles/343/making-ice-in-mississippi; Narvell Stickland, "Twentieth Century Mills: 1898–1953," chap. 5 in *A History of Mississippi Mills and Mill Villages*, accessed January 9, 2020, http://msgw.org/choctaw/cottonmills5.html.

10. "Fort Pillow Massacre," History.com, November 9, 2009, https://www.history.com/topics/american-civil-war/fort-pillow-massacre; "Port Hudson," American Battlefield Trust. accessed January 19, 2020, https://www.battlefields.org/learn/civil-war/battles/port-hudson.

11. Carol Anderson, *White Rage: The Unspoken Truth of Our Racial Divide* (New York: Bloomsbury, 2016), 3; Leed, *Mind of the Traveler*, 10; Jack Kerouac, *On the Road* (New York: Penguin Books, 1955), 133.

12. In "Concerning the Jews," *Harper's Magazine*, March 1898, Twain writes, "In the cotton States, after the war, the simple and ignorant negroes made the crops for the white planter on shares. The Jew came down in force, set up shop on the plantation, supplied all the negro's wants on credit, and at the end of the season was proprietor of the negro's share of the present crop and of part of his share of the next one. Before long, the whites detested the Jew, and it is doubtful if the negro loved him." For more on the sharecropping system, see Carol Anderson, *White Rage*, 44–45. See also Du Bois, *The Souls of Black Folk*, 109, on the role of "Russian Jews" in the sharecropping system.

Mobilities and Immobilities in The Souls of Black Folk

1. Henry James, *American Scene*, 307; David Levering Lewis, *W. E. B. Du Bois: A Biography* (New York: Henry Holt, 2009), 191, 192; Du Bois, *The Souls of Black Folk*, 5, hereafter cited parenthetically in text as *Souls*; Ralph Waldo Emerson, "The Transcendentalist" (1841) in *Transcendentalism: A Reader*, ed. Joel Myerson (New York: Oxford University Press, 2000), 377; Henry Louis Gates Jr., *Stony the Road: Reconstruction, White Supremacy, and the Rise of Jim Crow* (New York: Penguin, 2020), 198.

2. Ann Raine, "Du Bois's Ambient Poetics: Rethinking Environmental Imagination in *The Souls of Black Folk*," *Callaloo* 36, no. 2 (Spring 2013): 322, 326; Douglas quoted in Fussell, "Travel and the British Literary Imagination," 81; D. Lewis, *W. E. B. Du Bois*, 198.

3. D. Lewis, *W. E. B. Du Bois*, 47–49, 59, 57.

4. Ibid., 58; "from *here* to *there*": Tichi, *High Lonesome*, 4; Sarbin, "The Narrative as Root Metaphor," 4.

5. D. Lewis, *W. E. B. Du Bois*, 167.

6. Leed, *Mind of the Traveler*, 4.

7. Gates, *Stony the Road*, xiv; Doreen Massey, *Space, Place, and Gender* (Minneapolis: University of Minnesota Press, 1994), 23.

8. "Blend of detailed observation": D. Lewis, *W. E. B. Du Bois*, 198.

9. John Cox, *Traveling South*, 3; Gretchen Sorin, *Driving while Black: African American Travel and the Road to Civil Rights* (New York: Liveright Publishing, 2020), xii.

10. Sorin, *Driving while Black*, xi.

11. Gieseking, "Geographic Imagination," 7.

Henry James: The American Scene and the Geographic Imagination

1. Henry James, *The American Scene*, ed. John Sears (1907; repr., New York: Penguin, 1994), 3, hereafter cited parenthetically in text as *AS*; William James quoted in Leon Edel, *Henry James: A Life* (New York: Harper and Row, 1985), 588; Henry James quoted in Edel, *Henry James*, 589; Edel, *Henry James*, 589–91.

2. Graham Huggan, "Ultima Thule/The North" in *The Routledge Companion to Travel Writing*, ed. Carl Thompson (London: Routledge, 2016), 334, 332; Gieseking, "Geographical Imagination," 7; Tuan, *Space and Place*, 58; Said, *Orientalism*, 71, 54; quoted in Gieseking, "Geographical Imagination," 3; Derek Gregory, "Geographical Imaginary," in *The Dictionary of Human Geography* (Cambridge, Mass.: Wiley-Blackwell, 2009); Massey, *Space, Place, and Gender*, 3.

3. William W. Stowe, "'Oh, the land's all right!': Landscape in James's American Scene," *Henry James Review* 24 no.1 (Winter 2003): 47; Edel, *Henry James*,134; David L. Furth, *The Visionary Betrayed: Aesthetic Discontinuity in Henry James's "The American Scene"* (Cambridge, Mass.: Harvard University Press, 1979), 24; Ross Posnock, "Affirming the Alien: The Pragmatist Pluralism of *The American Scene*," in *The Cambridge Companion to Henry James*, ed. Jonathan Freedman, (Cambridge: Cambridge University Press, 1998), 228; Lisi Schoenbach, "A Jamesian State: The American Scene

and 'the Working of Democratic Institutions.'" *Henry James Review*, 30, no. 2 (Spring 2009): 169.

4. MacCannell, *The Tourist*, 27, 29; Gieseking, "Geographical Imagination," 3, 2, 7.

5. MacCannell, *The Tourist*, 45; Peter Buitenhuis, "Henry James on Hawthorne," *New England Quarterly* 32, no. 2 (June 1959): 207, 225, 221.

6. Dona Brown, *Inventing New England: Regional Tourism in the Nineteenth Century* (Washington, D.C.: Smithsonian Institution Press, 1995), 137–38.

7. Ibid., 143, 155.

8. Edel, *Henry James*, 45; Dona Brown, *Inventing New England*, 86.

9. Alan Trachtenberg, *The Incorporation of America: Culture and Society in the Gilded Age* (New York: Hill and Wang, 1982), 118.

10. Massey, *Space, Place, and Gender*, 3–4; Trachtenberg, *Incorporation of America*, 113.

11. Trachtenberg, *Incorporation of America*, 118; Massey, *Space, Place, and Gender*, 4; Perry Miller, *Errand into the Wilderness* (Cambridge, Mass.: Belknap Press of Harvard University Press, 1956), 201.

12. Gert Buelens, "Henry James's Oblique Possession: Plottings of Desire and Mastery in *The American Scene*," *PMLA* 116, no. 2 (March 2001): 116; Ross Posnock, "Affirming the Alien: The Pragmatist Pluralism of *The American Scene*," in *The Cambridge Companion to Henry James*, ed. Jonathan Freedman (Cambridge: Cambridge University Press, 1998), 229.

13. Olmsted quoted in Trachtenberg, *Incorporating America*, 109–110; see Stephen Miller, "Henry James's America," *The New Criterion*, 31, no. 10 (June 2013): 23–27.

14. James quoted in Edel, *Henry James*, 589; Charles R. Anderson, "Henry James's Fable of Carolina," *South Atlantic Quarterly* 54 (1955): 254; John H. Pearson, "Henry James, Constance Fenimore Woolson, and the Fashioning of Southern Identity," in *Witness to Reconstruction: Constance Fenimore Woolson and the Postbellum South, 1873–1894*, ed. Kathleen Diffley (Jackson: University Press of Mississippi, 2011), 76; Beverly Haviland, *Henry James's Last Romance: Making Sense of the Past and the American Scene* (Cambridge: Cambridge University Press, 1997), 186; Clifford T. Manlove, "James with Naipaul in Charleston, South Carolina: Modern Perception of 'The Tradition of the Transatlantic South,'" *South Atlantic Review*, 64, no. 4 (Autumn 1999): 62n2.

15. Quoted in Gieseking, "Geographical Imagination," 3.

16. Lowe, "Nineteenth-Century Southern Writers and the Tropical Sublime," 109, 95; Joseph Conrad, *Heart of Darkness*, ed. Robert Kimbrough (1899; repr., New York: W. W. Norton, 1971), 36.

17. Gieseking, "Geographical Imagination," 5; Tuan, *Space and Place*, 16, 99; Derek Gregory, *Geographical Imaginations* (Cambridge, Mass.: Wiley-Blackwell, 1994), 34; Yi-Fu Tuan, *Topophilia: A Study of Environmental Perception, Attitudes, and Values* (New York: Columbia University Press, 1974), 64; Urry, *Tourist Gaze*, 2nd ed., 1–2, 145; Massey, *Space, Place, and Gender*, 3.

18. Massey, *Space, Place, and Gender*, 3.

19. Ibid. See also Anna Despotopoulou, "'Terrible Traps to Memory': National Monuments, Collective Memory, and Women in Henry James," *Modern Fiction Studies* 63 no. 3 (Fall 2017): 429–51.

20. Rosalie Hewitt, "Henry James, the Harpers, and the American Scene," *American Literature,* 55, no. 1 (Mar 1983), 41; Haviland, *Henry James's Last Romance,* 2.

21. Haviland, *Henry James's Last Romance,* 44–45.

22. Henry James, "The Jolly Corner" (1908), in *Tales of Henry James,* ed. Christof Wegelin (New York: W. W. Norton,1984), 314. Hereafter cited parenthetically in text as "Jolly."

Epilogue

1. Scott Slovic, *Going Away to Think: Engagement, Retreat, and Ecocritical Responsibility* (Reno: University of Nevada Press, 2008), 28, 8, 9.

BIBLIOGRAPHY

Anderson, Carol. *White Rage: The Unspoken Truth of Our Racial Divide*. New York: Bloomsbury, 2016.

Anderson, Charles R. "Henry James's Fable of Carolina." *South Atlantic Quarterly* 54 (1955): 249–57.

Audubon, John James. *John James Audubon: Writings and Drawings*, edited by Christopher Irmscher, 1–156. New York: Library of America, 1999.

Austin, John. "The Collection as Literary Form: Sedgwick's Tales and Sketches of 1835." In *Catharine Maria Sedgwick: Critical Perspectives*, edited by Lucinda L. Damon-Bach and Victoria Clements, 158–70. Boston: Northeastern University Press, 2003.

Babcock, Charles F. "Rails West: The Rock Island Excursion of 1854." *Minnesota History*, Winter 1954, 133–43.

Bachelard, Gaston. *The Poetics of Reverie: Childhood, Language, and the Cosmos*. Translated by Daniel Russell. Beacon, 1960.

Badé, William Frederic. Introduction to *A Thousand-Mile Walk to the Gulf*, by John Muir, xiii–xxxi. Boston: Houghton Mifflin, 1916.

Bailey, Brigette. "Tourism and Visual Subjection in Letters from Abroad" and "An Incident at Rome." In *Catharine Maria Sedgwick: Critical Perspectives*, edited by Lucinda L. Damon-Bach and Victoria Clements, 212–30. Boston: Northeastern University Press, 2003.

Baker, Anne. "'A Commanding View': Vision and the Problem of Nationality in Fuller's Summer on the Lakes." *Emerson Society Quarterly* 44 (1st and 2nd Quarters 1998): 61–77.

———. *Heartless Immensity: Literature, Culture, and Geography in Antebellum America*. Ann Arbor: University of Michigan Press, 2006.

Bakhtin, M. M. *The Dialogic Imagination: Four Essays*. Edited by Michael Holquist. Translated by Caryl Emerson and Michael Holquist. Austin: University of Texas Press, 1981.

Baudrillard, Jean. "America." In *Defining Travel: Diverse Visions*, edited by Susan L. Roberson, 56–60. Jackson: University Press of Mississippi, 2001.

Baxter, David J. "The Dilemma of Progress: Bryant's Continental Vision." In *William Cullen Bryant and His America: Centennial Conference Proceedings 1878–1978*, edited by Stanley Brodwin and Michael D'Innocenzo, 13–25. New York: AMS Press, 1983.

———. "William Cullen Bryant: Illinois Landowner." *Western Illinois Regional Studies* 1 (Spring 1978): 1–14.

Baym, Nina. *American Women of Letters and the Nineteenth-Century: Styles of Affiliation*. New Brunswick, N.J.: Rutgers University Press, 2002.

Bercovitch, Sacvan, *The American Jeremiad*. Madison: University of Wisconsin Press, 1978.

Berkove, Lawrence. "Nevada Influences." In *A Companion to Mark Twain*, edited by Peter Messent and Louis J. Budd, 157–71. Oxford: Blackwell, 2005.

Berthold, Dennis. "Miss Martha and Ms. Woolson: Persona in the Travel Sketches." In *Constance Fenimore Woolson's Nineteenth Century*, edited by Victoria Brehm, 111–18. Detroit: Wayne State University Press, 2001.

Birdsall, Ralph. *The Story of Cooperstown*. New York: C. Scribner's Sons, 1925.

Blair, Sara. "Documenting America: Racial Theater in The American Scene." *Henry James Review* 16, no. 3 (Fall 1995): 264–72.

Blunt, Alison, and Robyn Dowling. *Home*. 2nd ed. London: Routledge, 2022.

Bode, Carl, editor. *The Portable Thoreau*. Viking, 1947.

Boyd, Anne E. "Tourism, Imperialism, and Hybridity in the Reconstruction South: Constance Fenimore Woolson's *Rodman the Keeper: Southern Sketches*." *Southern Literary Journal* 43, no. 2 (Spring 2011): 12–31.

Boylan, James. "William Cullen Bryant." *Dictionary of Literary Biography*, vol. 43, *American Newspaper Journalists, 1690–1872*, edited by Perry J. Ashley. Detroit: Gale, 1986.

Branch, Michael P. "William Cullen Bryant: The Nature Poet as Environmental Journalist." *American Transcendental Quarterly* 12, no. 3 (September 1998): 1–17.

Brehm, Victoria. "Castle Somewhere: Constance Fenimore Woolson's Reconstructed Great Lakes." In *Constance Fenimore Woolson's Nineteenth Century: Essays*, edited by Victoria Brehm, 99–110. Detroit: Wayne State University Press, 2001.

———. Introduction to *Constance Fenimore Woolson's Nineteenth Century*, 7–21. Detroit: Wayne State University Press, 2001.

Brehm, Victoria, and Sharon L. Dean, editors. *Constance Fenimore Woolson: Selected Stories and Travel Narratives*. Knoxville: University of Tennessee Press, 2004.

Bridwell, Margaret. *The Story of Mammoth Cave National Park Kentucky: A Brief History*. Mammoth Cave, Ky.: n.p., [1952].

Brown, Dee. *The American West*. New York: Simon & Schuster, 1994.

Brown, Dona. *Inventing New England: Regional Tourism in the Nineteenth Century*. Washington, D.C.: Smithsonian Institution Press, 1995.

Bruckner Cooper, Michaela. "Textual Wandering and Anxiety in Summer on the Lakes." In *Margaret Fuller's Cultural Critique: Her Age and Legacy*, edited by Fritz Fleischmann, 171–89. New York: Peter Lang, 2000.

Bryan, Jimmy L., Jr. "Introduction: 'Everybody Needs Some Elbow Room': Culture and Contradiction in the Study of US Expansion." In *Inventing Destiny: Cultural Explorations of US Expansionism*, 1–21. Lawrence: University of Kansas Press, 2019.

Bryant, William Cullen. "The Death of Slavery." In *William Cullen Bryant: Complete Poetical Works* (1876), Library of Early American Literature, 238–39. Seattle: Kindle Direct Publishing, 2020.

———. *The Letters of William Cullen Bryant*, vols. 1–2, edited by William Cullen Bryant II and Thomas G. Voss. New York: Fordham University Press, 1975–77.

———. "*The North American* on the Indian Question," *New York Evening Post*, January 9, 1830.

———. "The Prairies." In *William Cullen Bryant: Complete Poetical Works* (1876), Library of Early American Literature, 104–6. Seattle: Kindle Direct Publishing, 2020.

———. *Prose Writings of William Cullen Bryant*, vol. 2, *Travels, Addresses, and Comments*, edited by Parke Godwin. New York: D. Appleton, 1884.

Buelens, Gert. "Henry James's Oblique Possession: Plottings of Desire and Mastery in *The American Scene*." *PMLA* 116, no. 2 (March 2001): 300–313.

Buell, Lawrence. *The Environmental Imagination: Thoreau, Nature Writing, and the Formation of American Culture*. Cambridge, Mass.: Belknap Press of Harvard University Press, 1995.

———. Foreword to *Susan Fenimore Cooper: New Essays on* Rural Hours *and Other Works*, edited by Rochelle Johnson and Daniel Patterson, vii–viii. Athens: University of Georgia Press, 2001.

———. "Thoreau and the Natural Environment." In *The Cambridge Companion to Henry David Thoreau*, edited by Joel Myerson, 71–193. New York: Cambridge University Press, 1995.

———. *Writing for an Endangered World: Literature, Culture, and Environment in the U.S. and Beyond*. Cambridge, Mass.: Harvard University Press, 2001.

Buitenhuis, Peter. "Henry James on Hawthorne." *New England Quarterly* 32, no. 2 (June 1959): 207–25.

Buzard, James. *The Beaten Track: European Tourism, Literature, and the Ways to Culture, 1800–1918*. Oxford: Clarendon Press, 1993.

Byrkit, James W. Introduction to *Charles Lummis: Letters from the Southwest: September 20, 1884 to March 14, 1885*, xi–xlix. Tucson: University of Arizona Press, 1989.

Caesar, Terry. *Forgiving the Boundaries: Home as Abroad in American Travel Writing.*
   Athens: University of Georgia Press, 1995.
Campbell, Neil. *The Cultures of the American New West.* Edinburgh: Edinburgh
   University Press, 2000.
Capper, Charles. *Margaret Fuller: An American Romantic Life: The Public Years.*
   Oxford: Oxford University Press, 2007.
Cass, Lewis. "Removal of the Indians." 1830. In *The Cherokee Removal: A Brief
   History with Documents,* edited by Theda Perdue and Michael D. Green, 106–14.
   Boston: Bedford Books of St. Martin's Press, 1995.
Cesareo, Mario. "Anthropology and Literature: Of Bedfellows and Illegitimate
   Offspring." In *Between Anthropology and Literature: Interdisciplinary Discourse,*
   edited by Rose De Angelis, 158–74. New York: Routledge, 2002.
Channing, William Ellery. "Self-Culture." In *William Ellery Channing: Selected
   Writings,* edited by David Robinson, 221–66. New York: Paulist Press, 1985.
Child, Lydia Maria. "A Legend of the Falls of St. Anthony." In *Hobomok and Other
   Writings on Indians,* edited by Carolyn Karcher, 202–12. New Brunswick, N.J.:
   Rutgers University Press, 1992.
Clemens, Helen. "The Rebellious Life of Emily Post." *Biography Magazine,* Decem-
   ber 2000, 90–94.
Clifford, James. *The Predicament of Culture: Twentieth-Century Ethnography, Litera-
   ture, and Art.* Cambridge, Mass.: Harvard University Press, 1988. 94–107.
———. "Traveling Cultures." In *Cultural Studies,* edited by Lawrence Grossberg,
   Cary Nelson, and Paula Treicher, 96–112. New York: Routledge, 1992.
Cohen, Erik. "Phenomenology of Tourist Experiences." In *Defining Travel: Diverse
   Visions,* edited Susan L. Roberson, 29–55. Jackson: University Press of Missis-
   sippi, 2001.
Cohen, Michael P. *The Pathless Way: John Muir and American Wilderness.* Madison:
   University of Wisconsin Press, 1984.
Comer, Krista. *Landscapes of the New West: Gender and Geography in Contemporary
   Women's Writing.* Chapel Hill: University of North Carolina Press, 1999.
Conforti, Joseph A. *Imagining New England: Explorations of Regional Identity from
   the Pilgrims to the Mid-Twentieth Century.* University of North Carolina Press,
   2001.
Conrad, Joseph. *Heart of Darkness.* Edited by Robert Kimbrough. New York: W. W.
   Norton, 1971.
Cooper, Susan Fenimore. *Rural Hours.* Edited by Rochelle Johnson and Daniel
   Patterson. Athens: University of Georgia Press, 1998.
Cotera, María Eugenia. *Native Speakers: Ella Deloria, Zora Neale Hurston, Jovita
   González and the Poetics of Culture.* Austin: University of Texas Press, 2008.
Cox, James M. *Mark Twain: The Fate of Humor.* Princeton: Princeton University
   Press, 1966.

———. "Regionalism: A Diminished Thing." In *Columbia Literary History of the United States*, edited by Emory Elliott, 761–84. New York: Columbia University Press, 1988.

Cox, John D. *Traveling South: Travel Narratives and the Construction of American Identity*. Athens: University of Georgia Press, 2005.

Craik, Jennifer. "The Culture of Tourism." In *Touring Cultures: Transformations of Travel and Theory*, edited by Chris Rojek and John Urry, 113–36. London: Routledge, 1997.

Damon-Bach, Lucinda. "'My Readers Will Thank Me': J.-C. L. Simonde de Sismonde, Civil Liberty, and Transatlantic Sympathy in Catharine Sedgwick's Letters from Abroad to Kindred at Home (1841)." In *Transatlantic Conversations: Nineteenth-Century American Women's Encounters with Italy and the Atlantic World*, edited by Beth L. Lueck, Sirpa Salenius, and Nancy Lusignan Schultz, 3–22. Durham: University of New Hampshire Press, 2017.

———. "To 'Act' and 'Transact': Redwood's Revisionary Heroines." In *Catharine Maria Sedgwick: Critical Perspectives*, edited by Lucinda L. Damon-Bach and Victoria Clements, 56–74. Boston: Northeastern University Press, 2003.

Damon-Bach, Lucinda, and Victoria Clements, eds. *Catharine Maria Sedgwick: Critical Perspectives*. Boston: Northeastern University Press, 2003.

Davis, Mike. Introduction to *My First Summer in the Sierra*, by John Muir, xv–xxviii. New York: Modern Library, 2003.

De Certeau, Michel. *The Practice of Everyday Life*. Translated by Steven F. Rendell. Berkeley: University of California Press, 1984.

De Voto, Bernard. *The Year of Decision, 1846*. Boston: Little, Brown, 1943.

Despotopoulou, Anna. "'Terrible Traps to Memory': National Monuments, Collective Memory, and Women in Henry James." *Modern Fiction Studies* 63, no. 3 (Fall 2017): 429–51.

Dickinson, Emily. *The Complete Poems of Emily Dickinson*. Edited by Thomas H. Johnson. Boston: Little, Brown, 1960.

Dillard, Annie. *Pilgrim at Tinker Creek*. Toronto: Bantam Books, 1974.

Dimock, Wai Chee. *Through Other Continents: American Literature across Deep Time*. Princeton: Princeton University Press, 2006.

Dobson, Joanne. "Reclaiming Sentimental Literature." *American Literature*, 69, no. 2 (June 1997): 263–88.

Douglass, Frederick. *Narrative of the Life of Frederick Douglass, an American Slave, Written by Himself* (1845). In *The Classic Slave Narrative*, edited by Henry Louis Gates Jr., 243–331. New York: New American Library, 1987.

Du Bois, W. E. B. *The Souls of Black Folk*. New York: Penguin, 1989. First published 1903.

Dunbar, Seymour. *A History of Travel in America*. New York: Tudor Publishing, 1937. First published 1915.

Egan, Ken, Jr. "Poetic Travelers: Figuring the Wild in Parkman, Fuller, and Kirkland." *Western American Literature* 44, no. 1 (Spring 2009): 49–62.

Edel, Leon. *Henry James: A Life*. New York: Harper and Row, 1985.

Emerson, Ralph Waldo. *The Complete Sermons of Ralph Waldo Emerson*. Edited by Albert J. von Frank et al. 4 vols. Columbia: University of Missouri Press, 1989–1992.

———. "Experience." In *The Collected Works of Ralph Waldo Emerson*, vol. 3, edited by Alfred R. Ferguson, Joseph Slater, and Douglas Emory Wilson, 25–50. Cambridge, Mass: Harvard University Press, 1959–1972.

———. *Journals and Miscellaneous Notebooks of Ralph Waldo Emerson*, vol. 16, *1866–1882*. Edited by Ronald A. Bosco and Glen M. Johnson. Cambridge, Mass.: Belknap Press of Harvard University Press, 1982.

———. "Letter to Martin Van Buren, 23 April 1838." In *Transcendentalism: A Reader*, edited by Joel Myerson, 226–30. New York: Oxford University Press, 2000.

———. *Letters of Ralph Waldo Emerson*, 6 vols. Edited by Ralph L. Rusk. New York: Columbia University Press, 1939.

———. "Nature" (1836). In *Transcendentalism: A Reader*, edited by Joel Myerson, 124–59. New York: Oxford University Press, 2000.

———. "The Transcendentalist" (1841). In *Transcendentalism: A Reader*, edited by Joel Myerson, 366–80. New York: Oxford University Press, 2000.

Embury, Mrs. E[mma] C. "Essay on American Literature" (1835). In *Catharine Maria Sedgwick: Critical Perspectives*, edited by Lucinda L. Damon-Bach and Victoria Clements, 18. Boston: Northeastern University Press, 2003.

Faragher, John Mack. *Women and Men on the Overland Trail*. New Haven: Yale University Press, 1979.

Feltskog, E. N. Introduction to *The Oregon Trail*, by Francis Parkman, 11a–15a. Madison: University of Wisconsin Press, 1969.

Ferens, Dominika. "Native Americans, Chinese, and White Progressivists in the *Land of Sunshine*, 1895–1909." *American Transcendental Quarterly* 15, no. 4 (December 2001): 305–16.

Fetterley, Judith. "'My Sister! My Sister!': The Rhetoric of Catharine Sedgwick's *Hope Leslie*." In *Catharine Maria Sedgwick: Critical Perspectives*, edited by Lucinda L. Damon-Bach and Victoria Clements, 78–100. Boston: Northeastern University Press, 2003.

Fleischmann, Fritz. "Cultural Translation as Cultural Critique." In *Margaret Fuller's Cultural Critique: Her Age and Legacy*, edited by Fritz Fleischmann, 1–24. New York: Peter Lang, 2000.

Flint, Richard, and Shirley Cushing Flint. "Fred Harvey: Civilizer of the West." *New Mexico History*. Accessed March 17, 2024. http://newmexicohistory.org/people/fred-harvey-civilizer-of-the-west.

Floan, Howard R. "The New York *Evening Post* and the Ante-bellum South." *American Quarterly* 8, no. 3 (Autumn 1956), 243–53.

"Florida: Strange Aspect of St. Augustine—Climate and Productions—Its Unequaled Salubrity—Florida Winters—Summer in St. Augustine—Hotels Crowded—St. Augustine the Resort of Invalids—The Town Three Hundred Years Old—Inducements for Emigration to Florida." *New York Times*, April 28, 1860.

"Fort Pillow Massacre." History.com, November 9, 2009. https://www.history.com/topics/american-civil-war/fort-pillow-massacre.

Foucault, Michel. *Power/Knowledge: Selected Interviews and Other Writings, 1972–1977*. Edited by Colin Gordon. New York: Pantheon, 1980.

Fuller, Margaret. "The Great Lawsuit: Man versus Men, Woman versus Women." In *Transcendentalism: A Reader*, edited by Joel Myerson, 383–427. Oxford: Oxford University Press, 2000.

———. *The Letters of Margaret Fuller*, vol. 3. Edited by Robert N. Hudspeth. Ithaca, N.Y.: Cornell University Press, 1983.

———. *Summer on the Lakes, in 1843*. Edited by Susan Belasco Smith. Urbana: University of Illinois Press, 1991.

Furth, David L. *The Visionary Betrayed: Aesthetic Discontinuity in Henry James's "The American Scene."* Cambridge, Mass.: Harvard University Press, 1979.

Fussell, Paul. "Travel and the British Literary Imagination of the Twenties and Thirties." *Temperamental Journeys: Essays on the Modern Literature of Travel*, edited by Michael Kowalewski, 71–92. Athens: University of Georgia Press, 1992.

———. "Travel Books as Literary Phenomena." *Defining Travel: Diverse Visions*, edited Susan L. Roberson, 105–16. Jackson: University Press of Mississippi, 2001.

Fynaardt, Keith. "The Spirit of Place as a Usable Past in William Cullen Bryant's 'The Prairies.'" *Midamerica: The Yearbook of the Society for the Study of Midwestern Literature* 21 (1994): 50–58.

Gates, Henry Louis, Jr. *Stony the Road: Reconstruction, White Supremacy, and the Rise of Jim Crow*. New York: Penguin, 2020.

Geertz, Clifford. *The Interpretation of Cultures*. New York: Harper Collins, 1973.

Georgi-Findley, Brigitte. *The Frontiers of Women's Writing: Women's Narratives and the Rhetoric of Westward Expansion*. Tucson: University of Arizona Press, 1996.

Gianquitto, Tina. "The Noble Designs of Nature: God, Science, and the Picturesque in Susan Fenimore Cooper's Rural Hours." In *Susan Fenimore Cooper: New Essays on* Rural Hours *and Other Works*, edited by Rochelle Johnson and Daniel Patterson, 169–90. Athens: University of Georgia Press, 2001.

Gibson, James J. *The Ecological Approach to Visual Perception*. Boston: Houghton Mifflin, 1979.

Gieseking, Jen Jack. "Geographical Imagination." In *International Encyclopedia of Geography: People, the Earth, Environment, and Technology*, edited by D. Richardson et al., 1–8. New York: Wiley-Blackwell and the Association of American Geographers, 2017.

Gladding, Effie Price. *Across the Continent by the Lincoln Highway*. New York: Brentano's, 1915.

Goddard, Todd. "Mark Twain's Geographic Imagination in Life on the Missis-
    sippi." *Journal of the Utah Academy of Sciences, Arts and Letters* 95 (2018): 185–202.
Gougeon, Len. "Thoreau and Reform." In *The Cambridge Companion to Henry
    David Thoreau*, edited by Joel Myerson, 194–214. Cambridge: Cambridge
    University Press, 1995.
———. *Virtue's Hero: Emerson, Antislavery, and Reform*. Athens: University of
    Georgia Press, 1990.
Graham, Thomas. *Mr. Flagler's St. Augustine*. Gainesville: University Press of Flor-
    ida, 2014.
Gregory, Derek. "Geographical Imaginary." In *The Dictionary of Human Geography*,
    5th ed. Cambridge, Mass.: Wiley-Blackwell, 2009.
———. "Geographical Imagination." In *The Dictionary of Human Geography*, 5th
    ed. Cambridge, Mass.: Wiley-Blackwell, 2009.
———. *Geographical Imaginations*. Cambridge, Mass.: Wiley-Blackwell, 1994.
Griffin, Max L. "Bryant and the South." *Tulane Studies in English* 1 (1949): 53–80.
Griscom, Ludlow. Introduction to *Audubon's Birds of America*, popular ed., 15–30.
    New York: Macmillan, 1950.
Gross, Andrew S. "Cars, Postcards, and Patriotism: Tourism and National Politics
    in the United States, 1893–1929." *Pacific Coast Philology* 40, no.1 (2005): 77–97.
Gruen, J. Philip. *Manifest Destinations: Cities and Tourists in the Nineteenth-Century
    American West*. Norman: University of Oklahoma Press, 2014.
Guilds, John C. "Bryant in the South: A New Letter to Simms." *Georgia Historical
    Quarterly* 37 (1953): 142–46.
Gunn, Drewey Wayne. "The Monomythic Structure of Roughing It." *American
    Literature* 61, no. 4 (December 1989): 563–85.
Gussman, Deborah. "'Equal to Either Fortune': Sedgwick's *Married or Single?* and
    Feminism." In *Catharine Maria Sedgwick: Critical Perspectives*, edited by Lucinda
    L. Damon-Bach and Victoria Clements, 252–68. Boston: Northeastern Univer-
    sity Press, 2003.
Hamera, Judith, and Alfred Bendixen. "Introduction: New Worlds and Old
    Lands—The Travel Book and the Construction of American Identity." In *The
    Cambridge Companion to American Travel Writing*, 1–9. Cambridge: Cambridge
    University Press, 2009.
[Hamilton, Hurd D.] *History of Otsego County, New York*. Philadelphia: Everts &
    Farriss, 1878. https://archive.org/details/historyofotsegocoohurd.
Harding, Sandra. *Whose Science? Whose Knowledge? Thinking from Women's Lives*.
    Ithaca: Cornell University Press, 1991.
"Who Were the Harvey Girls?" Xanterra Travel Collection. Accessed March 18,
    2024. https://www.xanterra.com/stories/culture-lifestyle/who-were-the
    -harvey-girls-and-why-do-they-matter.
Haviland, Beverly. *Henry James's Last Romance: Making Sense of the Past and the
    American Scene*. Cambridge: Cambridge University Press, 1997.

Hawthorne, Sally A. "Francis Parkman." *Dictionary of Literary Biography*, vol. 235, *The American Renaissance in New England*. 3rd Series. Edited by Wesley T. Mott. Detroit: Gale, 2001.

Heitman, Danny. "Audubon the Writer." *Humanities* 32, no. 6 (November/December 2011): 22–53.

Hewitt, Rosalie. "Henry James, the Harpers, and the American Scene." *American Literature* 55, no. 1 (March 1983), 41–47.

Hines, Terence M., and Thomas Velk. "The United States Post Office Domestic Postal Money Order System in the 19th Century: A Nascient [*sic*] Banking System." January 2009. Accessed March 18, 2024. www.researchgate.net/publication/46475194_The_United_States_Post_Office_Domestic_Postal_Money_Order_System_In_The_19th_Century_A_Nascient_Banking_System.

Jackson, W. Turrentine, Rand F. Herbert, and Stephen R. Wee. *History of Tahoe National Forest, 1840–1940: A Cultural Resources Overview History*. Nevada City, Calif.: Forest Archaeologist, Tahoe National Forest, 1982. Cultural Resource Report 15. E-book.

Holbo, Christine. "'Industrial and Picturesque Narrative': Helen Hunt Jackson's California Travel Writing for the Century." *American Literary Realism* 42, no. 3 (Spring 2010): 243–65.

Hormuth, Stefan E. *The Ecology of the Self: Relocation and Self-Concept Change*. Cambridge: Cambridge University Press, 1990.

Horwitz, Tony. *Spying on the South: An Odyssey across the American Divide*. New York: Penguin, 2019.

Huggan, Graham. "Ultima Thule/The North." In *The Routledge Companion to Travel Writing*, edited by Carl Thompson, 331–40. Routledge, 2016.

Hunt, James B. *Restless Fires: Young John Muir's Thousand-Mile Walk to the Gulf in 1867–68*. Macon, Ga.: Mercer University Press.

Hurston, Zora Neale. *Mules and Men*. Philadelphia: J. B. Lippincott, 1935.

Irmscher, Christopher. *The Poetics of Natural History: From John Bartram to William James*. New Brunswick, N.J.: Rutgers University Press, 1999. Kindle.

Jackson, Helen Hunt. *Bits of Travel at Home*. Boston: Roberts Brothers, 1890.

———. *A Century of Dishonor: A Sketch of the United States Government's Dealings with Some of the Indian Tribes*. Minneapolis: Ross & Haines, 1964. First published 1881.

———. *Ramona*. New York: Grosset & Dunlap, 1884.

"James B. Eads and His Amazing Bridge at St. Louis." *History Gazette* (National Park Service). Accessed January 16, 2020. https://www.nps.gov/jeff/learn/historyculture/upload/eads.pdf.

James, Henry. *The American Scene*. Edited by John Sears. New York: Penguin, 1994. First published 1907.

———. "The Jolly Corner." (1908). In *Tales of Henry James*, edited by Christof Wegelin, 313–42. New York: W. W. Norton, 1984.

James, Ron. "Chinese in Nineteenth-Century Nevada." Accessed August 30, 2023. https://www.eventsnevada.com/ChineseInNevada.html.

James, William. "The Stream of Thought." In *The Writings of William James: A Comprehensive Edition*, edited by John J. McDermott, 21–73. University of Chicago Press, 1977.

Jarvis, Robin. "Travel Writing: Reception and Readership." In *The Routledge Companion to Travel Writing*, edited by Carl Thompson, 89–98. London: Routledge, 2016.

Johnson, Linck. "A Week on the Concord and Merrimack Rivers." In *The Cambridge Companion to Henry David Thoreau*, edited by Joel Myerson, 40–56. Cambridge: Cambridge University Press, 1995.

Johnson, Rochelle, and Daniel Patterson. Introduction to *Rural Hours: Susan Fenimore Cooper*, ix–xxii. Athens: University of Georgia Press, 1998.

———, eds. *Susan Fenimore Cooper: New Essays on* Rural Hours *and Other Works*. Athens: University of Georgia Press, 2001.

Kalayjian, Patricia Larson. "Disinterest as Moral Corrective in Clarence's Cultural Critique." In *Catharine Maria Sedgwick: Critical Perspectives*, edited by Lucinda L. Damon-Bach and Victoria Clements, 104–18. Boston: Northeastern University Press, 2003.

Karcher, Carolyn L. "Catharine Maria Sedgwick in Literary History." In *Catharine Maria Sedgwick: Critical Perspectives*, edited by Lucinda L. Damon-Bach and Victoria Clements, 5–16. Boston: Northeastern University Press, 2003.

Kelley, Mary. Foreword to *Catharine Maria Sedgwick: Critical Perspectives*, edited by Lucinda L. Damon-Bach and Victoria Clements, xi–xviii. Boston: Northeastern University Press, 2003.

Kennedy-Nolle, Sharon D. *Writing Reconstruction: Race, Gender, and Citizenship in the Postwar South*. Chapel Hill: University of North Carolina Press, 2015.

Kerouac, Jack. *On the Road*. New York: Penguin Books, 1955.

Kinneavy, James L. *A Theory of Discourse: The Aims of Discourse*. New York: W. W. Norton, 1980.

Kirkland, Caroline. *A New Home, Who'll Follow?* New Brunswick, N.J.: Rutgers University Press, 1990. First published 1839 under the pseudonym Mary Clavers.

Kolodny, Annette. *The Land Before Her: Fantasy and Experience of the American Frontiers, 1630–1860*. Chapel Hill: University of North Carolina, 1984.

Kucich, John. Introduction to *Rediscovering "The Maine Woods": Thoreau's Legacy in an Unsettled Land*, edited by John Kucich and James Francis, 1–22. University of Massachusetts Press, 2019. E-book.

Lackey, Kris. *Road Frames: The American Highway Narrative*. Lincoln: University of Nebraska Press, 1997.

"Lake Tahoe History." Accessed May 31, 2018. http://www.jobmonkey.com/casino/lake_tahoe_history.

Lancaster, Jane. Introduction to *By Motor to the Golden Gate*, by Emily Post. 1–9. Jefferson, N.C.: McFarland, 2004.

Leed, Eric J. *The Mind of the Traveler: From Gilgamesh to Global Tourism*. New York: Basic Books, 1991.

Leighly, John. "John Muir's Image of the West." *Annals of the Association of American Geographers* 48, no. 4 (December 1958): 309–18.

Lewis, David Levering. *W. E. B. Du Bois: A Biography*. New York: Henry Holt, 2009.

"Light the River." National Park Service. Accessed January 6, 2020. https://www .nps.gov/miss/learn/historyculture/rsongsligh.htm.

Limerick, Patricia Nelson. *The Legacy of Conquest: The Unbroken Past of the American West*. New York: W. W. Norton, 1987.

Loving, Jerome. *Mark Twain: The Adventures of Samuel L. Clemens*. Berkeley: University of California Press, 2010.

Lowe, John. "Nineteenth-Century Southern Writers and the Tropical Sublime." *Southern Quarterly* 48, no.3 (Spring 2011): 90–113.

Lummis, Charles F. *A Tramp across the Continent*. San Bernadino, Calif.: Adansonia Publishing, 2018. First published 1893.

———. *The Land of Poco Tiempo*. Albuquerque: University of New Mexico Press, 1952. First published 1893.

Lynch, Thomas. "The 'Domestic Air' of Wilderness: Henry David Thoreau and Joe Polis in the Maine Woods." *Weber Studies* 14, no. 3 (Fall 1997): 38–48.

MacCannell, Dean. *The Ethics of Sightseeing*. Berkeley: University of California Press, 2011.

———. *The Tourist: A New Theory of the Leisure Class*. New York: Schocken, 1989.

Mackinstosh, Will B. *Selling the Sights: The Invention of the Tourist in American Culture*. New York: New York University Press, 2019.

Madden, Etta M., and Martha L. Fitch. *Eating in Eden: Food and American Utopias*. Lincoln: University of Nebraska Press, 2006. E-book.

Maddox, Lucy. *Removals: Nineteenth-Century American Literature and the Politics of Indian Affairs*. New York: Oxford University Press, 1991.

Maddox, Notley. "Literary Nationalism in Putnam's Magazine, 1853–1857." *American Literature* 14, no. 2 (May 1942): 117–25.

Manlove, Clifford T. "James with Naipaul in Charleston, South Carolina: Modern Perception of 'The Tradition of the Transatlantic South.'" *South Atlantic Review* 64, no. 4 (Autumn 1999): 36–67.

Marcy, Randolph B. *The Prairie Traveler: A Hand-Book for Overland Expeditions* (1859). Bedford, Mass.: Applewood Books, 1993. First published 1859.

Marx, Leo. *The Machine in the Garden: Technology and the Pastoral Ideal in America*. London: Oxford University Press, 1964.

Massey, Doreen. *Space, Place, and Gender*. Minneapolis: University of Minnesota Press, 1994.

McLean, Albert F., Jr. *William Cullen Bryant*. New York: Twayne, 1964.

Melton, Jeffrey Alan. *Mark Twain, Travel Books, and Tourism: The Tale of a Great Popular Movement*. Tuscaloosa: University of Alabama Press, 2002.

Melville, Herman. "'Mr. Parkman's Tour': The Text of Melville's 1849 Review." *Mevilliana*, March 24, 2012. Accessed September 1, 2017. http://melvilliana.blog-spot.com/2012/03/mr-parkmans-tour-text-of-melvilles-1849.html.

Meola, Frank M. "A Passage through 'Indians': Masculinity and Violence in Francis Parkman's the Oregon Trail." *American Transcendentalism Quarterly* 13 (1999): 5–25.

Miller, Daegan. *This Radical Land: A Natural History of American Dissent*. University of Chicago Press, 2018.

Miller, Perry. *Errand into the Wilderness*. Cambridge, Mass.: Belknap Press of Harvard University Press, 1956.

Miller, Stephen. "Henry James's America." *New Criterion* 31, no. 10 (June 2013): 23–27.

Mitchell, Lee Clark. "Verbally Roughing It: The West of Words." *Nineteenth-Century Literature* 44, no.1 (June 1989): 67–92.

Morris, Elli. "Making Ice in Mississippi." *Mississippi History Now*. Accessed May 1, 2024. https://web.archive.org/web/20170323051824/http://mshistorynow.mdah .state.ms.us/articles/343/making-ice-in-mississippi.

"Moving the Mail." US Postal Service. Accessed March 19, 2024. https://about .usps.com/who/profile/history/moving-mail.htm

Muir, John. *My First Summer in the Sierra*. New York: Modern Library, 2003. First published 1911.

———. *A Thousand-Mile Walk to the Gulf*. Edited by William Frederic Badé. Boston: Houghton Mifflin, 1916.

Muller, Gilbert H. *William Cullen Bryant: Author of America*. Albany: State University of New York Press, 2008.

Neklason, Annika. "Poem of the Week: 'The Death of Slavery' by William Cullen Bryant." *Atlantic*, August 18, 2017. Accessed March 19, 2024,https://www .theatlantic.com/culture/archive/2017/08poem-of-the-week-the-death-of -slavery-by-william-cullen-bryant/622335.

Nevins, Allan. *The Evening Post: A Century of Journalism*. New York: Russell & Russell, 1922.

Newman, Lance. "Margaret Fuller's Summer on the Lakes, in 1843 and the Condition of America." *Transatlantic Romanticism* 38–39 (May 2005): 1–13.

Norwood, Vera. *Made from This Earth: American Women and Nature*. Chapel Hill: University of North Carolina Press, 1993.

Olmsted, Frederick Law. *The Cotton Kingdom: A Traveller's Observations on Cotton and Slavery in the American Slave States, 1853—1861*. New York: Mason Brothers, 1861.

O'Mara, Shane. *In Praise of Walking: A New Scientific Exploration*. New York: W. W. Norton, 2019.

O'Sullivan, John. "Annexation." *United States Democratic Review*, July–August 1845, 5–10.

———. "The Great Nation of Futurity." *United States Democratic Review*, November 1839, 426–30.

Ostrowski, Carl. "'I Stand upon Their Ashes in thy Beam': The Indian and Bryant's Literary Removals." *American Transcendental Quarterly* 9, no. 4 (December 1995): 1–13.

Packer, Barbara. "Travel Literature." In *The Oxford Handbook of Transcendentalism*, edited by Joel Myerson, Sandra Harbert Petrulionis, and Laura Dassow Walls, 396–407. Oxford: Oxford University Press, 2010.

Padget, Martin. "Travel, Exoticism, and the Writing of Region: Charles Fletcher Lummis and the 'Creation' of the Southwest." *Journal of the Southwest* 37, no. 3 (Autumn) 1995: 421–49.

Paes de Barros, Deborah. *Fast Cars and Bad Girls: Nomadic Subjects and Women's Road Stories*. New York: Peter Lang, 2004.

Parkman, Francis. *The Oregon Trail*. Edited by David Levin. New York: Penguin, 1982. First published 1849.

Patterson, J. B., ed. "Life of Ma-ka-tai-me-she-kia-kiak, or Black Hawk" (1833). In *Native American Autobiography: An Anthology*, edited by Arnold Krupat, 149–70. Madison: University of Wisconsin Press, 1994.

Paul, Rodman Wilson. Introduction to *Roughing It*, by Mark Twain., iix–viii. New York: Holt, Rinehart and Wilson, 1953.

———. *Mining Frontiers of the Far West 1848–1880*. New York: Holt, Rinehart and Winston, 1963.

Pearson, John H. "Henry James, Constance Fenimore Woolson, and the Fashioning of Southern Identity." In *Witness to Reconstruction: Constance Fenimore Woolson and the Postbellum South, 1873–1894*, edited by Kathleen Diffley, 73–89. Jackson: University Press of Mississippi, 2011.

Pearce, Roy Harvey. *Savagism and Civilization: A Study of the Indian and the American Mind*. Baltimore: Johns Hopkins University Press, 1953.

Perez, Emma. *The Decolonial Imaginary: Writing Chicanas into History*. Bloomington: Indiana University Press, 1999.

Perry, Lewis. *Boats against the Current: American Culture between Revolution and Modernity, 1820–1860*. New York: Oxford University Press, 1993.

Peterson, William J. "The Rock Island Railroad Excursion of 1854." *Minnesota History* 15, no. 4 (December 1934): 405–20.

Pfeiffer, David A. "Bridging the Mississippi: The Railroads and Steamboats Clash at the Rock Island Bridge." *Prologue Magazine* (National Archives) 36, no. 2 (Summer 2004). https://www.archives.gov/publications/prologue/2004 /summer/bridge.html.

Phillips, Kate. *Helen Hunt Jackson: A Literary Life*. Berkeley: University of California Press, 2003.

Pierson, George. "The M-Factor in American History." In *The Character of Americans*, rev. ed., edited by Michael McGiffert, 118–30. Homewood, Ill.: Dorsey Press, 1970.

"Port Hudson." American Battlefield Trust. Accessed January 19, 2020. https://www.battlefields.org/learn/civil-war/battles/port-hudson.

Posnock, Ross. "Affirming the Alien: The Pragmatist Pluralism of *The American Scene*." In *The Cambridge Companion to Henry James*, edited by Jonathan Freedman, 224–46. Cambridge: Cambridge University Press, 1998.

Post, Emily. *By Motor to the Golden Gate*. New York: D. Appleton, 1916.

Powers, Rebecca. "How America's Open Road Inspired Three Women of the 1910s." *Washington Post*. April 16, 2015.

Pratt, Mary Louise. *Imperial Eyes: Travel Writing and Transculturation*. London: Routledge, 1992.

Proshansky, Harold, et al. "Place-Identity: Physical World Socialization of the Self." *Journal of Environmental Psychology* 3, no. 1 (March 1983): 57–83.

Raban, Jonathan. *Driving Home: An American Journey*. Seattle: Sasquatch Books. Kindle.

"Railroad History (USA): Facts, Timeline, Definition." Accessed March 19, 2024. www.american-rails.com/railroad-history.html.

Raine, Ann. "Du Bois's Ambient Poetics: Rethinking Environmental Imagination in 'The Souls of Black Folk." *Callaloo* 36, no. 2 (Spring 2013): 322–41.

"Re-tracing John Muir's Famous Walks." Sierra Club. Accessed August 27, 2019. https://vault.sierraclub.org/john_muir_exhibit/geography/retracing.aspx.

Rhodes, Richard. *John James Audubon: The Making of an American*. New York: Alfred A. Knopf, 2004.

Ringe, Donald A. "William Cullen Bryant's Account of Michigan in 1846." *Michigan History Mind* 40 (1956): 317–27.

Rioux, Anne Boyd. *Constance Fenimore Woolson: Portrait of a Lady Novelist*. New York: W. W. Norton, 2016.

Roberson, Susan L. *Antebellum American Women Writers and the Road: American Mobilities*. New York: Routledge, 2011.

Rosaldo, Renato. *Culture and Truth: The Remaking of Social Analysis*. Boston: Beacon Press, 1989.

Rosowksi, Susan. "Margaret Fuller, an Endangered West, and Summer on the Lakes." *Western American Literature* 25 (1990): 125–44.

Said, Edward. *Orientalism*. New York: Vintage, 1978.

Sarbin, Theodore R. "The Narrative as a Root Metaphor for Psychology." In *Narrative Psychology: The Storied Nature of Human Conduct*, edited by Theodore R. Sarbin, 3–21. New York: Praeger, 1986.

———. "Place Identity as a Component of Self: An Addendum." *Journal of Environmental Psychology* 3 (1983): 337–42.

Satz, Ronald N. *American Indian Policy in the Jacksonian Era*. Lincoln: University of Nebraska Press, 1975.

Scharnhorst, Gary. "Mark Twain and the Literary Construction of the American West." In *A Companion to Mark Twain*, edited Peter Messent and Louis J. Budd, 309–33. Oxford: Blackwell, 2005.

Scheckel, Susan. *The Insistence of the Indian: Race and Nationalism in Nineteenth-Century American Culture*. Princeton: Princeton University Press, 1998.

Schivelbusch, Wolfgang. *The Railway Journey: Trains and Travel in the 19th Century*. Translated by Anselm Hollo. New York: Urizen Books, 1979.

Schoenbach, Lisi. "A Jamesian State: *The American Scene* and 'the Working of Democratic Institutions.'" *Henry James Review* 30, no. 2 (Spring 2009): 162–79.

Sears, John. Introduction to *The American Scene*, by Henry James, vii–xxii. New York: Penguin, 1994.

———. *Sacred Places: American Tourist Attractions in the Nineteenth Century*. New York: Oxford University Press, 1989.

Sedgwick, Catharine Maria. "The Great Excursion to the Falls of St. Anthony." *Putnam's Monthly Magazine of American Literature, Science and Art*, September 1854, 320–25. Ebook.

Shaffer, Marguerite S. *See America First: Tourism and National Identity, 1880–1940*. Washington, D.C.: Smithsonian Books, 2001.

Shores, James W. "A Win-Lose Situation: Historical Context, Ethos, and Rhetorical Choices in John Muir's 1908 'Hetch Hetchy Valley' Article." *Journal of American Culture* 29, no. 2 (2006): 191–201.

Sloane, David E. E. "Mark Twain and the American Comic Short Story." In *A Companion to the American Short Story*, edited Alfred Bendixen and James Nagel, 78–90. Oxford: Wiley-Blackwell, 2010.

Slovic, Scott. *Going Away to Think: Engagement, Retreat, and Ecocritical Responsibility*. Reno: University of Nevada Press, 2008.

———. *Seeking Awareness in American Nature Writing: Henry David Thoreau, Annie Dillard, Edward Abbey, Wendell Berry, Barry Lopez*. Salt Lake City: University of Utah Press, 1992.

Smith, Susan Belasco. Introduction to *Summer on the Lakes, in 1843*, by Margaret Fuller, vii–xxii. Urbana: University of Illinois Press, 1991.

Smith, Thomas Ruys. "The Mississippi River as Site and Symbol." In *The Cambridge Companion to American Travel Writing*, edited by Alfred Bendixen and Judith Hamera, 62–77. Cambridge: Cambridge University Press, 2009.

Smith, Virginia Whatley. "African American Travel Literature." In *The Cambridge Companion to American Travel Writing*, edited by Alfred Bendixen and Judith Hamera, 197–213. Cambridge: Cambridge University Press, 2009.

Sorin, Gretchen. *Driving while Black: African American Travel and the Road to Civil Rights*. New York: Liveright Publishing, 2020.

Spurlock-Evans, Karla J. "'Old' Sources for a 'New' History: Frederick Law Olmsted's Journeys in the Slave South." In *Olmsted South: Old South Critic, New South Planner*, edited by Dana F. White and Victor A. Kramer, 51–58. Westport, Conn.: Greenwood Press, 1979.

Stavans, Ilan, and Joshua Ellison. *Reclaiming Travel*. Durham, N.C.: Duke University Press, 2015.

Stein, Howard F. "The Influence of Psychogeography upon the Conduct of International Relations: Clinical and Metapsychological Considerations." In *Maps from the Mind: Readings in Psychogeography*, edited by Howard F. Stein and William G. Niederland, 181–207. Norman: University of Oklahoma Press, 1989.

Stephenson, William C. "A New Type of Nature Writing?" *Midwest Quarterly*, 36, no. 2 (Winter 1995): 170–90.

Stewart, Frank. *A Natural History of Nature Writing*. Washington D.C.: Island Books/Shearwater Books, 1995.

Stewart, Susan. *On Longing: Narratives of the Miniature, the Gigantic, the Souvenir, the Collection*. Baltimore: Johns Hopkins University Press, 1984.

Stowe, William. "The Literature of Travel." In *Henry David Thoreau in Context*, edited by James S. Finley, 120–29. Cambridge: Cambridge University Press, 2017.

———. "'Oh, the land's all right!': Landscape in James's American Scene." *Henry James Review* 24, no. 1 (Winter 2003): 45–56.

———. "'Property in the Horizon': Landscape and American Travel Writing." In *The Cambridge Companion to American Travel Writing*, edited by Alfred Bendixen and Judith Hamera, 26–45. Cambridge: Cambridge University Press, 2009.

Szeghi, Tereza M. "Scientific Racism and Masculine Recuperation: Charles Lummis and the Search for 'Home.'" *Intertexts* 17, nos. 1–2: 91–112.

Terrie, Philip G. "The Other Within: Indianization on the Oregon Trail." *New England Quarterly* 64, no. 3 (September 1991): 376–92.

Tompkins, Jane. *West of Everything: The Inner Life of Westerns*. New York: Oxford University Press, 1992.

Thompson, Mark. *American Character: The Curious Life of Charles Fletcher Lummis and the Rediscovery of the Southwest*. New York: Arcade Publishing, 2001.

Thoreau, Henry David. *I to Myself: An Annotated Selection from the Journal of Henry D. Thoreau*, edited by Jeffrey S. Cramer. New Haven: Yale University Press, 2007.

———. "Life without Principle." In *Reform Papers*, edited by Wendell Glick, 155–79. Princeton: Princeton University Press, 1973.

———. *The Maine Woods*. Edited by Joseph J. Moldenhauer. Princeton: Princeton University Press, 1972.

———. *Walden*. Edited by J. Lyndon Shanley. Princeton: Princeton University Press, 1971.

———. "Walking." In *Excursions*, edited by Joseph J. Moldenhauer, 185–222. Princeton: Princeton University Press, 2007.

———. *A Week on the Concord and Merrimack Rivers*. Edited by Carl R. Hovde et al. Princeton: Princeton University Press, 1980.

Tichi, Cecelia. *High Lonesome: The American Culture of Country Music*. Chapel Hill: University of North Carolina Press, 1994.

Tonkovich, Nicole. "Traveling in the West, Writing in the Library: Margaret Fuller's Summer on the Lakes." *Legacy* 10, no. 2 (1993): 79–102.

Trachtenberg, Alan. *The Incorporation of America: Culture and Society in the Gilded Age*. New York: Hill and Wang, 1982.

Treuer, David. *The Heartbeat of Wounded Knee: Native America from 1890 to the Present*. New York: Riverhead Books, 2019.

Tuan, Yi-Fu. *Space and Place: The Perspective of Experience*. Minneapolis: University of Minnesota Press, 1977.

———. *Topophilia: A Study of Environmental Perception, Attitudes, and Values*. New York: Columbia University Press, 1974.

Turner, Frederick Jackson. *The Significance of the Frontier in American History*. Chicago: American Historical Association, 1893.

Twain, Mark. *Adventures of Huckleberry Finn*. Berkeley: University of California Press 2003. Edited by Victor Fischer and Lin Salamo, with Walter Blair.

———. "Concerning The Jews." *Harper's Magazine*, March 1898. Internet Modern History Sourcebook, Fordham University. Accessed January 21, 2020. https://sourcebooks.fordham.edu/mod/1898twain-jews.asp.

———. *Life on the Mississippi*. New York: Harper and Row, 1981. First published 1883.

———. "Jim Smiley and His Jumping Frog." In *The Works of Mark Twain: Early Tales and Sketches, vol. 2, 1864–1867*, edited by Edgar Marquess Branch and Robert H. Hirst, 282–88. Berkeley: University of California Press, 1979.

———. *Roughing It*. Edited by Harriet Elinore Smith and Edgar Marquess Branch. Berkeley: University of California Press, 1993. First published 1872.

Stickland, Narvell. "Twentieth Century Mills: 1898–1953." Chapter 5 in *A History of Mississippi Mills and Mill Villages*. Accessed January 19, 2020. http://msgw.org/choctaw/cottonmills5.html.

Urry, John. *The Tourist Gaze*. 2nd ed. London: Sage, 2002.

Van den Abbeele, Georges. *Travel as Metaphor: From Montaigne to Rousseau*. Minneapolis: University of Minnesota Press, 1992.

Van Noy, Rick. "Surveying the Sublime: Literary Cartographers and the Spirit of Place." In *The Greening of Literary Scholarship: Literature, Theory, and the Environment*, edited by Steven Rosendale, 181–206. Iowa City: University of Iowa Press, 2002.

Vespa, Jack. "The Unsurveyed Interior: William Cullen Bryant and the Prairie State." *American Transcendental Quarterly* 11, no. 4 (December 1997): 1–24.

Wade, Mason. *Francis Parkman: Heroic Historian*. New York: Viking, 1942.

Walls, Laura Dassow. *Henry David Thoreau: A Life*. Chicago: University of Chicago Press, 2017.

Warner, Jennifer. *Minding Her Manners: The Life and Times of Emily Post*. Life Caps, 2014. Kindle.

Weaver, James. "Being in and Not Among: The Anti-Imperial Impulses of Helen Hunt Jackson's Bits of Travel at Home." *Legacy: A Journal of American Women Writers* 32, no. 2 (2015): 214–35.

Weingroff, Richard F. "The Lincoln Highway." *Highway History*. Accessed August 3, 2017. highways.dot.gov/highway-history/general-highway-history /lincoln-highway.

———. "The National Old Trails Road Part 2." *Highway History* (Federal Highway Administration). Accessed May 8, 2019. https://www.fhwa.dot.gov/infrastructure/not2.cfm.

Welter, Barbara. "The Cult of True Womanhood: 1824–1860." In *The American Family in Social-Historical Perspective*, 2nd ed., edited by Michael Gordon, 313–33. New York: St. Martin's Press, 1978.

White, Dana F. "A Connecticut Yankee in Cotton's Kingdom." In *Olmsted South: Old South Critic, New South Planner*, edited by Dana F. White and Victor A. Kramer, 11–50. Westport, Conn.: Greenwood Press, 1979.

White, Hayden. "The Value of Narrativity in the Representation of Reality." *Critical Inquiry* 7, no. 1 (Autumn 1980): 5–27.

White, Richard. *Railroaded: The Transcontinentals and the Making of Modern America*. New York: W. W. Norton, 2011.

Whitman, Walt. "Song of Myself." In *Leaves of Grass*, edited by Harold W. Blodgett and Sculley Bradley, 28–89. New York: W. W. Norton, 1965.

Wilkins, Thurman. *John Muir: Apostle of Nature*. Norman: University of Oklahoma Press, 1995.

Williams, Dennis C. *God's Wilds: John Muir's Vision of Nature*. College Station: Texas A&M University Press, 2002.

Williams, Eric. *Capitalism and Slavery*. New York: Capricorn Books, 1966.

Williams, Raymond. *The Country and the City*. New York: Oxford University Press, 1973.

Woolson, Constance Fenimore. "The Ancient City, Part I." *Harper's New Monthly Magazine*, December 1874, 1–25.

———. *Constance Fenimore Woolson: Selected Stories and Travel Narratives*. Edited by Victoria Brehm and Sharon L. Dean. Knoxville: University of Tennessee Press, 2004.

Worster, Donald. *Nature's Economy: A History of Ecological Ideas*. 2nd ed. Cambridge: Cambridge University Press, 1994.

———. *Under Western Skies: Nature and History in the American West*. New York: Oxford University Press, 1992.

Wright, Elizabethada A. "Keeping Memory: The Cemetery and Rhetorical Memory in Constance Fenimore Woolson's 'Rodman the Keeper.'" *Studies in the Literary Imagination* 39, no. 1 (Spring 2006): 29–54.

Wrobel, David M. *Global West, American Frontier: Travel, Empire, and Exceptionalism from Manifest Destiny to the Great Depression*. Albuquerque: University of New Mexico Press, 2013.

Ziff, Larzer. *Return Passages: Great American Travel Writing, 1780–1910*. New Haven: Yale University Press, 2000.

INDEX

129, 140, 250–51; and nature writing, 109, 160–4, 169; in newspapers, 3, 52; popularity of, 3–4, 32; women's, 18
tropical sublime, 295–96
Treuer, David, 320*n*10
Tuan, Yi-Fu, 39, 116, 145, 155, 165–66, 168, 284, 296
Tuckerman, Henry, 3
Turnbull, Dr. Andrew, 221, 253
Turner, Frederick Jackson, 56, 121
Twain, Mark, 4, 6–8, 10–11, 109, 110, 161, 176, 193, 203–04, 260–72; pilot, 263; *Adventures of Huckleberry Finn*, 8, 134, 140, 260–61, 270–72; "The Celebrated Jumping Frog of Calaveras County," 8, 128, 141; "Concerning the Jews," 269–70, 331*n*12; *Innocents Abroad*, 97, 128; *Life on the Mississippi*, 260–72; *Roughing It*, 128–143, 266

Urry, John, 74, 254, 296

Van Den Abbeele, Georges, 33
Van Noy, Rick, 35
Vanderbilt, George, 298
Vanderlyn, John, 211

wagon, 220
walking, 21–23, 167–68, 172–75, 236–37
Walls, Laura Dassow, 38–39
Warner, Susan, 2
Washington, Booker T., 273
wayfinding, 35, 40–41, 43, 45–46. *See also* mapping
Weaver, James, 145, 158
Weber, Max, 290
Webster, Daniel
Welter, Barbara, 319, n. 8
West, the idea of, 4, 6, 10–11, 40, 60, 71, 75, 78, 83, 84, 86; described, 109–202

West, New, 200
Western Paradox, 62, 64, 189. *See also* Worster, Donald
Westgard, A. L., 190–91
Whirlwind, Chief, 115, 121–26
White, Richard, 150
Whitman, Walt, 1, 11, 291
wilderness, 160
Wilkins, Thurman, 165, 249
Williams, Dennis C., 167
Williams, Eric, 228
Wilson, Alexander, 215
Wilson, Woodrow, 161, 199
Wisner, Sarah, 113–14
Wister, Owen, 193
Wood, Alphonso, 244
women, 78, 145–46, 229–30; Native American, 82, 145; pioneers, 81–82, 121; travelers, 100, 109
Woolsey, Sarah, 144
Woolson, Charles Jarvis, 92
Woolson, Constance Fenimore, 3, 5, 7–8, 10–11, 49, 65, 91–99, 107, 140, 161, 203, 250–59, 307; "The Ancient City," 252–259; "Detroit River," 91; "Felipa," 258; "Jeannette," 98; *Rodman the Keeper*, 258; "Round by Propeller," 93–98, 250, 257
Woolson, Hannah, 251
Wordsworth, William, 133
Worster, Donald, 30, 60, 83, 189, 248–49

Yates, Lorenzo Gordin, 181
Yosemite Valley, 109, 110, 144, 151–59, 160–71
Yulee, David Levy, 241–42

Ziff, Larzer, 4, 5, 140, 249, 262